MAKING
LAHORE
MODERN

MAKING LAHORE MODERN

*Constructing and
Imagining a Colonial City*

William J. Glover

University of Minnesota Press
Minneapolis
London

Portions of the Introduction, chapter 2, and chapter 6 are reprinted in revised form from "Objects, Models, and Exemplary Works: Educating Sentiment in Colonial Punjab," *Journal of Asian Studies* 64, no. 3 (August 2005): 539–66; reprinted with permission from the Association of Asian Studies. Chapter 5 is reprinted in revised and expanded form from "'An Absence of Old England': The Anxious English Bungalow," *HomeCultures* 1, no. 1 (2004): 61–81; copyright 2004 William J. Glover; reprinted with permission of Berg Publishers.

Maps, photographs, and drawings not otherwise credited were created by the author.

Published by the University of Minnesota Press
111 Third Avenue South, Suite 290
Minneapolis, MN 55401-2520
http://www.upress.umn.edu

Library of Congress Cataloging-in-Publication Data

Glover, William J.
    Making Lahore modern : constructing and imagining a colonial city / William J. Glover.
        p. cm.
    Includes bibliographical references and index.
    ISBN: 978-0-8166-5021-7 (hc : alk. paper)
    ISBN-10: 0-8166-5021-7 (hc : alk. paper)
    ISBN: 978-0-8166-5022-4 (pb : alk. paper)
    ISBN-10: 0-8166-5022-5 (pb : alk. paper)
        1. City planning—Pakistan—Lahore—History—19th century. 2. Architecture—Pakistan—Lahore—19th century. 3. Architecture, British colonial—Pakistan—Lahore. 4. Lahore (Pakistan)—Buildings, structures, etc. I. Title.

NA9253.L34G55 2008
711'.409549143—dc22

                                            2007031188

Printed in the United States of America on acid-free paper

The University of Minnesota is an equal-opportunity educator and employer.

12 11 10 09 08   10 9 8 7 6 5 4 3 2 1

CONTENTS

ACKNOWLEDGMENTS

It is a pleasure to express my gratitude to the many people and institutions who helped bring this book to fruition. Research would have been impossible without generous financial support from the University of California, the American Institute of Pakistan Studies, the Social Science Research Council, the University of Michigan Rackham Faculty Grant Program, and the Department of Architecture at the University of Michigan. I rewrote most of this book while I was a faculty fellow at the University of Michigan Institute for the Humanities, whose staff utterly spoiled me and my colleagues. All of us who had the fortune to be at the institute that year are indebted to Daniel Herwitz, its director, for establishing an intellectual environment with true interdisciplinary vitality. I thank Salima Hashmi, former principal of the National College of Arts in Pakistan, who provided me with professional affiliation and the opportunity to teach a course while I was conducting dissertation research on this project in Lahore. Thanks are due also to the staffs of the Punjab Provincial Archives in Lahore and the Oriental and India Office Collection in London, who were always helpful. I owe a special thanks to Muhammad Abbas Chughtai of the Punjab Provincial Secretariat in Lahore for his assistance in negotiating the records housed at that institute. I would also like to thank the staff and directors of the Dyal Singh Trust Library and the Punjab Public Library in Lahore, the Dwarka Das Library in Chandigarh, the Municipal Corporation of Lahore, the Board of Revenue offices in Lahore, and the District Commissioner's Office in Lahore for their assistance.

Work on this project began while I was a student at the University of California–Berkeley, where I was fortunate to have wonderful teachers and mentors. Dell Upton has influenced me most. Through his scholarly example, intellectual curiosity, and rigorous but constructive criticism, Dell has pushed me to ask harder questions, to recognize unsatisfying answers, and to remain both circumspect and happy in those rare moments when understanding begins to unfold. Thomas R. Metcalf helped me in numerous ways on this project, not least by opening so many important questions and insights into the colonial history of India in his own masterful work. On a more personal level, Tom has been extraordinarily generous with both encouragement and criticism at every stage of this project; I have benefited from his lucid and affectionate engagement with my work in more ways than I can adequately thank him for. In addition to asking me the hardest questions of anyone, Barbara D. Metcalf gave me perhaps the greatest gift a teacher can give to a student: she believed in me and expected me to believe in myself. Her creativity and openness to a project whose questions and approach were not her own made Barbara an extremely valuable interlocutor throughout. The late Allan Pred lived a commitment to creative and critically effective scholarship that inspired warmth and profound respect from all of us who were fortunate enough to come into close contact with him. I thank Allan, wherever he may be smiling down on us all, for giving me the initial encouragement to pursue this project in a way I could make my own and for modeling an ethics of attentiveness toward his students that I hope I can pass on to my own students in some small measure. Donald Moore has been a rigorous intellectual interlocutor and a valued personal friend; I thank him for so often setting aside his own struggles in life to help me bring clarity to my own. My friends and fellow travelers at Berkeley are now spread far and wide, but I still think of us as a community. My life would not have been the same without the warmth, friendship, and intellectual sustenance I found in the company of Arijit Sen, Sharad Chari, Steve Thorne, Anand Pandian, Kavita Datla, and Emily Merideth.

Among those I will always consider my teachers are two people whom I would especially like to thank. Gurinder Singh Mann literally walked me through the Punjab, helped me understand what was there, and shared his wisdom on less tangible things in ways that have shaped my life for the better. David Gilmartin provided valuable commentary during several stages of this project; I have not always been able to make good on his comments, but they helped me in a multitude of ways. Both David and Gurinder are living proof, for me, that genius, humor, and human kindness can all be found in the academy—and sometimes all in one person.

Friends and colleagues in Ann Arbor have challenged, inspired, and sustained me. I especially want to thank Arun Agrawal, Sunil Agnani, Kathryn Babayan, Tom Buresh, Scott Campbell, Kathleen Canning, James Chaffers, Caroline Constant, Nondita Correa, Geoff Eley, Rich Freeman, Danelle Guthrie, Rebecca Hardin, Rima Hassouneh, George Hoffman, Nancy Hunt, Webb Keane, Douglas Kelbaugh, Lisa Klopfer, Jayati Lal, Rama Mantena, Rahul Mehrotra, Christi Merill, Barbara Metcalf, Jonathan Metzl, Gina Morantz-Sanchez, Nadine Naber, Sumathi Ramaswamy, Hubert Rast, David Scobey, Parna Sengupta, Carla Sinopoli, Lydia Soo, Miriam Tiktin, and Jason Young for their friendship, support, and enabling insights. I thank Adela Pinch, Kali Israel, and Andrea Zemgulys for inviting me to present work in progress at the Nineteenth-Century Forum. I especially thank both Thomas Trautmann and Robert Fishman for generously reading portions of the manuscript in an early draft and providing constructive criticism. Finally, I am grateful to Pirasri Povatong, Itohan

Osayimwese, Omar Baghdadi, Sanjeev Vidyarthi, and Marty Baker for sharing the inspiration and discoveries of their own emerging research projects and for placing their confidence in me.

Friends in India and Pakistan extended their hospitality and intellectual generosity in measures too full to ever repay. Two remarkable gentlemen in particular, Najm Hosain Syed and Nadir Ali, sat with me for many long sessions and helped me make sense of Lahore's past. Members of Punjabi Sangat in Lahore introduced me to the wonders of Shah Husain's poetry, suffered through my readings in Punjabi, and graciously provided me with good company on numerous Wednesday evenings. Samina Choonara, Saida Fazal, Lala Rukh, Rabia Nadir, Shahid Mirza, Beatte Terfloth, Ayesha Nadir, Risham Syed, Sara Ahmed, Khizar Ahmed, and Sheik Abdul Waheed and his family all made me feel at home in Lahore; Khalid Mahmood, Naila Mahmood, Iftikhar Dadi, Elizabeth Dadi, and Khalid Nadvi did the same for me in Karachi. Amita Baviskar showed me around Delhi with great patience and humor, and a year or so later (on a snowy evening in Charlottesville, Virginia) she helped me understand a basic argument in this book in an entirely new way.

Pieter Martin at the University of Minnesota Press has been an ideal editor. The confidence he placed in this book right from the start made completing it that much easier. Anthony D. King read a draft of the entire manuscript and gave me precise and detailed comments that helped improve the book. Swati Chattopadhyay, from whose own scholarship I have learned tremendously, did the same thing. Whether standing next to her kitchen stove or coming to the end of her list of critical comments, I have benefited more than once from Swati's formidable talents. Diana Downing provided valuable assistance preparing the manuscript at a penultimate stage, and Kathy Delfosse did a superb job of final editing. I simply could not have finished this project without the talented and good-natured assistance of Sara Sarkasian and James DiMercurio, both of whom worked on this book's illustrations.

Finally, there are a few friends and family members without whose affection, guidance, and support this book would not have been possible. I first realized that Preeti Chopra was not entirely of this world when she announced to me, at the end of our first grueling year in graduate school, that in addition to completing all her coursework she had finished her first novel the evening before. More recently, Preeti sat with me at the Café Etoile in Madison, Wisconsin; she had painstakingly read every line of my manuscript and, over several hours at the café, unfolded a vision of how much better this book could be. I have not succeeded in doing all that Preeti suggested, but I will never forget that afternoon or the years of support and generosity that preceded it. Throughout the writing of this book, and throughout my entire life, I have enjoyed the love and support of both my parents, Alana Woods and Jack F. Glover. I thank Munis Farooqui, Clare Talwalker, and Lee Schlesinger for being such nurturing and brilliant friends. I am deeply grateful to Charles Hirschkind for his supportive and constant friendship and for un-self-consciously applying his intelligence to my intellectual confusions. After half a lifetime of friendship, Saba Mahmood has been the source of so much that is meaningful in my life that I hardly know where to begin to thank her. Most of all, perhaps, I thank Saba for challenging me to care for myself and for those who matter to me more fully no matter how consuming the work becomes.

Finally, Farina Mir has lived with this book since the very beginning. Her knowledge and intelligence have helped shape not only all of the book's main arguments but every line on every page. Farina has given me much more than her tireless willingness to help me think and write more clearly, however; she has given me, much more amazingly, that sense of contentment and repose in the world that comes only from a meeting of spirits.

INTRODUCTION

In 1809, a British officer in Lord Charles T. Metcalfe's diplomatic mission to Punjab described the province's capital city of Lahore as presenting a "melancholy picture of fallen splendour. Here the lofty dwellings and masjids [mosques], which fifty years ago raised their tops to the skies and were the pride of a busy and active population, are now crumbling into dust." After touring the plain surrounding the city, the same officer wrote that "on going over these ruins I saw not a human being; all was silence, solitude, and gloom."[1] Some twenty years later, in 1831, the young Lieutenant (later Sir) Alexander Burnes arrived in Lahore with a cargo of Arabian horses. The horses were a gift from King George IV to Ranjit Singh, the Sikh ruler of Punjab, as a gesture of friendship and cooperation. "On the morning of 18th June," Burnes wrote, "we made our public entrance into the Imperial city of Lahore, which once rivaled Delhi." As Burnes discovered, however, the legendary grandeur of the city was now a thing of the past: "The houses are very lofty," he wrote, but "the streets, which are narrow, [are] offensively filthy."[2] A few years later, in 1838, amateur numismatist (and recent deserter from the East India Company army) Charles Masson visited Lahore and concluded that "the extravagant praises bestowed upon [the city] by the historians of Hindustan . . . must be understood as applicable to a former city."[3] For these foreign visitors, as for many other early nineteenth-century travelers to Lahore, the city was a disappointment.

The decay these visitors witnessed was not the result of some unique historical calamity. Rather, Lahore shared a fate common to many Indian cities, especially those that expanded and contracted with the comings and goings of imperial courts. Lahore had indeed once been a bustling city, particularly during the late sixteenth through eighteenth centuries when Mughal emperors attracted commerce and residents to the city by making it an imperial and provincial capital. During the eighteenth century, however, when Mughal attention turned farther south to address threats from the Deccan, Lahore suffered heavily from successive destructive raids as a series of lesser Mughal governors struggled unsuccessfully to keep it within the Mughal realm. By the end of the eighteenth century, Sikh ruler Ranjit Singh consolidated his dominion over the province and fixed his court in Lahore's Mughal-era citadel. At no time during Ranjit Singh's nearly forty years of rule (1799 to 1839), however, did Lahore regain the population and wealth it had once had. Doing so would have been difficult indeed: At the turn of the nineteenth century, most of Lahore's residents huddled together for safety inside the city's walls. Outside those walls, the architectural rubble of more prosperous pasts ringed the city like deposits from a slowly retreating glacier.

After a brief half century of Sikh rule, Lahore was once again transformed by imperial circumstances. This time, however, it was the British Empire that caused the transformation. Following a series of intrigues, and later hard-fought wars (in 1846–47 and 1848–49), between the British East India Company and the Sikhs, the British annexed Ranjit Singh's former kingdom in 1849. With the transfer of power from the East India Company to Crown rule in 1858, Lahore became the capital city of Punjab Province in British India.

The alterations made to the city under British rule silenced perceptions of ruin. "Fortunately for the country and its people, times have now changed," wrote Syad Muhammad Latif, whose history of Lahore appeared in 1892. "Where desolation and ruin marked the surface of the land, luxuriant vegetation thrives, picturesque public and private edifices have risen, and gardens and plains, intersected by canals and metalled roads lined with shady trees, afford indubitable testimony at each step to the beneficent influence of a settled Government and good order."[4] From the mid-nineteenth century onward, the plain outside Lahore's city walls—only recently a desolate brickyard of ruins—was irreparably altered to make room for colonial institutions and residences. By any measure, the transformation was striking.

Even though Lahore came into the imperial fold late compared to other Indian cities, its metamorphosis during the late nineteenth century was rapid. The *Imperial Gazetteer of India* for 1908 provides a sense of the range of new institutions that structured urban life in Lahore by that time, most of them located in a several-square-mile "civil station" adjacent to the older walled city (Map I.1). In addition to the provincial government's executive and administrative offices, Lahore had three prisons (one exclusively for women), two British hospitals, and a large lunatic asylum located along the banks of the Ravi River. Although the literacy rate among the city's 200,000 residents was less than 5 percent in 1901, Lahore had 5 liberal arts colleges, 3 professional colleges, 28 secondary schools, 112 primary schools, and several religious institutions offering instruction. The largest manufacturing facilities in the city were a mill for spinning and weaving cotton that employed over 770 workers and the massive North-Western Railway workshops that employed over 4,500 in its machine shops, foundry, and cavernous engine sheds.[5] There were iron foundries, mechanized oil and flour mills, and scores of printing presses in the city; a cable tram carried passengers from Lahore's new railway station to "Charing Cross," an intersection at the geographic center of a new commercial district arrayed along Mall Road. At the end of the nineteenth century, Indian residents of Lahore sometimes called their city a "metropolis," using the

English term. As these people looked out over their city, they no longer felt the sense of abandonment and gloom of only fifty years earlier.

This book is concerned with the emergence of the modern Indian city as a distinctive social and material milieu shaped under British rule. While most of what follows is focused on colonial-era Lahore, and the arguments I will develop emerge from that particular context, the phenomena I examine were considerably more widespread. Even if Lahore's status as a provincial capital made it the focus of more than ordinary activity, most cities and towns in India underwent related changes during the same period. Colonial-era urbanization produced urban forms, infrastructures, functions, and ideas that were entirely novel in the subcontinent, even in those towns and cities that declined under British rule.[6] All across India, new types of buildings appeared in the form of factories, hospitals, prisons, lunatic asylums, clubs and racecourses, parks, arboretums, zoos, hotels, courthouses, museums, universities, cinema halls, gymnasiums, and so forth. Streets in cities were built to new standards, composed of new materials, and given new kinds of names and functions. Urban governance was institutionalized in the form of a "municipality" and effected through new regimes of record keeping and surveillance, new ways of classifying people and property. Spaces within buildings in the city even acquired new significance, as new kinds of rooms were added to older buildings and as people occupied them in new ways. In the growing suburbs of Indian cities a novel type of single-story house emerged, called a "bungalow," that stood apart from its neighbors, surrounded by its own sea of yard. Even as cities changed in these ways, new languages and concepts for describing and imagining them found their way into vernacular speech. Within the span of less than a century or so,

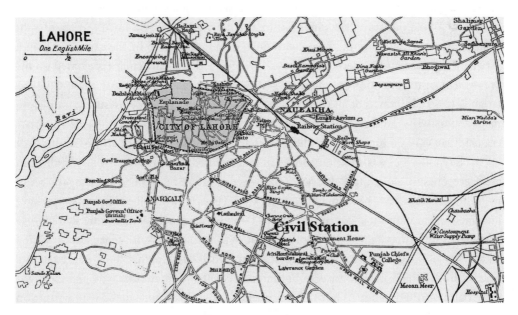

Map I.1. From a map of Lahore City and environs, circa 1910. From J. G. Bartholomew, A Literary and Historical Atlas of Asia *(London: J. M. Dent and Sons, 1913).*

India's towns and cities were thoroughly reworked. By the beginning of the twentieth century, therefore, to live in urban India meant something quite different than it had only two or three generations earlier.

Looking in detail at one city highlights the fact that urban change in colonial India was not a monolithic process: Preexisting peculiarities of history and culture, of climate and resources, and of the role a city played in the abstract hierarchy of broader state interests all mattered to the subsequent history of any particular city. Provincial capitals and older medium-size cities (like Lahore), for example, took a slightly different trajectory than the major port cities of Calcutta, Madras, and Bombay. Cities like Lahore may indeed be more broadly representative of urban change in British India than the latter three "presidency" cities,[7] despite the prominence of those cities in scholarship on India's colonial urban history. While my focus will remain largely on Lahore, therefore, this book is not only about that city.

MAKING A "MODERN" CITY

My use of the term "modern" to describe a city, in the title of this book and throughout its pages, refers to both an empirical and an imagined entity. Most scholars would agree that modern cities can be partially defined on the basis of functional criteria. Most important among these, perhaps, are the presence of zoning (with industry, commerce, administration, and residence all occupying more or less separate areas), of a nominally secular form of institutionalized governance whose jurisdiction is coextensive with the territory of the city (in English, this territory is usually called a "municipality"), and of the concentration of industrial and commercial activities in the city in service of a broader regional or national economy.[8] While most modern cities fail to attain all these criteria in full measure—for instance, many cities combine housing, industry, and commerce in the same area—in a very general sense, the modern city can be distinguished as a particular type based on the presence of, or the intention (often expressed legislatively) to enact each of, these three criteria. Note, in addition, that all these characteristics can be confirmed visually, located on maps and in bylaws, and assessed in quantitative and empirical ways. In this sense, a "modern city" can exist empirically regardless of its geographic location or cultural setting.

The modern city is simultaneously an imagined entity, however, as indeed all cities are. Here, questions of culture and geography become more relevant. While the number of ways modern cities have been imagined is coextensive with the number of people who have imagined them, I am most concerned in this book with a particular, broadly shared, idea or sensibility that has helped define modern cities as such. This is the sense, captured in a wide range of imaginative literature and humanistic scholarship, that the modern city is a place of both danger and promise, of both unprecedented human depravity and the highest of cultural attainments.[9] While this sentiment is most closely associated with writing on the nineteenth-century industrialized Western metropolis, this book traces, in part, how the same sentiment became a constitutive feature of urban discourse in colonial India.

In the modern Western metropolis, scholars have argued, the shock of the crowd and of suprahuman landscapes of industry, newly promiscuous forms of sociality, and an accumulation of both riches and poverty gave impetus to the idea of the city as a source of both danger and promise. Underlying both, and holding the potential for things to go badly or well in taut juxtaposition, was the experience of constant, inexorable, and irreversible change—in social relationships, in sources of authority, and in the materiality of everyday life.[10] The promise of inevitable change therefore held out the future as a privileged horizon of concern: The potential to control what the future would become provided an enduring motive for human intervention in urban life. It was assumed that the results of those interventions, moreover, would eventually be tangibly apparent, visible in the city's surfaces and activities, in the very way it looked and operated.

This sense that the city *itself* proffered an open-ended future and that the tangible features of the city—its people, streets, and buildings—would be in some sense diagnostic of that future's qualities is as much a characteristic feature of what I will call the modern city as are functional zoning, institutional governance, and the concentration of capital. Unlike the latter three features, however, this sensibility is less easily quantified, less obviously empirical, and less amenable to the language of measurement and description. In other words, understanding how modern cities have been imagined in different settings requires attending much more carefully to cultural narratives and intellectual preoccupations tied to particular geographies and histories.

Urban and architectural historian Zeynep Çelik acknowledged this task in her book on colonial Algiers.[11] In a passage juxtaposing Frantz Fanon's famous description of the "native" medina in a North African colonial city with architect Le Corbusier's description of Algiers, Çelik underscored how the same material setting can elicit radically different responses. For Fanon, the medina under colonial occupation was a "crouching village, a town on its knees, a town wallowing in the mire." For Le Corbusier, conversely, it was a district completely "in consonance with nature" that opened generously onto the sea, a place where "barbarians" could live "in solitude, in well-being."[12] Setting aside Çelik's analysis of the ideological differences embedded in these two descriptions, I point to her example for the way it illustrates the impossibility of locating a neutral, Archimedean point from which to comprehend any given city. Put somewhat differently, any city is constituted as much imaginatively as it is physically of bricks and mortar. Indeed, my premise throughout this book will be that these two features of a city cannot be dissociated from one another, either in scholarly analyses or in the lived experience of the people who inhabit it.

COLONIAL DIFFERENCE

My interest in the colonial history of a modern city thus raises the question of cultural difference. Such a city was composed of physical features that sometimes departed from and sometimes aligned with the empirical features of modern cities elsewhere, and it possessed

qualities in the imaginations of people who lived, worked, and passed through it that sometimes departed from and sometimes aligned with the same qualities imagined of cities elsewhere in the world during the same period. Therefore, coming to terms with the history of
that city requires attending to questions of difference and similarity, of what is culturally
specific and what is broadly shared, and of the processes through which architectural and
urban traditions become transferred, altered, or secured.

   A common response to these issues in scholarship on urban India has been to assess
the material forms of cities in terms of their adherence to or departure from Western models. This is a key feature of all "Westernization" hypotheses, which describe the Indian city
as a version—usually an inadequate one—of the modern Western city in its formal material qualities, styles of architecture, modes of fashion, and civil institutions, but a version
in which a lingering trace of the "local" manifests itself in the quirky, infelicitous, or naive
misappropriation of some Western principle or object.[13] This hypothesis allows material
objects to be assessed in isolation from the social practices that give them meaning and to
be made to function instead as signs of their users' or makers' cultural orientation.[14] Material objects that do not bear the marks of Westernization, or that do so only ambiguously,
can still be assimilated by a descriptive vocabulary that reifies a West/non-West distinction—they are either "Western" or they are not.

   This was an explicit assumption in an earlier generation of writing on "third world"
development, and while the Westernization hypothesis no longer retains much purchase in
scholarly circles, it is still a common explanation of cultural change in both the Western and
South Asian media. Perhaps the greatest weakness of this approach, for the purposes of this
study, is that if everything is assessed in terms of its conformity with a (usually vaguely
defined) "Western" trend or model, it becomes difficult to distinguish between phenomena
that may have little to do with a West/non-West relationship and those that directly result
from it.[15] As anthropologist Talal Asad powerfully argues, "The West is what it is in large
part because of its relationship to the non-West, and vice versa. And if by Western modernity one means the economies, politics, and knowledges characteristic of European countries, then much of this is incomprehensible without reference to Europe's links with the
non-European world." But this particular relationship does not and cannot account for
everything under the sun. As Asad points out, certain experiences "have nothing to do with
the West/non-West relationship. . . . There are experiences that have to do with other kinds
of relationships, such as the relationship of a given people to a distinctive past."[16] It will be
a fundamental premise of this book that formal similarities are only a starting point for
comparing different material cultural traditions. The fact that some of Lahore's colonial-
era buildings, streets, and patterns of occupation seem formally similar to Anglo-European
models thus provides an opening into questions of cultural difference rather than auto-
matic evidence of Westernization.

   Scholars from the disparate disciplines that now make up the field of colonial and
postcolonial studies have developed more sophisticated approaches to the question of
how cultural difference can be given an adequate analytical space in our scholarship. One

approach, which we might call "social constructionist," begins by eschewing all forms of cultural essentialism, or the idea that difference derives from timeless, pregiven, or unchanging cultural essences unmarked by processes of historical change and miscegenation. It is precisely the latter processes, according to cultural critic Stuart Hall (an influential representative of this approach), through which cultural difference is itself constituted as a relational, shifting, and always-incomplete "play" within a discourse on "identity." "Cultural identities come from somewhere, have histories," Hall writes, "but, like everything which is historical, they undergo constant transformation."[17]

For Hall, it is not that cultural difference does not exist per se—it comes, after all, from "somewhere." Rather, the opportunity to recuperate difference as some kind of "transcendental spirit inside us" has for him, and others, been foreclosed by the vicissitudes of time. Hall thus consigns the insight that difference is something that "already exists," that it comes from "somewhere" in particular, to the analytically fuzzy realm of "memory, fantasy, narrative, and myth."[18] While social constructionists avoid essentializing the concept of culture, I nevertheless find this approach limiting. Because of its tendency to frame cultural difference as a kind of rhetorical claim, it too quickly forecloses enquiry into forms of cultural difference that may operate outside the contours of rhetoric, including, importantly, those that may inhere in such nondiscursive media as buildings and other physical objects. The social constructionist approach also cedes too much ground, I believe, to the normative categories liberal humanism has provided for ordering difference within a single frame, including the important categories of "history," "identity," and "myth." Finally, by dismissing enquiry into how difference may in some ways be "real"—and thus avoiding the difficult task of translation that such an enquiry would entail—the category of the "real" is paradoxically reified as an unknowable yet omnipresent endowment.

A second approach to the question of cultural difference starts from a different assumption, namely, that "real," substantive, and "immiscible" cultural differences constitute an actually existing dimension of human experience that needs to be dealt with in our analyses. While some analysts have argued that rendering "untranslatable" cultural practices transparent within the hegemonic languages of Western academia amounts to an act of "epistemological violence," others have argued for the ethical necessity of doing just that.[19] While keenly sensitive to processes of historical transformation in the constitution of modern subjectivities, historian Dipesh Chakrabarty, for one, is unwilling to dismiss the existence of (and constitutive role played by) radically different life-worlds *within* modernity. Self-critically reflecting on his own previous research into the history of factory labor in Bengal, where laborers commonly invoked the agency of Hindu gods to facilitate a range of tasks at hand, Chakrabarty writes that "a secular subject like history faces certain problems in handling practices in which gods, spirits or the supernatural have agency in the world."[20] Chakrabarty's solution to these problems is not to cease and desist from writing history, however; nor is it to abandon altogether the task of "rough translation" required to make differences intelligible in academic writing. The latter choice Chakrabarty refuses largely on ethical grounds: "It may be legitimately argued that the administration of justice by modern institutions requires us to imagine the world through the languages of the social sciences," he reasons, since "one cannot argue with modern bureaucracies and other instruments of governmentality without recourse to the secular time and narratives of history and sociology" (72, 86).

At the same time, Chakrabarty urges historians to acknowledge both the "finitude" of history's secular outlook and the "scandalous" nature of "rough translations" required to render radical forms of cultural difference intelligible in social-scientific discourse (90). In my own work, I have come to a conviction that "immiscible" ways of life coexist empirically in modernity. Leaving aside for a moment my belief that radically Other ways of inhabiting the world are as much a feature of modern Euro-American experience as they are of that in South Asia, the urban restructuring of Lahore under British rule produced a constant juxtaposition of practices, epistemologies, and ways of inhabiting urban space that derived from diverse—and sometimes incompatible—practical and intellectual traditions. Consider, for example, Lahore resident Noor Ahmad Chishti, who was commissioned by a British official to write a history of the city in 1867.[21] As I show in chapter 6, Chishti's analysis, *Tahqiqaat Chishti: Tarikh-e-Lahor ka Encyclopedia* (Chishti's Inquiries: An Encyclopedia of Lahore's History), derived from an older Indo-Islamic tradition of historical writing that his patron saw as incompatible with the modern, objectivist history he desired. By calling his book an encyclopedia, however, Chishti registered his awareness of the necessity of engaging the older tradition with the protocols of the newly emergent tradition that arrived with the British. As many other examples in my book will show, the unavoidable juxtaposition of different life-worlds *within* the universalizing languages and practices of modern institutions was a defining feature of life in colonial Lahore. Addressing how those juxtapositions played out in the languages and practices of modern urbanism thus forms a central focus of this book. As Paul Rabinow similarly observes in his important study of French colonial North Africa, colonial urbanism was in large measure about bringing "modernity and difference into a common frame."[22]

My digression into a discussion of "difference" is prompted by the central role that the concept has played in current scholarship on colonial urbanism,[23] including two important recent monographs on cities in colonial India. A brief description of how these two works intersect with some of the ideas addressed above will help ground the discussion more concretely and clarify my own approach for the reader.

Jyoti Hosagrahar's 2005 book on Delhi, *Indigenous Modernities: Negotiating Architecture and Urbanism,* advances the concept of "indigenous modernity" to elucidate the city's colonial transformation into a "hybrid" city, one that juxtaposed both indigenous and extralocal elements in paradoxical and unstable combinations. In her well-researched and creative analysis, Hosagrahar shows how local customs, spatial practices, and knowledge traditions in the city both changed and were changed by a modern form of urbanism and scientific rationality that she sees as having been "imposed" on the city by the British.[24] Hosagrahar thus argues that Delhi's colonial urban forms were the result of local adaptations to Western ideals and were neither purely "Indian" nor purely "Western" creations. Instead, the products of colonial urban restructuring evinced "the irregular, the uneven, and the unexpected" through material juxtapositions of older and newer, local and foreign, elements.[25] Advancing a social constructionist notion of difference to account for Delhi's "hybrid forms of architecture," Hosagrahar underscores the "elusive, contradictory, tentative, negotiated, and fluid" meanings the city's residents attributed to the urban landscape.[26] The disjunctive, "indigenously modern" landscapes of colonial Delhi were thus unique, Hosagrahar implies, but no more so than those of any other modern city: "All modernisms are the consequence of negotiations of an imagined ideal with the particularities of a place and its socio-political context," she argues, "and hence [all] are *indigenous modernities*."[27]

Swati Chattopadhyay's 2005 book *Representing Calcutta: Modernity, Nationalism, and the Colonial Uncanny* is focused, rather differently, on the "structures of power and knowledge" that underlay diverse nineteenth-century representations of the city. Far from inhabiting a realm of pure "ideas," for Chattopadhyay the literary, artistic, and investigative modes of representation through which Bengalis, British, and others appropriated and lent meaning to Calcutta were constitutively grounded in the material fabric of the city and, indeed, directly helped produce it. Unlike Hosagrahar, Chattopadhyay sees British attitudes and practices as foundational to all subsequent developments in the city. The elite and middle-class Bengali protagonists who form the core of Chattopadhyay's analysis, however, "addressed, and at the same time bypassed" these British practices to craft "other ways of describing the self and community" and a distinctive spatial imagination.[28] In particular, she argues, Bengali nationalists both absorbed and internalized British anxieties over the "opacity" of native urban space—its difficulty of being mastered, its excess of sounds, smells, and textures— and turned them to strategic advantage: "The most powerful departures from British modes of representation [by Bengalis] were not geared towards illuminating the opaqueness that could not be accessed through Western modes of representation," Chattopadhyay writes, "but to strategically redistribute the opaqueness over a larger area."[29] The result was a recoding of everyday spaces and rituals in the city—formerly the objects of British disdain—as deep emblems of a Bengali national identity. While British and Bengali "representations [of the city] shared an acknowledgment of the power of vision," she argues, "the British anxiety of not being able to see through spaces was paralleled in Bengali discourse by a deep distrust of the merely visible."[30]

Chattopadhyay's approach to cultural "difference" in her eloquent and important book thus differs substantially from Hosagrahar's social constructionist perspective and aligns instead much more closely with the second approach discussed above. For Hosagrahar, "difference" in the colonial city emerges as the hybrid product of two (or more) dissimilar traditions that have reached some form of (usually uneven) accommodation through adaptation. For Chattopadhyay, conversely, "difference" is figured as a quality *internal* to the complex tradition of seeing and representation that came to be shared in Calcutta by colonizer and colonized alike. Put somewhat differently, Bengali nationalists crafted alternative (and oppositional) representational practices *within* a coherent colonial modernity whose trajectory was, nevertheless, contingent upon ongoing processes of "translation."[31]

A sensitive reader will discover my debt in this book to the theoretical interests both these authors have advanced. Like Chattopadhyay, I am most interested in understanding how a single, dominant, intellectual and practical tradition—which can be called "modern" urbanism—encountered the strange, the unfamiliar, and "newness" more generally in colonial India without entirely losing its coherence. I will argue in what follows that the tradition of modern urbanism brought to India by British colonialism did not simply replace preexisting practices and attitudes wholesale, creating everything anew in its own image. Rather, its protagonists had to demonstrate their relevance within, and establish effective articulations with, those "different," longer-standing, and sometimes incompatible practices and attitudes. Importantly, as the protocols of this new urban tradition reached deeper into local society, the protagonists of modern urbanism in India increasingly came from both the British and Indian communities.

MATERIAL AND MORALITY

I will conclude this introduction with a brief thematic sketch of the book's individual chapters, introducing the different settings and spatial scales I have found useful for answering the question of what made Lahore distinctive. Before doing so, however, let me turn to the question of what Lahore shared with other modern cities. Most important, I will argue, is that the changes I consider in Lahore were all part of a larger tradition of urban reform whose proponents emphasized a distinctive materialist approach to fostering societal development. The lay and professional people who proposed and carried out urban reforms in Lahore, both Europeans and Indians, shared an assumption that the material world embodied immaterial qualities that were both tangible and agentive. They were tangible because people who shared that assumption believed that no assemblage of material objects could exist without producing some effect on an observer. They were agentive because the effects objects produced were believed to have the power to shape human conduct. One further idea made this approach particularly valuable for the task of urban reform: the idea that material settings and their intangible qualities had lawlike regularities that could be known, adjusted, and applied.

Two important corollaries to this idea helped determine how its abstract propositions were applied practically. The first was a belief that the material world had the power to shape human conduct regardless of one's willingness to be shaped by it. There was a determinate connection, in other words, between a material environment and the mode of living it produced and corresponded to. British writer John Loudon articulated this belief in his 1833 encyclopedia of farm and garden design, where he wrote that "uncouth, mean, ragged, dirty houses, constituting the body of any town, will regularly be accompanied by coarse, groveling manners. The dress, the furniture, the equipage, the mode of living, and the manners, will all correspond with the appearance of the buildings."[32] Victorian essayist and parson Charles Kingsley, in a lecture on sanitation delivered at Bristol in 1857—the same year British troops waged an all-out battle to suppress a mass revolt among Indian troops—

articulated the same idea at the scale of an entire city: "The social state of a city depends directly on its moral state, and . . . the moral state of a city depends—how far I know not, but frightfully, to an extent as yet uncalculated, and perhaps incalculable—on the physical state of that city."[33]

A second corollary followed from the first. If one could discern the determinate relationship between a physical setting and the "mode of living" it produced, as many believed, then the former could be altered to change the latter. Put more simply, once the lawlike features of a setting's immaterial qualities were known, they could be harnessed to produce *particular,* desirable effects. The colonial actors I discuss in this book all believed that with conscious attention to design and organization, the ordinary material fabric of a city would continuously irrigate its residents with a flow of salutary effects. Moreover, most of them envisioned this process working almost effortlessly, as though it were an extension of nature itself.

The idea that urban society could be recursively shaped by and through material objects and arrangements of space was central to nineteenth-century traditions of urban reform across the Anglo-European world. It was central to nineteenth-century discourse on public health, sanitation, and disease, for example, a discourse that directly shaped how cities and buildings were planned. What I show below is that writings on public health and sanitation shared this feature with several other disciplinary genres, including works of architectural pedagogy, housekeeping manuals, and local urban histories, among others. The same idea, importantly, was central to most of the colonial urban projects explored in this book, from designs for model houses, institutions, and neighborhoods to didactic pamphlets extolling the virtues of domestic hygiene. Despite their differences in genre and detail, these projects were all designed to alter Indian society by changing the material settings of everyday life. These assumptions about the ability of cities' material qualities to affect society thus constitute one feature that Lahore shared with modern cities elsewhere.

Those assumptions have implications for how we might understand the nature of colonial power that these endeavors participated in. As a mode of social domination, the projects I discuss were designed to mold a person's sentiments and faculties of reason rather than to habituate their body to particular behaviors. The degree of coercion and control involved in them varied considerably; some were rigorously enforced, while others were fully voluntary. Even at the most coercive end of the spectrum, however, the methods considered in this book were largely meant to persuade toward, rather than force, social change. The ability to persuade, in turn, presumed the existence of a reflective subject, one whose capacity for reasoned judgment could be shaped and improved. For this reason, the practices I highlight in this book differ from what Michel Foucault calls "disciplinary" practices, a modern form of control that identifies the docile body (rather than the reflecting mind) as a site that can be "subjected, used, transformed and improved" through a process of "uninterrupted, constant coercion."[34]

As scholars of South Asia and elsewhere have shown, disciplinary practices were central to the working of colonial prisons, penal colonies, workhouses, and asylums, where movement was restricted and behavior closely monitored.[35] The same was not true of most settings I examine here, however. Rather than isolating the body's gestures and turning them into an "automatism of habit," the projects I explore worked through far-less-precise processes of emulation, self-conscious reflection on the material world, and contemplation of exemplary models.[36] As an expression of governmental power, these projects were designed to gradually obviate the need for more forceful approaches. David Scott has described this kind of colonial "governmentality" as one "concerned above all with disabling old forms of life by systematically breaking down their conditions, and with constructing in their place new conditions so as to enable—indeed, so as to oblige—new forms of life to come into being."[37] The material environments of everyday life were considered to be among the most important "conditions" enabling those "old forms of life," and their systematic rebuilding was the focus of a wide range of colonial efforts.

The propensity to think with and through the material features of a city in this way—to draw a determinate link between material and nonmaterial phenomena in an urban milieu—is not a "natural" habit of mind, of course. The assumption that, say, a physically decrepit building might bring about moral decrepitude in its inhabitants is formed over time and in reference to a particular setting and particular historical processes. Part of my task in this book, therefore, is to describe the particular kinds of connections people working on urban reform in India drew between human character and the physical environment and to place these in historical perspective. Central to understanding how these assumptions came to be shared, however, is to recognize the way those assumptions were supported by a distinctive materialist pedagogy that accompanied British rule in colonial India.

Early nineteenth-century religious, economic, and political thought in Britain and Europe provided the rationale for employing education in the work of colonial governance more generally. Historian Eric Stokes has traced the importance of education in colonial reform to the twin influences of British Evangelicalism and the ideology of free trade, both of which dominated early nineteenth-century theories of governance in India.[38] According to Stokes, Evangelical reformers felt that education would prepare Indian minds to accept Christian truth by "liberating the individual conscience from the tyranny of the [Hindu] priest."[39] Education would also remove the obstinate strictures of paganism, ignorance (rendered often as illiteracy), and civilizational decline that many in Britain thought India was mired in. Finally, by liberating Indian society from its attachment to "immemorial habit," education would create new "dispositions" and "knowledges" necessary for Indians to improve their material condition, not least by cultivating Indian taste for the products of British industry. For Stokes, this mingling of secular self-interest and religious fervor provided a lasting motivation for liberal reform in India, where "the passionate conviction that the ideals of altruism and the strongest claims of self-interest coincided."[40]

Continental and British empiricist philosophy, in turn, helped ground this conviction in the doctrine of man's fundamental "malleability." During the course of the nineteenth century, disparate notions about the character of human nature concurred in the assumption that, as philosopher Maurice Mandelbaum put it, "there are no specific ways of thinking and acting ... so deeply entrenched in human nature that they cannot be supplanted, either by the effects of the circumstances in which men are placed, or by means of man's own efforts."[41] Whether Indians should be strictly considered "men," in the sense implied by that doctrine, had been generally answered in the affirmative following John Locke's widely accepted attack on the theory of "innate" human endowments; consensus prevailed that Indians, like Englishmen, began life as malleable clay. These two activities—considering the effects of "men's" circumstances and the deliberate training of thought and action to address improvement in those circumstances—coalesced to provide a firm foundation for British reform in nineteenth-century India.

How did these abstract philosophical ideas inform the concrete work of urbanism in colonial India? The material environment of the Indian city was drawn into colonial discourse as both an object and a resource. This was due partly to respect for the knowledge gained through sensory experience of the material world and partly to the close connection drawn between "environment" and "moral improvement" in liberalism's deeply materialist outlook. A pedagogic technique that was developed at the beginning of the nineteenth century, the "object lesson," helps illustrate these points in more detail. The concept of object lessons migrated gradually away from the classroom into ordinary speech during the late nineteenth century and became a much-used metaphor for describing a diverse range of nineteenth-century reforms in India aimed at the development of human perceptive and moral capacities.

A DISCOURSE ON OBJECTS

Swiss educationist and social reformer Johann Pestalozzi (1746–1827) first developed object lessons as a teaching method. Pestalozzi's method entailed having children closely observe and then describe objects drawn from nature, objects he considered to be "pure."[42] By answering a series of scripted questions about an object's physical properties (Is the object rough or smooth? Is it heavy or light?), students gradually learned to connect their sensory perceptions to more-abstract scientific properties. A proponent of Pestalozzi's method summarized its purpose by drawing the following connection between attentive observation of objects and the cultivation of moral judgment, the end goal of the method:

> The senses furnish to the mind its means of contact with the external world. Through sensations the mind gains perceptions from the objects around it. Perceptions lead to conceptions of ideas, which are retained or recalled by memory. Imagination takes up these ideas, combines and presents them in new forms. Reason proceeds to investigate them by more definite modes, and judgment is the result.[43]

Pestalozzi's methods were widely adopted for use in Great Britain, Europe, North America, and eventually colonies in the British Empire. They were referred to in subsequent teaching manuals as "Object Methods," "Object Teaching," "Objective Method," and finally "Object Lessons." By the early nineteenth century, object lessons were adapted to the

Lancasterian system of schooling in Britain and the United States, which greatly facilitated their introduction into colonial school curricula in India.[44]

Historian Parna Sengupta has analyzed object teaching in India as occupying a nexus between Protestant Evangelicalism and nineteenth-century British theories of civilizational development. Sengupta writes that "to Protestant evangelicals, who were heavily involved in teacher training and primary schooling in Britain and its colonies, the falsity of other religions and faiths was partially attributable to their relationship to concrete objects and concrete ways of thinking."[45] Although object lessons subordinated the different epistemological status "objects" might have in different cultural systems to a primarily secular and empiricist notion of "concrete" versus "abstract" qualities (an example of the "rough translations" secular discourse imposes on Other practices), Sengupta argues that object theory nevertheless privileged a Protestant Christian belief that abstract thinking—as opposed to the fetishization of "inert" idols—was a mark of cultural advancement.

Pestalozzian pedagogy also had its secular supporters. Thomas Babington Macaulay wrote his famous "Minute on Education" while arguing to extend the Lancasterian method to a program for mass education in India. Macaulay's call to create an English-educated middle class in India "who may be interpreters between us and the millions whom we govern—a class of persons Indian in color and blood, but English in tastes, in opinions, in morals, and in intellect," is an adequate summary of the goals behind materialist reform in India more generally.[46]

The diffusion of Pestalozzi's methods, sometimes augmented with schoolroom disciplines adapted to the Lancasterian method (including codes of drill), is evidenced by the circulation of textbooks on "object teaching," published in large numbers from the mid-nineteenth century onward, to teacher-training schools in Europe and abroad. In 1885, a newly published manual on object lessons appeared in Lahore. The following year, the Punjab Textbook Committee prescribed the use of the Urdu text *Ashya ke Sabaq* (a literal translation of "object lessons"), by Umrao Singh and Lala Munshi Lal, for use in normal schools throughout Punjab and at the Teacher's Training College in Lahore.[47] As all these manuals make clear, object lessons were considered especially suitable for instructing nonliterate students, either young children entering school or, alternately, adults who had had no previous formal education. This combination of features made object lessons a potentially powerful device for training what colonial officials thought of as "childlike" Indian minds.[48]

FROM OBJECTS TO MODELS

In addition to appearing in teaching manuals in colonial schools, object lessons had another presence in colonial India. By the turn of the twentieth century, and occasionally earlier, the term "object lesson" was used extensively to characterize the result of seeing or otherwise physically experiencing some event that imprinted a vivid lesson on the mind. It is this second, more general sense of the object lesson that more directly characterizes the goal behind a number of reform projects discussed in this book. The migration of the term "object lesson" from specialized pedagogical discourse to ordinary speech paralleled the gradual abandonment of object teaching in schools. By the turn of the twentieth century, Pestalozzi's methods were largely considered outmoded. For one thing, by that time fewer people in general believed that "dispositions," "character," and "proper sentiments" were bound together with the physical environment in such determinant and mechanistic ways. In his 1999 book *Suspensions of Perception: Attention, Spectacle, and Modern Culture,* Jonathan Crary documents the rejection (by the 1880s in Europe and the United States) of earlier "passive" views of human understanding—which posited a subject passively receiving sensations through unwilled action—and the concurrent rise of models that emphasized, among other things, the role of "memory, desire, will, [and] anticipation" in perceiving and processing sensory information.[49] Late nineteenth-century developments in the relatively new field of psychology also helped discredit the earlier methods. The study of "behavior," in particular, led to the development of increasingly scientific methods to gauge the working of the mind. In the process, an earlier emphasis on "experience" was gradually replaced by a focus on "attention," "conditioned response," and various forms of selective awareness.[50] Nevertheless, we can also see the less-specialized use of the term "object lesson" in colonial documents as evidence of a broadening conviction, at least among English speakers, that objects from the material world had the power to instruct. Indeed, we might say that objects themselves increasingly bore the pedagogical burden without the need for a human instructor.

URBAN OBJECTS

This brief exposition of the object lesson is useful for understanding a key assumption underlying the kinds of projects this book is concerned with; namely, many officials engaged in the administration of public life in colonial India assumed the physical landscape of a town or city was replete with agentive—and therefore potentially educative—objects. These would include such things as buildings, natural landscape features, and the entire physical infrastructure that went into making a street. With conscious attention to design and organization, the ordinary material fabric of a village or city might be harnessed to a broader program of social improvement. In projects based on this assumption, reform would derive from a kind of somatic experience, one that worked tirelessly and pervasively on the sense faculties of anyone intently contemplating his or her surroundings. M. L. Dhingra, an Indian physician based in Edinburgh who wrote at the turn of the century, stated the principle succinctly: "The influence which surroundings exercise over the human mind is, I believe, enormous. . . . [It is] not a mere question of 'brickwork and mortar,' but an important civilizing endeavor."[51]

While object lessons were sometimes far afield from the practical issues involved in shaping Lahore's new neighborhoods and buildings, they illustrate that behind such mundane activities lay complex ideas about the relationship between human qualities shaped by a material universe and the intentions of those who saw that relationship as useful.

While intention is ever only a starting point for understanding a material cultural history of urban change, not least because intentions are quickly overturned by the actual uses material changes are put to, they provide a framework for understanding why people do what they do. In the chapters that follow, I aim to show how this and other frameworks helped produce an urban setting in north India where questions about the necessary, desired, or possible relationships that could exist between material and immaterial things, between human life and the world of urban objects, became a central preoccupation.

THE DESIGN OF THIS BOOK

If these frameworks were among the key features of a tradition of modern urbanism that Lahore shared with modern cities elsewhere, then how do I discern what distinguishes colonial Lahore from any other "modern" city? Each of the chapters in this book is a sustained attempt to answer that question in a different way. The chapters are organized thematically, and I make no claims to present anything like a comprehensive history of the city in what follows. Nor do I claim that the modern practices and modes of appropriating the city I concentrate on in this book were universally—or even broadly—shared. Like all historians, my account is limited both by the "finitude" of the questions I have asked of my materials and by the nature of those materials themselves. My choice to focus on what made Lahore distinctively "modern" was in this sense determined, in part, by the nature of the archive I availed myself of. Within that archive, the middle-class, mostly literate people who described their city as becoming modern were simply the loudest, most frequent, and most consistently recorded voices. While I attribute a significance to those voices that exceeds their presence in relative numbers among all of Lahore's colonial residents, neither I nor they can claim to have provided a definitive account of their city's colonial history. A brief preview of the thematic content of each chapter, therefore, will indicate which settings and processes I found most important for addressing the question of what made Lahore a distinctive modern city.

Chapter 1 addresses the question via genealogy, by examining the precolonial development of the city. The focus of the chapter is largely morphological, concentrating in particular on sixteenth- through eighteenth-century Mughal-era changes to the city. I argue that the colonial city of Lahore was built on a Mughal palimpsest, one that provided a generative principle of spatial arrangement and a cultural style of urban governance that the British both inherited and modified. The European accounts I cited above as remarking on the "ruins" in the plain surrounding the older walled city were essentially describing traces of the city's Mughal-era suburbs. Despite what these writers assumed, however, those traces were not inert. Mughal ruins and zones of settlement provided both building materials and building sites for most of Lahore's major colonial institutions. Within Lahore's city walls, the Mughal-era pattern of streets, buildings, and open spaces, along with a Mughal system for adjudicating urban property transactions, altered but little during the nineteenth and twentieth centuries. These and other elements of the Mughal-era city formed an obdurate presence, both materially and imaginatively, in what became modern Lahore. Chapter 1 thus approaches the question of what made Lahore distinct from other modern cities by attending to its distinctive genealogy.

Chapter 2 considers how Lahore's British officials conducted early enquiries into the settlements and landforms in and around Lahore, and how the knowledge they gained from these enquiries found its way into the various discursive genres that structured administrative discourse. As my analysis shows, British protocols of observation and description were only partially effective at appropriating and making sense of the range of objects the colonial state placed under its purview, even if colonial interventions that followed from those protocols betrayed an assumption that they were effective enough. The result was a logic of colonial intervention based on the kind of "rough translations" I have already mentioned, a logic in which different traditions of organizing and inhabiting urban and rural space were made to conform to a single, Anglo-European ideal. The attainment of that ideal was never entirely successful, of course, and the projects I explore in chapter 2 underscore how "rough translation" as an operating principle produced uneven levels of transformation across settings at different scales. The city's resulting lack of conformity with the Western urban models that were imposed provides another point of departure for answering the question of what made modern Lahore unique.

Chapter 3 considers in detail several major colonial institutions in the European district of the city (called the "civil station" in Lahore, as in other colonial Indian cities). Rather than viewing these institutions from the standpoint of how their builders intended them to function, I ask the reader to understand these institutions as the result of collaboration between the elite British and the Indian builders, patrons, and designers who made them a reality. The focus here is both on the changing practical and intellectual traditions through which buildings were imagined and designed in the colony and on the multiple ways the landscape that resulted refracted differentially through British and Indian attitudes about the meanings and uses buildings might support.

Starting from the premise that ordinary, vernacular buildings need not be analytically separated from architecture with a capital *A*, chapters 4 and 5 foreground commonplace domestic architecture in Lahore. Chapter 4 explores how the ordinary Indian townhouse in Lahore was altered in response to changing attitudes about public health, building technology, and domestic reform articulated in a range of vernacular discourses. Chapter 5 explores the bungalow as a social and architectural milieu whose physical features and social arrangements militated against the bourgeois ideal of domestic comfort that their British residents hoped to attain from them. When read together, these two chapters suggest that houses in the colonial city distributed homely comforts unevenly across the fault lines of race and class. While the same observation has been made of modern cities elsewhere, of course, the reconceived and retooled qualities of the Indian townhouse I discuss in chapter 4 and the British sense of domestic anxiety I discuss in chapter 5 were a direct result of material qualities, social arrangements, and racial dynamics particular to the Indian setting.

The final chapter of the book draws the previous sections together by considering the divergent strategies Indian writers used to comprehend and represent their city in literary works. The texts I consider, both fiction and nonfiction, help reveal the emergence of a sensibility about the city that, I have argued above, appears elsewhere at around the same time. In particular, I will argue that the gradual coalescence of a conviction that the city was useful for deciphering the present—its moral trajectory, its nodes of authority and disrepute—and, in turn, for imagining a possible future became a prominent feature of urbanistic writing during the city's gradual reconfiguration under British rule. This new mode of thinking about the city emerged in parallel with older ways of doing the same thing; importantly, however, while the latter modes of writing and thought diminished over time, they never fully disappeared. While those Indian residents who wrote about Lahore at the turn of the twentieth century could and did avail themselves of new epistemologies for making sense of an urban heritage, their works nevertheless bear traces of other ways of knowing and evaluating the city in terms that derived from older intellectual traditions.

AN URBAN PALIMPSEST

The Precolonial Development of Lahore

An entire past comes to dwell in a new house.
—GASTON BACHELARD, *The Poetics of Space*

1

From the air, Lahore appears today as a dense agglomeration of low-rise buildings spread across a large plain sparsely covered with vegetation. On all but the clearest of days, a thick haze of dust, smoke, and vehicle exhaust gives the city a murky yellow brown tint, making it, as one first sees it framed through an airplane window, look like a poorly focused sepia photograph. To the east, Lahore terminates a few miles short of the Indian border, made visible at night by a row of tungsten-lamp-lit steel observation towers that recede gradually into the distance. At the northern edge of the city one can make out the floodplain of the Ravi River and a broad grassy area most people still call Minto Park, despite the Pakistan government's having renamed it after Muhammad Iqbal, the symbolic poet-father of the nation. The oldest part of the city, called simply *Purana Shehr* (Old City), abuts the southern edge of Minto Park; on summer evenings its grassy fields are filled with city residents seeking cool breeze, open space, the companionship of friends, and the inexpensive pleasures offered by hawkers of cigarettes, plastic toys, and massages *(maalish)*. The Old City is encircled by a discontinuous line of older and newer masonry walls and a traffic-clogged circular road. The older walls exist by virtue of having clung tenaciously onto their sites, usually by providing the foundation for more recent, and more valuable, buildings. The newer walls seem to be continually under construction, one part of an anachronistic effort by the municipal government to underscore Lahore's medieval heritage. The streets in the Old City indeed largely follow routes laid out in the medieval era and seem carved as an afterthought from a solid mass of houses and shops. To the south of the Old City, in an area that was referred to during the colonial period as the "civil station" but that now has no particular name, building density decreases and roads become wider, straighter, and less heavily traveled. Further south still, beyond the civil station, suburban developments planned and settled in the last fifty years abut one another at odd angles. Informal squatter settlements *(katchi abadis)* occupy the interstices of this suburban armature; their unpaved roads and poorly constructed houses make up a large percentage of built space in the city.

Lahore's complex assemblage of streets and neighborhoods, along with the often abrupt transitions between them, is a source of familiarity and pleasure to some of the city's residents. Literary critic Sara Suleri Goodyear, who grew up in the city, wrote that Lahore's "streets wind absentmindedly between centuries, slapping an edifice of crude modernity against a medieval gate, forgetting and remembering beauty in pockets of merciful respite."[1] The city's complex spatiality has also been a source of confusion, however, for both residents and visitors. Reading accounts of Lahore written during the twentieth century, one is struck by frequent references to the city's elusive sense of order—including in those areas planned and built under British rule. The narrator of a 1927 report on the city described the colonial part of Lahore's civil station as being "well laid out with wide roads, though not, it would seem, according to any preconceived scheme."[2] A guidebook to the city written in the 1970s concluded that "the city cannot be divided into any hard and fast physical divisions. . . . [It is] a conglomeration of hundreds of *abadi*s [settled areas], colonies and settlements" that have "not grown under any specific plan."[3] Even Suleri, who otherwise took pleasure in the city's meandering qualities, had to admit that something about the city remained elusive: "Somehow one is always expecting to find Lahore," she wrote, "without [ever] quite locating it."[4]

This recurring sense of an older city partially hidden within a newer one, its presence hinted at by abrupt discontinuities of surface, by the remnants of distinct but unrelated plans, or by the sudden appearance of physical traces from the past, invokes the city as a kind of palimpsest. Like an actual palimpsest, Lahore bears the traces of many prior inscriptions, as well as of periods of erasure and overwriting; many elements of the city's previous inhabitations, in turn, have proved durable enough to be reused by later residents. The decision to reuse older fragments of the city sometimes derived from the logic of economy, a logic attached to older notions of the palimpsest as well: Reusing a parchment by erasing and writing over it was cheaper, after all, than "preparing new skin."[5] At other times the choice to reuse elements of the older city grew out of a sense that objects from the past were symbolically powerful, that they aided the imagination aside from (or in addition to) serving any utilitarian purpose. It will be the argument of this chapter that Lahore's precolonial urban spatial forms and traditions exerted an important presence, both physically and imaginatively, throughout the colonial period.

From a purely physical standpoint, the precolonial city inscribed an enduring pattern of paths, building sites, and actual buildings that subsequent generations used, altered, and built over without entirely erasing. British residents of nineteenth-century Lahore were acutely aware that they lived among and atop the physical detritus of a very old city. Rudyard Kipling, who lived several years in Lahore and worked as a reporter for the *Civil and Military Gazette* newspaper (from 1881 to 1887), described finding the "jawless skulls and rough-butted shank bones" of long-dead corpses jutting out from road-cuts and embankments after particularly heavy rains.[6] T. H. Thornton, an officer in the colonial civil service, found Mughal "coins and remains of jewellery" exposed by rains along "the *Moti Mahal*, or 'Regent Street' of old Lahore," an area in Lahore's mostly European civil station.[7] Abandoned older buildings were themselves drawn into colonial service in Lahore: The accountant general's office, railway headquarters, lieutenant governor's house, and Anglican church, among other key institutions, were all housed in retrofitted Mughal tombs.

For a wide variety of people and in many different ways, Lahore's precolonial buildings and spaces also asserted a symbolic presence during the colonial period. The numerous ruined and active tombs in the suburbs of the city continued to serve as repositories for memories of the city's important ancestors, as physical points of anchorage between a tumultuous present and an auspicious past, and as sites of collective celebration on saints' days and religious festivals. When British and Indian elites collaborated during the late nineteenth century in producing a new kind of civic landscape in the city, a development discussed most fully in chapter 3, they drew on a reservoir of visual forms and modes of patronage imbued with the stabilizing authority of antiquity. Lahore's precolonial monuments also became central features in a new genre of "local" urban history crafted by the city's Indian writers during the late nineteenth century. In these and other ways, the precolonial past of the city became more than mere detritus during the colonial period, more than so many rain-washed bones and coins and decaying or forgotten tombs.[8]

Later chapters in this book will show, on different scales and in different contexts, how British efforts to temper, control, or otherwise rewrite the significance of the city's past only served to ramify its importance in a range of counter discourses. In this chapter, however, I want to examine the city primarily as a physical object, analyzing some of the urban traditions that gave the city its formal character. The Mughal period in particular (especially from 1584 to the early eighteenth century) provided the most decisive influence on the city's subsequent form, since this was when many of the most enduring features of the city were established. A period of instability during the eighteenth century when the Mughals ceased using Lahore as a capital altered some, but not all, of these features. Large areas of Lahore's suburbs were abandoned during this time, and trade that once flowed steadily through the city was abruptly reduced. Stability returned to the city at the end of the eighteenth century, when Ranjit Singh made Lahore the capital of his Sikh kingdom. During the fifty years or so of consolidated Sikh rule in the Punjab (1799–1849), with Lahore as its administrative capital and nearby Amritsar as the commercial and spiritual capital, Lahore was selectively refurbished, though for the most part new constructions in the city were an extension of Mughal precedent. Therefore, when the British occupied Lahore in 1849 and replaced the Sikhs as the province's new rulers, they lived within a physical milieu whose basic features had been initiated under Mughal rule.

A second set of analyses in this chapter grows out of the premise that a city's physical form owes much to the legal traditions under which space and buildings are owned, bought and sold, and regulated and recorded in such things as codes, restrictive covenants, and deeds and other documents of ownership. In Mughal- and Sikh-era Punjab, these traditions were partially institutionalized through the offices of urban functionaries like the *kotwal* (head of town police) and *mohalladar* (neighborhood watchman) and by the court of the Muslim *qazi* (an official state judge to whom townspeople resorted more or less continually from the Mughal period until the early decades of British rule in north India). While the offices of the *qazi* and other urban officials in India were superseded by those of the British police and courts, precolonial modes of urban governance and property exchange provided a useful template (and sometimes actual personnel) for colonial-era urban institutions. My analysis in this chapter thus aims to sort out both the distinctive changes British rule brought to the city and the precolonial features of the city that continued to assert their relevance.

LAHORE AS AN IMPERIAL CITY

Unlike the important presidency capitals of British India—Calcutta, Madras, and Bombay—Lahore did not await the arrival of British rule on the subcontinent to become a prominent city. Indeed, Lahore's very location in the fertile and culturally diverse hinterland of the Indus River basin practically ensured that it would eventually become prominent (Map 1.1). All overland trade to India from the west came either through the difficult mountain passes of the Hindu Kush, whose foothills form the northwestern edge of Punjab Province, or through passes farther south on the route connecting Qandahar with Multan. Lahore lies directly on the ancient overland route that linked Delhi and points farther east with the Middle East, via Kabul and Iran. Because of its location on the east bank of the Ravi, a major north–south navigable waterway, Lahore was also an important node in riverine and overland trade between Kashmir in the north (over the Pir Panjal mountains), and the cities of Multan (near where the Ravi joins the Indus), Thatta, and seaports on the Arabian Sea to the south.

Overland and river-borne trade were only partly responsible for Lahore's eventual prominence as a city, however. Like other towns in the Punjab, Lahore was surrounded by a highly fertile agricultural zone where tobacco, indigo, and other products were produced for both trade and local consumption. Cotton and wool articles were manufactured in the city, as were long wooden riverboats, iron implements, and weapons. Lahore was also a major supplier of salt (shipped north to Kashmir), indigo (traded east with Bihar and Bengal), and horses. The Punjab's agricultural villages created a demand for the various kinds of urban services and manufactures that a city like Lahore could provide, including marketing, finance, and specialized agricultural equipment. In this way, rather than urban economies being parasitic on a largely self-sufficient hinterland, towns and villages in the Punjab were often mutually dependent.[9]

The most important reason Lahore became prominent, however, was its role as an imperial capital within a regional urban network. From the period of the Ghaznavid dynasty (circa 977–1186), for which, beginning in 1152, Lahore was the eastern capital, to the end of British rule on the Indian subcontinent in 1947, the Punjab's network of interlinked small, medium, and large cities was built on an imperial framework. The smallest unit in this urban system was the *qasba,* or small market town, providing services and manufactures that supported both agricultural and nonagricultural activities.[10] The *qasba* was linked administratively with several surrounding villages through the collection of agricultural revenue. It was also linked to these villages economically because it provided a market for surplus produce, credit, and manufactures of nonagricultural items.[11] Important *qasbas* in the vicinity of Lahore included Batala, Eminabad, and Kasur. *Qasbas* were in turn linked vertically to medium-size towns and small cities, places that had a broader range of administrative, manufacturing, trade, or service activities.[12] In the Punjab, important medium-size towns included Govindwal, Gujrat, Wazirabad, Ludhiana, and Ambala (Map 1.2). Finally, the largest cities in the system formed regional, and sometimes imperial, capitals. Such was the case with Lahore and Delhi in the Punjab, both of which served as imperial capitals for the Mughals and other pre-British dynasties. These largest cities combined market, manufacturing,

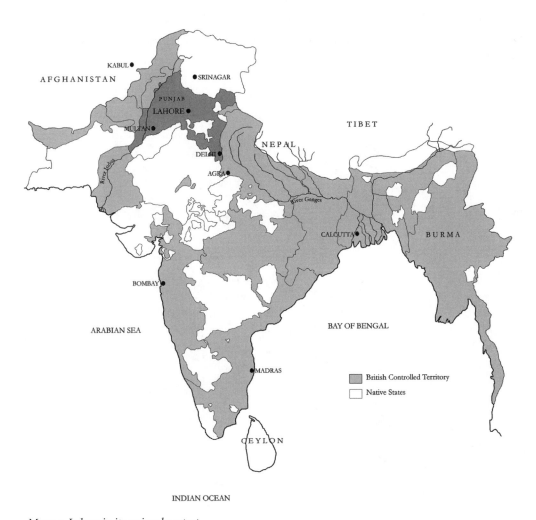

Map 1.1. Lahore in its regional context.

and administrative functions, and they often began as (and remained) important nodes in a network of transregional overland trade routes.

Like the urban system that Lahore was a part of, the basic morphology of Lahore and many of its most important monuments derived from imperial occupation and patronage. While archaeological evidence suggests that the city was founded as early as 1000 CE, Turkish and Afghan sultans of Delhi and emperors of the Mughal dynasty placed Lahore on medieval world maps. Despite having served as a capital during the Ghaznavid, Ghorid, and Sultanate dynasties, Lahore did not attract much mention in historical accounts prior to 1400. Abu Abdullah Muhammad Ibn Battutah (1304–78), an Arab traveler who described his experiences traveling from Morocco to China, knew about Lahore when he passed through north India but never visited the city.[13] Timur (d. 1405), better known in Europe as Tamerlane, bypassed the city during his historic raid into India (in 1398) and left the sacking of Lahore to a subordinate. The Mughal emperors Babur (r. 1526–30) and Humayun (r. 1530–56) both used Lahore as a base for mounting military campaigns, and both were careful to install loyal governors in the city, but they too spent most of their time elsewhere. While antiquarians might reasonably argue otherwise, Lahore attained widespread prominence only after the Mughal emperor Akbar (r. 1556–1605) shifted his court there from Fatehpur Sikri in 1584.[14]

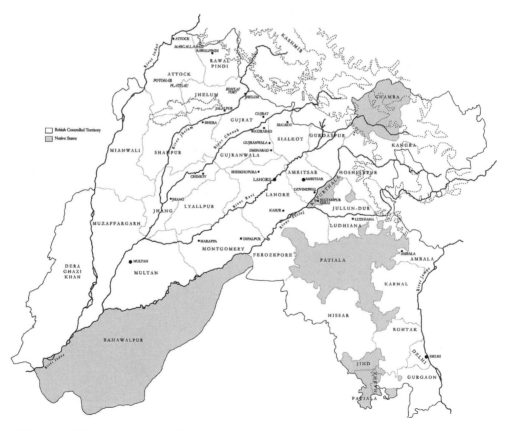

Map 1.2. Punjab Province during the Mughal period.

Prior to the Mughal period, Lahore was probably confined to the area west of the Shah Alami Bazaar and north of Bhatti Gate in today's Old City (Map 1.3). Tombs from the pre-Mughal era, including those of Malik Ayyaz (circa 1040 CE, near Taxali Gate), Ali Mukhdum Hajveri (circa 1072 CE, outside Bhatti Gate), Qutb ud-din Aibak (circa 1210 CE, in Anarkali Bazaar; see Map I.1), and Syed Muhammad Ishaq (circa 1400 CE, in the courtyard of Masjid [Mosque] Wazir Khan), all lie just outside the perimeter of this area and, since tombs were usually sited outside the city walls, they suggest limits to the original walled area. The Ghumti Bazaar (from *ghumpta*, "turning, revolving"), which runs in a gentle arc at the southern boundary of this area, may trace the city's original wall.[15]

Akbar had visited Lahore prior to moving his court there in 1584. On these visits, he slept in the house of Mahdi Qasim Khan, a court noble who lived on a mound in the city's ruined citadel.[16] Beginning in 1584, Akbar built a new palace on the same spot, now called the Lahore Fort, at the northern edge of the walled city, isolated from it by its own set of thick masonry walls. Akbar also rebuilt and fortified the city's wall, extending its compass eastward from Shah Alami to enclose a broad, sparsely inhabited area called the *rarra* (plain) *maidan*. The city's thirteen gates, all present today in their original locations (though not in their original configuration or materials), were built and named at this time. Just outside the easternmost arc of the expanded city wall Akbar established a grain market, Akbari

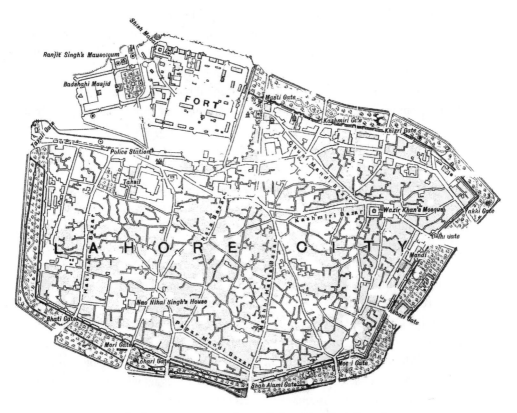

Map 1.3. The Old City of Lahore, circa 1889–90. Source: Lahore Municipal Committee.

Mandi, which is still used for that purpose today. Throughout Akbar's reign, court nobles were encouraged to build palaces, gardens, and religious institutions in and around the city, and Lahore grew rapidly, both in extent and population. Sixteenth- and seventeenth-century European travelers described Lahore as extensive and populous, its bazaars well stocked with valuable goods.[17] Abu Fazl, Akbar's court chronicler, called Lahore "the grand resort of all countries" and described it as a city "whose manufacturers present an astonishing display."[18] In the late seventeenth century, Venetian Niccolao Manucci described Lahore's markets as "crammed with foreign merchants."[19] In her history of Mughal cities, Indian historian H. K. Naqvi notes that travelers from the period compared Lahore favorably to Constantinople and described Lahore as "unrivaled by any Asian or European city in regard to its size, wealth, and population."[20]

All of the Mughal emperors following Akbar maintained some sort of relationship with Lahore, and most of them embellished the city with monuments. Akbar's son and successor Jahangir (r. 1605–27) and Jahangir's powerful wife Nur Jahan (1577–1645) were both buried in Lahore, in separate sepulchers in the suburb of Shahdara, on the west bank of the Ravi. Jahangir's son Shah Jahan (r. 1627–57) was born in Lahore, and in addition to remodeling his grandfather's palace, he built the Shalimar gardens a few miles east of the city (1634–42). A noble under Shah Jahan, Sheikh 'Ilm-ud-din Ansari (later known as Wazir Khan [d. 1634]), was responsible for the building of several important structures in Lahore, including the Masjid (Mosque) Wazir Khan inside Delhi Gate in the Old City (1634). The largest of Lahore's Mughal monuments was the Badshahi Mosque (1673), built by Emperor Aurangzeb, Shah Jahan's son and heir to the throne (r. 1657–1707). This mosque, with its buoyant white marble domes, prominent minarets, and immense paved forecourt, is considered by many to be Lahore's most significant Mughal monument.

Mughal grandees and prominent local zamindars also contributed important secular architecture to the city. The earliest large *havelis* (mansions) recorded in the city date from Akbar's reign, most of them built close to the Mughal citadel. These notable "mansions" were really massive walled compounds whose inner precincts contained a number of smaller buildings occupied by retainers, servants, and relatives of the principal family. Stephen Blake's work on Shahjahanabad suggests that Mughal-era *havelis* could house as many as five thousand residents and were thus often located away from principal streets in the city to find room for their massive size.[21] *Haveli*s of the principal nobles stood out from other residences in the city, therefore, by virtue of their sheer magnitude—in Lahore, the largest *havelis* occupied as much as 300,000 square feet of urban property, or roughly ten times the ground area of the wealthiest merchant's house.[22]

Houses and gardens erected by court nobles away from the city along the banks of the Ravi were another conspicuous feature of the Mughal capital. Like most towns and cities in north India, Mughal capitals were usually built on one side of a navigable river, and it was common to build houses, pavilions, and tombs, sometimes set within a formal garden, along the riverbank.[23] The most famous example is the mausoleum and garden complex built by Shah Jahan for his wife Mumtaz Begum in Agra, better known as the Taj Mahal (built from 1632–53). Especially in Lahore, Agra, and Delhi, there were many such gardens that, while more modest, provided varying residential, ceremonial, and mortuary uses.[24] During Aurangzeb's reign, the Ravi at Lahore threatened to change course and undermine the city wall; he initiated a lengthy engineering project to build the *Alamgir bund* (embankment) to divert the flow of the river. Major families from Lahore built houses alongside this embankment, in an area known as *band-i Alamgiri*.[25] A map of Lahore drawn in the late nineteenth century shows at least fifteen private gardens in this area, including the elaborate and much older Shalimar Bagh.

Population in the city reached its peak only when the emperor and his court were in residence. Despite the fact that most people associate the Mughal period with Lahore's walled Old City, the suburbs beyond these walls were considerably more populous than the districts within. Indeed, only nine of the thirty-six urban quarters (*guzars*) recognized in Lahore during Akbar's reign lay inside the city's walls. Urban geographer James Wescoat suggests that Mughal-era Lahore had a "distinctive Punjabi identity" in addition to its association with the imperial court; if the "urban identity of the city changed with people who lived there and the places they created," then Lahore's suburbs helped establish the ethnically diverse practices of place-making that were characteristic of its large population.[26] Suburban locales were sometimes founded by wealthy guilds (such as Jowhari Bazaar, named for the jewelers who founded it, or Mohalla [urban quarter] Lakhi Khan, founded by Khoja traders and moneylenders), or by officers in the imperial army (Mohalla Langar Khan, Mohalla Zen Khan). Other districts took their names from holy personages buried there, like Mohalla Pir Aziz (later called Mozang), or from auspicious natural features in the area, such as Mohalla Sed Sar, named after a tank whose waters were believed to heal skin ulcers.[27] Suburban expansion therefore added considerably to the city's area. During the reign of Shah Jahan, when Lahore's population probably reached its peak, the built-up area of Lahore's suburbs was perhaps six times that of the walled inner districts.[28]

Unlike Akbar's capital at Fatehpur Sikri or Shah Jahan's capital at Delhi, both of which were built in their entirety over a relatively short period of time, Mughal-era Lahore accumulated its major features piecemeal over a long period.[29] From Akbar's remodeling of the Ghaznavid-era city onward, there is little evidence to suggest that prescriptive codes or comprehensive geometrical strategies influenced the early history of the city's construction.[30] Instead, spatially circumscribed accretions, framed within immediate adjacencies, seem to have been the primary building blocks of Lahore's urban form. With the exception of the imperial palace, the bulk of urban construction in pre-British-era Lahore was developed in an ad hoc manner. This is not the same as saying that the city lacked any guiding formal principles, however. Rather, those principles were mostly concerned with immediate conditions—with adjacent property lines, with proximity to important people or places, or with what was taking place next door—rather than with cosmological diagrams or other large-scale schemata.[31]

Evidence to indicate the importance of proximal relationships in the spatial development of north Indian cities comes from several sources. Frenchman François Bernier's observations of the Mughal cities he visited in India while working as a physician in the court of Danishmand Khan (from 1656 to 1668), including Lahore, Agra, and Delhi, suggest the high level of importance the Mughals placed on a calibrated sense of proximity. Bernier described Delhi (Shahjahanabad) as well laid out, with a few straight principal streets and many smaller secondary streets leading off from these. The principal streets were lined with arcades of shops on both sides, prompting him to make a comparison with Place Royale in Paris, completed some fifty years earlier, "with this difference, however, that [Delhi's arcades] are only brick . . . [and do not have an] uninterrupted opening from one to the other, but are generally separated by partitions." Each shop on the principal streets had a warehouse for goods at the back that was accessed through a small arched opening. Above them, merchants built houses that "look handsome enough from the street," wrote Bernier, "and appear tolerably commodious within; they are airy, at a distance from the dust, and communicate with the terrace-roofs over the shops." Bernier observed that the city's wealthiest merchants kept their primary residences away from these markets, however, and that only a few of the city's smaller streets had houses of the same high quality as those found on the principal thoroughfares. The middling houses on Delhi's secondary streets were also large and airy; many of them incorporated small gardens and "good furniture." A few were built with stone or brick, though most were made of "clay and straw" and finished with "fine white lime." In addition to these larger houses, Bernier described "an immense number of small ones, built of mud and thatched with straw."[32] The latter housed members of the army and their servants and followers, and apparently they often caught fire—Bernier claimed that over sixty thousand houses were consumed by a conflagration in the city during the year prior to his arrival.

For Bernier, Delhi's arrangement of a few straight principal streets with well-built shops and houses, intersected by intermediate streets with more modest houses and surrounded by vast areas of mud-and-thatch dwellings set among irregular lanes and paths, called to mind a certain kind of order: "I always represent to myself Delhi as a collection of many *villages*," Bernier wrote, "or as a *military encampment* with a few more conveniences than are usually found in such places."[33] Bernier's invocation of the camp to describe the city hinged, in part at least, on the degree to which the two kinds of settings shared basic principles of spatial hierarchy. In a long descriptive passage on the imperial camp in one of his letters, Bernier emphasized the overlapping of social and spatial hierarchies, all grounded in a central organizing principle based on calibrated distances from the location of the Mughal ruler. He described the emperor's quadrangle of elegant tents and pavilions lying at the center of the rectangular camp, surrounded by a symmetrical array of subsidiary quarters housing the court's principal nobles. The latter quarters were laid out with strict regularity, such that "each nobleman may be placed at his usual distance from the royal square, whether on the right or on the left."[34] Social hierarchies in the camp, as in the imperial city, were thus reflected spatially through proximity, with the most important nobles located closest to the imperial court.

As was true of the imperial city, the interstices of the Mughal camp's formal layout were filled with the tents of "tradespeople of every description, of civil officers and other persons, who for various reasons follow the army." The density of smaller tents and quarters in the camp could lead to "uncertainty and disorder," Bernier wrote, since "the dust that arises often obscures [things], and it becomes impossible to distinguish the King's quarter, the different bazaars, or the tents of the several Omrahs." Even within the crowd and confusion, however, the basic principles of order underlying the imperial camp as a whole were present and broadly understood: "A slight acquaintance with the method observed in the quartering of the troops," Bernier advised his reader, "will enable you to go, without much difficulty, from place to place as your business may require."[35]

The spatial organization of the Mughal camp was most analogous to the precinct of the imperial palace in the capital city, where a semblance of the order and regularity of primary and subsidiary spaces within the imperial camp was given permanence in masonry construction.[36] Outside the Mughal citadel, however, the fixed hierarchies of the camp quickly broke down. Shah Jahan's capital at Delhi, or Akbar's newly planned city of Fatehpur Sikri, perhaps came closest to realizing the ideals of order that structured the camp, since both were intentionally constructed as capital cities over a short span of years. Even in Shah Jahan's Delhi, however, Bernier noticed "numberless streets" built at "different periods by individuals who paid no regard to symmetry." The analogy Bernier drew between the capital city and the imperial camp is even less pertinent for understanding older capital cities in the empire. In his description of Agra, whose foundation (like that of Lahore) predates Mughal rule, Bernier remarked on the absence of "uniform and wide streets that so eminently distinguish Delhi," since Agra had not been "constructed after any settled design." Interestingly, the lack of clarity in Agra's plan was reflected by a sense of confusion prevailing in the affairs of the court: "Nearly all the [streets in Agra] are short, narrow, and irregular, and full of windings and corners," Bernier wrote; "the consequence is that when the court is at Agra there is often a strange confusion."[37]

The city the Mughals built provided a palimpsest for all subsequent developments in Lahore, including those of the Sikh and British periods.[38] It was during this time that Lahore took shape as a densely settled walled urban core surrounded by a large area of suburbs spreading eastward and southward away from the city walls. Beyond the eastern suburbs, running in a line along the east bank of the Ravi, the walled garden complexes of Lahore's Mughal gentry established a durable pattern of elite construction that continued through the early years of the twentieth century. While these basic features would remain discernable in all subsequent alterations to the city, changes to the Mughal-era city were also quite distinct.

THE SIKH PERIOD CITY

As Mughal power declined in the Punjab during the seventeenth and eighteenth centuries, Lahore too declined in both population and wealth. By the time of Aurangzeb's reign, when conflicts in the Deccan turned the Mughal emperor's attention further south, the Punjab had grown increasingly remote from the center of imperial power. Aurangzeb held court in Lahore only briefly and spent most of his long reign on the move or in camp, pursuing the overthrow of the Marathas. Therefore, from the late seventeenth to the early eighteenth century, Lahore was ruled by a series of lesser Mughal governors appointed by the distant emperor. Following incursions into India by the Persian Nadir Shah and his successors (beginning in 1738–39), overland trade from the west, disrupted by warfare, was diverted south on a route through Qandahar that bypassed Lahore. At the same time, ports on the Arabian Sea near the mouth of the Indus gradually silted up, greatly diminishing the city's role as a center in north–south trade. During the late eighteenth century, successive bands of Sikh *misls* (armed groups from several hundred to several thousand strong) took advantage of the weakened Mughal province by launching attacks on Lahore, and by 1780 Lahore was partitioned among three Sikh chiefs, Gujar Singh, Lahna Singh, and Sobha Singh, who together split the city's revenue. Partly as a result of the instability in and around Lahore, the nearby Sikh-held city of Amritsar replaced Lahore as the region's primary commercial center. By the end of the eighteenth century, a traveler to Lahore described the city's entire population as living within the Mughal citadel, all other areas having been entirely deserted.[39] In only half a century or so, Lahore's population had declined dramatically, and its remaining residents were huddled within Akbar's walls for mutual protection while its once-populous suburbs lay abandoned and ruined.

For a brief half century, from 1799 to 1846, Lahore recovered under the patronage of Ranjit Singh and his successors. Ranjit Singh consolidated the Sikh *misldhars* (commanders) who had ruled more or less independently during the eighteenth century under a unified command, and in 1799 he established Lahore as the administrative capital of a new Sikh kingdom. Nearby Amritsar became the spiritual and commercial center of the kingdom in 1802, after Ranjit Singh's troops occupied the city and the maharaja announced his intention to extend patronage and protection to the city's leading groups.[40] A diminutive, perhaps brilliant, and fiercely energetic ruler, Ranjit Singh stabilized the Punjab's economy and checked British territorial expansion in the region for over thirty years.[41] He also trained and equipped an effective and modernized army (drilled, in part, by mercenary French officers Jean Baptiste Ventura and Jean François Allard, both of whom had served under Napoleon) and adapted earlier Mughal systems of governance to ensure a smooth flow of revenue.[42] At the time of his death (in 1839), Ranjit Singh ruled over the last large territory in India that remained independent of British rule outside India's several autonomous princely states.

While much of Lahore's Mughal-era fabric lay in ruins by the end of the eighteenth century, rebuilding efforts under the Sikhs were shaped by and indebted to Mughal practice. Ranjit Singh moved into the Mughal palace in Lahore's citadel upon taking over the city in 1799. By 1812 he had mostly refurbished the city's defenses by adding a second circuit of outer walls that followed the outline of Akbar's original walls and were separated from them by a moat. The maharaja also partially restored Shah Jahan's decaying gardens at Shalimar, and British maps of the area surrounding Lahore dating from the mid-nineteenth century show that walled private gardens—many of them bearing the names of prominent Sikh nobles—continued in the Mughal pattern under Sikh rule. The Sikh court continued to endow religious architecture in the city, including a number of Sikh *gurudwara*s (temples), Hindu temples, and mosques. In addition, prominent residents or merchant's groups built *dharamsala*s (rest houses), *serai*s (encamping grounds), and public wells.[43] The construction and endowment of religious and charitable institutions by prominent families in the city continued an older tradition of patronage. Like the Mughals, the Sikh state supported religious institutions in and around the city through revenue-free grants of land *(madad-i ma'ash)*.[44] Most of these grants were intended to be temporary; however, despite being technically nontransferable, grants occasionally lapsed into hereditary property.[45] In this way, the control of religious and other forms of endowed urban property often survived changes of rule, especially when those properties were associated with well-loved figures. Even when land grants reverted normally to the state through escheat, as historian Irfan Habib has shown, rulers often preferred to treat heirs of these grants favorably, sometimes by renewing endowments (although sometimes smaller ones) in their name, and almost always by distributing their proceeds generously.[46] Religious endowments under the Mughals and Sikhs thus served to link peripatetic and translocal imperial courts to local families and immovable properties in the city.[47]

A number of Mughal-era monuments in and around Lahore were altered or desecrated during the Sikh period, though few were entirely destroyed.[48] The large Mughal *haveli*s in the city were perhaps the first buildings to be altered, since the fortunes of their principal occupants often declined with the departure of the previous regime. Many *haveli*s in the Mughal-era city were built by *mansabdar*s, prominent officers of the Mughal court who enjoyed rights to the revenue from court-appointed lands *(jagir)* in return for an obligation to raise a specified number of soldiers (the number varied according to the *mansabdar*'s rank) when requested by the emperor. Under the Mughal system, *mansabdar*s were regularly rotated through different posts, which meant that at any given time most *mansabdar*s had little or no social connection to the area where they were posted and left few if any members of their family and entourage behind when they were transferred someplace else.[49] The departure of the imperial court from a city like Lahore would cause the departure of most the court's officers and thus the abandonment of their residential compounds.

Once the walls of a *haveli* compound were breached, encroachments quickly absorbed the buildings into the surrounding urban fabric, producing, in many cases, a new *mohalla*.[50] In some instances, these newly formed *mohalla*s would be named after the *haveli* whose lands they now occupied. Such was the case with Mohalla Pathran Wali in Lahore, which occupied the site of a *haveli* by that name built by Mian Khan, a governor in Shah Jahan's court.[51] The process of disassembly took place relatively quickly; by the time Ranjit Singh held power in Lahore, the largest *haveli*s of the Mughal grandees appear to have already been dismantled. In a memoir first published in 1831, Victor Jacquemont, a naturalist sent to India by the French Natural History Museum, wrote (erroneously) that "the nobles of the Mughal court must certainly have had their palaces outside the city for there is no ruin of any palace of importance within it." The *havelis* built by Sikh nobles, in his opinion, were "only large without being beautiful, built, like the commonest houses, of badly baked and badly cemented bricks."[52] Very few of the thirty or so *havelis* constructed in the walled city during Ranjit Singh's rule survive today, and among those that have, the houses of Khushal Singh, Dhyan Singh, and Nau Nihal Singh—all prominent members of Ranjit Singh's court—are the best preserved.

During periods of instability, buildings in the city's suburbs were also quickly abandoned, since whatever protection the city could provide against attack lay within the city walls. Houses and subordinate structures built of mud and straw or of unbaked bricks deteriorated quickly, and no known intact example of this type of structure remains from the Mughal period. More solidly constructed buildings such as tombs and other religious monuments lasted considerably longer, however, particularly when they were still used. "In our evening rambles at Lahore, we had many opportunities of viewing this city," wrote Alexander Burnes, who visited Lahore in 1831; "[outside the city walls] the mosques and tombs, which have been more stably built than the houses, remain in the midst of fields and cultivation as caravanserais for the travelers."[53] Based on travel accounts from the late eighteenth and early nineteenth centuries, however, the unused remains of other suburban buildings stood out like eerie carcasses. An English officer who met Ranjit Singh at Lahore in the 1830s noted that "for three or four miles before arriving at [Lahore] the country around presented one scene of ruins, nothing being visible but confused heaps of brick."[54]

Even though much of the built fabric of the Mughal-era city had fallen into disrepair by the time Ranjit Singh established Lahore as his capital, his decision to adopt Mughal urban administrative practices helped ensure that those parts of the city that remained but were altered, along with most new construction in the city, took shape according to earlier patterns. City form derives in part from the legal traditions governing the ownership and regulation of space and buildings.[55] Legal codes that control the layout of streets and buildings; restrictive covenants and other legal mechanisms to separate urban populations on the basis of race, ethnicity, religion, or nationality; and deeds and other documents of ownership annotate the boundaries and qualities of possession enjoyed by a building's inhabitants and owners. Legal traditions and styles of urban administration thus tie the production of physical form more or less directly to social concepts and practices prevalent in a region, and Ranjit Singh's decision to adopt Mughal precedent in administering urban areas ensured the continuity of certain formal urban patterns.

Urban administration under the Mughals was minimal, since all but the principal streets in a city were privately maintained, and taxes were only collected on goods sold in the city's markets. In the management of day-to-day urban affairs, the *kotwal* was a key figure. The *kotwal*'s main charge was to secure the peace of the city, organize its police, and ensure that the markets functioned properly. Abu Fazl's official chronicle of Akbar's reign, the *Ain-i Akbari*, suggests that the *kotwal* also conducted a kind of urban census, the *khana shumari*, which was a count of urban households and *mohallas* rather than individual residents.[56] The *kotwal* would appoint a reliable person as head watchman *(mir-i mohalla)* in each of the city's *mohalla*s, and he would in turn report to the *kotwal* on the daily comings and goings of people in the neighborhood.[57]

The office of the *kotwal* was continued under Ranjit Singh and under the British until after the rebellion of 1857, when sovereignty was transferred from the British East India Company to the British Crown and India's courts and urban administration were altered.[58] Under the British government, a *kotwal* came to be referred to as the chief officer of the police in a city or town, and *kotwali* was the name given to a police station or headquarters.[59] Similarly, the office of *mir-i mohalla* (or *mohalladar*) was continued by the Sikhs and later by the British, who gave the office a quasi-legal capacity. The *mohalladar*'s primary duties under the British included registering births and deaths that occurred in the *mohalla* and exercising general surveillance over the neighborhood.[60]

Throughout Mughal, Sikh, and early British periods of rule, the *kotwal* was subordinate to the *qazi*, who administered both civil and criminal law according to the principles of *shari'a* (Islamic legal interpretation). Under the Sikhs, the *qazi*'s court existed side by side with courts empowered to administer customary laws for other castes or religious communities in the city. Under British rule, the *qazi*'s role was confined to preparing deeds and other legal instruments and supervising Muslim marriages, funerals, and the like.[61] While formally excluded from colonial jurisprudence, they continued to provide an important function in the urban *mohalla*s of colonial north India.

The range of legal functions exercised by *qazi*s was diverse, including, among other things, executing deeds of sale *(bai'nama)* that vested absolute rights to property in the purchaser, mortgage contracts *(rahn-nama)* that could be legally redeemed in the event of default, rental agreements *(ra'iyatnama, kirayanama)* for consideration of cash or noncash forms of regular (monthly, quarterly, or annual) payment, and even declarations of infamy *(tazkara, mahzarnama)* lodged by anyone who thought their reputation had been damaged by another of the town's residents. Indian historian J. S. Grewal has translated and photographically reproduced an unusually rich collection of eighteenth- and nineteenth-century legal documents—called the "Bhandari collection" after the family who preserved them—executed in the *qazi*'s court of Batala, a small town located about sixty miles northeast of Lahore. They provide a useful window into practices underlying transactions in the region's urban land that extended from the later Mughal period through the Sikh period and into the early period of British occupation in the Punjab.[62]

The documents Grewal translated come from a period of several hundred years and demonstrate a continuity in the region of legal traditions governing land transactions that shaped urban form. Perhaps the first thing to note, in this regard, is that deeds to houses and other urban properties in the Bhandari collection show that throughout this period urban residents in the Punjab placed a premium on securing conditions for recovering mortgaged or rented property, which reflected an "extreme reluctance of the proprietor to relinquish his right of ownership," Grewal notes; "to tide over a temporary financial need one could resort to mortgage; and even when the hope of recovery from a financial setback was rather slight, one liked to cling to one's proprietary rights and preferred mortgage to outright sale."[63] This suggests both that urban property was available for purchase and sale and that it was an important and well-guarded asset for its owners. Proprietary rights were preferably transferred through inheritance, rather than sale, and a single property often had several cosharers in common. Not surprisingly, therefore, the documents also record the division of larger properties into smaller units over time, a practice that helped determine the density and social composition of individual neighborhoods. Properties could be subdivided by cosharers, whether they were related or not, and individual shares could be sold or mortgaged separately. Indeed, many documents in the Bhandari collection pertain to buildings divided into two or more sections. In one case, a shop was owned by two different parties, an uncle and a nephew who together purchased one half, and another individual who inherited the other half. The shop was being sold whole, however, to an individual purchaser—that is, a single owner replaced two unrelated former owners.[64] Individual rooms in a building could even be mortgaged separately from the building itself, and one document in the collection "involves the mortgage of an undivided half of a *haveli*."[65]

These examples show that buildings and properties that may have started out undivided were often carved into smaller sections over time. The size or "texture" of holdings in the city thus depended in part on the nature of occupation and proprietary rights recognized in the area. The Bhandari documents also make it clear that occupants of a divided house did not all have to belong to the same family, caste, or religious community. The long-standing notion in Indian urban-historical writing that the Indian city was made up of *mohalla*s whose residents shared uniform religious or occupational identities, therefore, is historically inaccurate for the time period under discussion.[66] During times of prosperity from the seventeenth and eighteenth centuries onward, a brisk market in urban land facilitated a process whereby some ancestral properties were divided and sold to purchasers from different caste and religious backgrounds.[67] In addition, attestations by witnesses on a single document are often made by persons from different caste and religious communities, underscoring the observation that the Muslim *qazi* adjudicated issues of urban property involving people from different religions. "For a Muslim dyer in document 32," Grewal writes, "those who appear as witnesses are Qadiri *sayyid*s [high-caste Muslims], a *Kakezai* [Afghan Muslim], a Muslim tent-maker, a Muslim dyer, Muslim masons, a *Khatri* [Hindu], and a *Brahman* [Hindu]." Evidence therefore suggests that communal categories "were not so 'closed' as they appear," according to Grewal, and that land transactions in the city could and did take place between people from widely varying social positions.[68] While *mohalla*s in Lahore and other towns to this day retain older names that suggest they may have initially been occupied by members of distinct caste or occupational groups or by people sharing a common place of origin, there is little evidence to suggest these areas remained homogeneous over long periods of time.

The *mohalla* was a useful indicator of location, however, and while not clearly marked, the boundaries of individual *mohalla*s were well known to local residents. A property could be fully described on the basis of the *mohalla* it was part of and the streets or buildings that were adjacent to it. A typical deed of mortgage from the Bhandari collection records the location of the sale property, a "shop built of burnt bricks and with a ceiling of seasoned wood," as a series of adjacencies along the cardinal directions:

> Boundaries of the mortgaged-shop mentioned in the text: Eastern: adjoining another shop of the mortgagor mentioned in the text, and Pira, the real brother of the mortgagor mentioned in the text. Western: adjoining (yet) another shop of the mortgagor, mentioned in the text. Southern: adjoining the street and the entrance. Northern: adjoining the wall of the *haveli* mentioned in the text.[69]

Indeed, adjacency and proximal relationships seem to have been the most important criteria governing the construction or alteration of properties in the city. The rights to alter or build on property in the city were negotiated and secured through reference to these criteria alone; larger-scale spatial considerations such as "ideal" or other kinds of abstract plans are never explicitly mentioned. Nevertheless, principles for altering and extending the material fabric of the city produced a characteristic spatial pattern over time.

To summarize, we can say that cities in north India from the Mughal period through the arrival of the British acquired their characteristic forms, in most cases, through a gradual process of accretion rather than by filling out a predetermined scheme. Proximal relations were the most important ones in this process, and these relations were negotiated and upheld in the social and legal practices governing property transactions in the city. Since urban property was valuable, the market for urban land led over time to heterogeneous neighborhoods and even to individual buildings in which people from different religious and social backgrounds were coresident. Proprietary rights based on inheritance fostered the gradual division of single properties into multiple smaller units, a process that helped establish the size of holdings.

Each of these processes was common to cities in the Punjab during both the Mughal and the Sikh periods, despite their separation by time, invasions, abrupt changes in population, and the accession to power of an entirely new ruling class. Along with the shock of the "new" as Sikh-era Lahore departed from its Mughal-era form—in the ruin of previously populous suburbs, the breakup and demise of the enormous *havelis* in the city, and the increasing ethnic and religious diversity in the city's neighborhoods as the Old City grew denser over time—there were many continuities with the city's Mughal past as well. With the arrival of British troops in the city in the mid-nineteenth century, those continuities grew dimmer but were never entirely broken.

THE BRITISH OCCUPATION OF LAHORE

We have seen how the Mughal-era city of Lahore provided both a durable physical template for all later developments and the remnants of a system of urban administration that Sikh and British rulers subsequently adopted and altered. These inheritances, while seldom conceptualized this way in British documents, continued to exert a force throughout the British period. The process of suburbanization established under Mughal rule in the city, for example, provided a spatial logic for establishing building sites that British officials directly adopted. Older systems of transacting property in Lahore's Old City continued more or less unaltered until the early decades of the twentieth century, when the city's inner *mohallas* were incorporated into a municipal system of regulations previously applied only to property in the civil station. Important religious monuments and places of public resort for disparate Indian communities in the city continued to be built and to draw devoted admirers; they enhanced the city and the status of those who endowed them. Indeed, as we will see in the final chapter of this book, these sites attained renewed significance when they formed the primary objects of interest for nineteenth-century Indian historians in the city, historians who together crafted a new genre of urban history. Lastly, actual buildings from the Mughal and Sikh periods were drafted into use for colonial purposes, in a practice that brought British and Indian architectural conventions together in complicated combinations. The material, symbolic, and administrative practices that organized British interventions in the city were thus deeply entangled with a longer history of urban change in the region, and that history's effects on the present were substantial.

The British occupation of Lahore took place in a protracted but concerted manner. Capitalizing on the disarray surrounding the succession struggles after Ranjit Singh's death and only partially diminished by a war fought against the Sikhs on their eastern frontier, the British rode into Lahore in February 1846 and garrisoned their troops in the citadel. Two unstable years later, they were drawn into a second war with the Sikhs at the southern city of Multan when that city's governor, Mul Raj, encouraged his troops to rebel. After a series of closely fought battles (whose intensity profoundly shocked overconfident British officers on the battlefield), the Sikh army was finally defeated in a battle at Gujrat, sixty miles north of Lahore. In March 1848, following the British victory, Dalip Singh, Ranjit Singh's teenage son and heir to the throne, was formally deposed in Lahore. The remaining Sikh regiments in the city were abruptly decommissioned and camped outside the city demanding severance pay. Within a year the Punjab was formally annexed to the British Empire and military sappers had begun leveling Lahore's city wall.[70]

During the first two decades following annexation, when both the personnel and capital needed for planning and constructing new buildings were scarce, the colonial government resorted to retrofitting existing buildings from the Mughal and Sikh periods for new administrative and social functions. Housing major new state functions in buildings long significant in the local landscape was no doubt a conscious decision. For one thing, Lahore's first colonial officials were perhaps more than normally willing to draw visible, material connections between themselves and the communities they ruled. Henry and John Lawrence, the first president and financial administrator of the Punjab Board of Administration, respectively, were known for addressing their subjects in the vernacular, cultivating firm but affective ties with Punjab's native "chiefs" and rulers, and eschewing the normal trappings and comforts of high imperial office—both men lived in converted Indian buildings throughout their terms of office in Lahore.

The British practice of converting existing buildings to new purposes in the city also continued a more long-standing practice in the region: namely, asserting the authority to rule by physically appropriating (and sometimes destroying) a previous ruler's buildings.[71] Recall that at the time of Ranjit Singh's accession to power in 1799, he moved his family and court into the Mughal palace and fort that had first been constructed by Akbar. Following his prohibition of Muslim prayer in the city's Badshahi Mosque, Ranjit Singh used the mosque as a storage magazine for weapons.[72] In another of many such examples, Jamadar Khushal Singh, an officer in Ranjit Singh's court, made his private residence in the Tomb of Muhammad Kasim Khan, one of Akbar's maternal cousins.

Finally, the kinds of buildings British authorities chose to reuse were most often those whose scale, architectural features, and siting resonated closely with Anglo-European notions of civic architectural grandeur. While the British army reused a row of barracks outside the Old City near Anarkali Bazaar that Ranjit Singh had originally built, most of the buildings chosen for reuse by the British dated from the Mughal era. Like the authoritative civic monuments familiar to Anglo-European urban tradition, Mughal buildings were often massive in scale, finely built and finished, and set apart from their surroundings as isolated objects in space. Mughal tombs, in particular, fit all these criteria well. "The Lieut.-Governor occupies a very comfortable tomb [in Lahore]," wrote British traveler J. Duguid, who visited the city in 1870; "the accountant general lives in one, and so do the railway officials. The reading-room is a handsome, and the principal English church, a spacious tomb." Another Mughal tomb, illustrated in Duguid's book with a camel coach and uniformed sentry standing out front, had been converted into a "police station, [with] a garden of mulberry trees behind" (Figure 1.1).[73]

What is more striking than the fact that the Punjab's new rulers (cost-effectively) appropriated the symbolically charged buildings of their predecessors is how long some of those appropriations lasted. The conversion of the Mughal-era tomb of Sharif un-Nissa, a noblewoman during Shah Jahan's reign, popularly known as Anarkali, was one such case (Figure 1.2). This Muslim tomb was first used as offices and residences for the clerical staff of Punjab's governing board. In 1851, however, the tomb was converted into the Anglican church in Lahore, a function it would continue to serve for more than thirty-five years. When it was converted, wooden pews replaced Anarkali's ornately carved marble cenotaph in the tomb's octagonal central chamber. A side recess provided space for an altar, lectern, and pulpit. Four years later, to meet the needs of the church's growing congregation, the Public Works Department built an outer staircase that provided access to expanded rows of seating in the arched recesses of the tomb's upper gallery. Anarkali's tomb was formally consecrated as St. James Church in 1857, with the bishop of Madras presiding.[74] The building remained in use as Lahore's official Anglican church until 1891, when a new cathedral was ready to be occupied. That same year, the tomb was converted once again into a document repository for the Civil Secretariat, a purpose it continues to serve today.[75]

Anarkali's tomb was only one of many buildings converted for use by the city's new rulers. At the time of annexation, John Lawrence moved into an eighteenth-century house near Anarkali's tomb originally built by General Ventura, the French mercenary commander

Figure 1.1. Mughal Tomb converted into a police station near Lahore, circa 1870. From J. Duguid, Letters from India and Kashmir: Written in 1870; Illustrated and Annotated 1873 *(London: George Bell and Sons, 1874), 156.*

employed in Ranjit Singh's army. This house was, in turn, converted into offices of the provincial Civil Secretariat. John's brother, Henry Lawrence, moved into the tomb of Muhammad Kasim Khan which, as we have seen, had been occupied earlier by an officer in Ranjit Singh's court. The first English resident to live in the tomb was Robert Macgregor, the province's first district commissioner. Lawrence replaced Macgregor as the tomb's resident; Robert Montgomery then replaced Lawrence when he became Punjab's lieutenant governor in 1859, and at that time the tomb was officially renamed Government House (Figures 1.3 and 1.4).[76]

Figure 1.2. The tomb of "Anarkali" (Pomegranate Blossom), popular name for Sharif un-Nissa, a noblewoman in Lahore during the reign of Shah Jahan in the late sixteenth century. This engraving was executed in 1873, when the tomb was used as St. James Church in Lahore. The illustration shows British residents of Lahore walking toward the church on a Sunday morning. Native bhistis (water bearers) are wetting the walkway outside the tomb using watering bags of oiled skin. Notice the Christian cross at the top of the dome. From J. Duguid, Letters from India and Kashmir: Written in 1870; Illustrated and Annotated 1873 (London: George Bell and Sons, 1874), 147.

Figure 1.3. Government House, Lahore, built around the tomb of Muhammad Kasim Khan. From Illustrated London News, November 27, 1869.

Figure 1.4. Government House, Lahore: photograph of the dining room in the original tomb chamber, circa 1910. Copyright The British Library Board. OIOC Photo 761/1/181; all rights reserved.

Figure 1.5. Baradari of Sheikh 'Ilm-ud-din Ansari (later known as Wazir Khan), viceroy of Punjab under Shah Jahan. A baradari *is a raised open pavilion usually placed in a garden, with three entries on each of its four sides; the word* baradari *comes from* bara *(twelve) and* dari *(door). At the time this building was first constructed, it sat in a large garden known for its date trees. When this photograph was taken in 1870, it was being used as a public library. Copyright The British Library Board. OIOC Photo 50/1 (112); all rights reserved.*

Similarly, Haveli Mian Khan, a large multipart house built during Shah Jahan's reign inside the Old City's Shah Alami Gate, was first used by the colonial government as a police *thana* (station). One section of the *haveli*, known as the Rang Mahal, was converted into a school for the American Presbyterian Mission, run by Reverend C. W. Forman. In 1886 Forman Christian College was opened in the same structure, only to be replaced by a post office when the college shifted to new premises outside the Old City in 1889.[77] The Mughal-era *baradari* (pavilion; literally, "twelve door") of Wazir Khan, a noble in Shah Jahan's court, was used for a series of different purposes. First converted into a settlement office by the military, the *baradari* subsequently became a telegraph office, museum, private book club, and public library (Figure 1.5).

Perhaps most prodigious of all conversions were those undertaken during the construction of the Lahore Railway Station shortly after the rebellion of 1857.[78] The Lahore station, built during a time when securing British civilians and troops against a future "native" uprising was foremost in the government's mind, looked like a fortified medieval castle, complete with turrets and crenellated towers, battered flanking walls, and loopholes for directing rifle and canon fire along the main avenues of approach from the city (Figure 1.6).[79]

Figure 1.6. The Lahore Railway Station, designed by William Brunton, C. E. in 1858. Notice the crenellated towers, battered walls, and loopholes in the station's parapets. This photograph was taken on the occasion of a visit to Lahore by Sir Louis and Lady Dane in April 1911. Dane was lieutenant governor of the Punjab from 1908 to 1913. Copyright The British Library Board. OIOC Photo 592/1/21; all rights reserved.

This daunting but anachronistic symbol of modernity was built on ground, wrote one nineteenth-century British commentator, "till lately marked only by memorials of Muhammadan bigotry and Sikh fanaticism."[80] Included among them was the mosque of Dai Anga, Emperor Shah Jahan's wet nurse, which the British converted first into a residence and later into the office of the railway traffic manager. Nearby was the tomb of Nawab Bahadur Khan, a highly placed member of Akbar's court, which the railway used as a storehouse. That same tomb had been acquired earlier by the railway from the army, who had used it as a theater for entertaining officers. The railway provided another nearby tomb free of charge to the Church Missionary Society, who used it for Sunday services. The tomb of Mir Mannu, an eighteenth-century Mughal viceroy of Punjab who had brutally persecuted the Sikhs while he was in power, escaped demolition by the railway but was converted nevertheless into a private wine merchant's shop by a Sikh proprietor (Figure 1.7).

Though early British residents of Lahore felt little compunction in physically converting and occupying Indian buildings, the broader material landscapes of which they formed a part were less easily rendered useful. It was not technically difficult to retrofit a Muslim tomb into a church; it could be accomplished using conventional constructional and engineering logic. As long as pragmatic necessity provided the logic, moreover, such interventions

Figure 1.7. Lithograph print of the tomb of Moin ul-Mulk (Mir Mannu), near Lahore Railway Station, circa 1760. Mir Mannu was a notorious persecutor of Sikhs during his reign as governor of Lahore. His tomb was converted into a wine shop during the late nineteenth century. The sign over the entry to the tomb-become-shop identifies the building as "Gurdit Singh & Co., General Merchants and Rum Agents." From Latif, Lahore: Its History, Architectural Remains, and Antiquities, with an Account of Its Modern Institutions, Inhabitants, Their Trade, Custom, &c. *(1892) (Lahore: Sang-e-Meel, 1994), plate 25.*

were relatively straightforward. But pragmatic necessity was not the only logic motivating British rule in the city, and necessity's purchase on the logic of colonial intervention became, over time, an increasingly minor force. With the transfer of Punjab Province to Crown rule following the events of 1857–58, a deeper set of engagements between British and Indian residents in the city than those established under the paternal leadership of Punjab's early administrators increasingly became the norm. As chapter 2 shows, the logic of colonial intervention in the city depended in critical ways both on the material settings the city (as well as the countryside beyond) presented and on the ways those settings were documented, imagined, and made sense of.

A COLONIAL SPATIAL IMAGINATION

British Knowledge of the City and Its Environs

2

For the first generation of colonial officials who occupied Lahore, the city and its immediate environs were unmapped and poorly known. There was, first of all, the walled inner district of the city, with its Mughal-era monuments and pattern of streets and houses. Outside the city walls, abandoned tombs, temples, and gardens coexisted with a number of populous enclaves that at one time had been contiguous with these ruins but that now formed more isolated settlements. Farther out, a few miles beyond the circuit of the city walls, the facilities and dwellings of people engaged in small-scale manufacturing blended seamlessly into a sparsely populated agrarian landscape whose scattered village sites owed all, some, or but little of their existence to the historical economy and political reach of Lahore.

Each of these different settings—Lahore's inner city, its suburban areas, and the agrarian and other types of villages that surrounded the city—were credited with separate and distinctive qualities in British writings on Punjab. At the same time, British officials asked whether, and if so how, these qualitatively different settings might relate to each other. The idea of an organic (if often troubled) relationship between the city, its suburbs, and the countryside beyond was, after all, a constant point of reference in nineteenth-century British urban theory.[1] As Raymond Williams showed many years ago, the country and the city have long been deeply imbricated in the changing "structures of feeling" that underlay British attitudes toward settled human society. Rapid industrialization, rural displacement, and the expansion of city populations into suburban locales, as people like Edwin Chadwick, Friedrich Engels, and George Godwin documented all too clearly in Great Britain at midcentury, brought the peripheral areas of Britain's great metropolises—not quite countryside, not quite city, and newly available for exploitation—into the same interpretive frame. "While our real social experience is not only of the country and the city in their most singular forms but of many kinds of intermediate and new kinds of social and physical organization," Williams wrote, "the ideas and the images of country and city retain their great force."[2] This approach to the physical world was too deeply etched in British thought not to have an influence on the way colonial officials thought about the Indian environment, even though their encounters with Indian landscape and society wrought changes in the way they perceived the relationship between country and city.[3]

British society in India could rarely isolate itself from its Indian context, although that was the motivation behind the hill station, the English club, and the British bungalow. As scholars have increasingly shown, however, even in these enclaves the ideal of separation was seldom realized.[4] The need to generate social and spatial arrangements for a life of racial interaction was far more pressing, continuous, and common a task for British officials in India than is often realized and was, more than any other factor, the driving force behind British efforts to understand, inhabit, and intervene in India's rural and urban landscapes.

For British officials in Punjab, the countryside would always remain more comprehensible than the city and thus easier to act upon. In the countryside there was less to appropriate and transform and fewer consequences as a result of intervening than in the city, and the villages of the countryside showed more evidence of stability and contentment than did the Indian city. More could be discerned about the countryside, too, without recourse to "native opinion" (which the British saw as a degraded kind of facticity) than was the case with the city, as Punjab's villages seemed analogous, in many ways, to older English villages. The rural agrarian villages in Punjab were also accessible to techniques of visual inspection. The inner city, on the other hand, remained problematic. Seen as a potential hotbed of disease and social instability, and notoriously difficult to observe and fathom, the inner districts of the city remained stubbornly resistant to colonial intervention. Throughout the British period of occupation in Punjab, for reasons we will explore more fully, the inner districts of its largest cities were almost entirely left alone.[5] The colonial state made its most significant investments in suburban tracts outside of cities. Newer settlements in these tracts were seen as less immured in the time-bound customs that made villages resistant to progressive change; they were largely free, as well, from the moral degradation British officials saw as endemic to the inner city. For these and other reasons, suburbs and other zones of newer settlement were key sites for colonial attempts to fashion a new form of civic space, one based on distinctive spatial principles and the equally distinctive moral sensibilities that were seen to accompany them.

A COLONIAL SPATIAL IMAGINATION

Chapter 3 will explore the urban and architectural qualities of those new spaces in greater detail; the empirical focus of this chapter is on early British enquiries into the social and physical arrangements that made up settlements and landforms in and around Lahore, with an emphasis on how the discursive conclusions colonial officials arrived at helped shape physical projects for social and environmental reform. While often undertaken in a spirit of scientific objectivity, those enquiries were grounded in preconceived notions about how society should properly inhabit a material setting, how the local environment affected human health and personality, and what the relationship was between spatial organization and moral development. In the written reports and other discursive media that accompanied those enquiries, subjective assessments about Indian culture and society intertwined with objective observations about material settings. This was as true of the observations penned in a sanitary inspector's field notebook as it was of the impressionistic descriptions of villages and cities found in colonial fiction and travel literature. What drew these disparate genres together was a tendency to conceptualize the unfamiliar settings that each was a response to in terms that were simultaneously sociological and spatial. This conceptual orientation exerted a powerful influence on the attitudes colonial officials formed about the material settings of Indian society and helped determine which elements they undertook to alter. The key point here is that colonial interventions directly depended on the way those settings were imagined, conceptualized, and assimilated into colonial administrative discourse.

Effective administration in colonial India hinged, critically, on the systematic observation and analysis of material phenomena on the ground in an effort to render them useful to a discourse on the proper distribution of objects in space. Solutions to particular problems could only be developed once relevant features of the material and social environment were rendered intelligible within the protocols of inquiry that structured administrative practice. These protocols were scientific in their basic method, disaggregating larger-scale phenomena into their component parts and then reassembling them into a variety of synthetic (and programmatic) constructions. The latter were often given shape through a mental or discursive image of the interrelationship of parts. In this and subsequent chapters of this book, I will use the concept of a "colonial spatial imagination" to characterize this process.

My use of the term "colonial spatial imagination" derives in part from the work of architectural historian Dell Upton, who uses the term "spatial imagination" to refer to the way a given group posits an ideal of the relationship between social and physical phenomena, envisioning "relationships among people as a synthesis of physical and nonphysical qualities." While traceable across a variety of discursive and nondiscursive domains—Upton links developments in early-republican city planning in the United States to developments in scientific taxonomy, museum display, merchants' accounting practices, the standardization of currency, and economic philosophy, among others—the spatial imagination never provides a simple prescription for social practice. As Upton writes, "[The] fusion of the material and the non-material" that characterizes the spatial imagination "can never be achieved in the real world, for [it] addresses the 'ought-tos' rather than the 'can-bes' of social and spatial life."[6]

My use of the concept of a spatial imagination also shares certain similarities with Charles Taylor's "social imaginary." Taylor defines the social imaginary as the way large groups of people—perhaps even whole societies—"imagine their social existence, how they fit together with others, how things go on between them and their fellows, the expectations that are normally met, and the deeper normative notions and images that underlie these expectations." Like the spatial imagination, Taylor's definition of the social imaginary describes the way "ordinary people 'imagine' their social surroundings," and the ways that imagination is expressed in "images, stories, and legends" rather than purely theoretical terms.[7] Commenting on Taylor's model, historian Mary Poovey describes the social imaginary as constituting a kind of "feed-back loop" in which "particular representations can influence institutional practices and vice versa, and explanatory paradigms that depend on abstractions can also be said to derive their power partly from the concrete images and stories these abstractions purport to explain."[8] Poovey's contribution to Taylor is useful in furthering something that both Taylor and Upton leave relatively undeveloped in their models, namely, a discussion of how "newness" or "change" enters into either of these social constructs as opposed to their role in reproducing particular social formations. If we can think of the spatial imagination as constituted through a recursive process, one in which both "concrete images" or settings and conceptual "abstractions" play constitutive roles, then we can see how an Anglo-European spatial imagination confronting the new and often strange spaces of India would be forced to gradually change.

This is an important point, since any given social formation will produce its own spatial imagination, its own distinctive syntheses of subjective and objective assessments, judgments, and observations. The colonial spatial imagination thus bears a historically specific relationship to its colonial field of production. Part of what made the colonial spatial imagination cohere, of course, was its distinctive interpellation of assessments, judgments, and observations rooted in Anglo-European contexts and histories. What made that imagination particularly "colonial," however, was its transposition onto, and engagement with, entirely new social and material terrains. In chapter 3 I will place more emphasis on how those transpositions and engagements gradually wrought changes in the largely Eurocentric imaginations colonial officials brought with them to India. In this chapter, however, I want to stay more closely attuned to those cultural assumptions and spatialized understandings of society that remained rooted in an Anglo-European framework.

In the context of colonial India, utilitarian thought and practice had a substantial influence on state policy; in the context of urban and rural reform discourse, that influence was almost complete. In utilitarian thought, the qualities of uniformity, regularity, and an easy concatenation of parts were perhaps the most symbolically charged metaphors for the operation of a just, productive, and morally advanced society.[9] Using a methodological counterpart to utilitarian theory, the colonial mode of observation derived from a scientific method that privileged classification and enumeration as a direct avenue to knowledge and that valorized what could be seen over things that remained hidden.[10] Classification and enumeration were important supports to the colonial spatial imagination, since they were essential steps in the process of rendering dissimilar things comparable to one another by emphasizing the range of shared features between them. Comparability, in turn, was the key to discerning how things articulated with one another, and thus how each element ideally occupied its place in a finite, patterned, and interlinked system.

The spatial imagination works to translate these kinds of social and spatial metaphors into actual physical geometries. I say "works to" because any particular translation has to claim its relevance over a range of other possibilities. The mid-nineteenth-century utilitarian theorist Alexander Bain, for example, urged that "in orderly arrangement of every kind, right lines are essential. We should never think of partitioning fields with waving fences, or making the ground plan of buildings of a zigzag curvature." Bain's explanation for this principle was that straight lines and regular forms "appeal to a primary sensibility of the mind," since the "neat, tidy, and trim gratifies us as part of Order." Like all translations from social metaphor to concrete geometrical figure, however, the "sensibility" being appealed to at any time is context dependent. In situations where "Order" or convenience are unnecessary, straight lines become "inherently unbeautiful," Bain argued, since they can just as easily suggest the "discipline of constraint." For the purpose of attaining some "desirable end," however, such as "partitioning fields"—or reforming the Indian physical landscape—regularity and uniformity of line were symbolically powerful figures. Notice how Bain's particularistic assertion that "right lines" are an essential ingredient of "Order" leaps fluidly into a more synthetic and generalized conception of the benefits order is associated with: "The rules manifestly founded on Utility," continued Bain, "are all those that protect the persons, property, good name of the members of each society . . . enforce justice . . . uphold veracity and integrity . . . maintain obedience to constituted authority; extend protection to the helpless, and so forth."[11] In the spatial imagination that underlay utilitarian thought, the regular, uniform, and predictable landscape was emblematic of a well-ordered society.

We can see a similar figural assumption in the writings of John Loudon, whose architectural treatises were highly influential in mid-nineteenth-century Britain. In a comment on the design of working-class houses Loudon combined the geometrical principles implicit in Bain's work with a theory of moral improvement: "The mere circumstance of familiarizing the mind with orderly arrangements, regular features, symmetry [or] means adapted to the end in view, either in building, in furniture, or in gardens, must have an influence on conduct. Order is the fundamental principle of all morals; for what is immorality but a disturbance of the order of civilized society."[12] This easy and reversible flow between specific geometries (regularity, symmetry) and synthetic social concepts (immorality, civilized society) illustrates the spatial imagination in action.

Building on the insights of Upton, Taylor, and others, I will argue below that a "colonial spatial imagination" shaped the way colonial officials—and, increasingly, Indian residents—conceptualized an ideal of desired relationships between colonial society and its material forms. In subsequent chapters I will explore this argument more fully in the context of architectural design, urban planning, and literary accounts of the city. In this chapter, however, I want to use the concept to understand how the city and the countryside entered colonial discourse and how the colonial spatial imagination shaped ideas about the way each would be controlled.

IMAGINING THE COUNTRYSIDE

We begin with the countryside and with the form of village life that helped define it in British discourse. Shortly after the official annexation of Punjab Province, a British surgeon named John Login was put in charge of recycling weapons kept in the magazine of the decommissioned Sikh army at Lahore. In a letter home to his wife, Login characterized his work in terms that became something of a leitmotif in subsequent British histories of the province: "We are now working hard in the magazine, breaking up old arms as fast as we can," Login wrote. "I had the pleasure of having the first swords brought in converted into capital scythes for mowing the grass in the soldier's gardens, which was coming as near 'pruning hooks' as circumstances permitted!"[13] The (only slightly altered) biblical motif of turning "swords into ploughshares" is reiterated often in imperial histories of the Punjab, reflecting both the abiding Christian ethos that underlies many of those histories and a widely shared belief by their authors that in the Punjab, settled agriculture would naturally replace nomadic warfare in the historical march from savagery to civilization.[14] R. Bosworth Smith, whose definitive biography of John Lawrence was published in 1883, availed himself of the same biblical motif when he wrote that the Punjab Board of Administration "literally as well as figuratively, beat [the Sikh army's] swords into ploughshares and their spears into pruning-hooks."[15] G. B. Malleson, in his personal account of the rebellion of 1857, wrote that Punjab's disbanded soldiers "cast their swords into plough-shares" following British occupation and threw their might behind the correct side.[16] In another of many such examples, Leslie Saunders, who revised Punjab's land-revenue settlements in 1869, wrote in his official report that "the warrior Sikhs [were] induced to turn from the use of the sword to the sickle by the liberal treatment displayed to them by Sir Robert Montgomery."[17]

The "swords into ploughshares" motif retrospectively frames a pronounced struggle to assert foreign rule in the Punjab as a story of peasants acquiescing peacefully to extralocal governance. As an accurate portrayal of what happened, of course, we can dismiss much of this idea outright. History is clear on this point: British rule in the Punjab provoked regular and widespread resistance throughout its century-long tenure. However, the way this motif couples a theory of colonial agency (divine ordination) with a sociological theory about Punjabi society (martial races poised on the brink of settled agriculture) provides an important insight into the way the Punjab's imperial rulers conceptualized Britain's role in the countryside.

It should not surprise us that the main focus of imperial attention in Punjab was its fertile countryside rather than cities like Lahore. Not only were Punjab's population and economy overwhelmingly agrarian, but British expertise was much more finely tuned for, and much more deeply invested in the management of, agricultural revenue than it was for managing urban processes.[18] Understanding Punjab's rural society, therefore, was an early priority for the colonial state. British efforts to analyze the structure and organization of rural Punjab led them to identify "tribes," rather than castes or religious communities (as in other parts of India), as the basic units of Punjabi society.[19] Under British rule, tribal "chiefs" would ideally sit at the head of Punjab's rural society, assisted in the day-to-day running of affairs by an elite cadre of British officials. The "tribe" was an indeterminate category, however, when applied to actual communities on the ground. British efforts to develop a legal and political system based on their understanding of indigenous practices in Punjab therefore often required them to construe tribal leaders where none had previously existed. Over time, whether real or manufactured, tribal leaders formed a privileged rural elite who mediated relations between the colonial state and local society.[20] Punjab's rural elites proved to be one of the most loyal subordinate aristocracies in the British Empire: Many among them organized small armies in 1857 to help the British defeat a rebellion triggered by mutinous sepoys that nearly brought British rule to a close. Punjab's "chiefs" were generously rewarded for their loyalty, receiving grants of land, titles, and other marks of distinction.[21]

For Punjab's early colonial administrators, then, the countryside proffered a vision of an incipient form of agrarian community whose features were broadly familiar from Britain's own imagined past. The point of departure was an idealized preindustrial Europe, since British representations of Punjab's "native chiefs" and landed peasant farmers readily suggested analogies with the feudal lords and yeoman peasantry of premodern England. If industrialization, enclosure, and urban migration had tragically disenfranchised the yeomanry in England, then colonization in Punjab presented an opportunity to protect, and thus preserve intact, a native version of this class, one whose idealized qualities in nineteenth-century Britain included docility, productivity, and a plain and virtuous thrift.[22] Colonization in Punjab thus held out to Britain the prospect of recovering a lost ideal: a contented rural world of peasant proprietors "securely embedded in communities of kin and neighbors."[23]

The imperial dimension of this ideal envisioned the British Crown at the apex of a single social hierarchy, one that incorporated both Indian and English subjects. Differences ascribed to racial and cultural attributes, rather than posing a problem, were considered both natural and inevitable as each person would take his or her rightful position within an all-encompassing "diversity of ranks."[24] Rural tribal and village social structures were therefore kept largely intact by the British, who gave the landowning classes primacy in Punjab's system of government through permanent settlements in land, legal prohibitions on the alienation of rural land from the "agricultural classes," and the incorporation of tribal, village, and religious leaders as intermediaries in the colonial government.[25] The goal was not to fossilize rural society in its current state of development, however. Rather, the colonial state intended to "lift" Punjab's rural communities, lock, stock, and barrel, into the civilizing system of British administration. "The maintenance of the tribe, the village, and the clan would not impede, but further the sort of progress that is most wanted in this part of India," wrote C. L. Tupper, who was chiefly responsible for defining the "tribe" as Punjab's main unit of society: "A tribe in the chains of its own customs, unrelaxed and unrefined, may stand still for centuries, but a tribe recognized and lifted into the system of British administration has, in the guardianship of the governing body, the best chance of disusing savagery and learning the wisdom of civilized men."[26]

VILLAGE SANITATION AND RUSTIC HEALTH

British attitudes toward Punjab's agrarian society and British policies in the countryside were partly informed by the way Indian society was imagined as inhabiting an asynchronous, less-developed version of Britain's own agrarian past. More empirical forms of assessment were equally important, however, in shaping those attitudes and policies. A survey of villages in the immediate vicinity of Lahore conducted in the summer of 1878 provides a good example of the latter.

The survey was undertaken to assess environmental hazards to British troops posted at Lahore's military cantonment at Mian Mir, several miles east of the city. It was one of several investigations conducted by the Indian government following the monumental 1859 study by a royal commission on the sanitary state of the army in British India.[27] The commission's report revealed, among other things, that European troops got sick and died at strikingly higher rates than their Indian counterparts, a discrepancy the report attributed largely to India's insalubrious (for Europeans) moral and physical environments.[28] The latter could be identified, isolated, and corrected more easily than the former. According to the dominant theories of disease at the time, threats to the health of British soldiers were likely to come from two sources in particular: the emanations of putrefying organic material and tainted or poisonous water.[29] Both of these could be found in abundance, it was feared, in the fields and villages that lay just beyond the formal limits of the military cantonment. As historian Mark Harrison writes, "Military imperatives were . . . vitally important in the process by which sanitary policing was extended to rural areas: Indian villages were seen as the foci of epidemics which, sooner or later, would take their toll on British soldiers."[30]

Military engineers had laid out the cantonment at Mian Mir, or at least they had conceived its layout. They oriented the cantonment's rectilinear road network to the cardinal directions, locating separate sites for Mian Mir's military, recreational, and commercial activities. Once these elements were in place, the major north–south streets were named after British officers (Elgin Street, Wellington Mall, Sir Hugh Rose Street, and so on), and the minor east–west streets were named after Indian cities in the new province (Amritsar Street, Gujrat Street, Rawalpindi Street, Murree Street). An oval park sat at the geographic center of the cantonment, with the Anglican church at one focal point of the oval and tennis grounds at the other (Map 2.1). Except for the names, it was a plan that would have fit anywhere, and one in which social and spatial hierarchies could be mapped onto one another and result in a close fit. Senior officers lived near the center of the cantonment, and subordinate personnel were placed outward from the center in order of decreasing rank. European and Indian infantry troops occupied separate quarters, north and south of the officers' quarters, respectively, and each group was housed according to its rank in identical barracks grouped in blocks of parallel "lines." In this way military engineers arranged for the fixing of goods and people in carefully measured arrays, using standardized spatial relationships and architectural devices designed to produce a predictable relation between a person's social position and his or her position in abstract space.

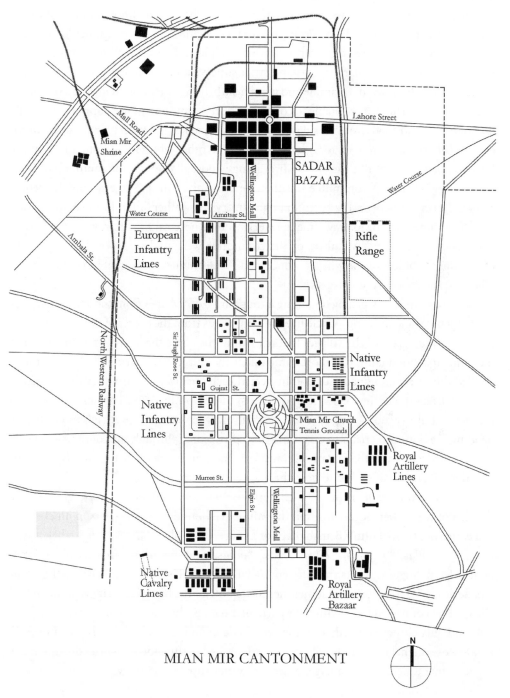

Mall Road
Mian Mir Shrine
Ambala St.
North Western Railway
Water Course
Amritsar St.
European Infantry Lines
Wellington Mall
SADAR BAZAAR
Lahore Street
Water Course
Rifle Range
Sir Hugh Rose St.
Gujrat St.
Native Infantry Lines
Native Infantry Lines
Mian Mir Church Tennis Grounds
Royal Artillery Lines
Murree St.
Elgin St.
Wellington Mall
Native Cavalry Lines
Royal Artillery Bazaar

N

MIAN MIR CANTONMENT

Map 2.1. Mian Mir Cantonment, Lahore, circa 1860.

Despite this attention to good order, however, the Mian Mir cantonment suffered heavily from epidemic disease. In 1861, less than ten years after its founding, the cantonment's "situation" was blamed for a severe cholera epidemic that killed almost 25 percent of the European troops stationed there, earning for itself the slightly inaccurate epithet "that plague spot" in at least one later reminiscence.[31] While people and goods within the cantonment were immersed in the orderly spaces and strict supervision of activities thought essential to maintaining both good discipline and good health, things that flowed into and out of the cantonment were far less amenable to control. Lahore's cantonment was supplied by a daily flow of people and goods from outside: Milk, water, vegetables, and fodder for animals; sweepers, *punkah* coolies (fan operators), grass cutters, and other laborers; and other less-visible forces, largely thought to be borne on prevailing winds, all came to the cantonment from surrounding villages. A committee was therefore organized in 1878 to examine the people and landforms present in the surrounding countryside, gather "useful information," and make recommendations for any remedial work deemed necessary to improve village "cleanliness and conservancy." Members of the committee were told to proceed so as "not to offend the prejudices of the villagers concerned."[32] Cleanliness, presumably, could be prejudicial to the concerns of villagers.

The committee began by obtaining a rough map of the area from the army's quartermaster general and drawing a circle five miles in radius from the center of the cantonment's oval park (Map 2.2). All the villages that fell within the circle that were not already within the municipal boundaries of Lahore came under the committee's scrutiny. The committee divided this circle into quadrants and inspected each quadrant in turn; they described the several villages under their consideration in just three working days. This initial gesture of geometrical abstraction—marking an abstract and geometrically precise boundary line, dividing the bounded area into quadrants, and proceeding through the countryside quadrant by quadrant—was the first of several efforts the committee made to simplify the complex material they were asked to describe and report upon.

The five-mile-radius circle the committee drew included some forty-eight villages, thirteen of which were located within the municipal boundary of the city. On nineteenth- and early twentieth-century British maps of Lahore, these places are variously labeled "villages," "*mohallas*," "*mandis*," "*kilas*," "*kots*," "*pinds*," and "*bazaars*," each term reflecting both different linguistic roots and different social origins.[33] The committee visiting the countryside around the cantonment sometimes made note of the historical origins of individual villages that connected them with their particular names; thus, Kot Lakphat was a village of "76 mud huts clustered together on the north side of an old mud fort *[kot]* now in ruins" (424). More often, however, the villages were described perfunctorily, in brief documentary passages that touched on drainage, sources of water supply, and the visible appearance of houses and people.

The types of building clusters that made up a village varied widely in the area the committee examined. For many settlements, like Pindi, the buildings were simply counted and briefly remarked upon: "Population 560; is a small village of 48 mud huts" (424). Several

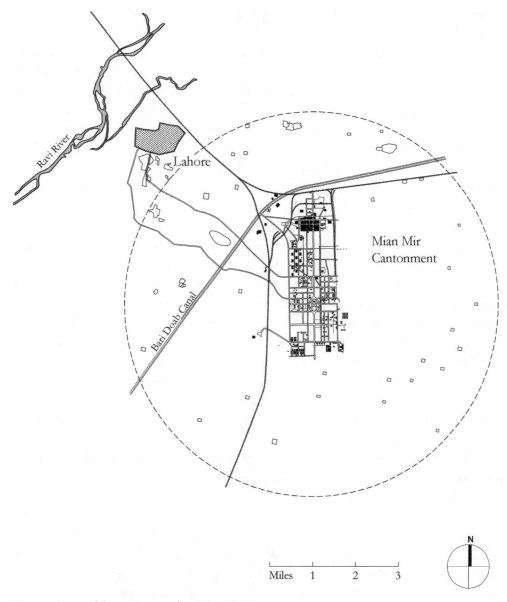

Map 2.2. Survey of the area surrounding Mian Mir Cantonment, 1879.

more were described as clusters of mud houses interspersed with a few more prominent brick ones. The village of Shadi Khui (probably *Shah di Khui*, or "Shah's Well"), like Debi-pura, was "a square mud wall enclosure, in which are about 20 huts with lots of room for more" (424). Kir and Shadipur were made up of "houses" disposed in two separate blocks a short distance apart. Charar was an example of a settlement, like several others, whose older core consisted of "several ruined tenements" (427). Fatagurh, with a population of 950 "souls," contained 262 houses, "of which most are built of brick masonry," and Bagwan-pura, an older village built by Mughal-era *arain*s (market gardeners) had "800 brick-built houses, many of which are two or three or four stories high" (429–30). While different histories of construction and use clearly underlay the different types of village organization the committee observed, the terms used to describe them were uninflected by those histories. Settlements in the plains surrounding Mian Mir were made up of "huts," "houses," and "tenements," and no new concepts to describe them were considered necessary.

In several ways, the inspecting committee described a method of organizing agricultural and living space in the countryside that was comparable to what might be found in Great Britain, if only in mirror image. Indeed, villages surrounding the cantonment were said to be organized in a manner "nearly the opposite" of their British counterparts. Whereas in Britain agriculturists occupied houses on individuated plots at the outskirts of the village center, in the hinterland of Lahore an agriculturist's house stood "jumbled up" with several others, "instead of being, *as it naturally should be* [British particularity stands in here for universal nature], situated by itself in the midst of its fields or lands" (432; emphasis added). To be precise, houses in the village were not houses at all, according to the committee, but jumbled arrays of more mundane spaces: "Each house is in fact a *farmyard*," the committee wrote in their narrative conclusion to the report (432; emphasis added). As evidence, the committee observed that animals, farm implements, fodder, and people cohabited building compounds, each "jumbled up with a number of others of like character in a very limited and altogether insufficient space" (432). Streets and lanes, familiar elements in the British village landscape, were in Punjab "mere passages, winding, narrow and irregular" (432). "Strange," it was said, were the interiors of village houses, where clear distinctions were made between areas occupied by animals and areas occupied by people in what was, nevertheless, a single contiguous space.

Pushing description beyond their original assignment, members of a similar expedition to the area surrounding Rawalpindi's cantonment during the same year (1878) dwelled at some length on the organization of a "typical" village house. This was a single-room structure, according to the committee, "about 30 feet by 12 feet wide and 8 feet high," fronting onto a small enclosed court and entered through a single opening on one of the long sides.[34] Inside, space was divided more or less equally between areas given over to livestock and areas used by people, a practice that was denounced continuously in subsequent efforts to reform rural housing. Each half of the "hut's" interior, according to its function, was conceived of and treated differently: "The interiors of huts present a strange mixture of tidiness, order, and simple decoration in the parts occupied by the family, and of neglect, filth and evil odors in the parts occupied by their cattle." The description of a "typical" house was drawn from a particular one, which the committee described in careful detail:

> The interior on one side of the doorway was occupied by a manger trough of mud built against one wall and a row of four or five tethering sticks. . . . space was allotted to the four cows we found standing in the courtyard, the sick one included, and its floor was one mass of mire, here and there collected into little puddles of putrid urine. . . . the interior on the other side of the doorway was occupied by the members of the family and their household goods. The floor was clean swept and neatly daubed with smooth mud

plaster. . . . Altogether the place appeared very neat and tidy and was doubtless the cher-
ished home of those we found occupying it.[35]

If the insides of houses presented a curious mixture of "order" and "neglect," then the
state of cleanliness outside the houses was considerably worse. The committee inspecting
the villages around Mian Mir wrote that "there is no attempt at regular or systematic conservancy, or indeed any conservancy at all immediately outside the dwelling rooms of the
inhabitants" (428). Most settlements were surrounded by hollows and excavations in the
earth where material for house construction had been removed. These hollows quickly filled
up with water and debris and were described as "soppy" and "miry," "stagnant" and "putres-
cent," as wide shallow puddles "of very filthy festering slush" (428). Village yards and passages were "encumbered" with litter and filth, "whilst the ground is soppy and saturated with
urine, and has an uneven surface with cow dung irregularly trodden onto it" (428). Even
the air in villages was "pervaded with foul smells" and "sensibly affected by the exhalations"
from urine, excreta, and litter. Here, described in the lively and emotionally powerful adjec-
tives used to evoke the danger of miasma, was the raw threatening material the committee
members were sent out to discover. They encountered it, they wrote, in "heaps" (428).

The committee empowered to discern threats to the health of troops in Mian Mir nevertheless drew an unexpected conclusion from their observations. Despite the disorganiza-
tion and filthy conditions described in these villages, the residents of these places seemed to
be considerably healthier than troops occupying the cantonment nearby: "In the whole tour
of inspection the villagers nowhere presented any sign of injury or suffering attributable to
the faulty conditions and modes of their daily life. On the contrary, as a whole, the villagers
everywhere presented the appearance of a remarkably healthy and generally prosperous and
contented people" (432, emphasis added). In the countryside, it appeared, conditions of life
needed little alteration. Unlike the case in the city, as we will see momentarily, rural ways of
life outside Lahore seemed to produce "contented" subjects who were "remarkably healthy"
(432). Evidence for the latter conclusion was apparent on the bodies of male villagers.[36]

In his narrative supplement to the 1881 Punjab census, Denzil Ibbetson wrote that the
"progeny" of village residents were "stronger and longer lived than the urban upper 'ten
thousand.' One has only to visit the *kachery* [district court] on a working day, and see in the
faces of the assembled crowd which of the two, the townsman or villager, is leading the
most healthy life. The city man of forty to fifty will be prematurely grey, his complexion
sallow, with every sign of old age about him; while his rustic contemporary will appear
brown, healthy and vigorous."[37] The report of the committee inspecting the villages around
the Mian Mir cantonment described most villagers as "physically robust and healthy" and
noted that "in almost every village visited by the Committee three or four or more gray-
beards, generally fine hale men, were observed amongst the groups of villagers assembled
to receive us" (425). In one village, the inspectors observed that "the oldest progenitor and
his son were equally adorned with flowing beards of snowy whiteness." A relative of these
men was described as "a fine robust fellow in the prime of life with a beard beginning to

grizzle" (425). In addition to beard hair, skin tone provided the committee visual evidence that the villagers enjoyed good health: A "76 year-old" man had not yet "lost the soft pliancy natural to the skin," one passage of the report observed, "though it was sufficiently wrinkled" (425). This evidence all reinforced the committee's unexpected conclusion: "None of the sanitary defects which the Committee have found to exist in the several villages inspected by them are of a nature to produce any special injury or general deleterious effect upon the health of those living in cantonments" (432).

Whether or not the assumption of good health on the part of the committee was accurate—based, as it was, on cursory visual inspection alone—the relatively healthier life of a "rustic" in comparison to that of someone occupying quarters among the sewage-saturated alleys, unswept passages, and foul drains found in the city was a familiar idea to nineteenth-century Europeans. As Steven Marcus reminds us in his study of Victorian Manchester, the English middle class was "abruptly disturbed" in the middle of the nineteenth century "by the realization that, to put it as mildly as possible, millions of English men, women, and children were living in shit. The immediate question seems to have been whether they were not drowning in it."[38] The same realization informed the assumptions held by the middle-class British inspectors sent out to document villages around Mian Mir. By the late nineteenth century, this assumption would attain the status of common wisdom. In the villages, "the people live an out-door healthy life," wrote Ibbetson in 1881; whereas "in towns, the people live by day and night in an atmosphere of impurity. . . . as for exercise outside the habitation in search of fresh air, the bare suggestion of this as beneficial made to an ordinary city trader would cause him to laugh at you."[39]

The ready association of rural life with good health and urban life with physical degradation was not universal, however. By the last quarter of the nineteenth century, the very real problems of poverty, poor health, and environmental degradation in England's agricultural villages was becoming increasingly visible. George Godwin, editor of *The Builder* magazine and a tireless advocate of housing reform in mid-nineteenth-century England, drew attention to the insanitary state of English villages as early as 1859, the same year the royal commission reported on the health of the Indian Army. An early adherent of the miasmic theory of disease, Godwin lamented the presence of "decomposing vegetable matter, stagnant horseponds, reeking ditches, ill-drained and undrained cow-sheds and stables" in every English village, and he exhorted his reader to look beyond bucolic stereotypes. In a book dedicated mostly to illustrating the perils of urban filth, Godwin nevertheless provided the following tableau of a typical agricultural village: "The place is without drainage. Pigs and dogs are kept: the people are dirty in their habits, and allow all kinds of refuse to collect: water flows down the hill, and lodges in pools, which become stagnant."[40] Thirty years later, journalist George Millen traveled throughout southern England to document the state of the rural poor, publishing his findings in a regular column in the *London Daily News*. The conditions Millen found differed but little from those the colonial inspectors had described in the countryside outside Lahore more than a decade earlier. Millen challenged the stereotypical rural image of "prosperous villages and charming little homes, embowered in orchards and flower gardens, and tenanted by a comfortable and contented peasantry, healthy, thriving, happy, and beyond all comparison better off than the corresponding class in our great towns." Instead, his columns described a rural landscape of "sordid" poverty, "tumbledown ramshackle, damp and draughty" houses, and intractable zones of disease.[41]

Works like these and others during the late nineteenth century served to link the English village to the industrial city conceptually, since problems of poverty, child labor, poor housing, and rampant disease were seen to be shared by both. Modernization and its deadly discomforts affected the village and the metropolis together in real time, in other words, just as solutions to those shared problems were seen to necessitate simultaneous reforms in both the countryside and the city. Despite the growing realization in England, thus, that the village and the metropolis formed an interconnected whole, colonial officials continued to see the Indian village as a more or less isolated phenomenon. Proposals to improve the "faulty conditions and modes" of daily life in rural Punjab, therefore, bore little relation to environmental reforms proposed for the city or its suburban districts.

While the village inspection committee recommended only limited intervention in Lahore's surrounding villages, rural sanitary-reform regulations were eventually passed. Beginning in 1888, proposals were put forth for a "Village Sanitation Act" in Punjab; it was passed three years later. The Village Sanitation Act of 1891 was administered by district-level deputy commissioners and extended only to villages with a thousand or more people. The act required that villages maintain their water supplies in good order, and it relied on a "*panchayat* [traditional village governing body] consisting of not less than three persons owning or occupying land in the village" to bring sanitary offenses to the notice of the government.[42] To repair an offense, a tax would be assessed on the village common lands in an amount determined by the district commissioner.

The opinions put forth by Punjab's various district commissioners on the institutional sites through which such a law might be enforced reveal the constitutive role their assumptions about village society played in formulating rural policy. Some commentators, like W. G. Waterfield, argued that only local officials could be relied upon to produce results, since villagers were inherently distrustful: "It is only the village police officer working under the Police Department and the Magistracy that could dare to interfere with the community, and they must be empowered to do so by law."[43] Others, including Punjab's lieutenant governor, J. B. Lyall, whose opinion proved decisive, argued that the same distrust of intermediary authority noticed by Waterfield in the villages under his control was reason enough to rely on more-central powers for the application of force: "Here, in this country of sturdy coparcenary communities of peasant proprietors, each village must in village affairs govern itself, or else be governed by orders issued by some high central authority. I think that no one who knows these villages will doubt the fact."[44]

The measures of Punjab's Village Sanitation Act of 1891 were enacted by force, rather than moral persuasion: "We have to deal with people in villages who are about as intelligent in spite of all our boasted education . . . as were the people of England at the time of the Conquest," wrote A. Harcourt, deputy commissioner of Jullundur, in his opinion on the original proposal; "I am aware of the old derisive cry that [not] everything can be done at the point of the bayonet. But force is at times necessary, for if it were not, why have law at all? And rules and regulations are after all the bayonet point sheathed in paper, and the cold steel, though concealed, is always in reserve."[45] As long as Punjab's villagers remained trapped in an earlier stage of civilizational development, colonial officials believed, their progress and general disposition could be safely controlled with a firm, authoritative hand. Problems arose in the countryside, however, wherever the ties of ancient custom had grown weak.

CREATING AN EXEMPLARY MILIEU

Despite the martial timbre of Deputy Commissioner Harcourt's comment, colonial policy in Punjab's agrarian villages aimed to maintain the status quo rather than alter the "modes and customs" of village life. There were a few settings in Punjab's countryside, however, where colonial interventions were much more directly engaged with the materials of everyday life. These settings included settlement camps for "criminal tribes" and canal-colony towns in newly irrigated tracts, both of which were novel products of colonial rule in the province. Here, model towns and villages were designed and built to act as exemplary milieus. Colonial officials believed that long residence in a particular locale solidified stubborn customs and made people resistant to change; similarly, they believed that the bonds of custom would be weakened in these other settings by spatial dislocation, or even by permanent settlement itself.

The earliest use of model villages in Punjab was as new reformatory settlements for wandering "criminal tribes," a term British officials applied to several groups of seminomadic pastoralists they considered genetically predisposed to crime.[46] As early as 1856, reformatories were established for these groups in an attempt to induce a settled, industrious lifestyle. In 1871, the government of India passed the Criminal Tribes Act, which helped standardize the regulation of reformatories. These reformatories were of two basic types, "agricultural" and "industrial," and a disciplined regimen of work was enforced at each. Once a group was settled in, officials drew up a register of names at each reformatory and called roll every morning and evening to ensure no one left without permission. Overseers could grant adult males permission to leave for no more than twenty-four hours. Women, in many cases, could not leave at all since, as one official argued, "while [women] remain free it is almost impossible to check crime, as they are the principal receivers of the stolen goods, and it is well known that they encourage and taunt the men to commit crime."[47]

The layout of a criminal-tribe settlement was designed to give an overseer a clear view into the quotidian details of residential life. Some settlements were built according to the "French Canadian plan," organized in long narrow strips of land, with a road running through the center of the settlement and with individual cottages facing the road (Figure 2.1). The advantage of this plan, according to its designer, was that by having houses placed close together, "there is not the *loneliness* of a farm house situated upon its own land"; he went on to note, of course, that "the road running through the center makes supervision

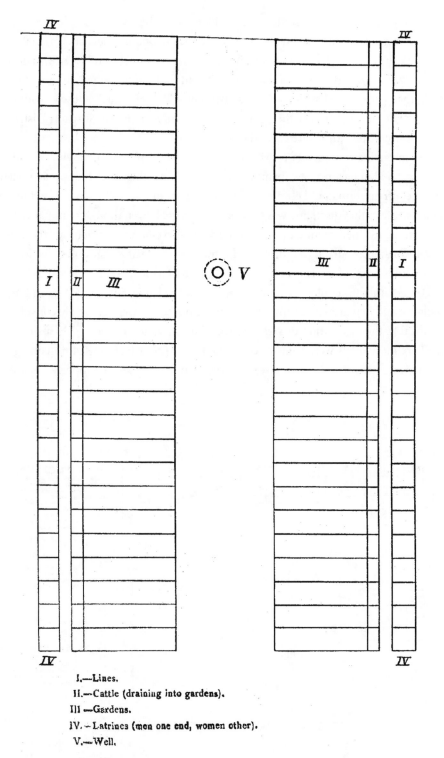

I.—Lines.

II.—Cattle (draining into gardens).

III —Gardens.

IV. – Latrines (men one end, women other).

V.—Well.

Figure 2.1. Criminal-tribe settlement plan for an agricultural village on the "French Canadian plan," Punjab, circa 1916. Source: Government of Punjab, Home Department Proceedings (Police), no. 10 (April 1916): 109.

comparatively easy."[48] In other settlements residents were housed in long lines of cell-like rooms roughly ten feet square, with separate lines joined to one another across a small walled courtyard (Figure 2.2). Whatever the particularities of plan, each settlement was designed to be quickly surveyed from a central location. If criminal activity relied on the art of concealment, then periodic inspections of the settlement—including each house—would make criminal activity impossible. At the Mina tribal reformatory in the Gurgaon District, for example, house inspections were carried out weekly.[49]

Criminal-tribe settlements can be seen as similar to prisons or asylums, and their success depended in part on new forms of discipline. Nevertheless, the idea that a particular spatial configuration could eliminate "the loneliness of a farm house situated upon its own land" suggests that discipline was only part of the goal. Even though criminal-tribe settlements were governed through a strict regime of surveillance, visibility in these settlements was considered an aid to moral development as much as a check on behavior. Mary Poovey reminds us that for nineteenth-century Britons, virtue was something that had to be demonstrated and thus could only develop when made visible. She writes that in England, "surveillance and ocular penetration of poor neighborhoods were generally considered to be as critical to the inculcation of virtue as was the cultivation of taste."[50] In a society like India, where individuals were considered prone to disappear from the moralizing gaze of their putative superiors—in this case, a reform-minded state—a properly constructed

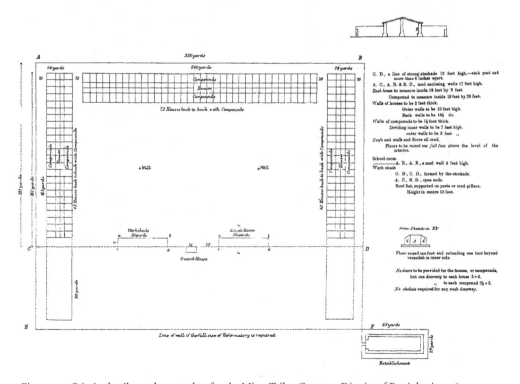

Figure 2.2. Criminal-tribe settlement plan for the Mina Tribe, Gurgaon District of Punjab, circa 1873. Source: Government of Punjab, Home Department Proceedings, no. 5 (October 1873): 775.

environment, one that pressed visibility into direct service of its goals, might itself prevent moral lapse.

A suitably organized environment was the primary vehicle for change in a number of other rural settings in Punjab as well. Beginning in the late 1880s and continuing into the twentieth century, the colonial state built several new villages in Punjab's canal-irrigated districts, villages based on model designs. Inundation canals had been a feature of Punjab's countryside for several hundred years. The British government began refurbishing many of these canals and building new ones shortly after taking formal control of the province in 1849. By the 1880s large tracts of irrigated land were available for cultivation, and the colonial government began granting agricultural plots to individuals and groups according to a range of different priorities.[51] These new canal-colony settlements provided an opportunity to accelerate desirable changes in agrarian society in Punjab's countryside since they presented an almost unfettered opportunity to alter the material settings of agricultural life. "For the British, as much as for earlier Indus Basin states, the link between canal building, agricultural settlement, and political control was central to the construction of state power," writes historian David Gilmartin; "agricultural settlement was important to the British not only for its role in the establishment of order, but perhaps even more critically, for its role in encouraging a general 'moral' transformation."[52]

Canal colonies, as these newly irrigated and settled areas were called, differed from other rural tracts in Punjab in significant ways. What made colonial officials judge village sites in these colonies to be more suitable for environmental reform than sites in older villages in the province was their assumption that newly settled towns lacked the binding ties of custom that characterized social life in the older villages. The residents who settled in Punjab's new canal colonies, therefore, were thought to be particularly susceptible to the moral effects that might be secured through a project of environmental reform. From the 1880s until the early 1920s, in the districts of Gujranwala, Gujrat, Jhang, Lahore, Montgomery, Multan, Shekhupura, and Sialkot, colonial engineers laid out new colony towns with broad streets, large house sites, and ample room for expansion.[53] The town of Lyallpur, for example, was built in 1896 according to the design of Captain Popham Young. The town was built in a gridiron pattern, with eight bazaars radiating from a central *chauk* (square). Separate quarters were provided for Hindus, Muslims, and, at the edge of town, low-caste sweepers, *gwala*s (cow-keepers), and tenants of the town farm.[54] The streets in Lyallpur were lighted, the town's water supply was kept clean, public latrines on a "modern pattern" were built both inside and outside the town's limits, and in the town's main square an imposing sandstone clock tower announced, in measured and regular intervals, the arrival of a new mode of life (Figure 2.3).

Standard village plans were developed for use in Punjab's canal colonies, each tailored to the type of settlers who would inhabit the village. All the plans were based on a grid, with separate sections earmarked for different religious groups and classes of laborer (Figure 2.4). Existing social hierarchies based on caste, religion, and race were left intact, in other words, but their spatial relations were reordered. As was the case in the military cantonment, these

Figure 2.3. Clock tower in Lyallpur (now Faisalabad, Pakistan), built circa 1896.

standardized spatial relationships produced a regular and predictable relationship between people's social positions and their positions in abstract space. Colony towns thus differed from Punjab's older villages by emphasizing sanitation, orderly arrangement, and a new kind of spatial hierarchy. In their uniformity of design, clarity of social and spatial hierarchies, and comprehensive accommodation for all members of village life, colony towns were particularly clear manifestations of the colonial spatial imagination at work.

By the turn of the twentieth century this new physical milieu, coupled with the social dislocation brought about by resettlement, was seen to be producing an effect. In 1907 a committee formed to report on canal-colony settlements noted that "the clear and orderly surroundings of the colony villages are having an *educative* effect on the people."[55] In highlighting the agentive power of the material environment on the shaping of human conduct,

PLAN OF PEASANT VILLAGE SITES
ON
JHANG AND BHOWANA BRANCHES

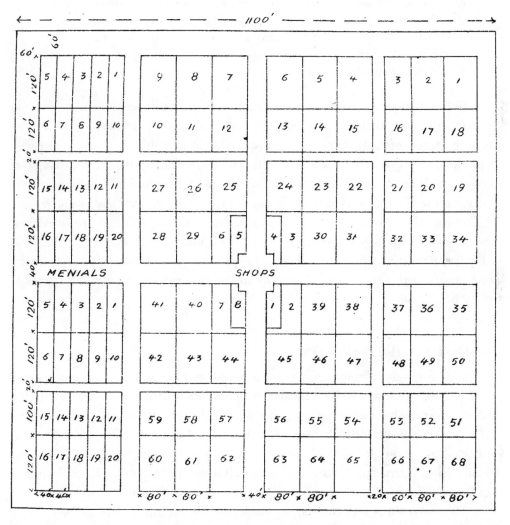

Figure 2.4. Typical canal-colony village layout plan for use in the Jhang and Bhowana irrigation tracts, circa 1900. From Government of Punjab, Gazetteer of the Chenab Colony, 1904 (1905) (Lahore: Sang-e-Meel, 1996), n.p.

colonial officials drew on the concept of the object lesson, which by that time had acquired its more general sense of a lesson resulting from seeing or physically experiencing some object or event that left a vivid impression on the mind. In 1905, the inspector general of civil hospitals in Punjab argued that spatial experiments in the newly developing canal colonies "ought to be object lessons" to others on the advantages of sanitary living: "Every family hutted would be an object-lesson that could not fail to have its effect in inducing others to take the step."[56] For one commentator, the new customs that appeared to be growing in canal-colony towns were evidence of a "natural" process:

> The conditions among which [canal colonists] find themselves are novel. They are far removed from the main body of their tribe; and it is understood that already there are signs that as the continuity of residence and community of conditions and needs are developing, new customs are already growing up which . . . are more or less common to the colony. . . . The process is *natural and inevitable,* but also, in [our] judgment, deserving of recognition and encouragement.[57]

This last comment underlines how much the supposedly determinant connection between material "conditions" and social "customs" had come to be taken for granted by the early decades of the twentieth century. For many colonial officials, progress in reform depended primarily on the efficacy of the material alterations themselves, something that could be methodically studied and applied. The officials who designed model villages, towns, and reform settlements worked by codifying and replicating standardized spatial ensembles, applying those ensembles to chosen settings, and monitoring the effects they produced. The designs all emphasized clear lines of sight, standardized components, and a hierarchical system of ordering. These physical devices were meant to instill both a new appreciation for rational ordering and the moral qualities attached to that kind of order in the colonial spatial imagination.

ASSESSING THE INNER CITY

When we turn to consider the city, a different set of emphases and aspirations are apparent. Unlike British attitudes about the Indian countryside, prevailing attitudes toward the Indian city were almost universally negative. As with the new settlements in Punjab's irrigated tracts, colonial officials believed that the material dynamism and social flux that characterized Punjab's growing cities weakened the long-sedimented bonds of kin and community that tied rural families together in a moral economy. Unlike the model communities British officials planned and built to shape a new kind of productive and civic life in Punjab's canal colonies and reformatory settlements, however, the Indian city was seen as far too opaque and too durable in its inferior condition to be easily reconfigured.

British commentators writing in the late nineteenth century attributed the filth and decrepitude of the city itself to cultural predisposition: The authors of an 1863 report concluded that "the habits of the natives are such that, unless they are closely watched, they cover the whole neighbouring surface with filth."[58] Rudyard Kipling's 1885 article on the sanitary condition of Lahore's Old City renders the filth of the city as the almost hydraulic effect of an imagined human tumult: "The dead walls," Kipling wrote, "the barred and grated windows, and the high storeyed houses, were throbbing and humming with human life, as you may hear a hive of bees hum ere they go forth to their day's work. Voices of children singing their lessons at school; sounds of feet on stone steps, or wooden balconies over-head; voices raised in argument, or conversation, sounded dead and muffled as though they came through wool; and it seemed as if, at any moment, the tide of unclean humanity might burst through its dam of rotten brickwork and filth-smeared wood, blockading the passages below. . . . By unclean corners of walls; on each step of ruinous staircases; on the roofs of low out-houses; by window, and housetop, or stretched amid garbage unutterable, this section of Lahore was awaking to another day's life."[59]

Because the conceptual linkage between living habits, filth, and morality remained strong in nineteenth-century British thought, the squalor of the city, a visible product of "the habits of the natives," was seen as emblematic of the less-visible moral degradation that characterized urban society.[60] In his famous report on the sanitation of British towns (1842), Edwin Chadwick observed that "tenements of inferior construction had manifestly an injurious operation on the moral as well as on the sanitary condition. . . . it appears to be a matter of common observation, in the instance of migrant families of workpeople who are obliged to occupy inferior tenements, that their habits soon become 'of a piece' with the dwelling."[61] John Loudon, in his influential encyclopedia of house and farm designs, wrote that "uncouth, mean, ragged, dirty houses, constituting the body of any town, will regularly be accompanied by coarse, groveling manners. The dress, the furniture, the equipage, the mode of living, and the manners, will all correspond with the appearance of the buildings."[62] George Godwin, whose depressing tableau of a typical English village we saw earlier, made the same point when he cautioned, "as the house, so the inmate. . . . Listen to the conversation, if so it may be called, of those inhabiting [a derelict building]: you would find it in keeping with the disordered, disruptured, disreputable locality."[63] This tight imbrication of morals, manners, and modes of living with the material culture of everyday life underpinned British assumptions that a city's material features were indicative of the moral development of society. Whereas the "modes and customs" of rural Punjab seemed poised to perpetuate a stable and contented peasant society, in the Indian city those modes and customs promised to perpetuate indecency, evidence for which could be amply found in the city's material culture.[64]

The main problem was the dense inner core of the city rather than the more sparsely settled suburbs of the civil station. Descriptions of India's inner-city districts were remarkably generic in the nineteenth century, and descriptions of Lahore were no exception:

> The Punjab is still India, and, when one has seen one Indian city, *one has seen the lot.* Narrow winding streets, where the mud often remains even in the dry season; some of them containing shops, whose windows, often protected by a penthouse, make them

still narrower; all the evil smells of these tiny factories, for most of the merchants manufacture themselves in front of their shops the articles they sell, either vases or ornaments of copper, sweetmeats, or vile pastry, or dyes; bulls, cows, goats, and donkeys
wander freely about; horses placed under a shelter which projects into the public street,
with their hind legs attached by two long cords to a post in the center of the street; half-
starved and ravenous dogs often covered with disgusting sores; here and there heaps of
brick, the ruins of former houses, and piles of dung which the neighboring inhabitants
have deposited; trees stretching across the road stripped of their leaves by passing camels
and elephants; such is the interior of Lahore.[65]

This conventional kind of narrative proceeds by describing fragments—narrow streets
that become "still narrower" yet lead nowhere in particular; animals wandering "freely
about"; things piled in heaps "here and there." The narrative depends on eliciting an emotional response in the reader in order to evoke the scene in its entirety, a response that sub-
stitutes for precise and connected mental images. The result is a spatial paradigm, but one
that lacks the predictable spatial sequences and hierarchy of order desired by the colonial
spatial imagination. In these and other European accounts, the inner city eludes knowability,
presenting a kind of visual opacity resistant to aggregate description. Crawford Roe, Lahore's
sanitary commissioner in 1897, wrote of his difficulty, even fifty years after the establishment
of British rule, in locating precisely where he was when he went out on inspection: "There
are practically no means of distinguishing one street or lane from another in many places,
except by the name of some wealthy man's house which may be in its immediate vicinity,"
Roe wrote; "all the main streets should be numbered, and the lanes leading off them in each
ward or division lettered. At the present time there is the greatest difficulty in determining
any special locality, as there are neither names nor numbers in many parts to distinguish
different lanes or streets."[66]

Even those who explicitly sought a totalizing description of Lahore, by indulging that
quintessentially European proclivity toward climbing a tall tower and having a look down,
often found the results wanting.[67] This is the vantage point a sweat-drenched narrator attains
in Rudyard Kipling's short story "The City of Dreadful Night" (1891) as he enters Lahore's
walled Old City late one torpid night in the punishing heat of summer.[68] Unable to sleep in
his house in the civil station, the narrator sets his "walking-stick on end in the middle of
the garden, and waited to see how [at random] it would fall. It pointed directly down the
moonlit road that leads to the City of Dreadful Night." Kipling takes the reader through the
debris-strewn plain and into the Old City through Delhi Gate, the preferred entry point for
European tourists. "Overhead blazed the unwinking eye of the Moon," Kipling wrote, thereby
enabling the reader to also see. The narrator encounters an abrupt shock to his senses as he
reaches the gate, and he nearly decides against proceeding farther: "A stifling hot blast from
the mouth of the Delhi Gate nearly ends my resolution . . . a compound of all evil savours,
animal and vegetable, that a walled city can brew in a day and a night." But he is intrepid,
and decides to continue until he arrives at the Mosque of Wazir Khan, one of Lahore's finest
Mughal landmarks.

During the nineteenth century the minarets of this mosque were popular with Europeans as a vantage point for taking in the city (Figure 2.5), and Kipling's narrator, too, climbs to the top of a minaret and describes what he sees:

> Turn to have a look on the City of Dreadful Night. Doré might have drawn it! Zola could describe it—this spectacle of sleeping thousands in the moonlight and in the shadow of the moon. The roof-tops are crammed with men, women, and children; and the air is full of undistinguishable noises. They are restless in the City of Dreadful Night; and small wonder. The marvel is that they can even breathe.

Next comes Kipling's effort at an encompassing gaze. The narrator describes the scene in its entirety, but just as he does so, description devolves once again into fragments:

> The pitiless Moon shows it all. Shows, too, the plains outside the city, and here and there a hand's-breadth of the Ravee [Ravi River] without the walls. Shows lastly a splash of glittering silver on a house-top almost directly below the mosque Minar. Some poor soul has risen to throw a jar of water over his fevered body. . . . two or three other men, in far-off corners of the City of Dreadful Night follow his example, and the water flashes like heliographic signals.

Kipling's narrator does indeed see and describe things in great detail. He observes human movement "in the pit-like courtyards of the houses" and the subdued "tumult" of people sleeping all across the roofscape. But the following passage contains the real impact of the story:

Figure 2.5. *Stereophotograph of Kashmiri Bazaar sold by Underwood and Underwood, Lahore, 1903. This stereo image was sold to a largely British market; when viewed through special glasses, the image would appear three-dimensional. The minarets of the Mosque of Wazir Khan, where Kipling's narrator in "The City of Dreadful Night" was perched, are just visible at the top of the image. Copyright The British Library Board. OIOC Photo 181(15); all rights reserved.*

Seated with both elbows on the parapet of the tower, one can watch and wonder over that heat-tortured hive till the dawn. "How do they live down there? What do they think of? When will they awake?" . . . A small cloud passes over the face of the Moon, and the city and its inhabitants—clear drawn in black and white before—fade into masses of black and deeper black.

In Kipling's story, and in the traveler's description presented earlier, the city's "excesses"—excessive heat, excessive complexity, excessive density of unanswerable questions—bore much of the emotional content, and pleasure, of the text.[69] That "excess" meant something entirely different, however, when it became the object of urban reform. To insert the space of the inner city into discourse on urban reform entailed a more empirically based practice of observation and description, one in which the city's component parts could be placed within an ordered whole and made to function according to administrative logic. What is notable, however, is the way the Indian districts of the city exceeded the limits of this more scientific mode of inquiry as well. This fact would make the inner city an object distinct from both the countryside and the suburban areas in colonial discourse. The modes of inquiry useful to a project of rendering order in the countryside—constructing encompassing spatial images to order description, drawing comparisons to known phenomena from English experience, inventing categories when analogies were inadequate—were insufficient to render the Indian city legible.

SPECIFYING SOCIETY'S CONTAINERS

This problem emerges clearly in early census-taking projects conducted in the city. The Indian census was a device that both enumerated and classified the main features of Indian "society" and also rendered its material containers transparent to this enumerative project.[70] The latter effect of the census has seldom elicited comment in historical analyses, in part perhaps because this feature of the census was only ever immanent in the device itself. Nevertheless, for the officials charged with conducting the census, specifying society's containers was a problem that had to be dealt with. In 1891 Edward D. Maclagan was in charge of directing the census in Lahore, and the problems he encountered relate directly to this point. Frustrated by the lack of fit between the English term "house" as a place of residence and the Hindustani term *ghar,* which he noted was used for both "house" and "family," Maclagan wrote that to send a census enumerator out to count "houses" was to send him "in search of a *social and moveable,* rather than a *structural and immovable* unit."[71] In other words, the term designating a material form that was coincident with the social practice of "residence" was at odds with the forms and social practices that term invoked in local usage. Both the social practice "residence" and the form "house" meant something different in India than what the census was prepared to account for.

For census purposes, "residence" implied the presence of a "household" of persons bearing a commensal relationship to one another. It was clear to Maclagan that something was amiss in this relationship among the range of phenomena he encountered while attempting to establish the precise number of households under his jurisdiction, and he traced the problem in part to his reliance on Indian interlocutors, mostly student canvassers. In Lahore, unpaid college students were selected to carry out census operations in the Old City.[72] Maclagan wrote that his Indian staff were erroneously prone to count men sleeping in lodging houses and dining in local public eating houses as "part of the family of the *tanur-wala,* or local cook, whose shop they patronized."[73] He observed that people often made their "residence" in eating houses, as well as in other kinds of shops, cattle pens, sugar mill–yards, boats, *serais*, schools, each others' houses, and a range of other places. The nomenclature of the census—and by extension, the concept describing the relationship between "house" and "residence" it was predicated upon—only confused matters further. Even when a "house" could be firmly established as a place of residence, English concepts were incompatible with the range of objects and spatial relations covered by that term. For example, the following obstacles arose to the practice of affixing a census number to the main entry door of each residence:

> In the first place, there are alleys or courts containing very often *hundreds of houses* and yet opening on to the street by a single doorway. The staff are greatly tempted to save themselves trouble by counting the whole of each such alley or court as one *house,* and there is nothing in the rules to prevent them. And again we meet often with upper stories of a building which open onto the street by a different door than the lower story, or open on to a different street altogether.[74]

Ten years later, Hugh Rose, who served in the same capacity as Maclagan had, was no better equipped than his predecessor to come to terms with the same problems. Referring to Maclagan's earlier census report, Rose wrote that "the term 'house' is, in towns, almost incapable of definition." Such too, according to Rose, was the case with the term "room," which meant something "vastly different" in local usage than what the census was designed to record.[75] Rose's summary report was a candid admission, in other words, that the thread linking observation with knowledge, cause with effect, was broken somewhere along the way.

Still, despite these awkward problems, the census was carried out, and "houses," "rooms," and other categories for which local usage provided such illusory substance took their accustomed place as key terms in a discourse whose immediate object was to characterize fundamental relationships between people and their physical place of residence. According to the 1901 census, therefore, the inner city of Lahore contained exactly 20,691 "houses." Given the nomenclatural complexities involved, it is hard to know exactly what that meant.

The way Lahore's census was carried out underscores the resilience of the observational methods we saw in the sanitary tour of villages outside Mian Mir, which, despite their ineffectiveness, attempted to render the landscape functional and legible. For purposes of the census, "houses" in Lahore were assimilated into an English conceptual field that admittedly had little relation to the objects it purported to describe and that depended on defining objects that were, according to its own terms, "almost incapable of definition."

As in the village survey outside the Mian Mir cantonment, the material fabric of Lahore's inner city was made intelligible for the census by establishing its nearest English equivalents in a process of translation or substitution that served to flatten differences between the two. However useful this flattening exercise was for purposes of governance, the differences it subsumed were precisely those that lend meaning to concepts like "residence" (or indeed "society") in a localized context. Finally, borrowing a phrase from Maclagan, the language of the census attempted to fix "social and moveable" phenomena in terms that presumed them to be, instead, "structural and immovable." For the colonial officials in charge of rendering the city transparent to discourse, there would always be a little more to Lahore than they could comprehend.

DURABLE POCKETS OF DISORDER

The Indian city presented a material space and assemblage of people and activities that resisted mechanisms, like the census, designed to render them more visible. For this reason, colonial intervention reached its limit of effectiveness at the gates of the walled inner city. The same was true wherever "fragments" of indigenous city cropped up in the city's suburbs, such as the numerous Indian *abadi*s (settled areas) situated in and around the civil station (Map 2.3). The colonial state repeatedly attempted to rework the basic features of the largest of these *abadi*s—places like Mozang, Anarkali, Gowal Mandi, and Kila Gujar Singh—but was able to realize little change.

Unlike late nineteenth-century urban reform projects in continental Europe, nineteenth-century urban reforms in India were usually small-scale interventions rather than wholesale demolitions or restructurings. Colonial officials argued that piecemeal reconfiguration of faulty streets, buildings, and neighborhoods along new lines would gradually produce new, more orderly habits. Urban reform often began, thus, by breaking problem areas into smaller, more manageable parts. Once an area was suitably isolated, new constructions could be inserted into the existing context as an inducement to transformation. The form these constructions most often took was that of the "model," and models were often referred to, in turn, as "object lessons."

Mozang was one such Indian neighborhood in Lahore's predominantly European civil station singled out for this type of improvement. In 1913 Punjab's sanitary commissioner, S. Browning Smith, argued at the Punjab Sanitary Conference that "the acquisition of crowded and insanitary collections of buildings which exist in many places in the suburbs of our larger towns and rebuilding on model lines would prove most valuable object-lessons, and possibly be remunerative.... Mozang, for instance, with a sewerage system in prospect, might be laid out as a model sanitary village, its danger as a center for the spread of epidemic disease abolished, and so prove of great educational value; other suburbs of Lahore suggest themselves for similar treatment."[76]

Smith's proposal went unheeded, but his assumptions were widely shared. The conference's keynote speaker, Michael O'Dwyer, the lieutenant governor of Punjab, commented

Map 2.3. Lahore's civil station, circa 1900.

on a range of buildings constructed by the colonial government that he believed worked much the same way. Among these, O'Dwyer listed model grain stores, soldiers' quarters in cantonments, police station houses, barracks, schools, and model housing schemes for railway employees, doctors, and teachers. O'Dwyer concluded by stating that "last but not least, no man ever serves a sentence of imprisonment in our jails without getting a wholesome if involuntary object lesson in sanitation."[77]

While model houses, grain stores, and soldiers' quarters were easily constructed, schemes for reforming urban neighborhoods like Mozang remained largely proposals on paper, since even though neighborhoods were a much more manageable size than the inner city itself, the high cost of purchasing land in these areas often made comprehensive redevelopment impossible. Mozang was a particularly thorny object for British administrators in Lahore, since its character and proximity to European dwellings had long posed a presumed threat to public health. The neighborhood's fate was thus in the balance almost continually from the 1880s until well after the turn of the twentieth century. As early as November 1887 the superintendent of works at Punjab's Public Works Department (PWD) wrote,

> [Mozang] is really a second city, having 10,000 inhabitants, right in the middle of the civil station, the present state of which is probably about as bad as can be imagined. . . . within an area of less than four acres are crowded some 10,000 people mostly in tortuous lanes and alleys thoroughly saturated with sewage. . . . the place is a hotbed of disease. . . . I suppose it is out of the question to propose moving this in every way objectionable feature out of the civil station [altogether]?[78]

Three years later, the city's superintending engineer wrote the following reply, noting how human excrement burned in Mozang's brick kilns contributed to "the particular Lahore smell":

> [The question has been asked:] "Has the removal of the village ever been contemplated and seriously considered?" There is no doubt this would be the best solution. A populous and dirty place like this, in the center of the civil lines of Lahore, is most objectionable; but I fear the cost of removal would be prohibitive. It is the home of a great many of the domestic servants of the station, and, according to the last census had a population of 7,300, but is now said to be over 8,000.[79]

What couldn't be accomplished in whole, however, could perhaps be accomplished in part. In 1890 Lahore's deputy commissioner, Colonel C. Beadon, pondered the prospect of removing Mozang outright: "The suggestion would, I think, be worthy of consideration were funds available for the purpose. I have, however, thought that even a *partial removal* of habitation would be a great improvement in the present condition of affairs." Beadon suggested moving some parts of Mozang to an area outside the settlement earmarked for extension. On a detailed map of Mozang he had drawn up, Beadon sketched—in pencil— the layout of a new residential settlement. Having calculated the cost of his scheme, how- ever, Beadon admitted it would not work: "I have roughly estimated that the project would itself cost Rs. 76,144, and even this sum is more than the Municipal funds could afford." The only option, given the budget, seemed to be a partial realignment of drainage channels and remedial improvements to Mozang's water supply. "The improvement of the village of Mozang, *if it cannot be removed,* is of very great importance to the station," he concluded, "and I should like to see the whole scheme carried through at once instead of piece-meal."[80]

Improvements were carried out piecemeal nevertheless. Rudimentary improvements to Mozang's drainage scheme took nearly three years to complete. One year after the pro- ject's completion, moreover, Mozang seems to have reverted to its original state: "This place [Mozang] has been partially drained, and the work was reported as complete in 1893," noted a sanitary inspector in his 1897 report; "the arrangement of these drains is so defective [however] that in many places they are already breaking away. . . . there is little doubt that sooner or later the whole thing will have to be done over again."[81] Even though rebuilding a neighborhood like Mozang into a "model sanitary village" might "prove of great educational value," as some argued, intervention in the costly and populous Indian neighborhoods of cities was often financially impossible. These seemingly durable pockets of urban disorder in Lahore's civil station presented insurmountable obstacles to large-scale urban restructuring.

Whereas elements in the countryside were resistant to—but ultimately more easily made available for—comprehension, the inner districts of the city were seen as fundamentally inscrutable. Uday Singh Mehta has shown that "the themes of opacity, mystery, and unfathomable inscrutability abound" in nineteenth-century British writings on India.[82] These perceptions set limits to the depth of affective engagement with, and the styles of interaction proposed for, social arrangements in the city. On a sliding scale from "resistant to comprehension" to "inscrutable," a countryside of sturdy "rustics" embedded in village houses and "huts" would occupy the former end of the scale and the inner city—comprehended not in shades of "black and white" but of "black and deeper black"—would occupy the latter. Even if the countryside could be lifted more or less whole into a colonial strategy of inclusion—as a subordinate component within a hierarchical whole—the inner city was fundamentally incompatible with that overall system and thus resistant to progressive modification. Throughout the entire period of British rule, the inner city in Lahore was never subjected to the same degree of direct intervention and reshaping as other settings in and around the city. Few British installations, and almost no British residences, were located in the Old City. The colonial municipal government rarely proposed or built a new street there. The few older streets that were widened by the municipality followed preexisting paths. When an Improvement Trust was formed in 1919 to oversee urban development in Lahore, districts within the Old City were left out of the plans.[83]

CONCLUSION

This chapter has used the concept of a colonial spatial imagination to help sort out why colonial officials intervened in some settings and largely avoided intervening in others. The concept also helps us understand how those interventions were organized, since we can see the spatial imagination as embedding the images and spatial paradigms that accompanied the colonial state's ideal of civic and moral advancement as something at least partially constituted through a proper physical milieu. These images and paradigms were not simply "imaginary," therefore; they worked their way through institutionalized projects of environmental reform, concretely shaping the projects' physical expressions. Using this logic, I have argued that the lack of colonial intervention in the inner districts of the city was at least partially an effect of the inner city's inscrutability, a quality that excluded it physically from the colonial state's modernizing reach. At best, intervention in the inner city (as in the Indian *mohallas* in the city's suburbs) would be attempted through piecemeal improvements, letting object lessons and model buildings accomplish whatever transformations they might.

Spatial complexity was only one of several reasons the colonial government intervened cautiously in the material fabric of the older city, of course. Complicated patterns of
property ownership in the Old City (as discussed in chapter 1) meant that purchasing land
for reconstruction was tedious and costly for a colonial municipal government that was
chronically short of funds. Colonial administrators also worried that interfering in Indian
quarters might provoke political unrest, a fear that was sometimes borne out.[84] Nevertheless, the hesitancy to intervene in the inner city cannot be fully explained by these other fac-
tors. After all, financial and political constraints were present in European cities that were
nevertheless subjected to intensive physical restructuring during roughly the same period
of time.[85] Although the aftermath of the uprising of 1857 led to numerous punitive demolitions in the older Indian quarters of some cities, including Delhi and Lucknow, material
alterations to most Indian districts were modest throughout the colonial period.[86] To this
day, the street pattern and density of construction in India's older urban districts, if not
always the buildings themselves, remain rooted in traditions that predate colonial rule.

Outside the inner city, however, there was more scope for the colonial spatial imagination to exert its influence. Throughout colonial India, the districts most directly shaped
by colonial power and knowledge, the primary zones of British engagement with the older
Indian cities' material and human phenomena, were the suburban areas outside the old
cities, usually called the civil station. In chapter 3 I will show how this several-square-mile
area in Lahore became the primary setting in British efforts to shape a new kind of urban
milieu, one whose realization depended heavily on the collaboration of a local elite.

COLLABORATIONS

Building an Elite Landscape
in Lahore's Civil Station

3

On the eve of annexation, Lahore's suburbs were made up of a flat, debris-strewn plain interrupted by a small number of populous *abadis*, the deserted cantonment and barracks of the former Sikh infantry (which, according to one British officer, "put to shame the humble huts in which the British Sepoy resides"), and a handful of still-serviceable tombs, gardens, and other large buildings in various states of disrepair.[1] This plain—which would be called the "civil station" in Lahore as in other cities of British India—was to be the site for a new kind of urban project in Punjab: the construction of a colonial provincial capital. As we saw in chapter 2, this more or less unpopulated suburban zone was the most promising among a range of other possible sites for establishing what British officials hoped would be an effective, and socially transformative, civic milieu—effective in the sense of adequately serving the military, administrative, and commercial needs of the new colonial province, and transformative in the sense of providing an urban setting whose material qualities might foster more decorous modes of interracial urban existence than could be provided by the degraded "native" city.

The colonial city of Lahore had its address in the civil station. The Old City, by far the most populous part of Lahore, was little more than a negative example in the minds of those who conceptualized, authorized, and built the colonial city. It would be wrong, however, to see the new city as embodying British authority in any simple way.[2] The civil station in Lahore depended in crucial ways on collaboration between British and Indian residents of the city. Though there has been a long-standing tendency in scholarship on colonial cities to emphasize segregation and spatial strategies of exclusion, a central argument of this chapter is that large portions of the colonial city were designed with the goal of invoking inclusivity in directly relevant and cognizable ways. As we will see, architectural styles, the choice of building sites and layouts, channels of architectural patronage, and even rules governing behavior in this new colonial city were all drawn upon at times to annotate the idea of inclusivity and (especially) collaboration among the elite residents of the civil station.[3] Among the kinds of authority British officers hoped the civil station would present to the Indian community, therefore, was the authority of benevolence—no matter how strained that presentation may have been under the asymmetries of colonial power.

We should remember that outside of colonial military cantonments, where rules encouraging racial separation were partially formalized in the 1860s, few if any legal prohibitions were placed on racial mixing in the business and residential districts of India's colonial cities.[4] Wherever government institutions, commercial enterprises, and places of public congregation were concentrated, mixing among races and social classes was both legally accommodated and necessary. In Lahore these kinds of activities were concentrated in a half-mile-wide zone stretching along Mall Road from the Civil Secretariat, near Anarkali's tomb, at one end to the botanical gardens at the other (see Map 2.3).

Considering how often British residents reused existing Indian buildings in the civil station during the first years of occupation, it is hard to conclude that concerns over how to represent an exclusive British presence determined architectural decisions. As we saw in chapter 1, with an abundance of abandoned large structures scattered throughout the civil station on *nazul* (state administered) property, the colonial government often chose to house major institutions in converted buildings rather than to build anew.[5] These institutions included the Civil Secretariat, which, as we have seen, was located in Ventura's former house; the Public Works Secretariat, housed in a converted barrack from Ranjit Singh's period; and the Accountant General's office, headquartered in a converted seventeenth-century mosque near the tomb of Shah Chiragh, just off Mall Road. In 1851, two years after the official annexation of Punjab, the seventeenth-century tomb of Anarkali was chosen to be the site of Lahore's Anglican church. Always considered less than optimal for the task, the retrofitted Mughal tomb nevertheless served as the primary religious gathering space for British residents in Lahore for more than thirty-five years.[6] Indeed, for much of the nineteenth century (and later, in many cases) colonial buildings in Lahore "looked"—and often were—traditionally Indian in their form, massing, and construction. Beginning in the mid-1860s, however, several new building projects in the city departed from this pattern. Most of these projects were financed with a mixture of provincial, municipal, and privately raised funds, designed by professional engineers, and intended for use by diverse members of the city's population. In the most general terms, these were perhaps the first of the projects that helped shape the newly forming landscape of the city in a distinctively "colonial" idiom.

COLLABORATIVE LANDSCAPES

The 1877 celebration of Queen Victoria's Jubilee in Lahore illustrates how the landscape of the civil station could be drawn upon to articulate a symbolic unity of purpose among different elite communities in the city. Events in Lahore during this India-wide celebration included a thanksgiving ceremony attended by both European and Indian residents in the new Anglican cathedral on Mall Road, an honorary dinner at Government House hosted by representatives of the city's Indian "corporations and societies," a night of entertainment for "600 Native ladies of the town" held by European "ladies of the Station" in Lahore's Town Hall and Museum, and, the following evening, a "grand display of fireworks" in the Lawrence Gardens.[7] As a gesture of loyalty, Punjab's "Princes, Chiefs, merchants, men of local note, and the public generally" formed a subscription to erect the "Victoria Jubilee Institute for the Promotion and Diffusion of Technical and Agricultural Education and Science" in Lahore, a complex that eventually formed the nucleus of the city's museum and the Mayo School of Art (completed in 1894).[8] As with hundreds of other buildings erected across India to commemorate the same event—including schools, hospitals, town halls, and science institutes—the creation of the Lahore Victoria Jubilee Institute embodied a process wherein urban artifacts could be drawn on to posit a vision of civic inclusiveness, even as that vision masked systematic structural inequalities that worked against realizing any such thing.

Victoria's Jubilee celebration drew several institutions and settings in Lahore's civil station together in a staged celebration of amity, good governance, and financial cooperation between Indian and British society. The physical landscape lent its power to that effort partly through its visual claims to comprehensiveness, claims that were a reflection, in turn, of the comprehensive nature of rule the landscape was drawn on to commemorate.[9] Underlying those claims, however, were a number of less-visible social and conceptual exclusions that were essential to the way they were secured. For one thing, the landscape of civic ritual enacted in the Jubilee was directed more at some viewers, foremost among whom were the city's indigenous mercantile and aristocratic elites, than it was at others. By the time that celebration took place in the city, these elites were the people for whom the landscape's claims to comprehensiveness had acquired a certain plausibility.

The efficacy of the urban landscape as a medium for conveying British ideology did not come about naturally. Rather, it was achieved through concentrated practical and intellectual efforts to persuade, instruct, and enforce upon people a new idea about what landscapes and monuments could do and mean in the city. This chapter will explore how some of these efforts unfolded, paying particular attention to the aesthetic and technical discourses that helped further the conviction, held by many, that the physical landscape could embed cultural values in powerful and largely novel ways. Whereas as we have already seen, circumstances during the first several years of British occupation of Lahore led officials to adapt older Indian buildings for use as colonial institutions, from the 1860s onward a number of well-financed, professionally designed, and highly visible projects in the city charted out new architectural and cultural terrain. It was in these latter projects that new ideas about how buildings and landscapes could acquire new forms of symbolic or rhetorical significance were most fully worked out. Importantly, however, as this new manner of both appropriating and appreciating the built landscape spread to more and more people in the city, both the scope of its application and the ideological purposes envisioned for architectural design expanded at the same time. No longer limited to actualizing a vision of British and elite Indian collaboration, the new high-style architecture of the city became a powerful resource for anyone who could afford to produce it.

The Lawrence and Montgomery Halls and the municipal garden that was eventually built around them were perhaps the first of these projects to introduce into the city a substantially new and carefully worked out formal and spatial landscape idea. The Lawrence and Montgomery Halls were both commemorative buildings, raised in honor of John Lawrence and Robert Montgomery (Figure 3.1). Lawrence Hall was built first, in 1861–62, on a site facing Mall Road near the eastern end of the developed portion of the civil station and directly across from Government House. The architect for the building, G. Stone, an engineer in the Public Works Department, designed the building in a "frigidly classical" style, in the words of one contemporary observer, who hastened to add that the "general effect . . . [was] not without dignity."[10]

Lawrence Hall was conceived as a social and entertainment space for Lahore's European community. The plan of the building was that of a conventional English banqueting hall, with a rectangular, double-height room on the ground floor surrounded above by a narrow colonnaded gallery on all four sides (Figure 3.2). Throughout the colonial period in Lahore, Lawrence Hall hosted a range of theatrical and musical performances by both local and traveling troupes. In a memoir of his life in the city during the 1860s and 1870s, Henry Goulding recalled, among other things, regular performances by a troupe of Christy Minstrels, "penny readings" given by the city's chaplain, "[a] famous party of dwarfs, General and Mrs. Tom Thumb, Miss Minnie Warren and Commodore Nutt, and a strong company of Japanese, the novelty of whose balancing and conjuring feats proved most attractive."

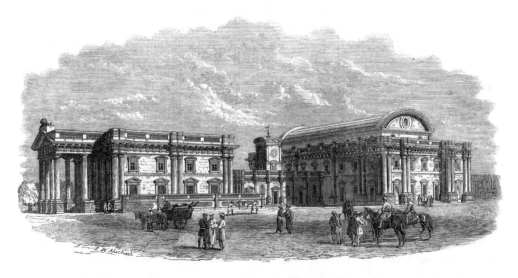

Figure 3.1. Lawrence Hall (left) and Montgomery Hall (right), conjoined by a passage. Notice the prominent clock tower at the midpoint of the joining passage. From Illustrated London News, *March 17, 1886.*

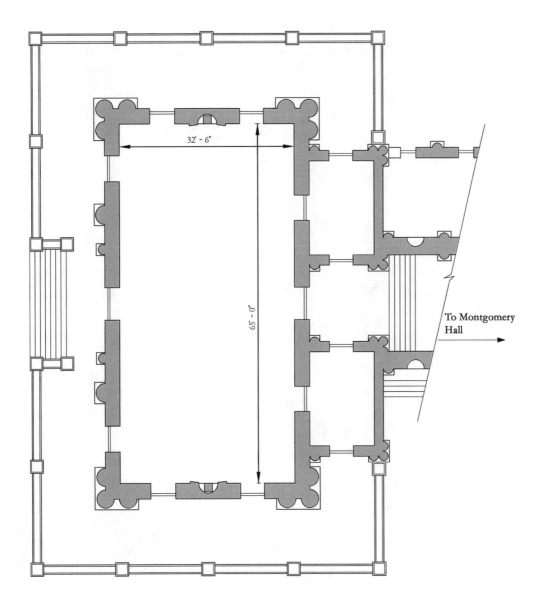

32' - 6"

65' - 0"

To Montgomery
Hall

N

Figure 3.2. Plan of Lawrence Hall, G. Stone, architect, 1861–62.

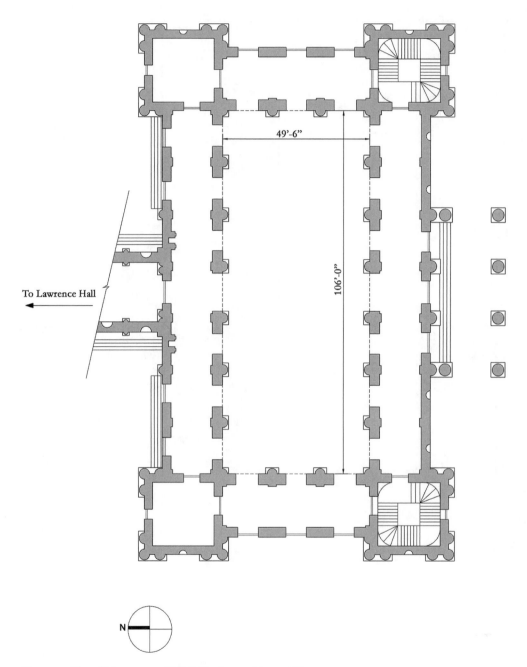

49'-6"

106'-0"

To Lawrence Hall

N

Figure 3.3. Plan of Montgomery Hall, J. Gordon, architect, 1868.

The Lawrence Hall thus formed a nucleus of polite European society in the city, a setting for hosting what Goulding called the "earliest endeavors to make a 'brighter Lahore.'"[11]

Montgomery Hall was completed a few years after Lawrence Hall, in 1866, and served a similar purpose. Unlike the earlier building, however, Montgomery Hall was financed entirely "from subscriptions raised from the Native Chiefs of the Punjab."[12] Montgomery Hall was larger, more complex, and more costly than the earlier building (Figure 3.3). The two were placed close to one another and were later joined by a hallway. Rather than forming a frontispiece to Lawrence Gardens by facing outward toward Mall Road, however, Montgomery Hall faced inward, toward the main avenue of what would become a large municipal garden on the grounds surrounding the buildings. In addition to its large central hall, the building housed a library and reading room, a teak dance and "rinking" floor (skating rink), and room for the Gymkhana Club. Lawrence Hall was devoted to the white community in Lahore; the spaces and program of Montgomery Hall allowed for racial interaction between British civilians and officials and the elites of Lahori society.

Lawrence and Montgomery Halls were both stylistically neoclassical, their facades framed by a row of engaged Doric columns that ran the full height of each structure. These columns were tripled at each corner to lend visual support to a massive frieze, cornice, and balustrade running the length of the roofline. At the front of Lawrence Hall, on a parapet above the entry, a Grecian urn was mounted on top of a marble panel inscribed with Lawrence's name (Figure 3.4). This traditional Anglo-European symbol of immortality suited the building's commemorative program. The brick exterior walls of both buildings were covered in a thick coat of burnished plaster, painted white and scored to look like the

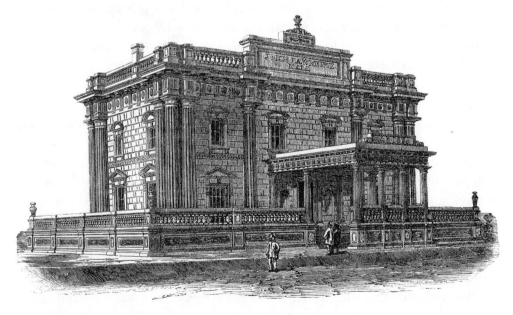

Figure 3.4. Lawrence Hall, as seen from the entry off Mall Road. Notice the honorary plaque and Grecian urn at the cornice line. From Illustrated London News, December 31, 1864.

much finer ashlar stone. With their exaggerated classical details, their use of classical com-memorative symbols, and their formally staged entrance from Mall Road, Lawrence and Montgomery Halls emphatically announced a social and visual distance from the local architectural milieu. Carefully isolated from the Indian city as much by their architectural treatment as by the Anglo-European forms of entertainment they housed, Lawrence and Montgomery Halls constituted a kind of urban "heterotopia" in Lahore, a physical setting detached from, and partially antithetical to, the organizing principles of its surroundings.[13]

A few years after Lawrence and Montgomery Halls were completed, they were joined by an eighty-foot passage with a prominent clock tower at its midpoint (see Figure 3.1). Portraits of living and deceased British officers of the province lined its interior walls; these men's putative accomplishment was to place the British Raj at the apex of Punjab's ruling hierarchy, whose aristocratic "chiefs and nobles" now played an important, if largely rhetor-ical, role in the new imperial system. The joining of Lawrence and Montgomery Halls thus helped materialize a metaphorical joining of interests between the elite European and aris-tocratic Indian patrons who donated the buildings to the city while presenting a tangible model of British and Indian elite collusion in vivid concrete form.

The Lawrence and Montgomery Halls complex was only one small part of a much larger isolated and controlled urban landscape. The construction of these buildings served as a catalyst for building a civic park on the surrounding grounds. Conceived as a major ornament for the province's capital city, Lawrence Gardens combined a public "pleasure ground" with a zoo and botanical garden, each element working in unison with the others to produce an integrated public landscape geared toward the cultivation of gentility (Figure 3.5). Like Lawrence and Montgomery Halls, moreover, the garden's major elements were all financed through a combination of provincial, municipal, and private funds from both British and elite Indian residents of the city. The Lawrence Gardens thus formed a carefully isolated space of controlled cultural interaction underwritten by elite collaboration.[14]

Both the botanical garden and the zoo in Lawrence Gardens drafted a controlled dis-play of exotic nature to the garden's overall didactic program. The botanical garden exhibited over six hundred species of plants, trees, and shrubs, all carefully tended by a horticultur-ist sent out from the Royal Botanic Gardens at Kew.[15] These species included American corn and cotton; English pansies, chrysanthemums, and camellias; orange trees from Malta; Ital-ian pomelos; and a small (largely unsuccessful) grove of apple and pear trees from Europe.[16] Each plant was labeled with both Latin and English names. In addition to maintaining the park's plantings of Anglo-European species, gardeners from Punjab University ran experi-ments in the garden's hothouses and fruit nurseries aimed at acclimatizing and introduc-ing new species of grain and fruit into the region. Successful results from these experiments were made available in the market or donated to charitable institutions in the city. Despite a stated aim to use the horticultural gardens for conducting experiments on possibly remu-nerative new agricultural crops for the benefit of the region, the garden's directors aimed "an important part of its efforts towards meeting the horticultural needs of the European urban-dwellers of Lahore."[17]

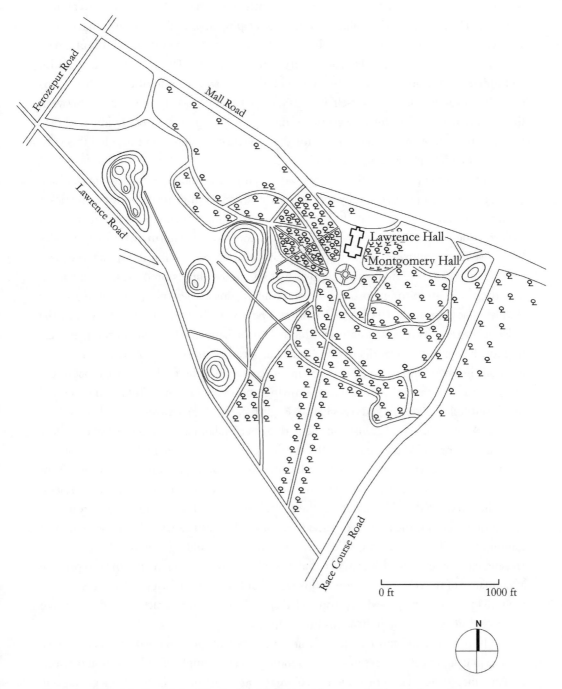

Figure 3.5. Plan of the Punjab Agri-Horticultural Society and Lawrence Gardens, Lahore, circa 1900.

Like other elements in the garden, the zoo depended to a great extent on donations from Punjab's indigenous aristocracy. While Indian membership in the Agro-Horticultural Society that ran the gardens was always low, it included some of the province's wealthiest residents. The maharaja of Patiala, in addition to helping finance the zoo's eventual expansion, gave a pair of ostriches to the collection. The nawab of Bahawalpur, who kept a residence near the garden, donated the obligatory lion and lioness.[18] The combination of British and Indian aristocratic patronage for the zoo linked the two communities together financially. The program of the zoo itself, however, forged a new kind of symbolic link between the region's new and old rulers. Keeping a "menagerie" was a long-standing imperial prerogative in South Asia, and the project for the Lawrence Gardens zoo exploited this connection while reframing its significance.

The final component of the gardens was a picturesque public pleasure ground, which combined irregular paths, carefully controlled vistas, and naturalistic plantings with cricket pitches and tennis courts. The maharajas of Patiala and of Jammu and Kashmir are reputed to have fielded cricket teams here, and mixed-race teams were the norm by the early decades of the twentieth century.[19] Not simply a space for unfettered rambling and sports, the pleasure ground was annotated with signposts that announced limits on conduct in the park, including bans on spitting, posting bills, and walking dogs. These physical and regulatory features—both the material cultural traditions underlying the park's formal design and the didactic thrust of its rules and natural exhibits—made Lawrence Gardens a prominent setting for the cultivation and display of Anglo-European gentility in the city, a secular code of public behavior and personal comportment seen as essential to the proper functioning of society. In her memoir of childhood growing up in Lahore, Elinor Tollinton described the "beautifully kept lawns and trees like an English park" of the Lawrence Gardens. Tollinton was accompanied on her visits to the park by her Indian nanny, and she makes it clear that the park provided a welcome outlet for domestic servants and students. "[In the garden there were] twenty tennis courts and to the delight of the nannies a bandstand from which twice a week there was military music provided by soldiers from the cantonment. Here the nurses told each other about their employers, and Indian students sat around in little groups committing to memory great sections of Shakespeare, in which they would be examined."[20] While Lawrence Gardens and the associated buildings could easily be seen as an isolated "island of Englishness," a racially segregated Anglo enclave designed to provide a semblance of the comforts of home, this would only be a partial view. Missing would be the role this landscape played as a controlled space of cultural interaction in the city, one heavily subsidized by elite indigenous philanthropy.

The planning and construction of Punjab Chiefs' College (renamed Aitchison Chiefs' College in 1886) in Lahore presents an even more explicit example of collaboration between Punjab's indigenous aristocracy and the colonial state. The Punjab Chiefs' College was one of several colleges designed for India's ruling princes across north India, beginning in the 1870s. The idea behind the chief-college system, first proposed by Lord Mayo in the 1860s, was to educate India's indigenous rulers in an English boarding-school environment, to create a series of "Indian Eatons" separate from the colleges and universities across India that admitted elites and commoners alike. In Punjab the indigenous aristocracy had long proven their loyalty to the British, not least during the rebellion of 1857–58 when these "chiefs" played a key role in helping Britain reestablish military control over the insurgency. At the ceremony laying the foundation stone for the new college at Lahore in 1886, India's viceroy Lord Dufferin acknowledged this past: "Nowhere else in India [but Punjab] are there to be found historical houses of a more illustrious antiquity, or a nobility that from age to age has been inspired by nobler aspirations or by traditions of a purer honor or of a more courageous or lofty bearing."[21] Despite these historical advantages, however, Punjab's indigenous aristocracy was seen by the British to be growing moribund in the face of a small but increasingly well-educated Indian middle class. Without their own rigorous modern education, argued Charles Aitchison, the college's main patron, Punjab's "hereditary leaders" were in danger of being superseded by members of the "middle and lower ranks of Native society." Dufferin elaborated the point:

> In these practical days of ours, when education is so largely diffused and when competition is so keen, nobility of birth, high descent, wealth and other adventitious circumstances cannot meet with their due recognition, or exercise the influence to which, under other circumstances, they might be entitled, unless they are reinforced by intellectual acquirements and by proper mental cultivation. . . . the people must have leaders along the path of moral and material advancement, and where can they be better found, or from whence can they be more conveniently drawn, than from amongst those great and illustrious families whose deeds in former generations have made the history of their province famous, and whose descendants I trust are bound, both by the material as well as by the moral pledges which they have given, to show a bright example of devotion to the public service.[22]

The chief-college scheme was conceived as an academic setting that would confer on the indigenous aristocracy both modern academic training and, importantly, new modes of personal character. Aitchison College replaced an earlier institution, the Wards' School at Ambala, which first opened in 1864.[23] At that time, owing to a shortage of funds and a lack of confidence in the new government's ability to oversee the education of Punjab's young "chiefs"—many of whom, because they were minors, were "wards" of the British government—a small day school was established in Ambala by the deputy commissioner. Students at Ambala received lessons during the day in several detached buildings, built with income from their own estates, and returned to their own homes in the evening. This arrangement was seen to create certain problems, however. The directors of the Wards' School complained that their students' domestic arrangements were "organized without regard to any particular system of discipline, according to the means and proclivities of the different families." The solution they developed was to make the school at Ambala as "home-like" as possible, "and in many cases the mothers of the boys came with their sons to dwell in the school compound and watch over them."[24]

Aitchison, who was the founding patron of the Ambala school, complained at the time that the "disposition of the buildings and the internal economy" of the school were primary "obstacles in the way of enforcing discipline and encouraging manly bearing and a public school spirit among the students."[25] The new school at Lahore would therefore mark a significant departure from its predecessor by housing all the students under one roof and allowing only a prescribed (small) number of personal assistants to accompany each student. In this sense, Aitchison College was conceived of as a kind of "total institution," a term sociologist Irving Goffman used to describe "a place of residence and work where a large number of like-situated individuals, cut off from the wider society for an appreciable period of time, together lead an enclosed, formally administered round of life."[26] In 1882 ten students from Ambala moved to Lahore along with their long-time principal W. A. Robinson, and two other students sent by authorities in Delhi joined them. These twelve students—six Sikhs, five Muslims, and one Hindu—were Aitchison College's first class, and they lived and studied in three rented houses on Abbot Road in Lahore while planning began for a permanent campus.

The inability to house students in a full-time campus residence had been a recurring complaint at Ambala. A similar problem was noted at Mayo College in Ajmer, a sister institution to Aitchison College completed only one year earlier. At Mayo College the problem of full-time residence was solved—against the preferences of the college's managers—by having each princely state build a separate residence for its ward.[27] All these buildings were substantial architectural undertakings, their large size and elaborate programs wholly reflective of the luxurious lifestyles their young residents were accustomed to: The raja of Alwar, famously, arrived for study at Ajmer with over two hundred retainers in tow. In contrast, students at Lahore would live together under a single roof, and limits were placed on the number of personal servants and horses allowed to accompany each pupil.[28]

Compared to the luxurious pavilions that served as individual residences at Ajmer, the boarding houses in Lahore were deliberately spartan. Since permanent residence required separate accommodations for cooking and dining based on religious custom, two separate blocks were provided, one for Muslim students and one for both Hindus and Sikhs. Once construction got under way, the Aitchison board opened admission to "scholarship" students and others from notable families with fewer financial means at their disposal. To accommodate the increased enrollment, a third block of housing was added for less-wealthy students. This third block was designed to appear identical to the other two on the exterior, but a different system of partitioning individual quarters on the interior increased accommodation from thirty-two to forty-four students.

While the college boarding houses were being designed, representatives from Punjab's Native States were asked to critique the plans. They were unanimous in their opinion that individual suites for the students were too small. The design that was finally approved gave each student in the full-tuition blocks one large sleeping room (sixteen by eighteen feet), a separate privy, and a "lamp room" for use by their private servants. In the third building, for scholarship students, rooms were designed as single-space cubicles, roughly nine by sixteen feet, each with its own attached bath. Cubicles in the scholarship block were separated from one another by seven-foot-high wooden partitions, leaving an open space above each room large enough for an iron catwalk or gallery, which was used by the *musahib* (warden or overseer) of the building to exercise "effective [visual] control over the conduct of the students" below.[29]

The Aitchison College campus, with its spatial and visual hierarchies of major and minor buildings, its well-landscaped grounds and playing fields, and its architectural accommodation of the differently ranked students, staff, and servants, embodied key elements of the colonial spatial imagination that guided British construction elsewhere in the city (Figure 3.6). The orderly and symmetrical layout of the grounds and the uniform visual treatment of each of the several functional types of campus buildings were a deliberate rejection of the disorderly "disposition of buildings and internal economy" of Aitchison's predecessor school at Ambala. The campus layout thus worked against British stereotypes of the typical Indian raja's palace as a mysterious, labyrinthine space that fostered an atmosphere of intrigue.[30]

In allowing for uninterrupted visual surveillance in the scholarship students' block and limiting the number of retainers each student could have, the designers of Aitchison College assumed architecture would help cultivate openness, discipline, and gentlemanly self-reliance in its students. If the orderly layout and regulation of activity in the college's residential blocks were intended to modernize habits of daily life, however, then the architectural

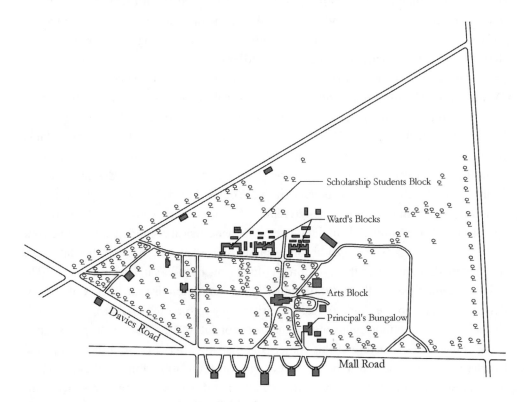

Figure 3.6. Site plan of Aitchison Chiefs' College, Lahore, circa 1889.

style chosen for the main building upheld a central role for tradition. Like most prominent architectural projects in colonial India, the design for Aitchison College was secured through a competition. In all, the college committee received twenty-nine anonymous competition entries sent by designers from across India. In the end, two entries appealed to the committee, each for a different reason. An entry labeled "Justicia" appealed to the committee for its "unusually pleasing and graceful" elevation. A second entry, "Non nobis solum," stood out for its efficient "ground plan and general arrangement of buildings."[31] The first scheme, with its "pleasing" elevation, turned out to be the work of Bhai Ram Singh, the head assistant to Principal John Lockwood Kipling at Lahore's Mayo School of Art. The second design was revealed to have been completed by Swinton Jacob, executive engineer of Jaipur State and architect of the recently completed Albert Hall Museum in Jaipur. Both designers had years of experience training and working with local craftsmen, and both built their reputations on an ability to adapt traditional design motifs to the requirements of modern institutional programs. Jacob's long years of experience—and perhaps his race and nationality— led the committee to choose him over Singh as principal designer for the combined scheme. At the committee's request, Jacob agreed to adopt Singh's elevations to his plan, and Jacob, Singh, and Kipling agreed to split the competition honorarium.[32]

Jacob's final design incorporated an eclectic array of architectural features from diverse sources, including pre-Mughal *chattris* (umbrella-like features) anchoring each inverted corner of the building, Mughal-inspired shallow-relief patterns in the brickwork on the lower story, interwoven arches and screens on the verandah borrowed from Umayyad Spain, and a large bronze clock of English manufacture on the domed octagonal tower rising over the building's center (Figure 3.7). The reference to "tradition," in other words, was not to any particular, well-defined stylistic corpus, but rather to a picturesque mélange of "oriental" and "Muhammadan" features that worked together to evoke an ecumenical "Indic" building.

The argument for using Indo-Saracenic design for an institution like Aitchison College had been tediously worked out a few years earlier in Ajmer, where Charles Mant's Indo-Saracenic design for Mayo College helped initiate a long-lasting trend. As Thomas Metcalf shows, eclecticism was a characteristic feature of Indo-Saracenic design more generally, a style of architecture that became the more or less "official" colonial style during the period 1870–90.[33] Indo-Saracenic design represented a more self-consciously "traditional" approach to modern imperial buildings than other neoclassical or modern alternatives, one that grew out of a growing imperial consensus, as Metcalf shows, that British rule needed to annotate its authority in the traditional visual forms of India's indigenous rulers.[34] The Indo-Saracenic style was thus a fitting choice for an institution like Aitchison College, one designed to incorporate Punjab's regional aristocracy into an imperial structure of rule rhetorically tuned to indigenous modes and forms of authority.[35] "As stone is placed upon stone in the visible structure of this edifice, and tier upon tier rises from the level plain," Charles Aitchison remarked at the ceremony laying the foundation stone for the college, "let it be our earnest hope that there may rise a still finer edifice in which the aristocracy of the Punjab shall be the polished corner stones, bright examples to their fellow countrymen of

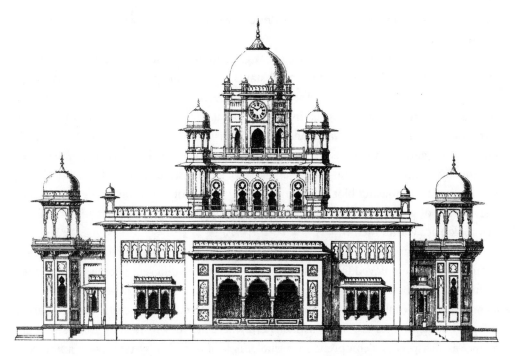

Figure 3.7. Elevation design of the Arts Block at Aitchison Chiefs' College, Swinton Jacob and Bhai Ram Singh, architects. Copyright The British Library Board. OIOC Photo 3153; all rights reserved.

true manliness, of the highest culture and the gentlest manners that the times can boast."[36] Consciously dedicated to shaping the "manners" and sentiments deemed necessary to bring the region's "natural leaders" into line with Britain's civilizing project, the planners of Aitchison College emphasized the efficient arrangement of functionally related parts, each designed for easy surveillance and imbued with the character of an authoritative past, to create a somatic, character-transforming landscape.[37]

The buildings and grounds of Lawrence Gardens and Aitchison College were carefully designed, in part, to posit a material model of the political relationship Britain desired with India's indigenous rulers. The use of different architectural motifs to elaborate this model grew out of differences between the two settings in timing, program, and ideology, which changed over time and sought to ground British authority, both symbolically and rhetorically, in British *as well as* Indian iconography. Each of these settings vividly annotated a putatively inclusive social and philanthropic agenda: By inscribing the names of elite donors on marble plaques affixed to the main buildings in both places, by combining British and Indian representation on the committees that governed, financed, and administered both institutions, and by soliciting an Indian "audience"—children of elite Indian families in the case of Aitchison College and Lahore's "municipal" public more generally at Lawrence Gardens—both institutions provided for the active participation of Lahore's British residents and indigenous elites in a new kind of controlled institutional landscape. An ordered visual display of the norms of social comportment, gentility, and attainment of knowledge that underlay British conceptions of civic urbanity was central to the way these institutions functioned.

At the same time, each setting used a range of architectural and spatial devices whose purpose was to mark differences in social status between people of different classes and races. At Lawrence Gardens, the key separation was between the Anglo-European world of entertainment and sociality housed in Lawrence Hall and the more socially promiscuous forms of mixed-race entertainment and passive instruction provided in Montgomery Hall, the botanical gardens, the pleasure grounds, and the zoo. At Aitchison College, the rhetorical equality between aristocratic and "scholarship" students, reflected in the identical exterior treatment of housing blocks accommodating each group, was belied by the unequal distribution of personal living space and disparate regimes of discipline and surveillance that took place within them.

Visual metaphors of inclusion thus predominated in these landscapes, even as the architecture was employed to precisely separate and order different people and activities. Inclusion could be evoked effectively, therefore, only so long as diverse members of the community were ranked within a single hierarchical system.[38] Architectural devices marked these social hierarchies in visibly distinctive ways, even as they worked to frame social difference as an aspect of a comprehensive whole. This hierarchical system was as ambiguous as it was informal, even if there were tacit rules holding it all together. Commenting on the desirability of legislating building design in the civil station, a senior member of the Lahore municipality underscored this point: "I should like to see [design controls] proposed, but these . . . will depend on the *social status* of persons applying for permission to build. It would be inadvisable, I think, to insist on any hard and fast rules."[39]

The lack of "hard and fast" rules, however, did not mean there were no rules at all. Excluding the myriad formal regulations governing urban space and conduct in the civil station—including injunctions on roadway encroachment, unlawful assembly, and the taxation of goods and services—informal rules were also present that structured the physical landscape and helped embellish it with meaning. Importantly, however, we should see these informal visual principles less as an element of doctrine or legal codification and more as a broad Anglo-European spatial sensibility shared by professional designers and amateurs alike. English novelist and social reformer Flora Annie Steel (1847–1929), who accompanied her husband to a number of small towns in Punjab where he was posted as a chief magistrate during the late nineteenth century, is an example of the latter. In a practice not uncommon in small out-of-the-way stations, Steel volunteered a design for the construction of a new municipal hall in Kasur, a small town located twenty miles east of Lahore (circa 1877). This important civic institution was the first building Steel ever designed; nevertheless, her description of the spatial devices she used to organize the different social groups she anticipated using the building reveals her familiarity with the spatial principles that organized more costly, professionally designed buildings in the colony. "I had provided a semi-circular sort of verandah [at the front of the municipal hall]," Steel wrote in her autobiography, "which had this advantage: that the real *rais* (nobles) could squat on the inside angle formed by two walls, the next in rank could similarly squat on the next step; and so on to the second, third, fourth steps (for the whole building was on a plinth), until the garden and the *hoi polloi* were reached."[40]

Steel's design for the Kasur municipal hall thus embodied an essential feature of Anglo-European architecture in India more generally, namely, the use of physical barriers to mark out social distinctions between differently ranked groups. The graded vertical elevation of spaces in the verandah she designed precisely mapped onto the graded social hierarchies she perceived among Kasur's Indian residents, each of whom she envisioned "squatting" (rather than sitting, as Europeans would be expected to do) in their rightful place. In most colonial buildings, this simple isomorphism between "elevated" people and the vertically elevated spaces intended for them was a regular formal principle. In more complex buildings, similar kinds of distinction were marked through the use of different kinds of ornament and materials and through careful attention to building placement and scale. Working in combination, these architectural strategies helped sort out social differences, while at the same time providing a physical model of their interrelationships. Though there were few "hard and fast" rules governing this abstract visual system, the landscape that resulted was both remarkably consistent and, to those familiar with the system, emphatically clear.[41]

The Punjab Chief Court, an imposing building situated roughly equidistant from either end of Mall Road and directly across from Lahore's Anglican cathedral, provides a

Figure 3.8. The Punjab Chief Court seen from Mall Road, circa 1900. Copyright The British Library Board. OIOC Photo 867/3(57); all rights reserved.

good example of these principles in a professionally designed building (Figure 3.8). The architect for the Chief Court, J. W. Brassington, was a consulting architect to the colonial government who had trained under Robert Chisolm in Madras. Chisolm was a leading exponent of Indo-Saracenic design and one of the first architects to successfully demonstrate its suitability for large public buildings.[42] When Brassington began his design for the Punjab Chief Court in 1881, he was already committed to the Indo-Saracenic style. Brassington's choice to design the court in the hybrid forms of this style, one later critic observed, "was appropriate in a way for an institution that administered laws which were in themselves an amalgam of English jurisprudence and Indian codes."[43] A stylistic program that drew northern Indian design motifs and British principles of planning together was only one of several ways the Chief Court posited the conception of a collaborative interrelationship between India's foreign rulers and their Indian subjects, however. The entire layout of the court complex worked toward the same end.

The Chief Court was built in the form of a quadrangle, with a courtyard at the center focused on a large marble fountain (Figures 3.9, 3.10). Litigants entered the public, or "front," area of the court complex off Mall Road on a broad path that ran through a garden. The garden served to isolate the court from the more mundane activities of the street and provided a space for litigants and their companions to interact with the hired pleaders

Figure 3.9. The Punjab Chief Court courtyard. This photograph was taken at the opening of an extension to the High Court complex in Lahore on October 23, 1923. Copyright The British Library Board. OIOC Photo 10/22(56); all rights reserved.

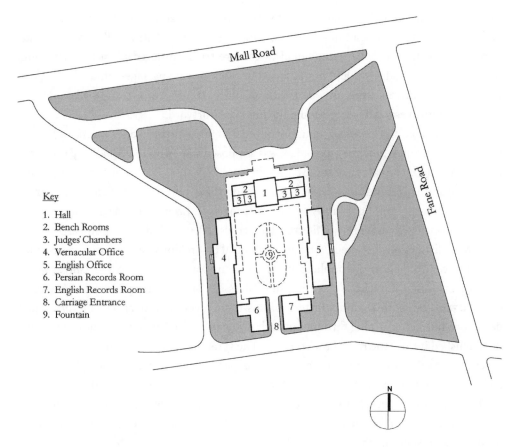

Figure 3.10. Plan of the Punjab Chief Court.

who would ultimately argue their cases in court. Judges, court officers, members of the bar, and high-level staff entered the complex from the private, or "back," side of the quadrangle through a gated "carriage entrance," a designation that pointed to deeply etched social distinctions in India between people who traveled on foot and those who rode or traveled in a conveyance. Spacious verandahs, both inside and out, served to link the public and private functions of the court together.

One wing of the quadrangle housed the jury room, the bar and bar library, a reading room, and the vernacular office with its staff of translators and clerks. On the opposite side were the chief registrar's offices, committee room, library, and the English office with its own staff of subordinate clerks. On one side of the carriage entrance at the back of the complex, annexed to the vernacular office, was the Persian records room. On the other side was the English records room, which was annexed to the wing containing the English office. Together these three wings housed the professional apparatus of the court. The fourth, or "front," wing of the quadrangle housed the main courtrooms where litigants came to seek legal remedy.

The front wing of the court focused on a large, expensively decorated central hall, which was approached through a projecting porch up a broad flight of marble steps. The steps elevated the entire building above its surroundings in a gesture of authority common to European and Indian tradition alike. On either side of the central hall were the bench rooms, or courtrooms, where individual cases were tried. Annexed to each bench room were two separate judge's chambers, accessed through private passages situated along one wall. Judge's chambers were provided with an office, retiring room, and bathroom and opened onto the verandah surrounding the interior courtyard.

The Punjab Chief Court was thus organized into three distinct zones: an enclosed public zone at the front where the rule of law was supposed to be applied equally by impartial judges; an enclosed private zone at the back split into "English" and "vernacular" wings housing the apparatus of professional legal practice; and a third, porous zone of encircling verandahs that physically and figuratively tied the two together. Each of the three separate zones was embellished with different architectural materials, a design choice that emphasized both functional distinctions between each zone and social distinctions between their occupants.

The central hall in the public zone of the court was finished most lavishly: marble flooring instead of hexagonal clay tiles, stone dressing on the ceiling instead of ordinary ceramic tiles, carved teak doors instead of less-costly deodar (cedar) panel doors, and a decorative tile dado running throughout each of the rooms in the public zone of the court distinguished it from the rest of the complex. The verandahs, in turn, were set off from the other zones by their distinctive ornamentation, in particular, by tracery panels placed above arched openings, derived from the mosque at Cordoba, the same pattern used down the road at Aitchison College. Marble was used for the tracery outside the judges' chambers and less-expensive terra-cotta panels were used everywhere else, a tactile and visual reminder of the elevated status of the court's chief officers.

The encircling verandahs—set off from the main rooms of the complex and the Chief Court grounds as much by the use of different materials and ornamental details as by their porous configuration—formed the first formal boundary between the tumultuous world of commerce outside the court and the rarefied world of justice within. At the same time, the verandahs provided an intermediary zone of circulation between the public and private functions of the court, a device that mitigated a conceptual disjuncture between a zone of professional procedures that recognized differences between "vernacular" and "English" subjects and a zone of public ritual that posited equality between the two.

Brassington's design for the Chief Court thus rendered abstract concepts about the nature of colonial law into a material model of the relationship between its constituent parts. With its lavishly decorated central hall, the Chief Court building spoke eloquently of the principles of liberal government, exalting the space where the rights of subjects were upheld impartially. At the same time, however, the back of the complex acknowledged that colonial governance relied on a range of classificatory procedures to separate Indians from the British on the basis of different languages, customs, and rights. Set apart from the promiscuous mixture of street life along Mall Road, the Chief Court complex was an argument, rendered in vivid forms and materials, that social promiscuity was superseded in the city by an orderly system of hierarchically related parts.

If the design of the Chief Court complex thus presented a tangible model of a colonial sense of order, then it also presented—like the other buildings discussed thus far in
this chapter—a novel assemblage of space and materials in its Indian urban context. The
efficacy of this new architecture, and especially its ability to rhetorically assert an ethos of
collaboration at its core, depended crucially on its being somehow understood. Buildings
like Lawrence and Montgomery Halls or the Punjab Chief Court were visually arresting
objects in their urban context. What people made of these buildings—what the buildings
evoked for different viewers or users in their material immediacy—was, of course, impossible to control. The new institutional buildings along Mall Road could evoke a range of
different impressions, as evidenced by two fictional college-age characters in a turn-of-the-
century Indian novel set in Lahore. The students encountered "the lofty pinnacles" of Aitchison College in the distance as they walked down Mall Road. "What a fine building," one of
the two says approvingly, gazing on the newly completed Indo-Saracenic structure. "Idle
waste of money," responds his friend, clearly peeved by all the building represents: "unscru-
pulous expenditure, the result of man's vanity and presumption, the outcome of his arro-
gance and hauteur."[44]

Architecture, once made concrete in the world (and thus available for visual assessment), can never be reduced to the meanings its builders intended to convey. However,
there was an assumption in British aesthetic discourse that the more a building's audience
and designer shared aesthetic precepts, the greater the chance the designer's intentions would
be understood. The more those intentions were accepted, the more efficacious the building
became. In the section that follows, therefore, I will trace in more detail the important role
education played in general, and the role technical and architectural education played more
specifically, in making the intentions and meanings of this new urban architecture the subject of explicit exposition.

ARCHITECTURAL PEDAGOGY

By the time buildings like Aitchison College and the Punjab Chief Court were under construction, Lahore had grown from a quiet provincial headquarters into a dynamic colonial
city. As Punjab's center of finance, education, and administration from the time of annexation onward, Lahore was a desirable posting for British and Indian officials as they passed
through the ranks of colonial bureaucracy, and it was an important setting for the development of a distinctive array of middle-class urban politics and lifestyles.[45] While urban population grew more slowly than rural population in Punjab throughout the last decades of the
nineteenth century, the population of Punjab's largest cities nevertheless increased steadily
at the expense of smaller towns. By the turn of the twentieth century, Lahore's population
had nearly doubled from what it had been when the province was first annexed, growing
from an estimated 120,000 people in 1849 to over 200,000 in 1901. Throughout this period
Lahore attracted new residents from across the Punjab and other areas of northern India,
many drawn by opportunities the city offered for education, commerce, and employment.

The source of Lahore's dynamism was not simply its increasing population and employment opportunities, however. By the last decades of the 1800s the city's population had
grown increasingly diverse as well. According to historian Kenneth Jones, "of all the cities
of the Punjab [recorded in the 1881 census], Lahore had the highest percentage of *strangers,*
of citizens born outside of the city and district."[46] Members of Punjab's indigenous gentry
remained prominent in the city, including those who received training at Aitchison College. There was also a small but prominent community of families in Lahore from Bengal
and the North-West Provinces (subsequently the United Provinces), most of whom had followed the British Raj to Lahore shortly after annexation to occupy positions in the new
administration.[47] By the closing decades of the nineteenth century, however, the prime
movers of Lahore's political, intellectual, and associational life were members of a newly
emergent Punjabi middle class, whose transformative effect on the city was disproportion-
ate to its modest numbers.[48]

For many residents of late nineteenth-century Lahore, a degree from one of the city's
colleges or technical institutes was the key to entering this middle-class milieu. The highest
demand, by far, was for baccalaureate degrees in the liberal arts. Government College, which
began offering classes in a converted *haveli* in the Old City in 1864 and subsequently moved
to a new, neo-Gothic campus in the civil station in 1877, was Lahore's premier liberal arts
institution. The college offered a two-year intermediate course and, following successful
completion of that course, both bachelor's and master's degrees.[49] Punjab University, founded
in 1869, and Oriental College, founded in 1863, both offered degrees in Indian literatures
and languages alongside training in English, Western science, and the humanities. The curriculum at Oriental College prepared students for bachelor's and master's degrees in Urdu,
Persian, Arabic, Punjabi, and Sanskrit, all taught according to the methods of European
philology. Punjab University's scope was somewhat broader; in addition to offering higher
degrees in "oriental languages" in both classical and vernacular forms, the university offered
degrees in law, medicine, engineering, and the sciences. Punjab University's statutes declared
its object to be the "diffusion of European science, as far as possible, through the medium
of the Vernacular languages of the Panjab . . . to associate the learned and influential classes
of the Province with the officers of the Government in the promotion and supervision of
popular education . . . [and to study] English language and literature, [with English] regarded as the medium of instruction and examination in all subjects which could not be
completely taught in the vernacular."[50] The curriculum and courses of study at Punjab University thus produced what one nineteenth-century writer described as the combination of
an "Oriental University . . . with an English University."[51]

University education in the city introduced new scientific and philosophical avenues
of thought to a small but increasingly influential group of the province's literate residents.
The unpublished memoir of Ruchi Ram Sahni, who studied at Government College in the
early 1880s and went on to become one of India's leading scientists—holding posts at the
Indian Meteorological Survey in Calcutta and Simla and as both lecturer and professor in
chemistry at Government College in Lahore—provides a glimpse into the excitement and

seriousness he and his cohort in Lahore felt as they delved into classic works of European thought:

> Two remarkable books, as they appeared both to [my friend] and myself, we also read together in our spare hours in the College verandah, or rather the vestibule. These were Mill's "Utilitarianism" and Bentham's "Theory of Legislation." They were, of course, not included in the college "course," but that was of little consideration for both of us. We read and re-read Mill's small book paragraph by paragraph, discussing, arguing, differing or agreeing in the end, as we went along. Now and again, we could not "do" more than a sentence or two in the course of an hour, for either we could not agree as to what the author's real meaning was or, for some other reason, the whole time was taken up with the discussion about all the implications of the passage or how far we could ourselves accept his lead. Now and again, we would deliberately take up our stand on opposite sides, so as to be able to thresh out a point as well as we could. As on such occasions I would, as a rule, undertake to support the Experiential view-point while [my friend] would become the exponent of the Transcendental School, we were sometimes nicknamed as such by our class fellows.[52]

Sahni's autobiography provides plenty of evidence that instruction at Lahore's colleges and universities was uneven in quality and that Indian faculty and students were regularly subjected to racial bias from British professors and administrators. Indeed, Sahni complained in his memoirs that the "deeper stirrings of the soul that should be the real purpose of education" came about in Punjab not because of its educational institutions but in spite of them: "My greatest complaint is that the teacher as we find him in the Punjab schools and colleges—with rare exceptions—[is] a soulless, mechanized robot whose only conception of education is limited by University examinations." Nevertheless, academic life in the city thrust new activities and modes of association into play that gradually shaped new subjectivities. "The Government school brought me into intimate association with a large number of young men of my own age drawn from various parts of the province," Sahni wrote; "I was thrown into the company of a large, miscellaneous group of young men . . . [from whom] I learnt so much in countless little ways. For one thing, I could see how the oddities and idiosyncrasies of speech, manners and dress were being rounded off by our association together. . . . this is a necessary training for a youth who aspired to take his fair share in the duties and responsibilities of citizenship."[53]

Only the best students acquired the level of proficiency in English that would allow them to debate the kinds of subjects Sahni and his friends discussed together after school in the vestibule of Government College. Fewer still could hope to rise to the level of prominence in the colonial bureaucracy that Sahni eventually attained. Nevertheless, as more and more students passed out of the university system in Lahore and took up positions in government, education, business, publishing, and other fields, the scope for addressing local issues and concerns within Lahore's colonial framework grew correspondingly wider. By the closing decades of the nineteenth century, as technical education took its place alongside training in the liberal arts as a popular vehicle for social advancement, local concerns and issues became noticeably more prominent in urban and architectural discourse as well.

Technical education in Punjab was offered in a diverse array of British-sponsored institutions, most of which took relatively longer to consolidate than those offering degrees in the arts and sciences. While drawing, mapping, "mental arithmetic," and the fundamentals of hygiene were added to Punjab's primary school curricula in the last decades of the nineteenth century, technical training at higher levels was rare and uneven in quality. The North-Western Railway in Lahore opened a technical school in 1889, restricting admission to the children and relatives of artisans employed in their workshops. Essentially a feeder institution for the railway, the school gave students a practical knowledge of English, basic drawing skills, and instruction in the use of railway-related tools. Education stopped, however, when the student reached sixteen years of age, if not sooner, and graduates were funneled directly into service in the railway's cavernous workshops. Racial prejudice no doubt played a role in the indifference with which training was carried out at the railway school, since a large percentage of employees and their families were Anglo-Indians, a community for whom British society held low expectations. The mixed-race Anglo-Indian community in the city was subject to the disdain of both white and elite Indian society, as was the area of the city where the railway had its shops. M. E. Fyson, who grew up in Lahore, described visiting the house of a distant relative near the workshop "set among shabby vegetable gardens, with grimy factories rearing their chimneys round about—no better than the outskirts of a midlands town." Her relatives were "hospitable to a degree," Fyson wrote, but they nevertheless "lived in the hopeless Eurasian half-world which is neither here nor there, nor ever can be."[54]

Other small technical institutions existed in the vicinity of Lahore, including schools at Kasur, Hoshiarpur, Amritsar, and Gurdaspur. These smaller schools had mixed success—the Gurdaspur and Hoshiarpur schools closed a few years after they opened—and their curriculum was limited, in most cases, to carpet-weaving, sewing, and carpentry. As the director of public inspection wrote in his 1884–85 report on their operation, these smaller technical schools had a "tendency to degenerate, either into charitable institutions, or into factories supported by public funds."[55] Schools like these, moreover, did not train students to fill posts in the colonial services. Rather, Punjab's lower-level technical schools were designed to "check the growing tendency of boys in the ordinary schools of the country to desert their hereditary occupation and help to swell the class of men who seek for Government service."[56] While providing a venue for the dissemination of new material and mechanical techniques and equipment practices in a small number of craft-based enterprises, these schools played only a peripheral role in the development of the new urban architecture.

Higher education in architectural design in Punjab, like elsewhere in India, was at first a subsidiary field of study in schools of engineering.[57] All the students who became professional architects in Punjab, whether they were British or Indian, were trained in a curriculum whose main goal was to prepare engineers for employment in the Public Works Department (PWD). While the architectural profession in India would not be formalized until the early twentieth century, engineers in the PWD were often called upon to design buildings. Indeed, all the official colonial institutional buildings in nineteenth-century India, and most of the more prestigious private commissions, were designed by engineers who worked for the PWD.[58] Henry H. Locke, the first principal of Calcutta's school of art and a staunch advocate for improving colonial architectural design, observed in 1873 that "the natives of this country who take degrees at our universities in Engineering do so in the great majority of cases for the purpose of entering our Public Works Department, and in this department *they perform the work of builders rather than engineers*. . . . even if they do not prepare the designs [for buildings], they are frequently called upon during the progress of the work to supply directions as to details involving the preparation of working drawings and requiring a knowledge of architectural forms, which, I fear, very few of them possess."[59]

While students in engineering schools studied the basic functional parameters of building design, including structural mechanics, construction, material science, and technical drawing, little attention was given to more advanced issues of formal aesthetics, architectural history, or theory. For those who were concerned about India's modern architectural development, therefore, the engineering curriculum was part of the problem. Locke described the problem passionately:

> At present the graduate in Engineering may say, and justly, that his culture was less an object of university care than was that of his brother, the BA or MA. With the one much heed was taken to ascertain the possession among other things of some acquaintance with the literature of the past. . . . [The civil engineering candidate, however,] was examined in mathematics, mechanics, natural and experimental science, laws of forces, strength of materials, and so forth—the mere nouns and verbs of the art of building; but one may search the series of University Examination papers in vain to find a single question bearing upon the way in which the great masters in this art have used their vocables. . . . The University asks the BA candidate to "describe the constitution and functions of the Amphictyonic Council," "the nature of Lieinian Rogations," and bids him "give an account of the dictatorship of Sulla"; but she does not inquire what the future builder knows of the Parthenon or Erechtheium, or the grand proportions and constructive glories of the structures of Vespasian or of Titus.[60]

Given the circumstances, any interest shown by colonial engineers in acquiring basic education in architectural design was both welcomed and supported. A small number of British assistant engineers in India and of those bound for colonial service from the Royal Indian Engineering College in England received financial support to travel to Europe on "architectural" sketching tours during the 1880s. These trips were considered desirable since, as one official in the Bengal Public Works Department wrote, "there are so few officers in the Public Works Department who can be said to possess much proficiency as architects."[61]

While Punjab University in Lahore began offering courses in engineering in 1873, it took several years before the education at Lahore was good enough to allow students to qualify for positions in the PWD. Throughout the 1870s and into the 1880s, most of the engineers in the provincial PWD were trained at the more prestigious College of Engineering at Roorkee. Among the many engineers in Punjab who received their training there, two in particular stand out. The first was Kanhayalal (d. 1888), a native of Agra who entered the College of Engineering at Roorkee in 1852 and served most of his career in Lahore. Kanhayalal rose to the position of executive engineer in the PWD, where he oversaw construction of Government College, Lawrence and Montgomery Halls, the Lahore Central Jail, and the Senate Hall of Punjab University, among other buildings. He also wrote professional descriptions of each of these buildings, and several other projects completed in Punjab, in Roorkee's *Professional Papers on Engineering* series, which began publishing in 1863. In addition to his professional papers, all of which were written in English, Kanhayalal also wrote a Persian history of Ranjit Singh (1876), a Hindi history of Guru Nanak (1877), and an Urdu history of Lahore (1872). His other major nontechnical published work was a series of moral essays written in Persian entitled *Gulzar-i-Hind [The Indian Rose Garden].*[62]

The other significant figure was Ganga Ram (later Rai Bahadur Ganga Ram) (d. 1925), who graduated from Roorkee with a degree in civil engineering in 1873, the same year Punjab University began offering courses. The son of a police officer from a village near Amritsar, Ram would become a well-known figure in the city and one of Lahore's richest and most generous philanthropists; a women's hospital bearing his name exists in the city to this day. Ram first attracted notice at the 1877 Imperial Assemblage in Delhi, an event organized to celebrate Queen Victoria's assumption of the title empress of India. In his capacity as assistant engineer, Ram was given the task of designing a large amphitheater to seat attendees at the event's main ceremony: the reading of Victoria's royal proclamation by Edward R. Lytton, viceroy and governor general of India. Ram designed a semicircular stepped amphitheater, nearly eight hundred feet in diameter, that encircled a raised throne for the viceroy at its center. In spite of the fact that the Imperial Assemblage was meant to symbolically secure the loyalty of India's aristocracy through a modified Mughal ceremony, the *darbar,* and despite what British observers of the assembly described as a "dazzling" array of indigenous costumes and princely trappings, Ram's design for the amphitheater lacked any reference to Indian motifs. According to James Talboys Wheeler, a witness at the assemblage, the amphitheater had "nothing oriental" about it.[63] The amphitheater was divided into thirty-six radial compartments, like equal divisions of a celestial compass, each with a separate entry distinguished by its occupant's ruling insignia. The design thus emphasized both the distinctive and separate character of India's ruling chiefs and their unified subordination to the imperial power at the center.

Ram's work on the amphitheater attracted the approving attention of Lytton's successor, Lord Ripon (viceroy 1880–84). When Ram forwarded a novel request, in 1882, to travel to England to study architecture and "practical engineering," he did so with Ripon's support. In a letter accompanying Ram's request, senior members of the Punjab PWD announced their support for the idea as well: "[Ram] is said to be a good English scholar, and better read than most natives in the theory of his profession, and has the power, more than is usual with natives, of applying practically what he has learnt by study. We are gratified by this spontaneous expression of a desire for self-improvement." The letter continued: "One of the great drawbacks to our native Engineers is a poverty of invention in design. This is more especially the case in designing buildings, in which they do not rise above the type of the Indian bungalow or the Indian barracks, which are their models for all European dwellings. They have seen nothing and aim at nothing higher."[64]

Ram's request was approved by the government, and in April 1883 he traveled to England accompanied by Lala Balmokhand, another Indian engineer from Punjab who was included in the project during the intervening period. When he returned in 1884, Ram took up a position as assistant engineer in Lahore. In this position, he oversaw the construction of Lahore's High Court, Anglican cathedral, and Aitchison College buildings. At the completion of the Aitchison College project, he was promoted to executive engineer, a position he held until he retired. During his tenure as Lahore's executive engineer, Ram oversaw the construction of many of Lahore's most prestigious monuments, including the museum, the Mayo School of Art, the General Post Office, the Albert Victor Wing of Lahore's Mayo Hospital, and the Government College Chemical Laboratory. In addition to his role as an engineer, Ram patented several design innovations, including a reinforced brick floor and roof system, a design for interlocking bricks for use in constructing wells, and a slide rule that quickly calculated the necessary dimensions of structural beams, girders, and trusses.[65] He also wrote *The Pocket Book of Engineering for Sub-Divisional Officers, Mistrees, and Contractors* (1889), a small leather-bound book full of details on construction and engineering equations; the strength, quality, and Punjabi names of scores of tools and materials; the prevailing price for every common type and trade of construction; and model designs for a range of simple buildings of the sort an assistant engineer might be expected to build.

While Kanhayalal and Ganga Ram exerted their influence over the design of several buildings in Lahore in their official and unofficial capacities, both remain best known for their accomplishments as engineers. In addition, because both completed their training at Roorkee, neither of them received academic training attuned specifically to Indian architectural knowledge. The same was true of students in Punjab University's engineering program, despite the fact that the engineering course was offered within the university's Oriental College. In his annual report of 1883–84 on the Mayo School of Art, Principal John Lockwood Kipling (Rudyard Kipling's father) wrote that the absence of any reference to "Oriental" art and architecture in the engineering curriculum "seems anomalous in a college that has Eastern poetry, literature and metaphysics for its chief studies."[66] This latter "anomaly" would form a central object of Kipling's attention in his role as principal of the Mayo School.

Kipling would eventually propose that Punjab University's engineering courses be transferred to the Mayo School of Art, where students would have access to coursework in freehand drawing, carpentry, ornamental design, and architectural drawing, all based on the close observation and analysis of regional building traditions. Kipling was well aware that these students would be "the future designers of municipal and other buildings"; his plan was to instill in them a "touch of the feeling for beauty that distinguishes all purely native buildings."[67]

The Mayo School of Art was one of four official art schools in India sanctioned by the central government (Figure 3.11). Like the other three schools—in Calcutta, Bombay,

Figure 3.11. Courtyard of the National College of Arts (formerly the Mayo School of Art), Lahore. The building at the center houses studios and exhibition space.

and Madras—the Lahore school was centrally administered from the South Kensington Museum in London, whose curriculum and textbooks were also adopted.[68] Kipling, who had previously taught at the J. J. School of Art in Bombay, was an ardent enthusiast of the arts and crafts movement, and he played an important role in that international movement's coterie of professional promoters and theorists.[69] Kipling's tenure at the Mayo School coincided with Lahore's most active period of building since the city had been incorporated within the British Empire and with the ascendance of Indo-Saracenic design as a quasi-official style reflecting a new, more general interest in Indian architecture. The architectural training Kipling devised for students at the Mayo School represented a sharp departure from training available in India's other engineering programs.

In addition to providing training in fine arts, traditional crafts, and architecture, institutions like the Mayo School were designed to play a role in developing the economic viability of the industrial arts in India. Students and faculty in these programs were active participants in a series of Indian exhibitions and international exhibitions held at regular intervals during the late nineteenth century, colonial venues where "native" crafts were sold in an effort to generate potential new markets and where imperial racial and ethnological science provided the logic for a new form of architectural spectacle.[70] These institutions also had more lofty goals, however, framed outside the narrow confines of imperial marketing logic. It is these latter goals, and the pedagogy that framed them, that connect most directly to changes in the way Indian buildings were seen to embody symbolic and rhetorical qualities.

In a correspondence that took place in 1873 over the scheme for an India-wide system of industrial arts training, British administrator and amateur ethnologist Richard Temple asserted his conviction "that the tendency of instruction in a school of art should be to develop art and to produce a knowledge and love of truth and beauty: not to develop industry, nor to produce marketable commodities." Temple argued that the focus of arts training should be the total development of the pupil rather than a simple transference of technical and manual skills: "In the education terminology of the day, the curriculum should be *gymnastic* and not *technical;* should tend to elevate the pupil, to expand his mind, and to render him capable of receiving, and knowing, and retaining and appreciating—not to teach him petty knacks nor to strengthen his fingers and put him in the way of making money by means of aimless mannerism or stolid reproduction."[71]

The surest path to meeting this goal, in the opinion of Temple and others, was to create a graded sequence of courses that moved from the basic analysis of "form"—and, importantly, its delineation through drawing—to more complex training in modeling, sculpture, painting, and composition: "Students should begin with the design of simple forms in pencil or monochrome, and passing on to the design of more complex forms, groups, and the like, might end with the composition of drawings, groups in plaster, terra cotta, marble, &c., and, lastly, of pictures in water-colours and oils."[72] For Temple, the need for a methodology to train Indian students in the "love of truth and beauty" derived from his belief that British rule had destroyed the nonrational, "instinctual" approach to artistic production that characterized Indian culture. Since the "instinct" had been lost, he reasoned, the path forward was to replace it with a rational knowledge of the universal sources of artistic beauty. "The inevitable tendency of our rule is to repress native genius and originality," Temple wrote, and "it behooves us, therefore, since the original instinct is lost, to mould the opinions and tastes of the natives on a rational system. Rules and laws exist and are known, founded on an analysis of the impression received by educated minds from the inspection of certain forms and colors and combinations, which show the reason why those impressions are produced." Those universal laws, moreover, were capable of being taught: "The 'line of beauty,' the 'law of preponderance,' harmonies and contrasts of color, and the rules of composition can no longer be looked upon as matters of taste or of fancy, but are regarded as established principles. These laws can all be learnt, illustrated, and applied, and on them practical rules can be founded."[73]

For Temple and others involved in the creation of India's art-school system, therefore, the path to higher forms of artistic thought and practice, to the soul-changing development of "a knowledge and love of truth and beauty," was a rigorous grounding in the lawlike principles that underlay all great art. The key to accessing these broader principles and to cultivating the ability to embody and reproduce them in original work was "drawing" in all its several forms, including freehand sketching, tracing, and projective geometry, among others. "Before we can compose we must be able to delineate," Temple wrote, for "the existence of ideas will never amount to a composition if the power of expressing the ideas be absent."[74]

Drawing did not only provide a systematic means for communicating formal ideas, however, such as those inscribed on an architectural plan. By cultivating faculties of perception more broadly, by encouraging students in the "habit of close, accurate and sustained analytic observation," drawing was also thought to provide access to a more comprehensive and rational appropriation of the world.[75] In this sense, drawing instruction was more than a means toward regularizing graphic communication; its more important role was to cultivate new kinds of subjectivity: "The arts, as regards teachableness, differ from the sciences in this—that their power is founded not only on facts which can be communicated, but on the *dispositions* which require to be created."[76]

Kipling's innovation at the Mayo School was to ground this character-reforming pedagogy in the indigenous material culture of the province. The curriculum at Mayo School combined training in traditional crafts practiced in the region with instruction in aesthetic theory and in technical and freehand drawing. Students in every course were required to apply their drawing skills to local building ornaments and forms, sketching the street architecture of Lahore's Old City and preparing original designs for traditional crafts, calligraphy, and buildings. Kipling's approach thus marked a significant departure from the style of training available in most other technical schools, since the latter seldom if ever directed attention to Indian objects, art traditions, canonical texts, or methods.[77]

The impact of this change was felt more fully in the field of architectural design, perhaps, than in any of the other courses of study offered at the school, which included clay modeling (primarily for architectural sculpture), carpentry, painting, carpet and textile design, and engraving. For one thing, students in the latter disciplines were never expected to master drawing to the same level of proficiency as students pursuing architectural training, since mastery of the highly formalized graphic conventions of architectural design was more critically central to success in that field than graphic communication was to any of the other crafts. In addition, local methods of practice in the other crafts—enhanced by various kinds of technical refinement—remained the primary focus of the craft curricula, whereas architectural methodology at the school, lacking any accepted Indian source to model itself on, derived almost wholly from European practices. Put somewhat differently, while Lahore's Indian architecture provided models for the students to emulate, architectural training at Mayo School privileged Western conventions of drawing and design methodology.

Drawing in Kipling's curriculum was thus seen as a kind of intellectual filter, a way to transcend rote methods of design based on an unreliable (and increasingly diminished) indigenous "intuition." Drawing elevated building design to the status of an expressive cultural art, a product of an intellect trained in the rules and "laws" of artistic beauty. The Mayo curriculum left the theoretical and technical bases of architectural training largely intact, therefore, but broadened the range of relevant examples students were required to learn from to include exemplary local buildings. At the Mayo School, the indigenous architecture of the city was discursively relocated to occupy a central position in colonial design discourse.

It remains for us to assess how effective the Mayo School was at transforming architectural practice in the province. It is certain that several students from the school went on to practice architecture in Lahore and elsewhere, both as employees of the provincial PWD and as private practitioners. Kipling was often pessimistic, however, about how fully many of these students had acquired an appreciation for the loftier goals of their training. One of the key problems, in his opinion, was that students often took classes just long enough to acquire the delineating skills needed for employment as draftsmen and never completed the higher-level courses in design and composition. The lure of remunerative employment was great for many of the school's students, since the majority came from very poor families: "Most of those who leave the school leave it from the junior classes," Kipling wrote, "chiefly to follow their fathers' crafts."[78] While Kipling was sympathetic toward this kind of student, students from the educated "service" classes who failed to complete their training were subject to his disdain: "The worst type of pupil is the youth who has a contempt for manual work, who hopes to acquire easily the knack of tracing or copying an engineering drawing, who comes late and leaves early, who has a desultory and dawdling habit of doing what is set before him, who does not even affect an interest in it and who yet complains that he ought to receive a more liberal stipend, or be placed in some well salaried appointment."[79]

Students who left Mayo School before matriculating often found well-paying jobs. In his annual report on the school for 1891–92, Kipling wrote that of the students who left, "some diverge from the lines in which [their] training would be of use; but most of them find ready employment as Draftsmen or Designers in the Public Works, Archaeological, Railways, and Local Boards' Offices; as Masters in Industrial Schools; as Surveyors; and as Overseers."[80] The steady trickle of students outward from the school thus marked both a success and a failure. Even though students were taught well enough at the school to obtain stable employment in government or private service, abandoning the pursuit of higher artistic skills and sensibilities for the security of a monthly salary was precisely what the school aimed to prevent.

Despite Kipling's frequent lament that his students often valued their training more as a vehicle to economic gain than for its broader artistic goals, both the curriculum of the Mayo School and its mode of operation were closely tied to the colonial economy: "From the training of art and craft teachers, carpet designers, decorative painters, and surveyors, to the supply of carpenters, architectural draftsmen, wood carvers, and hereditary traders, education [at the Mayo School] was administered according to the annual registers of state employment and commerce in the province."[81] Both students and faculty at the school participated regularly in remunerative projects in Lahore and other cities as part of the normal work of the school. A representative survey of projects done for hire by Mayo School students includes decorating the corridor connecting Lawrence and Montgomery Halls; designing honorific banners used at the 1877 Imperial Assemblage in Delhi; preparing maps, plans, and illustrations for the *Civil and Military Gazette* and other publications; selling student artwork at colonial exhibitions; supplying reproductions of furniture and other crafts to the South Kensington Museum; manufacturing and installing wall coverings, frescoes, mantles, and furniture for use in churches, museums, and private houses; designing copper badges for railway employees; building a wooden construction model of the Chief Court while it was under construction; and undertaking various decorative work on the Chief Court and other buildings in the city. While the school received little income from these commissions, and in some cases took no payment at all, the inevitable effect of these activities was to transform a theoretical and practical knowledge of Punjab's "native traditions" into a marketable commodity. The principal circuits through which this exchange flowed, moreover, were those most closely allied with the private, commercial, and governmental interests of the British community: the museums, exhibitions, *darbar*s, churches, town halls, court houses, and English publications that together made up the key institutions of colonial knowledge and control.

The rewards for completing the Mayo School's curricular program, however, were often greater than those available to students who dropped out. Graduates of the Mayo School found easy employment in the colonial engineering services, and their skills were generally admired. A typically approving comment came from F. J. E. Spring, executive engineer for a large bridge over the Chenab River near Multan, who hired a draftsman from the Mayo School to work in his drawing office: "[The Mayo School student] is just the class of man we much need in the Public Works Department," Spring wrote to Kipling, calling special attention to the student's command of drawing: "The old style of 'Tracer' . . . has as a class no real knowledge of the things he draws and thinks of them only in the plane of his paper, whereas your Lahore carpenter draughtsman sees the things he is drawing as they actually are, and is therefore the man we have long wanted."[82]

In addition to finding lucrative employment in the colonial government for gradu-ates, Kipling recruited his best students to serve as faculty in the school. Foremost among them was Bhai Ram Singh (d. 1915), a native of Rasulpur (Gurdaspur District) in Punjab and a graduate of the Mission School at Amritsar, where he had studied carpentry.[83] Singh joined Mayo School during its second year of operation, and his talent for design soon attracted the attention of Kipling, who made him head of carpentry and cabinet work. Singh's career at the college was capped by his promotion to principal in 1909. In 1883 Singh sub-mitted a design for the Punjab Court at the International Exhibition in Calcutta that was noticed approvingly by Queen Victoria's son, His Royal Highness the Duke of Connaught. Shortly afterward Singh was hired, under the direction of Kipling, to design and build over 270 wooden panels for a billiard room and hallway at the prince's home, Bagshot Park, in England (1885–87). During his long career Singh often worked in conjunction with Kipling; together the two designed Lahore's museum (1883) and, as we have already seen, with Swin-ton Jacob, Aitchison College (1885). Singh was also the lead designer of Khalsa College in Amritsar (1892), an elegant complex of Indo-Saracenic buildings and perhaps his most crit-ically acclaimed work (Figure 3.12). Singh's most prestigious commission, however, came from Queen Victoria herself. The queen commissioned Singh to design and fabricate, in an "Indian" style, the banquet, or "Durbar" room, for Osborn House on the Isle of Wight. In 1891 Singh was sent to England to oversee construction on the room. Upon his departure two years later, Singh wrote to Kipling with barely concealed pleasure that the queen "gave me Her portrait and a gold pencil case on Christmas Day."[84]

Like Ganga Ram and Kanhayalal before him, Bhai Ram Singh was an exception rather than the rule. All three men built their highly successful careers on a body of work whose patronage and purposes were closely allied to imperial methods and goals. All three received substantial material and symbolic rewards for their service to Britain's colonial project: Kanhayalal was awarded the honorific title *rai bahadur* and served as the vice president of

Lahore's Municipal Committee; Ganga Ram was also given the title of *rai bahadur* and, in 1922, was knighted by order of the British Crown; Bhai Ram Singh, in addition to being promoted to principal of the Mayo School, also enjoyed the personal patronage of Queen Victoria and the prince regent. It would be a mistake to assume, however, that the gradual transformation of skills and attitudes directed toward building design that each of these men embodied and expressed, in all their variety, remained solely contained within the compass of British interests. Both the skills that allowed this new generation of architects to deftly negotiate the regulatory environment of municipal planning reviews and PWD contracts and the growing conviction among Indian architects that buildings were in some sense reliable signs of the people who made them—that buildings were a kind of touchstone to cultural identity—were things that could be, and often were, appropriated for use in projects that had different goals and aims.

A HINDU CIVIC INSTITUTION

In the final section of this chapter, I will develop this point by describing a project for a new college campus in Lahore whose patrons often openly defied colonial rule and whose very inception was a pointed response to the perceived inadequacy of colonial institutions of higher education. The project was a new campus for the Dayanand Anglo Vedic (DAV) College, designed by Ganga Ram and Bhai Ram Singh. The DAV College was organized and run under the auspices of Lahore's Arya Samaj, a socioreligious reform organization based on a renewed appreciation for the principles of Vedic Hinduism.[85] The Arya Samaj was only one of several voluntary social associations formed in late nineteenth-century Punjab, most of which had their headquarters in Lahore.[86] The leading figures of the organization were members of Lahore's well-educated middle-class community, including at least five M.A.

Figure 3.12. Khalsa College, Amritsar, Bhai Ram Singh, architect.

degree holders, a lawyer, and two medical doctors.[87] Nearly all had trained at Government College, and several held high positions in the colonial bureaucracy. Despite the fact that the Arya Samaj leadership decided against sending delegates to the first conference held by the Indian National Congress, the organization's politics and goals were straightforwardly nationalist.[88] Lala Lajput Rai, a major figure in the Indian nationalist movement who was tried, convicted, and deported for sedition following nationalist protests in Lahore in 1907, joined the Arya Samaj in 1882 and was one of its most active early members.

The DAV College, founded originally in 1886, was explicitly designed to counter what its founders saw as the increasing Anglicization of students trained in the British colonial university system. Rather than dismissing English education outright, however, the college attempted to take the literary and scientific advances Western education had made available and reframe them as truths revealed far earlier, and in more profound ways, in the ancient Vedas. Students from DAV College nevertheless consistently scored well in the India-wide colonial schedule of examinations. The college offered courses in both English and indigenous languages, including classes in English and Sanskrit literature, philosophy, ayurvedic medicine, and physical and chemical science. DAV College also offered technical training in tailoring and carpentry and, beginning in 1896, a degree course in civil engineering.

Lala Lal Chand, the first president of the DAV College Trust and Management Society, outlined the goals of the new institution in an 1886 draft proclamation. At the heart of the matter, Chand argued, was British education's tendency to create an elite educated class that moved "by itself"; one that was "incapable of materially influencing, or being influenced by, the uneducated masses." To address this problem, the DAV College would "make provision for the efficient study of the national language and literature, and [to] carefully initiate the youthful mind into habits and modes of life consistent with the national spirit and character." The primary objects of the college, in Chand's words, were "to weld together the educated and uneducated masses by encouraging study of the national language and vernaculars; to spread a knowledge of moral and spiritual truths by insisting on the study of classical Sanskrit; to assist the formation of sound and energetic habits by a regulated mode of living; to encourage sound acquaintance with English Literature and to afford a stimulus to the material progress of the country by spreading a knowledge of the physical and applied sciences."[89] As was true at Aitchison Chiefs' College, founded around the same time, the planners of DAV College sought to attain these goals by combining an expressive and carefully conceived campus landscape with a program of institutional life that fostered a "regulated mode of living."

From the very beginning, the college founders made efforts to cultivate habits of thrift and regularity in the student body. A majority of the college's students lived in boarding houses located on or near campus, first in a converted building located in the Wachowali Bazaar in the Old City and later in two converted *kothi*s (houses) on the college's new grounds. Their intention was to create a disciplinary milieu aimed at molding "the whole life of the student," according to Chand, rather than stuffing the student's mind with mere facts.

To this end, students' daily routines were regulated hour by hour, from early morning exercises and prayer to regulated study hours and evening codes of drill.[90] Boarders ate together in a common eating hall, unsegregated by caste, and a range of organized sports formed an important component of daily activities. DAV students were among the first in the city to form a rowing club, using boats of their own manufacture for races in the Ravi River.

Prior to construction of the new campus, college classes were held in the Arya Samaj *mandir* (temple) near Shah Alami Gate, inside the Old City. John C. Oman, a popular professor of science at Government College (1877–97) and later principal of Khalsa College in Amritsar (1898–99), was invited to attend a ceremony at the temple in 1879. Arriving at Lohari Gate from his house in the civil station, Oman "had to quit [his] carriage," he wrote, "for it could not go into the narrow crowded thoroughfares of the native quarter which lay within the gate." His careful description of the temple and ceremony merits quoting at length:

> On the doorway [to the temple] was a board bearing, in large English characters, the words "Arya Samaj" and below that, in smaller characters, the same words in Hindi and Urdu. Ascending a flight of stairs and passing through a narrow passage we entered an open space or court, bounded on one side by high and on the remaining three sides by low buildings. The place of meeting was a very humble one, with unsightly walls all round and the open canopy of heaven overhead. In one corner was a recess, perhaps six feet square, roofless like the other portions of the court. Here preparations had been made for the performance of the *Hom* sacrifice. Floor-cloths had been laid down for the visitors to sit upon, and festoons of leaves had been hung in great loops right round the enclosure. . . . At one end of the open court was placed a small table covered over with a white cloth of English manufacture. Upon it were ranged three brass vases containing flowers. At this table the lecturer stood when, in his appointed turn, he addressed the audience "on the wants of our country." Somewhat in advance of the table, i.e., a little nearer to the centre of the court, there was a small carpet, and a very low table, just a few inches high. These were for the use of the guru when he read to the audience out of the Vedas. At the other end of the court three or four musicians were squatted tuning their instruments in a listless fashion. A little way behind them I noticed the Society's charity-box, marked in English and two vernacular languages, the uppermost line and the largest characters being English.[91]

Oman's description underscores both the plainness of the temple's architecture and its frank intermingling of Hindu and Anglo-Christian religious accoutrements (the open court and raised dais for the *Hom* ceremony, on the one hand, and the potted flowers and collection box, on the other) and liturgical features (the reading of Vedas by a Guru, and an address on "the wants of our country" by a "lecturer"). The same blend of Anglo-Christian and Hindu settings and rituals and the same emphasis on simple forms and materials that characterized the Arya Samaj *mandir* were carried over into the planning and design for the new DAV College and residences.

The construction of DAV College took place slowly owing to litigation over the new site, lack of sufficient funding, and internal disputes within the organization itself. Throughout the construction process, however, the college's leaders kept their focus on producing a distinctive campus architecture that spoke transparently of their broader political and religious convictions. After a long period spent raising funds by private subscription—and refusing any grants-in-aid from the colonial government—the college's founders purchased property near the provincial secretariat and, in 1909, finally began construction. The core of the new college was made up of two educational blocks: a "Science Block" housing chemistry, physical sciences, and engineering classes, and an "Arts Block" housing a library and classrooms for instruction in English, Sanskrit, history, mathematics, and philosophy. In addition to these two main academic buildings, the college provided on-campus housing for one hundred students in two converted bungalows that already existed on the site. Next to these houses, two lines of rooms were built for the college's sweepers and servants, and a low, raised outdoor platform for open-air worship ("Samadh") was built at the back of the site (Figure 3.13).

The Science Block was the first building completed, based on a design by Rai Bahadur Ganga Ram, who had retired from his role as executive engineer in the provincial PWD and now served as the college's honorary director of engineering. The Science Block was a long

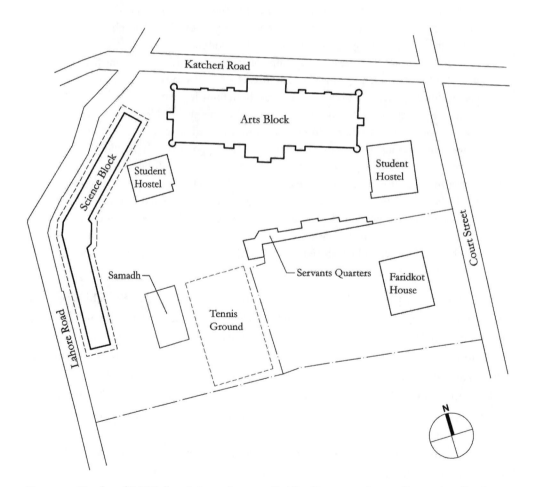

Figure 3.13. Site plan of DAV College, Lahore, circa 1910. Faridkot House occupies an adjacent plot of land.

single-story building with a large octagonal lecture hall at its center. Two symmetrical wings, one on either side of the central hall, provided space for classrooms and offices. The building's plan formed a shallow *V*, conforming to the lot lines and streets nearby. Surrounding the entire structure was a ten-foot-wide open verandah, shaded above by a sloping shed roof and punctuated by small dormers at the entry to each classroom.

Aside from a modest molded-brick decorative frieze running along the cornice and several small pyramidal-roofed cupolas covering the chimneys of fireplaces that warmed each classroom in the winter, the Science Block had little decorative ornament (Figure 3.14). Several visible features of the building announced its up-to-date construction, however, including operable ventilating windows placed high on the exterior walls, modern laboratory equipment in the block's apparatus rooms, and exposed brick jack arches in the ceiling that revealed the rolled-steel beams supporting them. The exposed structure, ventilating windows, and matter-of-fact treatment of the building's exterior might be seen as a reflection of the continuous shortness of funding for the building, something that made progress on the structure "exasperatingly slow," according to Chand.[92] When we consider that Ganga Ram had been sent by the Indian government to study architecture in London, however, and that he was instructed by both his education and his patrons to emphasize the expressive rather than purely functional potentials of architectural design, the straightforward quality of the building's design might also be conceived of as rich with allusions to the rational program of study it was meant to accommodate.

The design of the Arts Block, begun in 1911 and completed one year later, provides further evidence that the patrons of DAV College saw architectural design as an expressive medium for publicly identifying themselves as a Hindu, civic-minded body. The managing committee commissioned Bhai Ram Singh from the Mayo School of Art to design the building in a "Hindu classical" style.[93] Singh's original design for the building was sanctioned by the civil station subcommittee of Lahore's Municipal Committee in 1907 (Figures. 3.15, 3.16). The committee lacked the funds to realize the initial design, and the permit lapsed one year later; a new set of drawings was submitted in 1910, when the funds for construction were in hand. Singh's revised design scaled back the overall dimensions of the original proposal, partly in response to municipal officials' concerns that the building was too close to the main road. The plans for a revised Art Block were drafted by Ganga Ram, with Singh contributing a redesigned exterior facade.

Singh's original design was more in keeping with the eclectic, pan-Indic, Indo-Saracenic scheme he used at Aitchison College. The architectural details of the final design were drawn

Figure 3.14. Elevation drawing of the Science Block, DAV College, Lahore. Rai Bahadur Ganga Ram, architect. Source: Lahore Municipal Corporation.

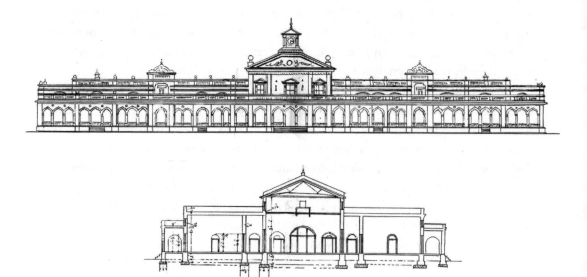

Figure 3.15. Elevation and section of Bhai Ram Singh's first design for the Arts Block at DAV College, Lahore. Source: Lahore Municipal Corporation.

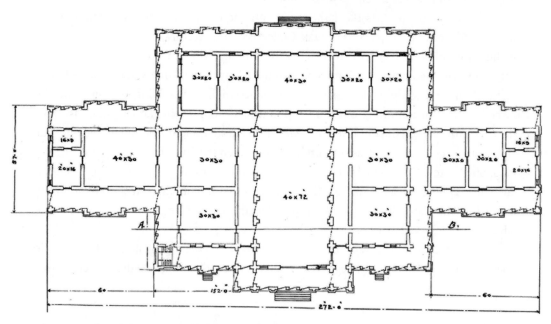

Figure 3.16. Plan of Bhai Ram Singh's first design for the Arts Block at DAV College, Lahore. Source: Lahore Municipal Corporation.

from Hindu religious buildings, with a large masonry *shikhara* (a stepped vertical mass rising over a temple's inner sanctum) towering over the building's main central hall (Figures 3.17, 3.18). The much more explicitly "Hindu" treatment of the facade in Singh's revised design upheld the College Board members' conception of themselves as the "regenerators" of an Aryan Vedic tradition.[94] Singh's final design thus helps confirm the presence, by the first decade of the twentieth century, of a widely shared attitude that buildings should both reflect and embody the cultural aspirations of their builders. The "Hindu classical" design of the Arts Block, rather than reflecting a retrogressive or isolationist retreat into some purified and abstract Hindu tradition, one uninflected by exposure to Western traditions

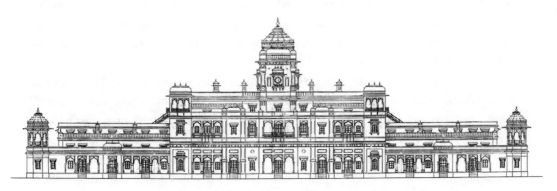

Figure 3.17. Elevation of Bhai Ram Singh's second design for the Arts Block at DAV College, Lahore. Notice the shikhara *form of the central clock tower, Ram's use of shallow-domed* chattris *at each of the building's corners, and decorative bracketing beneath the open verandahs on the second level. Source: Lahore Municipal Corporation.*

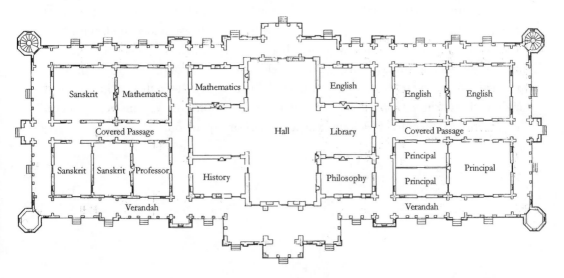

Figure 3.18. Plan of Bhai Ram Singh's second design for the Arts Block at DAV College, Lahore. Source: Lahore Municipal Corporation.

of building, was part of a new, modernist architectural practice. Like Aitchison College, the DAV College Arts Block was a complicated architectural essay, one that combined the authority of India's architectural past with a pedagogical program aimed at the future. The "oriental" courses the building housed—including Vedic philosophy, Sanskrit literature, and ayurvedic studies—were conceived not as relics of a distant and moribund past but as living traditions, founded on the most advanced scientific principles, and as key sources of renewal for a properly functioning, modern Indian nation.

I began this chapter by arguing that the newly constructed colonial districts of Lahore made up a landscape that was as notable for the way it announced and embodied forms of social inclusion and collaboration between different elite communities in the city as it was for the way it registered social hierarchy and cultural difference. A new approach to architectural design, one that emphasized a close connection between building forms and the cultural qualities of those who made them, helped ground the symbolic idea of collaboration in tangible material forms. What I have attempted to show in this chapter is how that new approach took hold, both through new kinds of aesthetic and technical training and through a rhetorical (at least) commitment on the part of the colonial government to producing an urban milieu in the civil station, a milieu whose architecture presented persuasive visual support to the idea that the city was a collaborative enterprise. The design of DAV College—both its symbolic references to a distinctly Hindu and civic social formation and its adoption of the Anglo-European spatial idea of the isolated total institution—illustrates that this new approach to architecture became equally useful to an Indian middle class for its own politically oppositional projects. The very idea of inclusivity embedded in the formal qualities of Lahore's most notable colonial institutions made taking that step seem natural: The idea that architecture could be a powerfully expressive cultural medium existed independently of any *particular* cultural claim. That idea, along with the pedagogies, material cultural practices, and repertoire of formal aesthetic choices that accompanied its arrival, transformed the conceptual bases upon which the city was understood, at least for the small but powerful community of British and Indian residents who together effected that transformation. Not everyone in Lahore held this view, of course, nor was it the only approach people took to thinking about, and building, the city. In the striking institutional buildings that anchored space in Lahore's colonial civil station, however, this new, modern, and powerful architectural idea found particularly clear expression.

CHANGING HOUSES

Rethinking and Rebuilding Townhouses and Neighborhoods

4

The construction of Lahore's civil station did not take place in a vacuum. Changes to the city's architecture took place throughout Lahore, even in places far removed from Mall Road. Few British observers noticed those changes taking place. Fewer still saw them as representing anything other than the demise (for better or worse, depending on the observer) of a traditional "Indian" way of life. This was particularly true of changes taking place in ordinary Indian houses in the city. Throughout the late nineteenth and early twentieth centuries, Lahore's Indian residents gradually reworked both the forms and meanings of their homes in response to new technical and aesthetic ideas and to changing attitudes about how families should properly inhabit the physical space of the home. Changes to an earlier set of residential building practices in the city were gradual and selective during the late nineteenth century, as the architecture of the home was drawn into a new discourse on proper forms of urban living. The changes had an impact on the interior arrangement and furnishing of houses, led to the use of new technologies, and altered the meaning of house facades. These small changes produced large effects, altering aspects of traditional urban form in the city, such as the way houses were placed on the street, and changing people's expectations about the range of non-residential uses an *abadi* should provide. For all these reasons, changes to Indian domestic architecture in Lahore exerted a powerful force on city development more generally. Despite how little comment these changes elicited in British circles at the time, it is clear that the stakes were considerable. By the late nineteenth century, ordinary houses and other small-scale vernacular buildings were deeply implicated in questions about the role architecture could play in shaping a colonial milieu.

UNSTUDIED SIMPLICITY

To demonstrate the latter claim more fully, we start in England at a lecture delivered by C. Purdon Clarke on the evening of May 25, 1883, at London's Society of Arts. The title of Clarke's talk was the "Domestic Architecture of India," a subject that was relatively novel at the time since, although India's ancient and medieval architecture had long been a subject of interest in England, "nothing had hereto been said," according to one attendee at the talk, "as to the ordinary domestic architecture of India."[1] Clarke's presentation was based largely on his observation of the residential architecture in Lahore's Old City, and to give the audience a visual sense of his subject, Clarke passed around photos and drawings of houses and shops in the city prepared by Kipling and his students at the Mayo School of Art.

It was obvious from Clarke's presentation that he admired the ordinary buildings of Lahore, everything from their charming "unstudied simplicity" to the way they effectively tempered Punjab's extremes of heat and cold with their intelligent use of building mass, carefully placed perforations, and orientation on their sites. Equally important to these buildings' success, in Clarke's opinion, were the distinctive customs and social relations through which their construction was realized. Each house came about through "the enterprise of the owner," he noted, rather than through speculation or government initiative. Patron and worker were bound together through ties of trust rather than written contract; progress on construction was encouraged through idioms of hospitality rather than financial incentives. While building accounts were kept loosely, each person involved in the construction project—the owner, the *mistri* (overseer), the craftsmen, and the common laborers on the site—nevertheless upheld his role in a hierarchical relationship whose successful functioning was interrupted by nature alone:

> [The owner] engages a "mistri," who is at once architect and clerk of the works. Materials are purchased by the "mistri" and the owner, or his agent or servant in company. Wages are paid to common labourers daily, and to craftsmen at irregular intervals. The accounts invariably get complicated, by reason of advances, and what a London tradesman calls the "dead horse" [wages paid in advance] is never fairly worked off. When any difficult work is in hand, or a spurt necessary, the workmen are treated with tobacco, sherbet, or sweetmeats.... Once begun, the work steadily goes on, and no notice is taken of the many holidays. Rain only stops it. (738)

Clarke believed he was describing a "living tradition," to use his own words, one whose material expression was inseparable from the culture that produced it. For Clarke, the value of Lahore's domestic architecture derived from its grounding in both local forms and materials and from the "artistic spirit" he saw animating the inner essence of Indian culture. Equally important was the idea that this living tradition expressed its power most fully in situ; Lahore's "ordinary domestic buildings" could not be easily imitated or reproduced elsewhere with similar effect: "[The charm of these houses] is not easily translatable. A vast sweep of brickwork, pierced here and there with an opening, filled with perforated terra-cotta, or jeweled, so to speak, with a carved balcony, or a bit of painted wall, whose tiny details give an air of space and size by contrast, looks quite splendid in the sunlight, but it is not easy to draw it successfully, and it was never in any strict sense designed, but grew in an organic and altogether inimitable fashion" (739). For Clarke, this was an architecture and way of life whose integrity needed protection from the contaminating influences of Western building methods and overregulation by municipal codes. If a building act to regulate the design of houses was enforced in Lahore, he argued, then "the class of buildings represented in the photographs and sketches would be doomed" (742).

At the conclusion of his lecture, Clarke summed up what he saw as the main value of directing his audience's attention to India's "living" vernacular traditions. "If as much were done to investigate and preserve the living traditions of Indian handicraft as is now devoted to the more speculative work of archaeological research," he urged, "[then] we would be soon in possession of the key to much puzzling matter, both in the arts, social relations, and politics of the people of India" (740). In other words, for Clarke, the "puzzling matter" that bound Indian art, social relations, and politics together could be solved by knowing and preserving traditional forms.

Sitting in the audience that evening, only days after having arrived in London to pursue architectural training at the behest of the Indian government, was the young engineer from Lahore, Ganga Ram, whom we encountered in chapter 3. At the end of Clarke's speech, Ganga Ram rose to acknowledge Clarke's claim that Indian culture writ large provided the foundation of India's architectural genius: "The Hindoos, every one knows from past history, were at one time a civilized nation," Ram began, "and all their habits and customs were really based on some reason" (740). Where Clarke saw continuity, however, Ganga Ram saw decline. In Ganga Ram's opinion, people in India "had fallen into ignorance"; if earlier customs persisted, then they did so only in moribund and unreflective ways. For this reason, the idea that India's vernacular architecture wanted no correction from outside the cultural system that sustained it was, for Ram, open to question.

Ram agreed that houses in Lahore were well adapted "to the climate and convenience of the people"; however, based on his few short days in England, he claimed to have "no doubt [that] there were many knick-knacks" present in English houses "which could be introduced into [Indian] buildings, [that] would tend greatly to the comfort and convenience of the people" (740). Ganga Ram's speech struck a chord among several British members of the audience, people who perhaps shared Clarke's sense of his subject's importance but disagreed with his basic conclusions. When Ganga Ram had finished, a member of the audience named Juland Danvers rose to support Ram's point, agreeing that Indian builders had much to learn from "the usages and contrivances, and the combination of science and art, to be seen in this country" (742). Mr. Pedder, identifying himself as someone who had "lived in a good many houses in India," stood up to concur, arguing that surely there was something to be done "in the way of practical improvement in Indian architecture" (743). The Reverend J. Long, addressing Clarke directly, asked whether "some of the details of the architecture of India might be usefully adopted in this country" as well, noting that England was "so overrun in the present day with horrid structures, erected by jerry builders, that any improvement would be a great boon" (742).

Clarke responded to these questions by stating that it was not his intention "to advise English people to orientalise their houses." Rather, he urged his listeners to search for renewal in their own national traditions, to let each culture preserve its genius intact. The chairman of the meeting, Sir George Birdwood, rose to back Clarke up.[2] In Birdwood's opinion, the highly cultivated artistic feeling "of the Hindus" gave rise to a domestic architecture as beautiful and spontaneous "as the spreading hawthorns and laburnums in the summer sunshine of St. James's park," something that came about from "the sympathetic manner in which [Indian] builders seem to feel their way to what they are doing" (742). For Birdwood, the continuation of an ancient artistic spirit in India derived from the immobility of Indian culture and its resistance to outside change. The idea that "knick-knacks" from England could enhance a "native" dwelling, therefore—as Ganga Ram and others had proposed—was for him entirely out of the question. "I hope that the native gentlemen from Lahore who had addressed [us] would not be misled by the idea that they could learn anything in England for the improvement of the indigenous domestic architecture of the Punjab," Birdwood concluded; "it would be most mischievous if they were influenced by any such idea" (745–46).

The debates that ensued from Clarke's presentation that night, and from Ganga Ram's (and others') polite but provocative disagreements with him, help chart out the contested cultural terrain that underlay British and Indian discourse on the role ordinary vernacular buildings might play in constituting colonial society. At the most general level, that discourse revolved around the question of transferring British forms into Indian domestic buildings. Would this improve the "convenience" of the Indian dwelling, as Ganga Ram and others argued, or lead to the dissolution of a "living tradition"? If that tradition was a product of both formal material features and intangible cultural essences, what happened to the intangible essences when the material features of India's domestic architecture were changed from outside? The debate in play that evening, in other words, revolved around the question of what kinds of susceptibilities were exposed in a culture when its architectural forms were altered. Before returning to evaluate how that question was answered by different groups in the city, and what unexpected forms those answers sometimes took, I want to devote some detailed attention to understanding the nature of the alterations themselves.

INDIAN HOUSES IN THE OLD CITY

Clarke illustrated his lecture by showing elevations and plans of buildings he described as "mostly modern" (741). While Clarke claimed that some of the buildings he showed were "perhaps two hundred years old," he surmised that many of Lahore's "traditional" houses were no more than twenty years old. The implication of his comments, therefore, was that few if any changes stood between houses two hundred years old and houses of more recent construction. Anecdotal evidence suggests that Clarke was partially right; the basic layout and construction of houses like those he presented were illustrative of a fairly long-standing tradition of building in the city. A range of other nineteenth-century commentators had no hesitation in describing a "typical" Indian residence, though the same people seldom noted changes taking place in those houses at the time. I want to begin with a more detailed description of the "typical" urban Indian house in Lahore, therefore, drawing on anecdotal accounts, field observations, and permit applications for buildings that date from the late nineteenth century, concentrating on their basic layouts and mode of construction and the uses to which they were put.

In the Indian districts of Lahore, including the Old City and native *abadi*s outside the city walls, the most common form of residence was an attached row house, or a house placed "cheek by jowl" between two other buildings with no space left between them. In most cases, each house had its own separate exterior walls rather than sharing a common party wall with the neighboring property, though shared walls were sometimes used (Figure 4.1). The outer walls of the house marked the boundaries of individual plots, while the city's streets formed a more or less stable perimeter to blocks of private holdings. Houses were built beginning at the street edge itself, with no space for a sidewalk or other passage separating buildings from streets. Not every house fronted onto a main street, however, and many were constructed within the interior of a block. The latter houses were accessed by narrow lanes, or *gullee*s, that usually broadened out at the end into an open space *(katra)* shared by the residents of each building that opened onto it. In most cases, the only space open to the sky on an individual plot besides the roof (which was invariably used for living space as well) was a small open courtyard near the center of the house. A majority of houses in the eighteenth and early nineteenth centuries drew water from a private well located in the courtyard.

Houses in Lahore's Old City varied in height from a single story to as many as five or six stories, and many houses also had a basement room or rooms *(sardkhana* or *tehkhana)* well below the surface of the street that were often used as cool spaces in the summer heat. While houses came in many shapes and sizes, the most common form was a narrow, roughly rectangular building with its short dimension fronting the street. The maximum width of houses depended on the maximum span allowed by the wooden roof and floor beams, since most houses in the city were one structural bay wide. This building practice kept the maximum width of houses to around eighteen feet, though houses as narrow as five or six feet were common, even when several stories high (Figures 4.2, 4.3). Given the density of the built-up area in the city, when the need arose for more space on a lot, houses and shops were expanded vertically.

No statistical data exists from before the twentieth century, but single-room dwellings may have been the most common form of house in the city during the late nineteenth century. Lala Kashi Ram, a resident of Lahore who wrote a sanitary primer for Indian readers in 1884, described the general features of the type:

> They (the people) in four out of five cases, live in separate huts, but owing to the dearness of the ground the huts consist merely of one small room, with a small courtyard

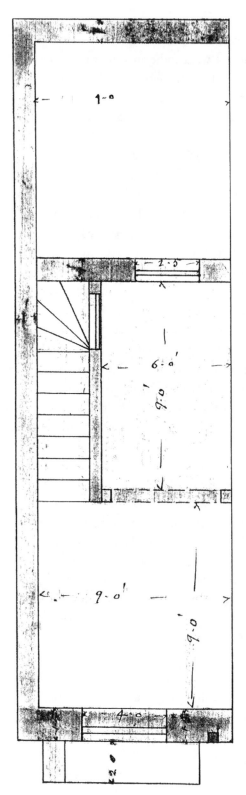

Figure 4.1. House in Lahore, 1893. Note that the shared wall on the right side of the plan is drawn as a single line. The front entry to this house is at the bottom edge of the illustration. The plan shows a two-foot-wide tharra (raised platform) running the length of the facade. Source: Lahore Municipal Corporation.

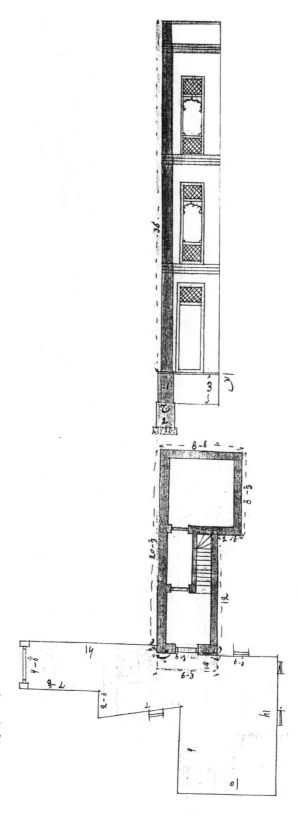

Figure 4.2. Narrow three-story house in Lahore, plan and elevation, circa 1880. This house is six feet three inches wide at the front entry. Source: Lahore Municipal Corporation.

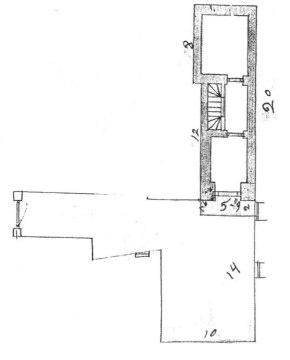

Figure 4.3. Narrow three-story house in Lahore, plan and elevation, circa 1880. This house is five feet nine inches wide at the front entry (compare to Figure 4.2). Notice the indication of decorative infill panels over the apertures in the elevation and the indication of a perforated brick screen at the roof level. Source: Lahore Municipal Corporation.

about 10 feet square, often the floor of the dwelling is below the level of the street. In this room and courtyard a family, consisting of from three to six persons, sleep, eat, cook, work, and perform the offices of nature.[3]

Kashi Ram's reference to "one small room" suggests that he was describing single-story buildings. Two- or three-story buildings with a single room on each floor are also found in archival records, often with a shop *(dukaan)* on the ground floor and living quarters above. In multistory one-room buildings, the stairway to the upper floors was given its own separate entry off the street and, for reasons discussed below, isolated from the room on the ground floor by a solid partition (Figures 4.4, 4.5). While these small, one-roomed buildings probably made up a large percentage of residences in Lahore's Indian districts in the nineteenth century, few buildings of this kind can be found today in the older sections of the city, and they remain difficult to trace in the city's archival record.

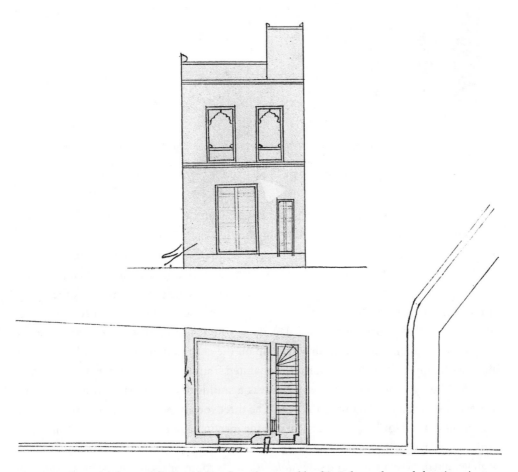

Figure 4.4. One-room house with shop (dukaan) *on the ground level in Lahore, plan and elevation, circa 1880. The stairway to an upper story is at right in the plan. Notice that the stairway can be entered from the street separately from the shop. Source: Lahore Municipal Corporation.*

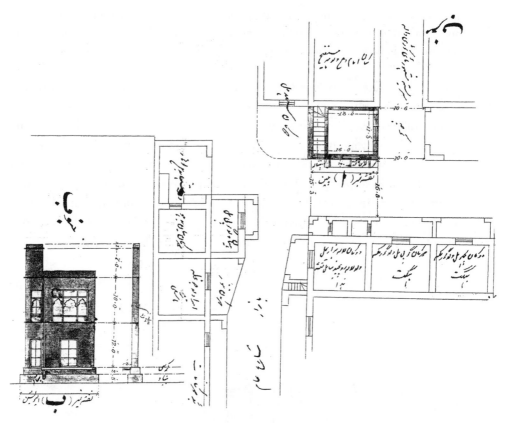

Figure 4.5. One-room house in Lahore, site plan and elevation, circa 1880. The stairway to an upper level can be accessed only from the street. Source: Lahore Municipal Corporation.

Applications for building permits for houses with two rooms on each level are more common in the late nineteenth century (Figures 4.6–4.9). In most cases, the rooms of a two-room plan were roughly equal in size, and a movable partition on the interior separated one room from the other. The house was thus divided approximately in half, with one room located at the front of the lot toward the street or lane outside and the other room placed at the back. Like one-room houses, two-room houses could be one or several stories tall, with each floor repeating the basic layout of the one below. As with one-room houses, in two-room buildings that combined a shop on the ground floor with a residence above, stairways to upper floors were invariably separated from the rooms on the ground floor.

A third type of common residence was a multistory building with a three-room sequence on each level (Figures 4.10–4.14). The three rooms included, on the ground floor, a front room used for business purposes or for meeting guests *(baithak);* a central courtyard *(sahen)* partially open to the floors and sky above and sometimes bordered by an open verandah placed along one side *(dalaan);* and a room or rooms at the back (*kothi*s or *kothri*s) used for any number of purposes, including storage. Larger houses of this type often included a foyer *(deorhi)* as part of the entry sequence, a room that was used, among

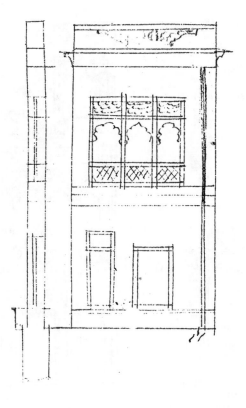

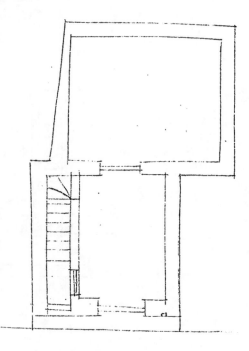

Figure 4.6. Two-story, two-room house in Lahore, plan, elevation, and partial section, circa 1880. In this building the stairway communicates both with the interior rooms on the ground floor and to the street outside, through a separate doorway. Source: Lahore Municipal Corporation.

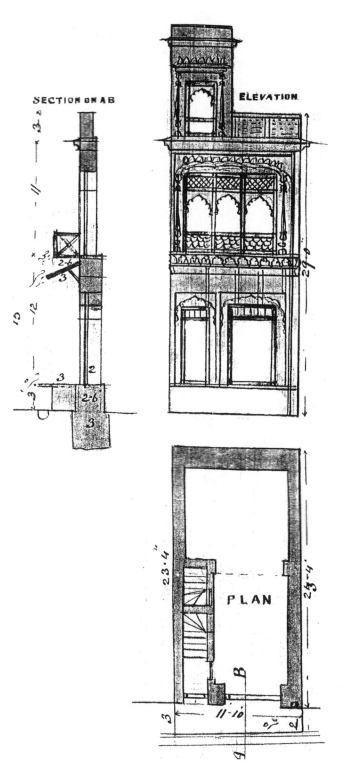

SECTION ON AB

ELEVATION

PLAN

Figure 4.7. Two-story, two-room house with rooftop barsati (covered pavilion) in Lahore, plan, elevation, and partial section, circa 1880. The second-level street facade has a jharoka (projecting bay window). Note the second stairway behind the front stairway, which probably leads to a basement (sardkhana). Source: Lahore Municipal Corporation.

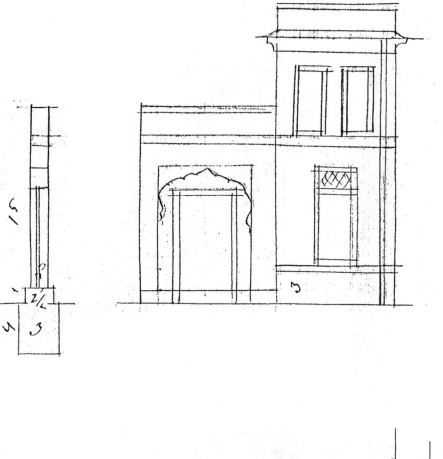

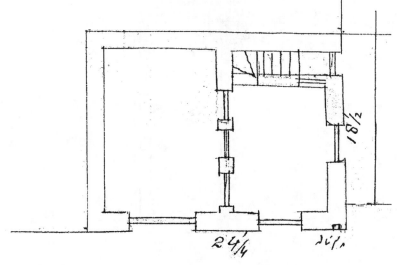

Figure 4.8. Two-story, two-room house with semiopen barsati *on a corner lot in Lahore, plan, partial section, and elevation, circa 1890. Source: Lahore Municipal Corporation.*

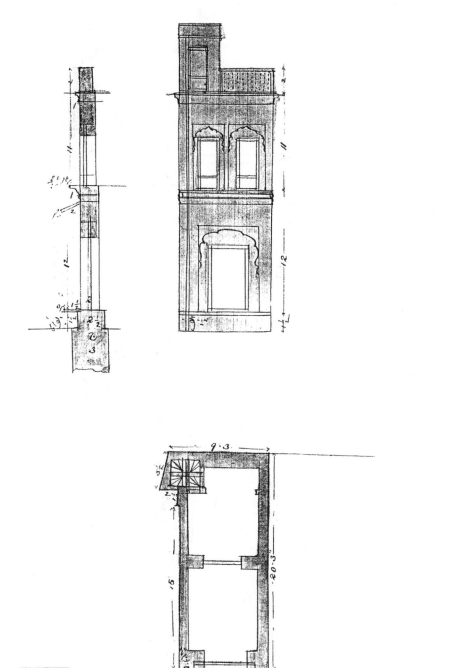

Figure 4.9. Two-story, two-room house with internal staircase in Lahore, plan, partial section, and elevation, circa 1890. Source: Lahore Municipal Corporation.

other things, as a reception area for guests or clients. Like one- and two-room houses, the plan of upper stories in a three-room house repeated the ground-floor plan almost exactly, except that on upper floors a narrow balcony spanned one side of the open courtyard providing connection between the front and back rooms. Alternately, the upper floors and roof were made solid except for a small opening *(magh)* centered over the courtyard below and covered with a wooden grill for safety.

The stairway in a three-room house might be located in the interior of the building, at the front of the building, or occasionally in both places. In all but the most expensive and grand dwellings in the city, the stairway was treated as a purely utilitarian device. As we have seen, separation between the inner rooms of the house and the stairway was a recurring feature of all houses, a design that allowed "sweepers" to reach a rooftop latrine without passing through the main rooms of the house. Other portions of the roof were used for sleeping and socializing in the evenings during good weather, and in some cases a small covered structure *(barsati)*, open on one or more sides, provided a sheltered sleeping area on the roof during the rainy season.

Night soil from rooftop latrines was collected in small earthen vessels *(gumllas)* once a day, usually in the morning, by "sweepers" who customarily received one *chapatti* (unleavened bread) as payment. Liquid waste from the latrine was channeled to drains in the street through a vertical notch *(parnala)* in the house's outer walls rather than through internal piping. By the closing decades of the nineteenth century, builders sometimes covered *parnalas* with tin sheets to keep the sewage from splashing openly onto the street below (Figures 4.15, 4.16).[4] British observers widely denounced the *parnalas*, covered or not, as a building device. Sanitary inspector Crawford Roe complained that in Lahore "house drains are rarely, if ever, joined on to the sewers, the bath, cooking, and all water used for domestic purposes, including a good deal of urine, pours out of holes in the walls. . . . I have frequently seen it gush out in volumes, falling like a fountain, and splashing the stinking liquid all over the streets and the persons passing below. A few houses have bits of tin over these escape holes to lessen this shower, but the majority have nothing of the kind."[5] Comments like Roe's, in addition to repeating a widely shared characterization that the Indian quarters of the city were filthy, also reveal the relative independence each house maintained from larger systems of urban infrastructure. The lack of horizontal interconnection between houses, their use of independent rather than shared party walls, and the self-contained nature of their structural systems suggest much the same thing. While closely packed together as part of the city's dense material fabric, individual houses nevertheless maintained fairly closed boundaries between themselves and both neighboring structures and the spaces (streets, lanes, and courts) shared among them.

CONSTRUCTION MATERIALS

Almost every house in Lahore, whether meant for British or Indian residents, was made primarily of brick. Bricks were made locally at numerous kilns in and around the city and

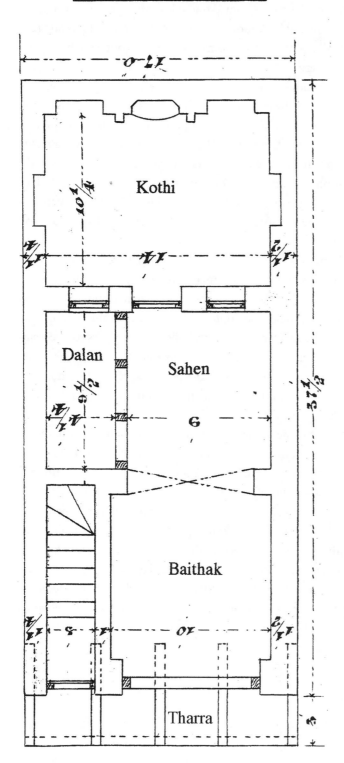

Figure 4.10. A typical three-room sequence, plan view. Measurements are given in feet and inches. The front entry of the house is at the bottom of the drawing. Note that the stairway opens directly onto the tharra *and is accessed through a separate entry. This building is also illustrated in Figure 4.11. Source: Lahore Municipal Corporation.*

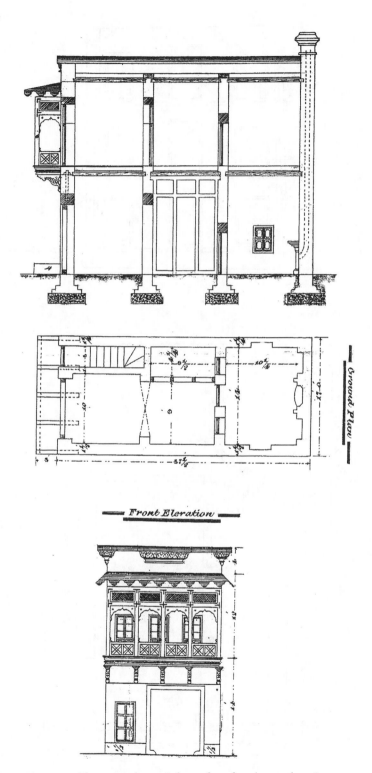

Figure 4.11. Three-room house, Lahore, plan, elevation, section, 1893.
Source: Lahore Municipal Corporation.

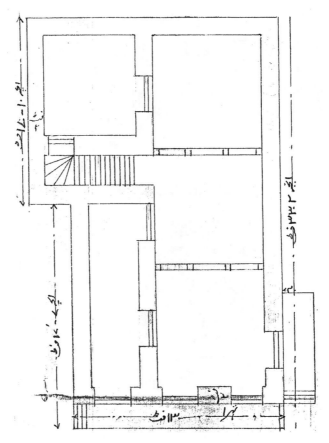

Figure 4.12. Three-room house, Lahore, plan and elevation, circa 1885. Notice the tharra *at the bottom of the plan and the internal staircase. The narrow space at the left of the main rooms is an entry foyer (deohri). Source: Lahore Municipal Corporation.*

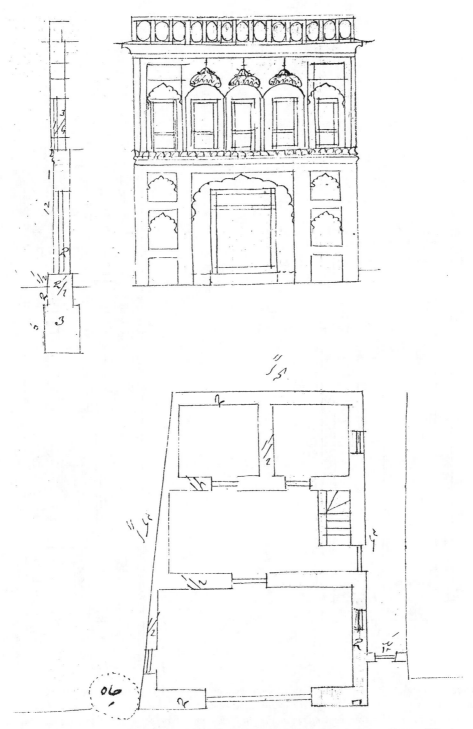

Figure 4.13. Three-room house, Lahore, plan, partial section, and elevation, circa 1890. A small kucha *bund, or gated entry, into the* kucha *(cul-de-sac) beyond is located in the lower right side of the plan. Note that the front of the house (the street elevation) is at the bottom of the plan. On the left, at the front of the house, the draftsman has used dotted lines to indicate a well. The "back" of this house has two small* kothis, *or storage rooms. Source: Lahore Municipal Corporation.*

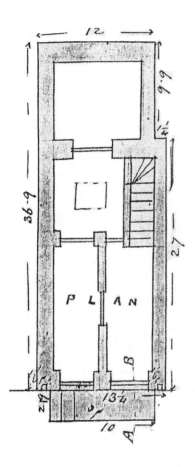

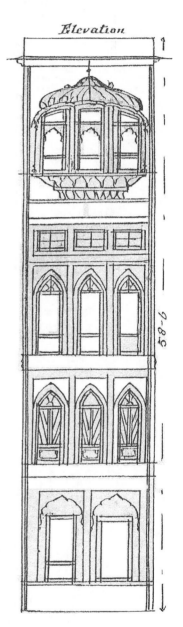

Figure 4.14. Four-story, three-room house in Lahore, plan and elevation, circa 1890. The elevation drawing depicts an eclectic late nineteenth-century decorative scheme, with pointed window lights, decorative mullions, transom lights over the windows on the third level, and a large decorative jharoka *(projecting bay window) at the upper level. Source: Lahore Municipal Corporation.*

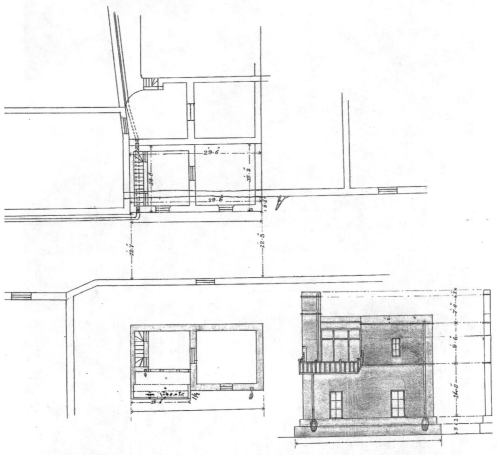

Figure 4.15. House elevation and site drainage plan, Kucha Sar Basta, Lahore, 1892. The plan in the upper half of the drawing shows a preexisting drain (dashed lines) that will run under the ground-floor platform of the new house. The elevation depicts parnalas (drainage channels) running vertically along either side of the facade. In the original permit drawing, blue ink was used to indicate water flowing through the drains and onto the street below. Source: Lahore Municipal Corporation.

Figure 4.16. Cloth shop in Delhi, circa 2000. Note the parnala *in the center of the upper portion of the photograph partially covered with a sheet of tin taken from an oil can.*

varied in cost according to size, shape, and degree of firing. Prior to the late nineteenth century, the most common brick in use was a flat, thin unit sometimes called a *lahori* or *lakhauri* brick. The *lahori* brick came in a range of different sizes, but two in particular were common: large (7 × 4 × 1.25 inch) and small (5 × 3 × 1 inch). A thicker English standard brick (2¼ × 3⅝ × 7⅝ inch) was manufactured in Punjab Province by the 1880s, but less-costly local bricks with their distinctive shapes were used for construction well into the twentieth century.[6] Walls built from local bricks were made unnecessarily thick from a structural standpoint, a technique that both eliminated the need for formal structural calculations and ensured that the house was well insulated from Punjab's punishing summer sun. In the best buildings, kiln-fired bricks were set in lime mortar, while less-expensive structures were made from sun-dried bricks set in mud plaster.[7] Lime for plaster and mortar was produced locally by burning *kankar*—calcitic nodules found at shallow depths in the soil—in conical kilns fueled with patties of dried cow dung. Mortars of tremendous strength and luster were sometimes made by adding horse hair, rice husks, lentils, and other "secret" ingredients to the lime.

Masons used a *pansal*, or water gauge, to level house foundations and laid local bricks in thick courses *(radda)* with little or no decorative surface pattern rendered in the bond itself. On street facades, exterior brickwork on houses or shops was usually plastered with mud or lime and whitewashed. Exterior surfaces on exposed side and back elevations, however, were commonly left unfinished. House facades in residential districts of the city were often quite plain, with the exception of decorative carving on the wooden door and frame *(chaukat)* at the entry and on wooden window frames or projecting balconies *(jharoka)* on the upper stories. In the main bazaars of the city, the latter could be very elaborately carved and decorated, and it was not unusual for a single building to have a separate *jharoka* at each level (Figure 4.17). The *jharoka* was a kind of projecting bay window, usually made from wood but sometimes made of plastered brick, with a rectangular or semihexagonal plan. They usually had three arched openings on the front face and a single opening on each of the two sides. The openings were partially filled in with fixed wooden lattice screens *(pinjra)* or with solid wood panels that could be slid in and out of grooved jambs. *Pinjra* work in the Punjab was especially fine, with some screens made up of as many as two thousand pieces, all mortised or doweled together and held tight within a wooden frame (Figure 4.18). Entry doors were made from two separate wooden leaves mounted on pivots rather than hinges. When the leaves were pulled shut, a raised piece of carved wooden trim *(bini)* attached to one of the leaves covered the joint (Figure 4.19). Door frames were often intricately carved with geometric and floral patterns, and sometimes with animals and gods. Lintels were often treated differently from the rest of the frame, and they were sometimes decorated with deities in Hindu houses or Quranic inscriptions in Muslim houses. In addition to carved wooden features on the facade, finer houses often used decorative pilasters, bracketed cornices, incised floral panels, and cuspate lamp niches as ornaments. All these features could be cut directly from the finished brick surface, rather than applied, and finished with a thick coat of lime plaster.

Figure 4.17. Street scene, Kashmiri Bazaar, Lahore, circa 1910. This street led from Delhi Gate to the Mosque of Wazir Khan, and for a long time it has been the central commercial bazaar in the Old City. Note the elaborate jharokas on shop-house facades on both sides of the bazaar. Copyright The British Library Board. OIOC Photo 297/1(54); all rights reserved.

Figure 4.18. A multipart jharoka *with fine* pinjra *work, Lahore, circa 1890. Copyright The British Library Board. OIOC Photo 405/3(44); all rights reserved.*

Wood was used sparingly in Lahore's houses owing to its scarcity and cost. In addition to ornamental balconies, screens, doors, and window frames, wood was used for beams, joists, and purlins. Builders preferred to use deodar, teak, mango, or *sheesham* (rosewood) for structural members, since all these woods are resistant to rot and white ants. Larger beams were milled or shaped by hand, while smaller "scantlings" (purlins) and rafters could be either milled or left rough. It is not uncommon to find failed floors and roofs on older houses, since builders seem to have used as little material as possible to economize on costs. Floor surfaces on the ground level and stairs were commonly made from bricks set edgewise *(karanja)* in a mortar bed, while upper floors and roof surfaces were usually made from tile over a bed of gravel and were often finished with a thick bed of plaster. Interior walls were also finished in whitewashed plaster, and in finer houses plaster trim with either a flat or shaped profile was used at the ceiling line. Most houses had a range of smaller and larger built-in shelves and recessed storage spaces on the interior, features that were easily accommodated within the overly thick wall (Figure 4.20).

The builders of Lahore's traditional houses thus worked with a small number of locally available materials, primarily brick, mortar, and wood. Since bricks and masons were cheap and wood and carpenters were dear, masonry walls tended to be overdesigned in a structural sense while wood members were sometimes underdesigned. The structural system of

Figure 4.19. Raised wooden trim (bini) joining two leaves of a door in Lahore's Old City, date unknown. Notice the geometric pattern on the door leaves and the brass star-shaped studs running along the bini.

Figure 4.20. Built-in shelving and fireplace surrounds in a ruined structure near the Old City, circa 2001. Notice the chandaans (ventilating apertures) placed high in the walls and the plaster finish on walls. This building probably dates from around 1910.

houses was simple, relying on single wooden spans between brick bearing walls with wooden frames and lintels bracing openings. Ornamental refinement was limited primarily to openings, carved wooden doors and *jharokas*, and the occasional lamp niche in the front facade. Most of this ornament, moreover, was conventional, drawn from a shared but limited pool of figural elements that distinguished Hindu households from Muslim households but annotated little else about the householders. As we will see below, late nineteenth-century changes to this basic pattern included the development of new structural features and the increasing use of exterior ornament to announce the status of the household.

USING HOUSES

Houses in the city often accommodated more than one generation of a family and more than one type of use, especially in commercial areas where houses were combined with a shop on the ground floor. In multistory buildings, the stairway separated the residence from the shop or office, a device that kept the mixing of sexes to an absolute minimum in the commercial parts of the city. Writing in 1890, an Indian author from Delhi, a city comparable to Lahore in social composition, emphasized that "respectable" families unfailingly segregated work from residence and women from men: "In the large towns there are no shops in the family quarters, and no respectable families living in bazaars. The partition of sexes during business hours is complete, and you never see a woman in charge of a shop except it be . . . some poor hapless, helpless creature without friends or relatives in some odd corner."[8]

On the ground floor, shops were opened to the street outside during business hours by swinging the double leaves of a large wooden entry door inward on their pivots and moving the goods for sale out onto a narrow *tharra*, or raised platform, that ran the length of the street facade.[9] Most shops had a wooden awning above the *tharra*, and during business hours a cloth was unfurled from its lower edge to keep the shopkeeper out of the sun. Shopkeepers sat on the *tharra* while conducting business, and customers stood in the street (Figures 4.21, 4.22). Indeed, "sitting" and "selling" were synonymous in some linguistic registers: During the colonial period, city authorities required shopkeepers, stallholders, and "sitters" to keep their premises in a clean state; to describe a woman "sitting" in the bazaar was to imply that she was a prostitute.[10]

Shops in the bazaar deployed various strategies for attracting customers, including lavish or colorful displays of goods and verbal or visual assurances that their wares were good and their prices fair. Eliza Scidmore, an American who visited Lahore during the winter of 1902, described a tour through the city, noting "the cloth dyer stirring his vats, wringing out lengths of cloth and festooning them over the front of his shop" and "the printer, next door, stamping block patterns on turban ends . . . [and elsewhere] heaps of oranges and pale bananas, red Kashmiri apples, and green Kabul grapes [forming] set color studies on every fruit stand." Scidmore described the half-mile stretch of bazaar between Delhi Gate and the Sonehri Masjid (Golden Mosque) as "the heart of Lahore," where every alcove and shop was "set for theatrical effect and overflowed to the street."[11] Herbert Compton, writing at around the same time, noted shopkeepers attesting to their fairness and integrity by "ostentatiously" suspending their empty scales before the customer "to demonstrate that they hang evenly."[12]

Away from the main bazaars, where purely residential buildings predominated, the facade and rooms on the street level differed from shops in the bazaar. Gone for the most part were the raised *tharras* along the street, and a single entry door (sometimes raised a few steps above the street) led into the ground-floor rooms. Every level of the house flexibly performed some sort of domestic function, and each of the upper floors made accommodation for what was usually more than one generation of a family living together in the same structure. Ground-floor rooms were sometimes used as work spaces and were sometimes rented out or used for storage, but they were seldom used for living, since the lowest floor of the house was considered the least desirable space. "The rooms on the ground floor are dark and gloomy," wrote Jya Ram, an employee in the Punjab government, "and are often occupied by poor people who cannot afford to hire better houses. In some cases it is left untenanted to provide room for building materials, fuel and dry forage."[13] Gopal Das Bhandari, a member of Punjab's Sanitary Board, wrote that "the lower parts of the houses

Figure 4.21. Street scene inside Lohari Gate, Lahore, circa 1904. Copyright The British Library Board. OIOC Photo 1007/7/844; all rights reserved.

Figure 4.22. Street scene outside Masjid Wazir Khan, Lahore, circa 1904. Notice the merchants seated on a platform at the edge of the street. Copyright The British Library Board. OIOC Photo 50a(16); all rights reserved.

[in Punjab's cities] cannot with any decency have a place within the term 'human habitable premises.'"[14]

Those who could afford a multistory dwelling, therefore, preferred to live above the street on an upper floor. "Suppose you are in the actual heaven of an upper story where a middle class Hindu family resides," Jya Ram wrote in his description of a Delhi house; "one or two poor prints representing Hindu Gods and Goddesses and a looking glass adorn the walls of one of the verandahs. . . . there is little furniture except small square seats called *pirhas* for the women; a few *charpais* [short four-poster beds or cots with woven string platforms] lying naked in the *kothas* [rooms] with piles of cloth on them or standing along the walls and basking in the sun; and a few durries and mats."[15] Most household furniture was lightweight and movable, allowing for use in different rooms according to the need, the time of day, the season, or who was present at any given time.

Individual rooms were also flexible in use, with the same spaces being used for different purposes at different times. For example, the desire on the part of many families to physically separate the women of a household from male visitors (a practice called *purdah*) could be accomplished even in small houses that lacked a separate area for women *(zenana)*. When male visitors called, women would simply move out of sight, where feasible, to a separate room farther back from the street or to another level of the house. Seasonal changes in the way spaces were used also received architectural elaboration. During the summer, members of a household were likely to sleep outside on the roof, which was also where women would spend most winter days. Beds could be easily moved onto the roof for sleeping and stored vertically along one wall to provide extra space during the day. In the cooler winter months, beds would be moved downstairs and laid out at night in an inner room of the house. "The general habit of sleeping on the roof in the hot weather leads to constant competition [in the cities]," wrote Hugh Rose in his report on the 1901 census, "it being an object of ambition to secure absolute privacy by raising one's house higher than one's neighbors."[16] Perforated brick walls from three to five feet high ran along the edge of the roof, providing visual privacy and allowing for the unimpeded circulation of breezes.

On the rare occasions when Europeans toured the interiors of Indian houses, they commented on the general lack of furnishings: "The furniture in most of the city houses is of the barest description," wrote Gordon Walker in the 1893 *Gazetteer of the Lahore District;* "a piece of carpet or a munj mat, a few wooden boards, some reed stools about half a foot high, woven with cotton thread, and a number of ordinary cots complete the furniture of an ordinary trader's house."[17] Compton made the exaggerated claim that Indian houses had "no furniture" whatsoever: "Chairs and tables are unknown in Indian native life, not to mention glazed windows and chimneys. . . . Cover the floor with mats or carpets and you have finished his house-furnishing." For Compton, the absence of furnishing made it difficult to distinguish the houses of the rich from the houses of the poor, and both lacked "that spirit which lends enchantment to our own idea of home life." These observations reflect a widely shared sentiment among the British community that the Indian house lacked the comforts and middle-class refinements that distinguished the English "home." "To summarize the Indian home," Compton wrote, "you may say that it affords shelter from the sun and rain, and supplies that amount of privacy which walls can afford. But when you seek for comfort, taste, and decoration, you seek in vain."[18]

ARCHITECTURAL CHANGES TO INDIAN HOUSES

The preceding section laid out the recurring patterns of use and appearance of the ordinary city house. The relatively simple and ubiquitous repetition of a one-, two-, or three-room plan on each level allowed for the flexible use of each space and on each level of the house and set a simple but enduring pattern for all subsequent expansions. Isolated both from its neighbors and from the street outside by structure and plan, no less than by its internal plumbing, the aggregate form of Lahore's urban houses traced out both the limits of individual property ownership in the city and a zone of interaction between members of the household and the sweepers, sellers, customers, and renters who moved regularly across their threshold. Ornament on houses was conventional, minimal, and concentrated mostly around windows and doors. The exterior facades of houses bore little burden in terms of annotating the status of households: "The size and quality of houses do not vary with the means of their occupants," one British commentator noted; "decayed gentlefolk live in corners of large old houses. Rich traders sometimes live in hovels."[19] The British assumption that the interiors of houses should reflect the taste and character of the family was seen not to fit the Indian house: In the houses of rich and poor alike, furniture was minimal, lightweight, and movable, unadorned alcoves provided for storage, and there was little evidence of the "tasteful decoration" that indexed British notions of domestic comfort and respectability.

Each of these things underwent change during the late nineteenth and early twentieth centuries, though change was selective, gradual, and uneven. Houses with all the general features described above continued to be built, of course, as should be made clear by my use of colonial documents to describe them. Nevertheless, it would be inaccurate to characterize the vernacular architecture of Lahore as unchanging or sedimented in timeless forms. On the contrary, owners and builders of houses in the city often valued innovation and were quick to adapt their buildings to accommodate new architectural ideas.

The Indian house in late nineteenth-century Lahore was both praised by British observers for its "unstudied simplicity" and denigrated for its lack of "comfort, taste, and decoration." Both of these assessments relied on partial—largely visual—evidence, a lack of familiarity with the domestic routines and material qualities of Indian houses, and an Anglo-Victorian bias toward the material coordinates and symbolic importance of the concept of "home." When we look at changes made to Indian houses during the same period, however, we find that the notions that domestic architecture was "unstudied" in any simple sense or that Indian homes lacked attention to comfort and taste are largely misplaced. Beginning in the late nineteenth century, Indian domestic design underwent significant changes in response to discourses on urban sanitation, the availability of new technologies and materials, new aesthetic concerns circulating through both architectural curricula and print media, and discussion of the proper formation of the "modern" family. Traditional craftsmen and *mistris* were joined by sanitarians, religious reformers, architects, publishers, magistrates, elected officials, and purveyors of goods of all sorts, who together placed the production of city houses into a much wider discursive field. Changes were not simply confined to the individual architectural artifact; the newly reworked house became the building block for a new kind of suburban development in the city, in a process whose ineluctable force was marked by the formation of a town planning body in Lahore in 1919 to guide suburban expansion.

One of the most powerful forces driving changes in residential design in Lahore was a vigorous discourse, furthered in manifold ways, on urban sanitation and public health.[20] The connection between urban buildings, streets, and public health was the subject of both official regulations and unofficial commentary and concern. In official circles, sanitation and public health were vested chiefly in the municipality. The Lahore Municipal Committee (LMC) was formed in 1862, twelve years after the central government passed the Municipal Act for all of India that mandated the establishment of such committees. In the early years of the LMC, both British and Indian members were appointed by the district commissioner, who was always British. Close government control over the affairs of the committee ensured that only prominent (and loyal) Indian residents were asked to serve. Even when positions on the committee became subject to popular election, following reforms in 1882, Indian members of the LMC were drawn, by virtue of qualifying criteria, from the middle and upper classes.[21] The bulk of the committee's work focused on conservation and taxation, and until the mid-1880s little attention or control was exercised over building construction in the city.

A revised act was extended to Lahore in 1884, however, that provided legal mechanisms for the LMC to regulate construction practices, oversee the erection of buildings within municipal limits, and require the submittal of building plans prior to construction.[22] Building plans were scrutinized for evidence of structural integrity, and site plans were required to show building alignment with the street (to prevent encroachment on public property) and the means for disposing of wastewater to a central drain. Builders submitted a form with their plans giving the date of application, the name of the applicant and the applicant's father, and the *mohalla* (rather than the street) in which the building was being erected. The general thrust of the required plans, therefore, was to ensure that issues of safety and sanitation were attended to. In this way, building applications assigned responsibility for upholding public health to families and individuals belonging to named areas of the city. They also required owners to include hired draftsmen in the process of construction, where previously only a *mistri*, specialized craftsmen, and common laborers had been involved in the task. As we saw in chapter 3, more often than not draftsmen in the city were trained at the Mayo School of Art, where instruction in technical drawing was indissociable from a pedagogy that emphasized a close relation between architectural form and social identity. Like all such putatively neutral regulatory documents, therefore, building permit applications provided a discursive link between technical and social domains, one that connected the efficient disposal of waste, however distantly, to the cultivation of "artistic" sensibility.

A further development brought sanitary discourse more fully into processes of house production beginning in 1887, when provincial sanitary boards were set up across India, with responsibility for both rural and municipal sanitation. From 1887 onward, biannual inspection reports on municipalities were filed with the municipal committee by a provincial sanitary engineer.[23] These reports were street-by-street, *mohalla*-by-*mohalla* graphic descriptions of the city's sanitary failings, written in a style of exhortatory rhetoric first crafted by people like Edwin Chadwick in midcentury England.[24] This excerpt from the conclusion of a report on Lahore by Crawford Roe, sanitary commissioner of Punjab in 1897, is typical of the genre's exhortatory style and reliance on (and grounding of authority in) the power of sensory observation:

> Let anyone visit some of the places I have mentioned [in this report], breathe its air, taste its water and eat its food; let him enter some of the yards, taking care where he treads, and follow the guidance of his olfactory nerves into some of its recesses, and then reflect whether such sickening evils as one hour's enquiry will have shown him ought to be the habit of the masses of the people, and whether it is not a blot on civilization that

such things exist in the midst of us, and the interests of human life remain almost uncared for.[25]

Part exposé, part exhortation to action, and sometimes part picaresque humor, sanitary reports helped translate the indigenous quarters of Indian cities into the emotive and pseudoscientific verbal imagery that gave sanitary reforms in England at the time their purchase on middle-class activist sentiment. Intended primarily for official channels of communication, both the style of writing and the normative prescriptions found in these reports found their way into vernacular pamphlets and treatises. As early as 1868, the sanitary commissioner of Punjab, A. C. DeRenzy, established programs in Lahore, Amritsar, Delhi, and Multan to train *hakims* (native medical practitioners) in "the diagnosis of disease, general hygiene, and disinfecting arrangements."[26] And while the colonial government resisted suggestions to create sanitary commissions made up solely of Indian members, colonial officials readily admitted that native medical practitioners and systems of medicine were far more popular and widespread in Punjab than Western allopathic practitioners.[27]

In Lahore, beginning in the late 1880s, Urdu pamphlets and treatises on urban sanitation, public health, and a range of infectious diseases (including plague, smallpox, and fevers) were published by Indian authors in the city.[28] Many of these publications included lithographic images of familiar urban settings, highlighting both "good" and "bad" arrangements and practices. An Urdu treatise on the prevention of plague written in 1890, after the rat flea had been isolated as the vector of that disease,[29] provided illustrations of animals living in residential quarters, leaking sacks of grain piled on shop-front *tharra*s, unwashed dishes piled carelessly in cooking areas, and telltale inscriptions on the outer walls of buildings documenting the number of plague rats killed on the premises (Figures 4.23, 4.24).[30] These works cast familiar urban imagery into a new network of statements about how urban settings and mundane daily practices should be reorganized to prevent the spread of disease. By combining scientific arguments with detailed descriptions and visual depictions of customs and habits that led to ill health, public health discourse drew the space of the home and the urban neighborhood into the picture as crucial sites for both the production, and prevention, of sickness and death.

Vernacular publications helped address lacunae in official discourse on the city, since the colonial government rarely made detailed enquiries into the physical space of Indian residences. Lala Kashi Ram, author of an 1884 pamphlet published in both Urdu and English, drew attention to the colonial government's reluctance to intervene in the private spaces of the city's Indian residents. "We see that the public thoroughfares of towns which have been under the supervision of municipal establishments are generally clean," Kashi Ram wrote, "but the Government could not venture to permit its officials to look after the private dwelling quarters, and these . . . are as dirty as ever."[31] Kashi Ram, who subscribed to the miasmic theory of disease, saw structural features of houses, from their insufficient handling of human waste to their inadequate provision of natural light and ventilation, as complicit in the generally poor state of health and high mortality in the city: "The urban population

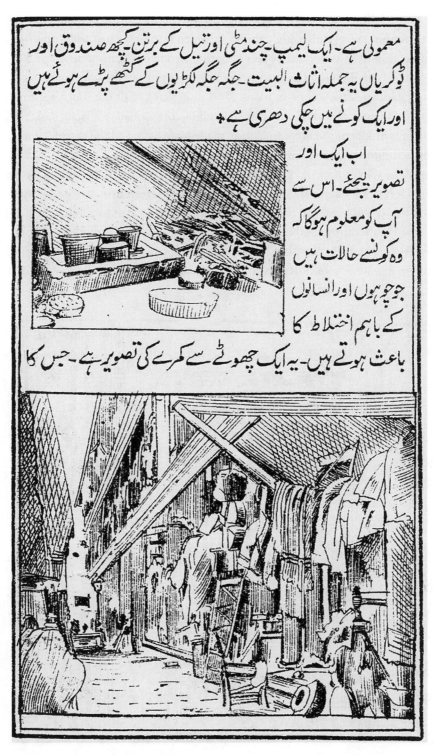

معمولی ہے ۔ ایک لیمپ ۔ چند مٹی اور تیل کے برتن ۔ کچھ صندوق اور ٹوکریاں یہ جملہ اثاث البیت ۔ جگہ جگہ لکڑیوں کے گٹھے پڑے ہوئے ہیں اور ایک کونے میں چکی دھری ہے +

اب ایک اور تصویر لیجئے ۔ اس سے آپ کو معلوم ہوگا کہ وہ کونسے حالات ہیں جو چوہوں اور انسانوں کے باہم اختلاط کا باعث ہوتے ہیں ۔ یہ ایک چھوٹے سے کمرے کی تصویر ہے ۔ جس کا

Figure 4.23. Page of lithographs depicting an untidy kitchen (top), and residential street in the city. From Gulam Nabi Adir, Chuha aur Plague, Billi aur Chuha, aur Mohafiz-e-Jaan Tika *[Rat and Plague, Cat and Rat, and a Guard] (Lahore, 1890), n.p.*

lives in towns having narrow and tortuous lanes, with overcrowded, damp, ill-ventilated and dirty houses several stories high, the air of which is impregnated with impurities arising from . . . exhalations from the bodies of both men and cattle, from privies reeking with liquid excreta, from dung-hills or heaps of filth of all sorts, from the stagnant sewage which, owing to faulty construction or in many cases utter want of drains, does not find a free exit."[32] M. L. Dhingra, an Indian physician in London, complained that faulty design exposed the occupants of Indian dwellings to bad air, inadequate light, and the harmful emanations of fermented filth uncovered during the excavation of foundations: "While everybody is thinking of the water problem," Dhingra wrote, "houses continue to be built in violation of every principle of sanitary architecture. . . . buildings are erected on 'made soil,' there is no provision for air and light, and the condition of privies is such as to allow of easy percolation of fœcal matter through the roofs. It is small wonder, then, if dwellers of these overcrowded areas, with their nutrition already below par, fall an easy prey to one or other of the zymotic diseases."[33] Kashi Ram warned his readers that "the soil on which [Lahore]

Figure 4.24. Lithograph depicting inner-city alley annotated with graffiti indicating the number of plague rats killed in the area. From Gulam Nabi Adir, Chuha aur Plague, Billi aur Chuha, aur Mohafiz-e-Jaan Tika *[Rat and Plague, Cat and Rat, and a Guard] (Lahore, 1890), n.p.*

presently stands is no more than that of a graveyard and a collection of the debris of decayed animal, vegetable and all sorts of filthy matter heaped together in the course of many centuries. . . . it is in these dwelling quarters of towns and cities, overcrowded, unventilated, unsewered, and often undrained, that fevers originate and find a congenial habitat."[34]

These ideas, circulating in both English and vernacular writings, informed building practice in direct ways. By the turn of the twentieth century, builders had taken measures to improve drainage and sanitation in houses by attending to internal and external plumbing, increasing the amount of light and air by adding ventilating apertures (*chandaans*) in the upper portions of rooms, placing larger and more numerous windows in walls, and providing manual fans to help air circulate through the house. These changes gradually produced a new look in the residential architecture of the city, as *chandaans* and other types of ventilators proliferated, transom lights appeared above doors, and walls were pierced by larger and more numerous (often glazed) windows (Figures 4.25, 4.26). In his census report on Punjab in 1911, Pandit Harikishan Kaul remarked that "within the last ten years, a wonderful improvement has been made in the design of houses generally. . . . Windows are now very often put up in rooms which formerly had but one opening. Little grated apertures for admitting fresh air [*chandaans*] are also being introduced, and where there is an educated boy in the house he manages to stick up a ventilator whenever the rebuilding of the ancestral habitation is undertaken."[35] The same report noted that "the plinths of some newly built houses [have been] made rat-proof," a measure designed to reduce the risk of plague, and that the old system of building damp and unhealthy "underground cellars (*sardkhana*) for the excessively hot days of summer has been completely abandoned, as the adoption of *pankha*s (fans), [and] the use of ice and other cooling beverages" helped moderate the interior climate of houses. The newly revamped urban house thus stood out from its neighbors visually, as a "modernized" dwelling attuned to the physical health of its occupants.

In addition to focusing on the physical features of neighborhoods and houses, things that could be changed to improve public health, Indian writers and pamphleteers also drew attention to social and religious customs that led to poor hygiene. The practice of treating the sick and mourning the dead in houses, rather than hospitals or other specialized spaces, was of particular concern. Lala Kashi Ram described the cramped quarters of a typical Indian house, where a patient "lies on his bed and, if suffering from cholera, passes his evacuations from stomach and bowels. The other inmates sit all around on the same floor which only the minute before was flooded by the sufferer. One of the anxious relatives will now rise to get water to relieve the sick man's burning thirst, will take a vessel, wipe it with the body clothes which have been in contact with the contaminated floor and then dip it into the family supply of water, with hands reeking of the sick man's discharges." If the patient died, the author wrote, then the requisite mourning feast that followed exposed twenty or thirty other female friends and relatives to the cholera "poison"; some of them would inevitably carry it to their own homes and into "the stomach of the first member of the family requiring the aid of her clothes as a dish cloth."[36] Kashi Ram's focus on the questionable practices

Figure 4.25. A "modern" house in the Old City of Lahore, circa 1920s.

Figure 4.26. House and shop in Gowal Mandi, in Lahore's civil station, circa 1920s.

of women members of the household during the mourning ritual found echoes in other genres of literature that indirectly helped reshape domestic space.

A WOMAN'S DOMAIN?

The now-extensive literature on women's reform in nineteenth- and twentieth-century India has demonstrated the centrality of the physical space of the home, and of the discursive trope of women as the "spiritual essence of the home," in contemporary reformist litera-ture.[37] Reformers did not speak with a single voice, of course. In addition to drawing on different bases of religious authority to ground their views, Sikh, Muslim, and Hindu re-formists pursued different ideals, had different expectations, and judged by different criteria the competence required from women in a modernizing colonial context.[38] What all these groups shared, however, was a conviction that in their roles as mothers and wives, women were a critical component of a modern ideal of respectable middle-class domesticity. The mostly male authors exhorted a middle-class female audience to become "better compan-ions to their husbands, better mothers to their children," and more rational and effective managers of the household.[39] With regard to the latter goal in particular, the space of the home was seen as a crucial site for inculcating the new habits of thrift, discipline, and hygiene that gradually became hallmarks of the modern, respectable family.

For example, the customary seclusion of females in middle- and upper-class families was challenged on both sanitary and moral grounds in the city. Indian reformers complained that women's constitutions were dangerously weakened by denying women in *purdah* access to physical exercise outside the home and sequestering them in the dark and ill-ventilated quarters of the *zenana*. Public health statistics documenting high rates of female mortality in the city were sometimes adduced to support the point. "Imperfect ventilation is . . . a characteristic feature in all Hindu dwellings," wrote an unnamed author in the *Indian Mag-azine and Review* in 1891; "the sitting and reception rooms, intended for the male members of the family, are comparatively spacious; as is the *dalan* or hall for the celebration of the *puja*s and festivals that take place on the premises. . . . But in the *untuppoor* (*zenana*, or female apartments), in which the men are apt to sleep half their time away, a very limited number of cubic feet of air are allotted to each individual; and in the immediate neigh-bourhood are the cooking rooms, which have no proper outlet."[40]

While problems of light and ventilation could be resolved through architectural means, problems that stemmed from "custom" required the more difficult restructuring of habits. "It is to be hoped that our enlightened countrymen will try to relax the rigidity of the *pur-dah* system in their own families," wrote Lala Kashi Ram, "and permit their female relatives to frequent such quarters the atmosphere of which is calculated to refresh both the soul and the body." Nevertheless, Ram continued, "let it not be understood that I mean to advise them to imitate exactly the custom of the ruling race in this matter. . . . the moral atmos-phere of our country is full of impurities much more injurious than those the townswomen inhale within the precincts of the *zenana*."[41]

Writers never reached consensus, however, on whether the social practice of *purdah* should be retained or discarded or on whether the physical space of the *zenana* was desirable or not. Literary works like *Majalis un-Nissa* (Assemblies of Women), written in Lahore in 1874 by Khwaja Altaf Husain (better known as Hali, or "up to date"), used a conversation between *purdahnashin* (observers of *purdah*) women in a typical household in Delhi as its primary vehicle for conveying new ideals of domestic management, the obligations of marriage, and relations with one's family and servants. In Hali's work, the *zenana* was taken for granted, something underscored by his use of a dialect peculiar to the *zenana* in north India (*begamati zuban*).[42] Maulvi Abd-ul-Halim's novel *Badunisa aur Uski Musibat* (Badunisa and Her Misfortunes) (1898), on the other hand, was representative of several works that condemned the system of *purdah* altogether by showing how an irrational adherence to strict rules of segregation could lead to family ruin. In a case of mistaken identity caused by the veiling of two new sisters-in-law, the wrong husband slept with the wrong wife, thus dismantling both women's (and thus the family's) honor.

At stake in domestic reform literature was the formation of new domestic sensibilities, a complex of personal qualities, habits, and sentiments that would be cultivated and disciplined in the newly remade spaces of the home. While the physical space of the home forms the setting for most of these works, the architectural implications of this literature are harder to assess. The home that emerges in women's reform literature is seldom a wholly reconfigured space. Instead, it is a newly *reorganized* space, one whose rooms are kept clean and orderly and whose occupants are thrifty, diligent, and socially respectable. Perhaps the most direct architectural implication of this literature is its tendency to encourage the specialization of rooms for particular purposes and the fixing of activities and objects in space. "All the people of the house should make a habit of keeping each thing in its own place," wrote Maulana Ashraf 'Ali Thanawi in his *Bihishti Zewar* (Heavenly Ornaments), a guide to good conduct for young Muslim women written in the early 1900s. "Anyone who takes an item out to use should put it back in the same place, so that no one has to ask around and look all over to find it."[43] Fixing activities in space and making material alterations to accommodate them was presumed to enhance a woman's household efficiency. In Nazir Ahmad's book, *Mirat ul-'Arus (The Bride's Mirror)* (1869), the protagonist's attention to thrift and good order made the house a self-regulating "machine."[44] The *Mirat ul-'Arus* follows the activities of two young brides in the same household in Delhi. One is tempestuous and lazy and brings ruin onto the house, and the other (Asghari) is prudent, thrifty, and considerate. At one juncture in the book, the "good" bride Asghari is constrained to run the household on a mere twenty rupees per month following her father-in-law's transfer to Lahore. Left alone with her mother-in-law, her delinquent husband, and three servants, Asghari methodically transforms the house:

> Out of the five rupees which were left over [at the end of each month] there were gradually purchased two large platters, weighing five and ten seers, a tray, some small spoons, two drinking-vessels, one complete tea-set, and so on. Also she had two boxes made, and two chests of drawers—one for the kitchen and one for the store-closet—and

two new beds were furnished. In a word, out of her twenty rupees, Asghari furbished up the house to such an extent that in outward appearance it assumed a look of considerable grandeur. Thrift and good order were introduced by her into everything. . . . Whatever things were in the house used formerly to be left lying about in wonderful misarrangement, like cabbage-leaves or radishes. Now everything was in the right place. If you ask for the bundle of clothes, they are all tied up and arranged in order, with the clothes neatly folded inside them. Every vessel in the closet where the grain is stored, and water kept, is carefully covered up. The dishes, clean and bright, are put away in their proper places; those of china and copper apart. It was as if the house were a machine, with all its works in good order, and the key of the machine in Asghari's hands. Whenever she turned it, the machine began moving of itself.[45]

The new image of an orderly, functional, and spatially specialized household—with its "kitchen," "store-closet," and array of specialized receptacles—shares an affinity, perhaps, with other settings being created outside the home at the time in response to the colonial spatial imagination. These included anything from hospitals, schools, barracks, and factories to the space of the civil station itself, where residences were spatially and functionally separated from shops, roads made provision for the separation of vehicles and pedestrians, and written and unwritten rules asserted their claims over conduct. Put somewhat differently, despite the perception that colonial authority stopped at the threshold of the private home, the publicly enacted colonial spatial imagination produced effects beyond the public realm. Partha Chatterjee, among others, has argued that the "inner" domestic sphere in colonial India was increasingly isolated from the "outer" world of public life in indigenous discourse, producing a split between the "home" and the "world." In nationalist writings, Chatterjee argues, "the world *(bahir)* is the external, the domain of the material; [while] the home *(ghar)* represents our inner spiritual self, our true identity. The world is a treacherous terrain of the pursuit of material interests, where practical considerations reign supreme. It is also typically the domain of the male. The home in its essence must remain unaffected by the profane activities of the material world—and woman is its representation."[46] The regular illustration of the inner spaces of the home in newspapers, magazines, and the like—as well as its reorganization according to publicly aired opinions on sanitation, hygiene, and moral improvement—suggests that the isolated and private nature of the domestic sphere was more a figure of desire than reality. In addition to its role as the locus of "spiritual" culture, in other words, the newly organized and efficiently run home was equally a device for shaping the new public sensibilities that advanced family interests in colonial society.

STATUS AND THE NEW HOUSE FACADE

Alterations to the Indian house during the late nineteenth and early twentieth centuries were first and foremost concerned with the management of its interior and were only secondarily concerned with its outer appearance. In addition to the proliferation of household goods and appurtenances that eased the task of household management, new concepts about the function of rooms also emerged to mark a departure from previous practice. Perhaps the best illustration of what this entailed is found in a book of house plans published by an architect in Amritsar in the 1930s entitled *Joshi's Modern Designs*. In his introduction to the book, author and architect K. C. Joshi noted that "there are so many standard and authoritative books in the market on various subjects dealing with buildings and designing that the edition of a new book on the subject would ordinarily appear redundant. But some of them are too technical and the others have been written by specialists in certain branches of the science and art of building, dealing with their own branches of the subject only." Joshi's book, in contrast, was meant to be comprehensive, suiting the needs of the specialist builder as well as the lay "citizen with a few thousands to invest in a house of his own."[47] The book included chapters on the history of architecture, principles of concrete and brick construction, and a range of sample designs that could be used by the reader planning a house "of his own."

Perhaps the most striking aspect of Joshi's designs for "modern" inner-city row houses is how little their internal arrangement of rooms departs from older planning traditions. The first plan illustrated in the book is for a three-room house, whose description should be familiar from the discussion above (Figure 4.27):

> This is a three-storied building of artistic design meant generally for people living in congested areas in cities. Only the frontage faces the road. This suits shop keepers who in order to have full supervision over the household do not keep a shop separate from the residence. . . . The shop faces the road where the business is transacted and a suitable staircase is on the side entirely partitioned from the shop to observe strict privacy and not to interfere with the transaction at the shop as well as ladies coming down and going up stairs. (132–33)

In two designs for a house without a shop on the ground floor, a "sitting room" is provided "for the reception of friends where the *purdah* is observed" (136) (Figure 4.28). Another plan mentions that the "staircase ascends quite uninterruptedly," something Joshi suggested was best "for well to do citizens" (138). Indeed, what seems to have changed most in the interim between the late nineteenth century and the writing of Joshi's book was a fixing of spaces for separate uses; room designations had previously been more flexible. "It is a pity that most people on account of their poverty cannot afford to have separate bed rooms," Joshi wrote; "in most cases they have to content themselves by turning their sitting, drawing and reception rooms into bed rooms at night" (116). The labels Joshi used for rooms on his plans differ from the simple designations for rooms found in plans submitted to the municipality twenty or thirty years earlier. In Joshi's book, the traditional term *dalaan* is replaced with "verandah"; *kothi*s become "bedrooms" and "store rooms"; Joshi uses the terms "drawing room" *(kamra araam)*, "sitting room" *(baithnay ka kamra)*, and "ladies room" *(zenana baithak)* for spaces that would once have carried the single designation *kamara* (room) (Figures 4.29, 4.30).

Not only were spaces more specialized, but strategies for keeping different types of people separated from one another were also prominent. "[A] passage *[andarooni rasta ya gulli]* is a necessity in modern buildings, as it keeps the suites of the rooms independent of each other. This is a kind of *way,* which ensures the privacy and movement in the rooms" (117). The most important separations for Joshi were separations between men and women, and his text often invokes the interest of "orthodox" families in keeping clear separations between the sexes:

> It is desirable in new-fangled people to set the drawing room in the heart of the building on the front, as it will open into all the rooms and provides diversion; but to the contrary, the orthodox families, where the ladies observe *purdah,* simply despise this situation of the drawing room, as it interferes with the privacy of the ladies and their movements. In such cases it is best to have the drawing room on one side with a verandah on the front and a lobby on the other leading from the verandah to the inner apartment. The lobby preserves the privacy of all the rooms to which it leads and is indispensive *[sic]* in an orthodox family. (116)

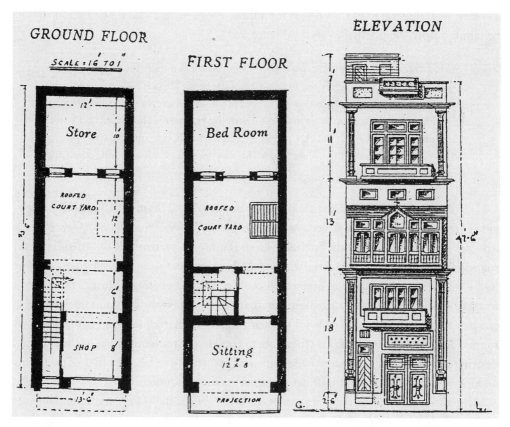

Figure 4.27. Plan and elevation for a three-room house. Notice that each set of windows has a ventilating aperture (chandaan) *above it. The wooden grilled opening* (magh) *in the center of the house on the first-floor plan covers an opening through each floor to the floor below. From K. C. Joshi,* Joshi's Modern Designs *(Amritsar: Ber Badhar Joshi, 1937), 133.*

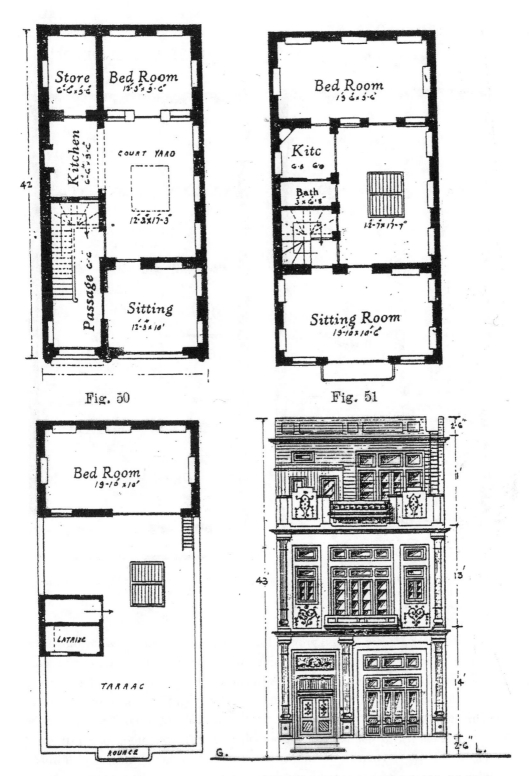

Store
6'-6"x5'-6"

Bed Room
12'-3"x5'-6"

Kitchen
6'-6"x5'-6"

COURT YARD

12'-3"x17'-3"

Passage 6'-6"

Sitting
12'-3"x10'

Fig. 50

Bed Room
13'-6"x5'-6"

Kitc
6'-8"x6'-0"

Bath
3'x6'-8"

12'-7"x17'-7"

Sitting Room
13'-10"x10'-6"

Fig. 51

Bed Room
13'-10"x10'

LATRINE

TARRACE

ROUNCE

G.

43'

2'-6"

13'

14'

2'-6"
L.

Figure 4.28. Elevation and plans for a house without a ground-floor shop. From K. C. Joshi, Joshi's Modern Designs (Amritsar: Ber Badhar Joshi, 1937), 135.

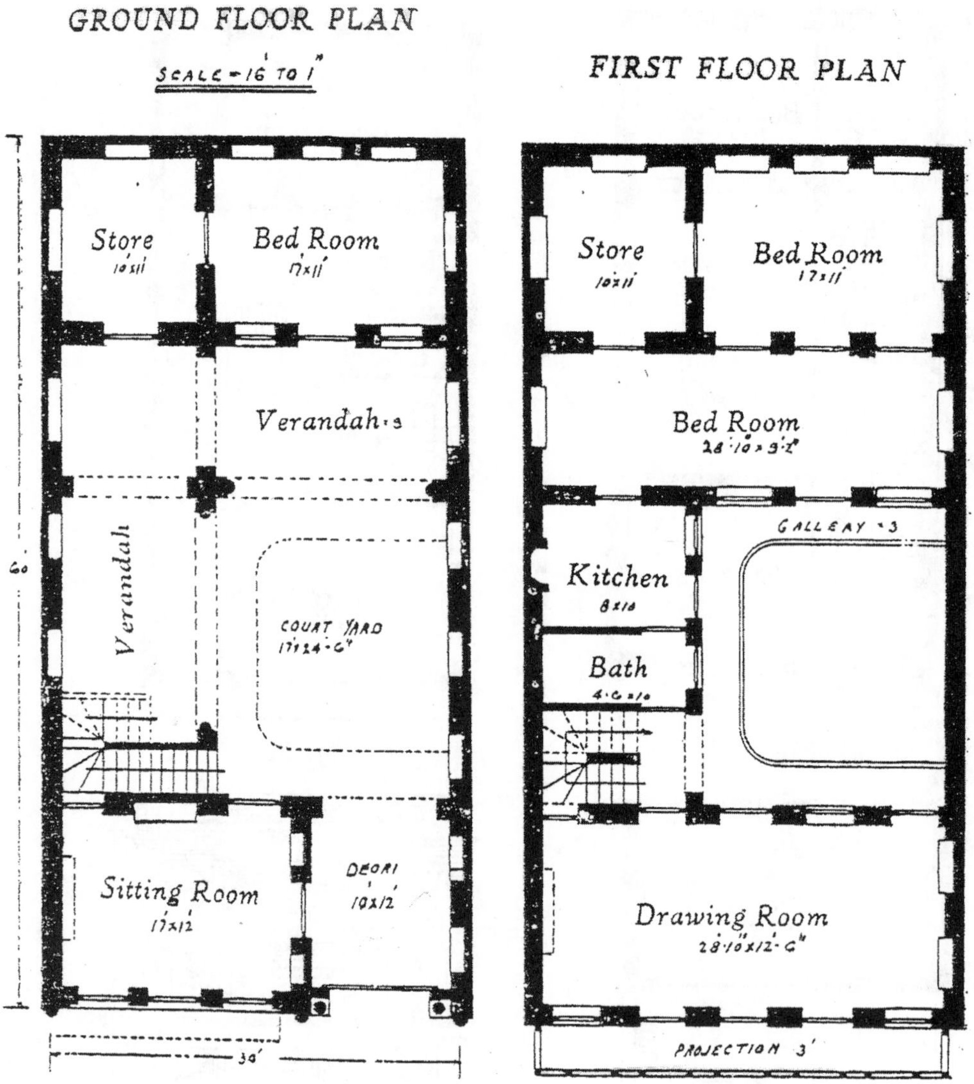

GROUND FLOOR PLAN

SCALE - 16 TO 1"

FIRST FLOOR PLAN

Store
10x11

Bed Room
17x11

Store
10x11

Bed Room
17x11

Verandah-3

Bed Room
28.10x9.2

Verandah

GALLERY -3

Kitchen
8x10

COURT YARD
17x24-6"

Bath
4.6x10

Sitting Room
17x12

DEORI
10x12

Drawing Room
28.10x12-6"

30'

PROJECTION 3'

Figure 4.29. Ground- and first-floor plans showing specifically designated spaces. From K. C. Joshi, Joshi's Modern Designs *(Amritsar: Ber Badhar Joshi, 1937), 138.*

While *Joshi's Modern Designs* provided ample visual material for use by those who desired to be "up-to-date," there was no contradiction between those desires and more "orthodox" and long-standing traditions of spatial use in the house. Many of Joshi's plans, for example, included a space for worship in the house *(puja ya parastish kamra),* something the author described as important to practitioners of all faiths and which bore on the "honesty and integrity of character" of the householder (119). Accommodating "orthodox" rules for the segregation of men and women fit as easily into Joshi's scheme, in other words, as did providing space for the newly introduced "motor cars" and designing for a cinema hall that would afford "all the necessities of a modern luxury" (284).

Joshi's book also reflects basic changes in the ornamental program of house facades by the 1930s. All of Joshi's row-house designs illustrate facade ornamentations that derive from Western neoclassical decorative traditions. Neoclassical pilasters, applied cornices and friezes, and decorative plaster festoons embellish these facades, and suitable designs for each of these features are appended to the end of the text (Figures 4.31, 4.32). Each of the houses Joshi illustrated were, in turn, linked to the type of resident the author considered them most suitable for, including specialized building plans for "shop-keepers," "citizens with a big family," "well to do gentlemen," "gentlemen of high culture," "advanced families," "high class [upper walay darjay kay] families," and, in one case, "a palatial bungalow intended for [the] premier [raisa] class." Joshi's facades are described, in turn, as "handsome," "imposing," "simple," "attractive," and "majestic," all of which suggests that Joshi's pattern book was sensitive to the kinds of social messages the newly "modern" house might bear in its outer appearance.

Until the turn of the twentieth century, it was uncommon for urban families to display wealth in visible or obvious ways. "Every day in large civil cases, in suits for dower, in dealing with ward's estates, in cases of elopement, thefts, burglaries, murders, and a thousand other

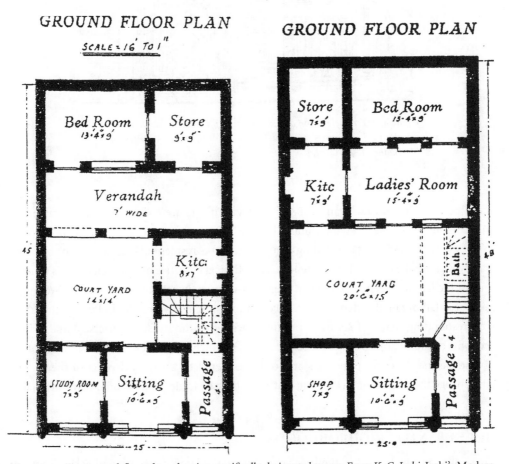

Figure 4.30. Two ground-floor plans showing specifically designated spaces. From K. C. Joshi, Joshi's Modern Designs (Amritsar: Ber Badhar Joshi, 1937), 136.

FRONT ELEVATION

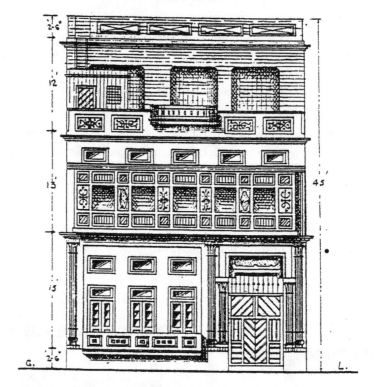

Figure 4.31. Front elevation of a single house illustrating facade
ornamentation. From K. C. Joshi, Joshi's Modern Designs *(Amritsar:
Ber Badhar Joshi, 1937), 139.*

ways," wrote Edward Maclagan in 1889, "the civil officers are constantly being confronted
with this enormous wealth lying [hidden] in the coffers of the people."[48] Joshi's book points
to a new desire on the part of building designers to make residential buildings in the city out-
wardly register the status of their owners. The physical evidence of this transition is ubiquitous in the late nineteenth- and early twentieth-century urban fabric of the city. We might
say that as Lahore matured into the fixed center of colonial government in Punjab, there was
a corresponding fixing of status in building facades in the Indian districts. While British
accounts of the city often emphasized the lack of predictability between the size and stature
of a house and the corresponding status of its residents, by the early decades of the twentieth century the display of wealth and status on house facades had become conventional.

HOUSES INTO NEIGHBORHOODS

I have shown how houses in the inner city during the late nineteenth and early twentieth
centuries were gradually altered in response to new technologies, new attitudes toward

public health and urban hygiene, vernacular reformist discourse, and new assumptions about the relationship between household appearance and social status. While basic typologies of internal arrangement remained remarkably consistent throughout this period, the external appearance of houses, and what was and could be said about them—what their rooms were used for, what they reflected about their occupants, and the role the house played in creating urban subjectivities—all underwent substantial alteration.

These changes were equally significant in houses built outside the Old City, in new neighborhoods developed during the late nineteenth and early twentieth centuries. As we have seen, at the time Lahore was first occupied by the British, several Indian *mohallas* and *abadis* were situated in the civil station. Largest among these were the neighborhoods of Mozang, Naulakha, and Kila Gujar Singh, each of which held several thousand residents. Throughout the last half of the nineteenth century these neighborhoods continued to grow in population. Beginning in the late 1880s, other Indian neighborhoods began to form in the civil station, built both by newcomers to the city and by residents of the Old City moving outward.

In a period of twelve years from 1868 to 1881, population in the civil station (including the neighborhoods above) increased approximately 30 percent, from 26,000 to nearly 34,000 people.[49] In 1890 a member of the sanitary board in Lahore attributed the recent population increase in the civil station to a "larger number of natives living in the suburbs."[50] In 1893, citing the desire by many residents to leave the unsanitary conditions of the Old City behind, another officer claimed that "any educated member of the native community who can afford it builds himself a house outside."[51]

FRONT ELEVATION

Figure 4.32. Front elevation of a row house illustrating facade ornamentation. From K. C. Joshi, Joshi's Modern Designs *(Amritsar: Ber Badhar Joshi, 1937), 147.*

A 1914 guidebook to the city described houses in the civil station as being "spread a considerable distance around. . . . most of the houses occupied by Lahore society are recent and have been built well within the last fifteen or twenty years. But the demand for houses still presses and landlords are active in meeting it." The guidebook's author, A. H. Pook, attributed the extramural growth of the city to "recent expansions in the executive and legislative departments of government, the strengthening of the chief court, the increased establishment required to control a Buildings and Roads Department with a charge so extensive and widespread as that of the present day, and, in particular, the recent extraordinary growth of trade and commerce and of the departments which deal with canal irrigation, railway, posts and telegraphs."[52]

These new settlements growing up around the old city differed from *mohalla*s in the inner city in terms of their overall siting, organization of streets, and density of construction. They differed in these same respects, too, from the nearby zone of civil-station bungalows occupied primarily by European residents. "In [Punjab's] cities and towns, houses are built cheek by jowl, i.e., wall to wall and back to back," wrote H. A. Rose in 1901, "but in the modern extensions of town, [houses] are as far as possible erected at a small distance from one another." Increasing pressure for space in the civil station led to denser configurations, however, something Rose drew attention to in the same report: "Where the rush is great and the area available limited, houses are springing up on the intervening spaces and consequently, the distance between these outlying houses is also decreasing."[53] Indeed, as the Indian quarters interspersed throughout the civil station grew in population, they seemed to evince an almost organic propensity to acquire the properties of the indigenous city itself: "The houses which are being built on the outskirts of the towns are built on *no principle*," wrote A. E. Barton in 1913; "a man will build a house wherever he can get a plot of land with utter disregard of its surroundings and the future development of the *abadi*. The result is that other men come and build their houses round him haphazard so the result is no better than the interior *abadi* of the town in point of congestion and bad sanitary arrangements."[54]

Concern over the future of spreading settlements prompted the Lahore Municipal Committee to commission a special report on urban expansion in 1908. At that time, complained the report's author, no complete survey of the Old City and civil station existed. Without such a plan, Halifax argued, the city could do little to ensure that development took place in the proper way. Referring to what plans he had available, Halifax noted areas of the city that were suitable for the houses of "Indian gentlemen," including the area between Temple and Ferozepur roads in the center of the civil station and vacant property in Gowal Mandi, near the Old City. "We might try and get one or more capitalists to come forward and lend us what we want for the acquisition of [these sites] to be repaid in a year or two with say 6 per cent interest," Halifax wrote, "on condition that we reserved selected plots for the people who found the money and with a view to our laying out the site into streets and dividing it into lots to be auctioned for the building of houses thereon in accordance with prescribed plans."[55] An earthquake that year centered in Kangra (a few hundred miles north of Lahore) diverted resources to unplanned repairs and brought an end to any grand schemes, but the idea of creating something like an overall urban plan for the city was kept alive.

What that plan should look like, however, was slow to come into focus. At a sanitary conference in Simla in 1913, Punjab's lieutenant governor, Michael O'Dwyer, characterized the options. The choice, in O'Dwyer's opinion, was between a low-density settlement pattern with wide streets and houses on individuated lots and a much more densely settled pattern of houses and shops more in keeping with "the people's ideal." O'Dwyer wrote that "you [conference attendees] have advocates among you of broad streets and bright well-ventilated houses; on the other hand, you are reminded that the traditional huddling together of poky little huts secures the highly prized objects of seclusion and mutual protection."[56] Another conference attendee noted that "the people (and also the municipal commissioners from whom they are drawn) have a strong prejudice in favor of huddling buildings together. They are quite seriously aggrieved when provision is made for unusually wide streets . . . [which] cause great heat, and render possible the accumulation of dust over very wide surfaces. The people's ideal . . . is the narrow winding lane, closed in, by preference, at the top with scraps of matting. Sometimes, on a day when a fierce hot wind is blowing, even the Englishman understands why the covered lane is preferred to the open boulevard."[57]

By 1919 a committee had been formed in Lahore to consider the planning of Lahore's growing suburbs.[58] In 1922 the Town Improvement Act was passed in Punjab establishing the legal framework for municipal improvement trusts.[59] From 1924 to 1926, Lahore was mapped at the scale of 330 feet to the inch, and surveys were carried out by Basil M. Sullivan, a consulting architect with the Punjab government and a member of Lahore's Improvement Trust Committee. In a report published in 1927, Sullivan described Lahore as "a 'live' and growing city," noting that the city's population had increased 22 percent from 1911 to 1921, to 257,295 people. Sullivan noted the existence of fourteen "layout plans" for sites in the civil station, but he disparaged their apparent effectiveness. "It is probably no exaggeration to say," he wrote, "that in the areas covered by the fourteen layouts, more houses are without roads and drains than with them."[60]

Sullivan's report was advisory, and the Improvement Trust Committee, working with the Lahore Municipal Committee, accomplished little for the first several years. Beginning in the early 1920s, however, Indian residents began building suburban settlements in Lahore's civil station with little oversight by government officials. In new developments like Kishan Nagar, Gowal Mandi, Ram Nagar, and Farooq Gunj, Indian residents crafted a model of urban residence and commercial organization largely on their own terms.[61] Each of these settlements was laid out in a gridiron of broad streets lined with multistory row houses (with shops on the ground floor on the major arteries) and provided for schools, religious buildings, and other shared amenities. The style of houses built in these areas predates the publication of Joshi's pattern book but would have fit harmoniously within its pages (Figure 4.33).

Figure 4.33. Street of houses in Purana Anarkali, an Indian suburb developed in the 1930s.

FROM NEIGHBORHOOD TO MODEL TOWN

While these new neighborhoods established an early but enduring pattern of planned sub-urban developments in the city, each of them relatively self-contained and subject to spa-tial restrictions based on private landholding, a much more comprehensive scheme was envisioned for Lahore at around the same time. This new settlement, Model Town, was built by middle-class Indian residents of Lahore—largely retired employees of the provincial and municipal governments—with funds collected through private subscription.[62] Prakash Tandon, author and former chairman of the board of Hindustan Lever, Inc., spent time in Model Town in the house of his retired father during the late 1930s and early 1940s and wrote about this experience in his memoir, *Punjabi Century*. Tandon's book provides a rare, and perhaps unique, retrospective sketch of social life in Model Town shortly after the set-tlement's inception. In Tandon's opinion, "Model Town was a place, the like of which had never been and will never be seen again."[63]

Model Town embodied many of the planning ideas developed by Ebenezer Howard in his book *Garden Cities of To-morrow*. Diwan Khem Chand, a barrister who studied for the bar in England in 1909, was the guiding force behind Model Town's creation and an admirer of Howard's ideals. Howard's garden city was meant to combine the restorative elements of the countryside (gardens and open space) with institutions appropriate for a decentralized civic society (small industry, shops, professional services, schools, and the like). While not trained as a physical planner, Howard published a series of diagrams in his book showing the garden city as having a circular plan, with radial streets, circumferential boule-vards, and a large open park at the center.[64]

Model Town's founders may have also received support from the Scottish town plan-ner Patrick Geddes, who visited Lahore during the winter of 1917, prior to the formalization of town planning in Punjab. Geddes held a number of official and unofficial positions in India between 1914 and 1919, including professor of civics and sociology at the University of Bombay and planning consultant to numerous municipalities and princely states.[65] In the latter capacity, Geddes wrote about fifty town-planning reports for several different Indian cities. These reports express a relatively sympathetic approach to the indigenous quarters of Indian cities, arguing for their conservation and improvement through "conservative surgery" rather than for wholesale demolition or slum clearance. The reports also address the growing need for housing outside the crowded quarters of Indian cities, however, and the model Geddes had in mind for new suburban developments clearly drew on Howard's garden city. In his 1917 report on Lahore, Geddes identified several sites outside the city suitable for planned "garden village" suburbs that had much in common with the garden-city model.[66]

In a publication that predated his trip to Lahore, Geddes wrote approvingly of Howard and the garden-city movement generally, and he cited the Hampstead Garden Suburb out-side London as a "great object lesson" worthy of imitation. While in Lahore, Geddes con-ducted a survey of the central city and surrounding neighborhoods and submitted a report to the Municipal Committee praising a new Indian suburb growing up outside the developed portion of town.[67] Whatever Geddes's role may have been, Howard's ideas were clearly circulating in Lahore around the time of his visit, and five years after Geddes filed his report, the planning of Model Town was well underway.

Just as Howard had envisioned for his garden-city scheme, the land for Model Town was purchased by a limited partnership company, the Co-operative Model Town Society, Limited. According to the bylaws of the society, house plots and open space were held in common, and individual houses were privately owned. The planners of Model Town took Howard's abstract ideas for the garden-city plan literally, turning the circular geometry and radial streets of his sketched diagram into a blueprint for actual construction (Figure 4.34). Each segment or "block" of Model Town had a park at its center, where buildings for public use were erected. These included schools, a mosque, a Sikh *gurudwara,* and Hindu temples in alternate blocks. Model Town also had its own library, school, *baraat ghar* (for hosting wedding parties), hospitals (male and female), post office, police station, cooperative store,

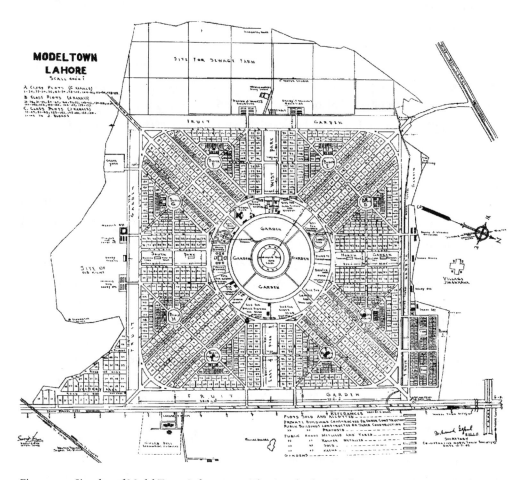

Figure 4.34. Site plan of Model Town, Lahore, 1949. The city of Lahore is about six miles northeast of this settlement. Source: The Co-operative Model Town Society, Limited.

and separate women's and men's clubhouses, the latter outfitted with billiard rooms, card rooms, and a formal dining hall.

For the first several years, electricity was produced at the society's own generating plant and water was provided to residents from several jointly owned tube wells. At the outer edges of the town, in addition to land given over to gardens and orchards, the society's planners built *dhobi ghats* (places for washing clothing), menials' and washermen's quarters, a Hindu cremation ground, and both Christian and Muslim cemeteries. Still farther away, outside the geometrical limits of the scheme, land was given over to a large sewage farm, a slaughterhouse, and plots for small-scale factories. These features made Model Town largely self-sufficient, and the day-to-day governance of the town was run locally by elected members of the society.

The first houses constructed in Model Town drew on the formal type of a British bungalow, with shade-filled verandahs, strict axial symmetry in both the facade and floor plan, and ample open space around the dwelling; auxiliary functions (such as servants' quarters and vehicle storage) were provided for in smaller structures placed at the rear of the house along one edge of the lot (see chapter 5). Tandon suggested that these buildings were familiar to Model Town's founders because many of them had occupied this kind of house during their years of peripatetic service in a series of government postings. Tandon described the early houses as stylistically "curiously alike," even though dwellings were more or less prestigious according to their proximity to the club on one side of the great circle (farthest away from Lahore) or to the area set aside for commercial activity on the other (Figure 4.35).[68]

Model Town's houses also departed from the British bungalow typology, however, in small but significant ways:

> Each house was divided into two parts by a huge vestibule in the middle. On one side were dining and drawing-room and an office room; on the other side the bedrooms, with dressing-rooms and bathrooms. The front verandah overlooked a lawn surrounded by flower-beds and cypresses. Here male visitors were received. On the other side was a verandah, where meals were served except on winter evenings, and an enclosed paved courtyard, the women's domain, with kitchen and storerooms. . . . *In its own way the house was like the British bungalows in front and grand-uncle's house at the back.*[69]

The zoning of domestic space in the house into male and female domains was accomplished more through use than through alteration of the bungalow's plan (Figure 4.36). Other differences, however, involved more physical kinds of changes. A study of building permit applications currently housed in the society's offices reveals that a common modification was made to these houses from the mid-1930s onward. As we saw above, Indian houses were often occupied by more than one generation of a family simultaneously; however, the single-level layout of the bungalow did not always make adequate provision for the coresidence of what were, in effect, separate households. Consequently, many Model Town residents added a second floor to their dwellings after some time, the new level often repeating the ground-floor plan exactly (Figure 4.37). Thus Model Town houses were expandable vertically in complete, replicated units, just like townhouses in the city.[70]

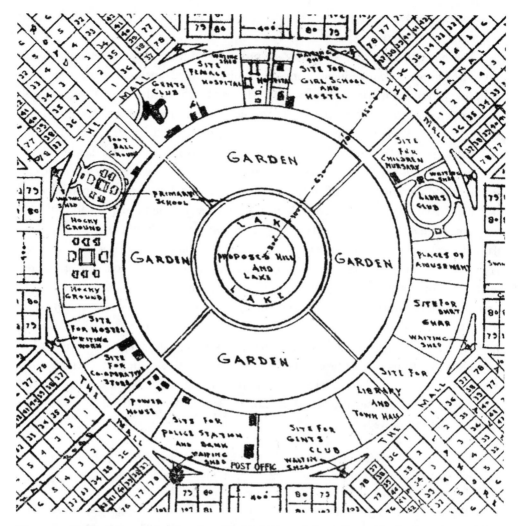

Figure 4.35. Detail of the central park and garden, Model Town, Lahore. Source: The Co-operative Model Town Society, Limited.

With very few exceptions, therefore, Model Town was a remarkably faithful repro-duction of Howard's progressive ideal—more faithful, perhaps, than Howard himself would have attempted. There is little doubt, moreover, that the physical organization of Model Town, along with the benefits that Howard argued would spring from such a scheme—the removal of social problems endemic to both cities and impoverished agricultural areas, and ultimately, the ushering in of a higher stage of civilization—place Model Town firmly within the tradition of materialist reform we have been considering thus far. Like the crim-inal tribe settlements and model agricultural villages discussed in chapter 2, Howard's gar-den city (and with it, Model Town) was a vivid statement of the widely shared belief that "reforming the physical environment can revolutionize the total life of a society."[71]

Certainly, a little-known English resident of Lahore named Esmee Mascall would have counted herself among those who shared that belief. Mascall grew up in Lahore as a young girl while her father worked for the North-Western Railway. In her memoir (written in 1907 or 1908), Mascall speculated about the kinds of attachments Lahore's Indian residents had to their traditional material environment and the disruption a scheme like Model Town might cause. Mascall wrote, "One can't imagine anything but furious resentment had the British authorities razed to the ground the ancient piled-up houses in that rabbit warren of narrow streets, and re-housed the City population in something so alien to their way of life as a neat Western-type 'New Town' environment." Such an "alien" change in environment,

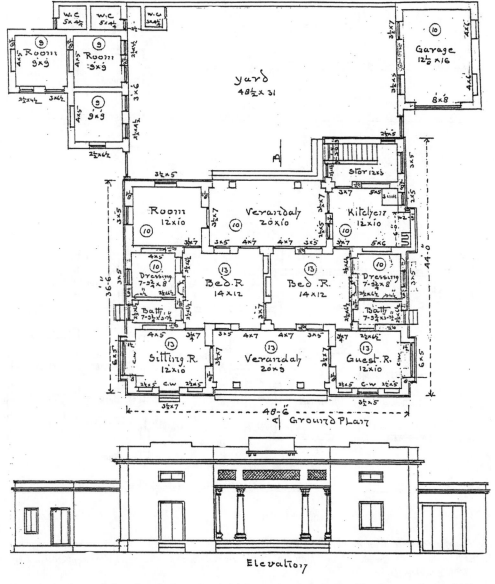

Figure 4.36. Plan and elevation of a house in Model Town, circa 1931. Source: The Co-operative Model Town Society, Limited.

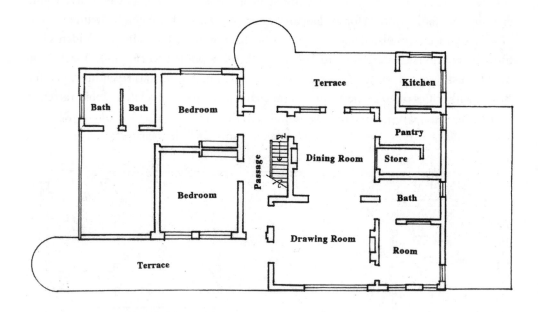

Proposed Second Level Plan

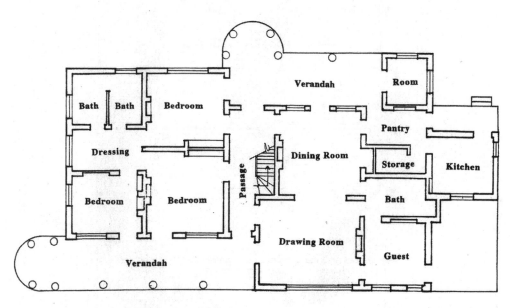

Existing Ground Level Plan

Figure 4.37. Ground- and second-level plans of a house being remodeled in Model Town, Lahore, circa 1940. Notice how closely the new second-level plan repeats the original floor below. Source: The Co-operative Model Town Society, Limited.

she feared, might destroy the inner substance of Indian culture—or at least its stereotypical outward expression: "Wouldn't the ancient Indian crafts have died out," she asked, "divorced from the crowded Indian way of life?"[72]

Mascall's statement would have an air of commonsensical good judgment about it, like most of the rest of her memoir, to anyone raised on the assumptions explored in this book. By the early decades of the twentieth century, as we have seen, this group would include Europeans and Indians alike. Nevertheless, Tandon's account of Model Town does not support those assumptions very well. In his memoir, Tandon emphasized the "traditional" or "conservative" way residents continued to lead their lives in Model Town, despite the changed environment they themselves had created according to a progressive British model. "All the old men began their day early," Tandon wrote, and spent the first hours of the morning outside walking, a practice observers of social life in Lahore's older neighborhoods repeatedly noticed as well. Women and men took afternoon walks separately, husbands and wives included, and Tandon observed "no real mixing of the sexes." Despite having two clubhouses fashioned after English models, there was "no club life" in Model Town to speak of, and the only social events Tandon claimed to have attended were religious holidays, "weddings, and head-shavings."

Despite the conservative social practices Model Town seemed to promote, however, none of its residents had a problem with the town's formal geometry. Ironically, it is only Tandon's Swedish wife Gaard who gets singled out in his account as somehow violating, if only gently, this affection for a certain kind of order. Growing tired of her father-in-law's rigorously symmetrical placement of the sitting-room furniture, Tandon's wife made nightly attempts to rearrange things along less orderly lines. Her efforts were frustrated, however, by Tandon's "old servant, [who] restored the order every morning until she gave up."[73]

CONCLUSION

Model Town's planners, in seeking out the spatial and material coordinates for a new kind of urban community, had no hesitation in adapting for the purpose Howard's garden city, a scheme whose intellectual roots may have been foreign but whose principles and assumptions had been made familiar over time in a multitude of colonial projects. At the same time, Model Town illuminates an important limit to the assumptions these projects were based on. Rehousing Lahore's Indian residents in a "neat Western-type 'New Town' environment" did not result in the destruction of an "Indian way of life" as some would, and did, predict. Despite the formal and institutional similarities between Model Town and Howard's garden city, Tandon's account emphasized both the radically new nature of this settlement *and* its residents' attachment to older ideas and institutions. Rather than overturning old customs and habits, the residents of Model Town took as much of the garden-city model as they wanted or needed, holding on to those elements of family and social life they wanted to preserve intact.

I began this chapter by arguing that the changes to vernacular and small-scale architecture in the city—and the many fields of discourse those changes engaged, grew out of,

CHANGING HOUSES

and altered along the way—constitute an important dimension of the process that made Lahore a modern city. By tracing changes in the ordinary houses of Lahore—both changes in their architectural treatment and their impact on suburban development—we gain a better sense of the role Indian residents played in that process than we could by limiting our focus to colonial institutions alone. Nevertheless, while my analysis above underscored British perceptions that "traditional" domestic architecture in the city eschewed progressive change, the inaccuracy of those perceptions did more than denigrate the agency of Indians in producing a distinctive urban modernity. They also marked out the contours of a widely shared anxiety about the implications of cultural hybridity, about the susceptibilities exposed in a culture when its most deeply private, personal, and culturally distinctive settings were altered through cultural mixing. As we will see in chapter 5, those anxieties were not limited to concerns over the impact of "Westernization" on Indian culture. Similar anxieties were expressed about the opposite effect: The impact that living in an Indian architectural milieu had on British culture.

ANXIETIES AT HOME

The Disquieting British Bungalow

5 Like many British officials who lived in India, William Owens Clark kept a diary.[1] Clark, who served as, among other positions, the chief judge of the Punjab High Court in Lahore (from 1898 to 1909), had a scientific bent of mind. His diary is most notable in this regard for its obsessive recording of the weather. Throughout the entire twenty-nine years of his sporadic diary entries (which span from 1877 to 1906), in addition to noting the condition of the sky and whether and how much it had rained, Clark regularly recorded the temperature at various times of day both inside his house and outside on the verandah. His measurements show that throughout the scorching hot days of summer, the encircling shade of the verandah kept the inner rooms of his house several degrees cooler than the temperature outside. Clark's repetitive recording of this fact suggests a certain attentiveness on his part to the way architectural features of his dwelling moderated the impact of climate on comfort.

In Clark's entry for August 11, 1878, just below his usual notes on the midday temperature ("90 degrees") and amount of rainfall ("Very heavy fall of rain about 8 am. Three and four-tenths inches between noon and 2:30 pm. Country flooded."), Clark made a neat pencil sketch of a floor plan entitled, simply, "Design for a house" (Figure 5.1). Nothing in this or any other entry tells us much about the reason Clark drew the design, though I am inclined to see in it an effort to pass time on a soggy monsoon afternoon when the prospect for accomplishing any normal kind of work would have been nullified by the deepening pools of rainwater in the streets outside. Whatever the circumstances of its production, Clark's design was for a slightly better house, more than likely, than the one he lived in at the time. I say "slightly" because the plan he sketched departed but little from the conventional house someone like Clark would have occupied.

As one might predict, Clark's preoccupation with the climate found graphic expression in his design. In addition to large, clear compass points marked on the perimeter of the drawing, Clark drew an open verandah (1) on the house's southwest corner beneath a deeply shaded overhang. On the north and east sides of the house, where the midday sun would be less intense, the verandah disappears altogether except for a narrow covered entryway. These features point to Clark's sensitivity to the architectonics of thermal comfort, but his sensibilities about an entirely different form of comfort are equally present in the design. Simply put, this was the comfort of propriety, of having the right sorts of things placed in the right kinds of relationships with one another.

For example, the covered entry on the northern wall, though not explicitly labeled, is unmistakably meant for servants. Clark's note beneath the drawing locating the unseen "cook room and outhouses away to North E." makes this all but certain. Servants would inevitably use the "back" entry of the house, making the southern facade the "front." Clark indicates as much (without explicitly saying it) through the most economical of means: a slight symmetrical curve in the line marking the southern verandah points toward a noted, but unseen, "avenue to South." These three simple words, along with the slight penciled gesture toward a portico, suffice to evoke the formal entry to a modest, but gentrified, estate. Each of the bedrooms in his plan has its own private dressing room and bath, while the most public room of the house—the *kutchery* (literally "court," but also the common term for a room

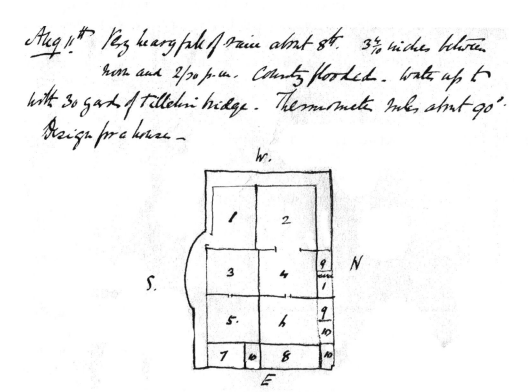

Figure 5.1. Page from the diary of William Owens Clark, chief judge of the Punjab High Court, 1898–1909. The rooms shown here are (1) verandahs, (2) kutchery (room to conduct business with visitors), (3) sitting room, (4) dining room, (5) and (6) bedrooms, (7) and (8) dressing rooms, (9) storerooms, and (10) bathrooms. Copyright The British Library Board. OIOC MSS Eur A148/1; all rights reserved.

to conduct official business with visitors)—was separated from the most private bedrooms by an intervening dining room.

The notes that accompany Clark's drawing refer more explicitly to his sense of desirable material refinements. According to his notes, the ceiling of the new house would be covered with reed mats set in "chuna" (*chunam,* lime cement) to provide something "like a plaster ceiling." The floors of the house would be covered with brick tiles rather than the more common surface of packed clay, except at the base of each unmarked fireplace, where Clark envisioned a surface of "enameled tiles" instead. Rather than using common and flimsy split bamboo "chicks" as coverings for doors and windows, Clark imagined using more costly but durable "perforated tin doors," which would allow breezes to enter the house freely while keeping everything (and everyone) else out. While the "ottoman and sofa" in Clark's imaginary sitting room would be made out of inexpensive local wicker *(kanak),* he envisioned them "covered with chintz" like the furniture at "Cla—— [indecipherable]," a place no doubt fondly tucked away in Clark's memory.

Clark's informal little sketch, the product of perhaps an hour's diversion, is noteworthy for how much implicit and explicit information it contains about an ordinary British official's house in the colony. With tremendous economy of means, his sketch evokes a complicated mapping of distinctly British notions of domestic propriety onto an equally distinct colonial artifact. The plan Clark drew is recognizably that of a bungalow, the most common form of expatriate house used by British residents in India. It is decidedly not, moreover, the plan of a house in England.

The travel account of Nawab Mehdi Hasan Khan, the chief justice of Hyderabad, who visited London in 1890, offers a better description of the latter. "I am very much amused to witness English home life," Khan wrote, noting that he considered "home" to be "a word employed chiefly in the elevated style" in England:

> I had heard the word so often that I was anxious to see an English home and real home life. This is a small cozy house, tastefully furnished. . . . Throughout the central parts of London there are large buildings of five or six stories, rented either by flats or rooms. In many cases these buildings are separated from the street in front by railings, with a small gate in front leading up a short flight of steps to a door which is numbered. Inside, generally, the dining room is on the ground floor, the drawing room on the first, and the bedrooms above. Beneath the ground floor are the rooms for servants and the kitchen. This is the kind of abode in which our retired Lieutenant Governors live.[2]

Khan's account highlights the "elevated" status of the English home in the minds of that island's inhabitants, just as it alludes to differences between English homes in England and English homes in colonial India. Whereas the typical retired lieutenant governor's London row house (as described by Khan) was seen as "small" and "cozy," the active lieutenant governor's residence in India at the time was certain to be a much grander affair. Such a house in India was not simply the residence of a loyal and well-placed government servant but also, according to Thomas Metcalf, "a representation of the authority of an imperial power and the residence of that power's representative in the colony."[3]

While this may have been true for India's largest official residences, it would not have been true of the far humbler structures that were home to the vast majority of British residents in India. Clark's design was a representative example; most officials' houses were much simpler indeed. "They were sitting in the verandah of 'the splendid palace of an Indian Pro-Consul,'" one of Rudyard Kipling's stories begins, in a passage dripping with sarcasm: "In plain English it was a one-storied, ten-roomed, whitewashed mud-roofed bungalow, set in a dry garden of dusty tamarisk trees and divided from the road by a low mud wall."[4] Nevertheless, as a visible feature of the landscape, these simple homes shared some of the physical and symbolic gestures of exclusivity that characterized the empire's largest official residences. Small or large, most British houses were isolated from their Indian surroundings by walls and gates; most were set in large open lots; and most were raised honorifically above their surroundings on a stepped plinth. Even simple houses were sometimes adorned with neoclassical or Gothic-revival ornament, features that alluded both to extralocal sources of cultural authority and to contemporary fashions in the distant metropole.

The ordinary colonial bungalow was much more than a symbolic visual form, however. It was also a key site for practicing a kind of expatriate domesticity aimed at cultivating the values, tastes, and dispositions that separated ruler from ruled.[5] The bungalow was seen as a refuge from the strange and unfamiliar world outside; a bulwark against losing one's "culture," going "native," or simply surrendering to a slow process of dissipation.[6] The material culture of the building itself was considered essential to its effectiveness, to its ability to preserve family virtue. And preserving family virtue—indeed, improving that of the local population—was a subject of explicit concern: "Britons were quite open in their efforts to impose their values on local domestic arrangements," write John and Jean Comaroff in their study of colonial Africa, "and they never doubted that buildings embodied particular moral principles of conjugality and kinship."[7]

The colonial bungalow can therefore be thought of as an important component of rule, and not only as an isolated zone of British repose. The transplanted European in a colonial domicile, through an industrious application of effort, could enact the ideals of cleanliness, thrift, and order required to run both the home and the empire effectively, and parallels were often drawn between these two: "We do not wish to advocate an unholy haughtiness," wrote Flora Annie Steel in her 1888 book, *The Complete Indian Housekeeper and Cook,* "but an Indian household can no more be governed peacefully, without dignity and prestige, than an Indian Empire."[8] The bungalow, along with its compound and coterie of servants, was regularly used as a metonym for empire. The housebound narrator of Rudyard Kipling's humorous sketch "The Private Services Commission" (1887) refers to himself as the "State" and to the staff of his bungalow compound as a faction-ridden colonial population in miniature.[9] In a closing passage of the story, the narrator brings a halt to his staff's petty factional infighting by drawing a line across the tennis court that stands between his bungalow and the servant's quarters beyond and delivering an ultimatum:

Oh people! On the side of the line which is furthest from my house you may scream and fight and bully and intrigue as you will, for at this distance your voices cannot reach me. But if I hear noises—unseemly noises—which break my rest, I shall know that you have crossed the line and evil will follow. The *khansamah* [head male servant] through whose hands my money passes has cheated the punkah coolies, who are rustic folk unable to protect themselves. These therefore I shall myself pay. The *khansamah* has also cheated you as you cheat one another, and all collectively rob me. Therefore I shall not now dismiss the *khansamah,* nor shall I dismiss you. Once a week because the weather is warm, I shall sprinkle *phenyle-ke-diwai* [phenyl disinfectant] in and about the *serai* and shall severely punish all uncleanliness; because this is a danger to me. (241–42)

Having thus established order, Kipling's narrator enjoys the fruits of a well-run domain. "Curiously enough," he concludes, "my people are happy. I think this must be because they are allowed free scope to develop their national characteristics" and are kept guessing what high-handed action their master may take next (242). Keeping his servants guessing is an apt metaphor, indeed, for the distancing postures adopted by the British in India more generally to keep rulers aloof from the ruled. Facile claims, like Steel's or as implied by Kipling, of an isomorphism between empire and bungalow compound did not always end by evoking mastery, however. They were equally likely to hint at the anxieties of alienation and an inability to assert control. As this chapter will show, a wealth of evidence suggests that the colonial home in India was a place both familiar and strange to its occupants, a source of both homely comfort and disquieting anxiety.[10] Even as the English home in colonial India provided a setting for cultivating the dispositions that authorized colonial rule, they also gave presence to a kind of "Indian-ness" that both undermined those dispositions and produced a range of discomforting effects. What tied these two opposed senses of home life together—homely comfort and disquieting anxiety—was the architecture of the colonial residence itself, a material and social artifact with distinctive qualities. Rather than being a simple symbol of an idea of British power and authority, the colonial bungalow was a complicated setting where the attitudes and practices of colonial authority met with—and never fully overcame—a range of stubborn obstacles.

OCCUPYING COLONIAL HOUSES

Although the European community in Lahore never exceeded a few hundred people at any time during the nineteenth century, the city's British residential district was considerably larger in area than the entire Old City. The heart of the civil station was coterminous with the "bungalow area," a term used unofficially by the early twentieth century to describe the main form of residence found along Abbott, Davis, Cooper, Durand, Empress, Egerton, Fane, Ferozepur, Hall, Cust, Lake, Lawrence, Club, Jail, Mayo, Montgomery, Masson, Napier, Race Course, Sanda, Temple, Thornton, and Warris roads. A survey conducted during the 1911 census found that houses in the civil station occupied lots averaging 2.25 acres; the corresponding figure for the Old City was 0.027 acres, or roughly 1 percent of the civil station average.[11] The spacious lots in Lahore's civil station formed a landscape that was as conspicuous for its lavish consumption of space, therefore, as it was for the presence of Europeans.

As was the case in most cities occupied by the British in India, the most common type of British residence in Lahore was a bungalow, a detached single-story house surrounded by a large compound that was fenced or enclosed within walls.[12] A small minority of British officials and civilians lived in other types of accommodation in the city, including dormitories ("chummeries") and residential hotels. According to one former British resident of Lahore, residential hotels had become popular in the city by the early decades of the twentieth century, once "permanent or quasi-permanent residents of the station . . . acquired the *hotel habit.*"[13] Hotels in the city that offered long-term accommodation included Faletti's, Nedou's, and Charing Cross Hotel, all of which were located near the civil station's geographic center.

However, residential hotels were used primarily as temporary quarters for people waiting for a bungalow to be vacated. In 1897 Lady Maynard, the American wife of longtime Indian civil service officer John Maynard, wrote home to her mother in Virginia from her temporary quarters in Lahore's Charing Cross Hotel. Even the hotel, she wrote, was built like a bungalow: "In the February *Review of Reviews* there is an interesting article on Rudyard Kipling which I presume some of the family must have read. The engraving of the Kipling bungalow [in Lahore] gives you a most accurate idea of an Indian bungalow. Everything in Lahore is built on this plan; even this hotel is exactly like it, only it has two long wings which project from either side"[14] (Figure 5.2).

The hotel described by Lady Maynard shared another feature with the bungalow she was soon to occupy: Both were rented quarters. Since most colonial officers moved every

Figure 5.2. Rendering of Rudyard Kipling's bungalow in Lahore, circa 1897 (since destroyed). Architect unknown. From Review of Reviews, *February 1897.*

few years (or more frequently), housing for the European community was almost always rented.[15] In the case of government officers, the resident paid rent from a part of his or her monthly salary earmarked as a housing allowance. Some bungalows, especially those located in military cantonments, were built by the colonial government for its officers and employees, and standard plans were produced by the PWD for the purpose.[16] In larger cities throughout India, however, bungalows were often built by Indian businessmen and landowners who rented them to both British officers and civilians. Within Lahore's civil station (outside the military cantonment at Mian Mir), the latter was usually the case, and building permit applications housed in the Lahore Municipal Corporation record room reflect a preponderance of Indian owners over Europeans on applications for the construction of new bungalows at the turn of the century.

There were multiple reasons for the predominance of Indian landlords over British landlords in the city. For one thing, Indian landlords often owned the building plot outright and could build without the added expense of acquiring land. For another, Indian businessmen were willing to accept lower returns on their invested capital than British businessmen. In towns across Punjab that served as district headquarters, it was common practice for the district commissioner, district superintendent of police, and civil surgeon (the top three government officials in district towns) to rent housing from wealthy Indian landlords, since it usually made economic sense to do so. Responding to a question about officer housing in the Punjab in 1896, an official in Punjab's civil secretariat wrote,

> We know that in most Punjab Stations outside Lahore the DC [district commissioner] can usually secure an excellent house for Rs. 80/mensem. . . . Native landlords are only too glad to receive as little as 3% return on capital invested in house property. Were a house of this class purchased or built by Government the rental under existing rules would probably be not less than Rs. 250/mensem, a sum altogether beyond the means of a DC, who would naturally not be prepared to pay more than the customary sum.[17]

Even when government bungalows were affordable and available, the quality of housing left little scope for individual tastes. In 1904 Lieutenant Governor Charles M. Rivaz, in response to the often-raised question of whether officers could consult on the design of their own dwellings in cases where a new building was sanctioned, assigned such decisions to higher authority. "Questions of plan, accommodation, and etc. should not be left to the idiosyncrasy of the officer immediately but only temporarily affected," Rivaz wrote, "but should be settled by superior authority, i.e. in the case of Commissioners by Government, Divisional Judges by the Chief Court, of Deputy Commissioners by the Financial Commission, of Police Officers by the Inspector General of Police, and of other offices by the heads of their respective offices."[18] Basic features of British residence were thus tied to the peculiarities of colonial political economy (with its schedule of approved rates and salaries), colonial administrative procedures (which encouraged frequent transfers), and the control landlords exercised over their tenants (including setting rental rates, providing regular or irregular maintenance, and making housing available in the first place). All these features gave rise to a number of problems for those who conceived of the home as a space for reflecting and helping instill in its occupants the outward marks of decorum and refinement that helped distinguish between ruler and ruled.

TASTE, MORAL CHARACTER, AND THE BUNGALOW

The colonial bungalow was nevertheless a critical site for cultivating the distancing postures, refinements in taste, and class-based moralities that underwrote inter- and intraracial relations in the city. The connection between taste, morality, and domestic design is a well-established theme in nineteenth-century British social history.[19] Beginning in the 1840s, schools of design were established in Britain in an effort to elevate the standards of "taste" of the urban working classes—whose morals were deemed most in need of improvement— by training them to appreciate good design in home furnishings, tableware, and other arts of home decoration.[20] At the same time, architects both at home and abroad discussed the social and moral benefits accrued by surrounding oneself with articles of daily use that exhibited the qualities of polish, refinement, and good taste, qualities also desired of the owners of those same articles. An English commentator in an 1873 London trade journal argued that mundane household objects could be more influential than the monumental designs of architects:

> There can be no doubt that altogether, independently of direct intellectual culture, either from books or society, the mind is molded and colored to a great extent by the persistent impressions produced upon it by the most familiar objects that daily meet the eye . . . and though the cathedral may produce an immense impression on a crowd, and even for the time on the human minds composing it, it will often happen that a comparatively utterly insignificant article in the house really does more in the way of impressing, or even molding, the human intelligence with which it is in almost persistent contact.[21]

The felicitous use of domestic design to secure a measure of moral integrity was predicated on the ability to control basic features of the home space itself. This ability, however, was sharply limited in the colony by the continual shifting of residences and by whether previous tenants—or the whims of an Indian landlord—had kept the house in good repair. F. S. Growse, a colonial government servant, trenchant critic of the PWD, and amateur architect of some note, recorded in his memoir (1886) that he actually turned down a transfer to another station in India simply because the house he would occupy left "no scope for the exercise of individual taste." "I declined [the transfer]," Growse wrote, "solely on account of the house there, though it had been built by no less distinguished a character than Mr. A. O. Hume, and at enormous cost to the owner. . . . [It was] an impossibility to put up pictures or hangings, or to give the interior anything of a home-like appearance, and I therefore—on this account alone—declined the transfer. A plain, roomy, weather-tight barn would have suited me far better."[22]

Not only was the carcass of the building often simply inherited, but the same was often true of more intimate items. Being more or less constantly on the move meant that whatever one possessed by way of "household decoration" had to be relatively mobile, disposable, or not liable to be missed when left behind. Furniture built according to European designs and tastes could be procured from local craftsmen, but most such furniture was seen as inferior in quality. Lockwood Kipling complained that "[carpenters in Punjab towns] turn out piece after piece [of furniture] which, usually copies of copies to begin with, have all the defects of the first copy gradually magnified till soon all technical merit is lost . . . at best [the] work is spoiled by a certain want of finish. [The carpenter] exhibits a tendency to leave his work crooked in line and unfinished in joints."[23] Lady Maynard, whose description of Charing Cross Hotel was cited earlier, wrote to her mother that "you would be astounded if you could see the make shift way people live in this land. It is difficult to realize that English people with their great love for comfort, are willing to put up with such things. . . . the doors, for instance, have no locks, you have to paw at them with your nails until they see fit to allow themselves to be opened. The beds have no springs or mattresses and only occasionally a head or foot board." Despite the good-natured tone of her letter, the conditions she found herself living in were "rather amusing in one way," Maynard wrote, "but provoking in another."[24]

Furnishings of higher quality were scarce in most cities and were often acquired on the cheap at moving sales or at sales accompanying European funerals. By the latter half of the nineteenth century a genre of "ladies" periodical literature and household decoration guides had emerged to address a market for cheap furnishings and economical decoration ideas, and the classified section of English newspapers in Lahore, as elsewhere, regularly advertised furnishings for sale (Figure 5.3).[25] Marriage trousseaus provided another avenue for acquiring the proper sort of furnishings, especially when a marriage was arranged prior to the new bride's journey to India. In an unpublished account of her grandmother's betrothal and subsequent marriage to Lucas White King, an officer in the Indian Civil Service, A. G. N. Verity devotes long passages to the letters the young lovers sent back and forth between India and England as they decided together what the new bride should carry with her: "We shall want a piano, plate, crockery, [and] house linen," wrote her husband, "things we cannot do without." In addition to these items, Verity's grandmother arrived in India with saddles and a harness for a horse-drawn dogcart, bolts of light cotton and silk fabric, multiple sets of breakfast and dinner plates, and an assortment of personal effects, including twelve plain and twelve "trimmed" skirts, seven pairs each of shoes (including a pair for tennis), gloves, hats, and thirty-six pairs of "knickers" with an equal number of camisoles.[26]

Keeping a proper home, with its requisite furnishings and appliances, was one way of distancing expatriate home life from what Europeans perceived as the promiscuous and degraded context of the Indian city. Even among the white community, however, differences in status were open to view, and the bungalow was an equally important site of social anchorage for marking and maintaining those differences. Esmee Mascall's memoir of growing up in Lahore in the early twentieth century illustrates the way basic domestic rituals that Europeans were familiar with from home, once adapted to the different material and social

GRAND SALE THIS-DAY.

300 HOGSHEADS OF BASS' AND ALLSOₚ PALE ALE,

100 PIPES CHOICE CAPE AND MADEIRA WINES,

EX-SHIP "ZENOBIA."

AND A VARIETY OF FRESH EUROPE GOODS, BY THE LATE ARRIVAL

TO BE SOLD BY PUBLIC AUCTION.

BY TULLOH AND COMPANY,

At their Auction Rooms, Tank Square, This-Day, Saturday, the 10 Feb. 18—.

A SELECT AND EXTENSIVE INVOICE OF

COWARD'S PERFUMERY AND MEDICINES,

500 CANISTERS HERMETICALLY SEALED FRESH SALMON,

43 BARRELS OF FRESH AMERICAN FLOUR.

An entire Invoice of Grocery and Oilman's Stores.

CHEDDER AND PINE CHEESE—PRIME YORKSHIRE HAMS.

Contents of 3 Cases of splendidly cut and plain

TABLE GLASS-WARE AND CROCKERY.

A further Selection from an Extensive Invoice of ARGYLE TABLE LAMPS.

And a quantity of British PIECE GOODS & superfine COTTON HOSIERY—A case of GINGHAM UMBRELLAS.

ENTIRE PACKAGES OF SUPERFINE TOWN CLOTHS, ASSORTED WOOLLENS, CASSIMERES AND DRILLS.

And an Assortment of Morrocco Skins.

At 12 o'Clock in the Horse Compound,

300 Hogsheads Bass' and Allsop's *PALE ALE* and 100 Pipes *CHOICE WINES.*

400 Crates of empty QUART BOTTLES, and 500 Gross of fine VELVET CORKS,

And a variety of other Articles as fully detailed within, &c.

EXTENSIVE SALE THIS-DAY,

Of Landed and Miscellaneous Property—Stationery—New and Second-hand Books,

VALUABLE OIL PAINTINGS, &c.

TO BE SOLD BY MESSRS. ———— AND COMPANY,

This-day, THURSDAY, the 24th December, 18—.

---

125 Reams of superfine FOOLSCAP and 15 Reams superior PRINTING DEMY.

100 BUNDLES OF BEST OFFICE QUILLS.

AN ENTIRE INVOICE OF NEW BOOKS.

TWELVE HIGHLY VALUABLE OIL PAINTINGS.

AN EXTENSIVE ASSORTMENT OF ACKERMAN'S AND REEVE'S DRAWING MATERIALS;

AND A COLLECTION OF PLAIN AND HIGHLY COLOURED ENGRAVINGS.

Fresh invoices of Milroy's superior SADDLERY—Rogers and Son's superfine CUTLERY.

SINGLE AND DOUBLE BARRELLED GUNS.

A CASE OF DUELLING PISTOLS (! ! !)

A CONSIGNMENT OF BEAUTIFUL MIRZAPORE CARPETS.

ELEGANT DRAB AND BEAVER HATS—LONDON-MADE SHOOTING SHOES.

PRECISELY AT 12 O'CLOCK,

THE WELL-KNOWN INDIGO CONCERN, IN THE DISTRICT OF B——

VALUABLE HOUSES, SHOPS AND LANDS,

Situate in Tank-square, Cossitollah and Intally.

THE LATE MR. ————'S SCHOONER "EMMA."

AFTER WHICH

A QUANTITY OF NEAT HOUSEHOLD FURNITURE.

As fully detailed within. Orders faithfully executed.

Figure 5.3. Advertisement for items for sale, originally published in the Mackenzie, Lyall and Company auction catalog in Calcutta in 1851. Note the entry for "neat household furniture" at the bottom of the page. From Colesworthy Grant, Anglo-Indian Domestic Life: A Letter from an Artist in India to His Mother *(1862) (Calcutta: Subornorekha, 1984), 38.*

circumstances of home life in Lahore, threw status negotiations between Europeans into new kinds of relationships. Mascall wrote,

> I must describe the dinner-party of those days because one saw nothing quite like it in England. Table servants of the invited guest would turn up to help wait at table, bringing with them, very likely, anything in the way of silver and cutlery of which the host might be in short supply for a dinner of seven courses and ten or twelve table guests. Nothing was said about this beforehand, but when the host saw unfamiliar items on his table—and these of course were recognized by one or other of his guests—it was *just an amusing joke,* and the guest's servant saw to it that all the borrowed items went back safely.[27]

Mascall's dissembling comment that a shortage of cutlery "was just an amusing joke," compared with what such a situation might represent in England, highlights the altered sense of social impropriety. Such, too, was the case when creating a proper setting for polite dining, one that would reflect on the skills of an English hostess in telling ways. "If you had a new *khitmatgar* [parlorman] who had perhaps been in service with a bachelor," Mascall wrote, "you might find rather a dreadful decoration on the table in place of the English-style silver vases with flowers. . . . one had to be tactful and warn the man well beforehand that vases of flowers were the right thing for the English Sahib's table."[28]

Another British woman resident in Lahore (circa 1915) related an incident in her memoir where similarly mundane features of the house were drawn subtly into a commentary on distinction: "The baths [in our bungalow] were made of tin and filled with boiling water from old kerosene tins," the author wrote; "it did not even seem strange when my father, as an act of devotion to my mother, imported an English porcelain bath which was filled with the kerosene tins as before. A number of ladies came to refresh their memories and admire this object in its alien setting. An Indian friend who had not seen such a thing before gazed for some time and finally remarked, 'he must love you very much.'"[29]

Rudyard Kipling's short stories returned often to the theme of how the bungalow frankly revealed social position. Consider the predicament of Martyn in Kipling's short story "William the Conqueror" (circa 1890). The building Kipling described was no doubt similar to many he would have known from his years living in Lahore, where this story was also set:

> As an Acting District Superintendent of Police, Martyn drew the magnificent pay of six hundred depreciated silver rupees a month and his little four-roomed bungalow said just as much. There were the usual blue-and-white striped jail-made rugs on the uneven floor; the usual glass-studded Amritsar *phulkaris* [embroidered cloths] draped to nails driven into the flaking whitewash of the walls; the usual half-dozen chairs that did not match, picked up at sales of dead men's effects; and the usual streaks of black grease where the leather punkah-thong ran through the wall. It was as though everything had been unpacked the night before to be repacked next morning. . . . Thus did people live who had such an income; and in a land where each man's pay, age, and position are printed in a book, that all may read, it is hardly worthwhile to play at pretenses in word or deed.[30]

Furnishings and architectural features of the bungalow are prominent in this passage, and they work to reinforce Kipling's emphasis on Martyn's lowly status. Kipling suggests that maintaining an air of civility in a house whose architectural features constantly miti-gated against it was an ongoing battle for those "who had such an income." There is ample evidence to suggest, however, that people like Martyn shared their predicament with resi-dents of much higher standing. Even relatively fine bungalows were often perceived as poorly planned, simply appointed, and difficult to maintain.

THE CONSTRUCTION OF BUNGALOWS

In 1910 the crown prince of Germany visited India and stayed in a government bungalow near Delhi, by then Punjab's largest city. In anticipation of the prince's visit, the sanitary commissioner, Major E. Wilkinson, conducted a walk-through tour of the bungalow in order to certify its suitability for the visiting dignitary and his entourage of more than sev-enty people. Wilkinson's detailed notes from the tour provide a glimpse into the kind of housing meant to be, quite literally, fit for a prince at the time:

> Ventilation [in the house] is imperfect, the windows not having been well arranged.... The bathrooms have linoleum over a rough stone floor (rather than glazed tiles) and the walls (as also those of some of the other rooms) are whitewashed rather than painted. Some of the baths are provided with long enameled tubs, others with ordinary galva-nized tubs, and although all have water taps, these are for cold water only.... There are only ordinary, dry pattern, commodes instead of water closets [in the bathrooms]. The waste water of bathrooms, etc. is discharged into sumps just outside the buildings from which it has to be dipped.... The kitchen is small and dirty. It is only provided with ordinary *chula*s [open stoves] for charcoal. There is only one water tap and there is no proper sink for washing cooking vessels, etc. There is a small sink in the floor below the tap, but this is quite unsuitable.[31]

Wilkinson ordered a number of remedial improvements to the house, including in-stalling underground drainage pipes to carry away wastewater, adding a sink and range in the kitchen, and installing tile on the kitchen and bathroom walls. While these types of deficiencies could sometimes be remedied, however, other problems were much harder to solve. Foremost among these, perhaps, was the decidedly "Indian" look of the bungalow's basic architectural details—including those commented upon by Kipling above—since bun-galows' materials and manner of construction helped assimilate them visually into a local, Indian, architectural idiom.

With few exceptions, the structure and finish of bungalows were exactly the same as those of Indian residential buildings in other parts of the city, including those explored in chapter 4, even if the design and layout of bungalows and the social uses they accommodated were markedly different (Figure 5.4). Bungalows were built using local labor, and labor was organized by Indian contractors. Many bungalows, indeed, were designed by Indian archi-tects, who nevertheless worked according to English tastes and specifications. The customary techniques and materials of each of the main building trades involved in bungalow con-struction—excavation, masonry, carpentry, and tile work—had long been in use in north

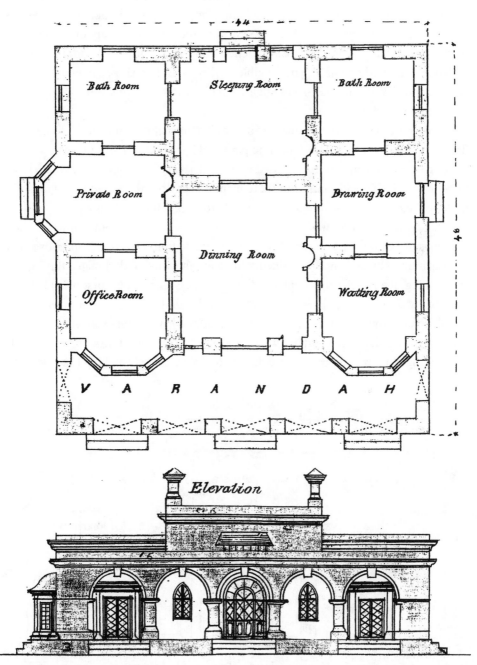

Plan

Bath Room Sleeping Room Bath Room

Private Room Drawing Room

Dinning Room

Office Room Waiting Room

V A R A N D A H

44

46

Elevation

Figure 5.4. Elevation and plan drawings for a bungalow in Lahore, circa 1905. Source: Lahore Municipal Corporation.

India, and their members often learned their trade through apprenticeships in guilds with hereditary rights to membership.[32] The basic design of bungalows changed far less quickly than that of the Indian townhouse, although there were changes in construction practice introduced during the colonial period, including the gradual substitution of engineered standards for rules of thumb in the sizing of structural members, the adoption of new methods of iron construction from European practice, and the use of glazed windows in place of grilled or shuttered openings. The tangible qualities of a bungalow's physical fabric, however, remained rooted in Indian, not English, architectural conventions throughout the colonial period in Lahore.

Like houses in the Indian quarters of the city, the majority of Lahore's bungalows had flat roofs covered with clay tiles or lime plaster (Figure 5.5). The roof's outer surface was built up over a thin layer of compressed earth underlain by masonry tiles. Wooden battens three to four inches wide and from six to eight inches deep were used as ceiling and floor joists, spaced roughly one foot apart. Where battens met the brick supporting walls of the house, a receiving pocket was made in the wall by leaving a brick out. Similarly, like most buildings in Lahore, the bungalow's supporting walls, foundations, and interior partitions were all built of brick. Lahore's distinctive brick architecture predominated throughout the city, leading one traveler to complain, "I must confess that when I first beheld [Lahore] I was greatly disappointed. Everything is brick; confounded brick, walls, houses, pagodas, temples of any and every description, confounded brick. Go where you will, the bricks still stick to you. Up this street, with its wretched pavement of loose stones, and down that with its tottering old dwellings made since the day of Adam, there is nothing but brick."[33]

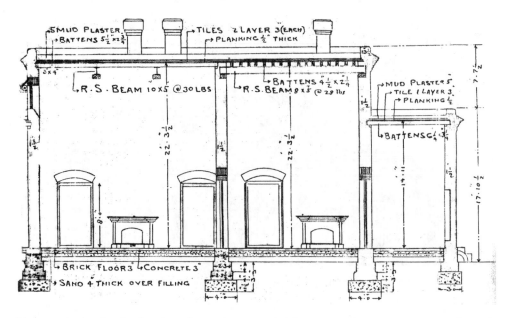

Figure 5.5. Section drawing for a bungalow on Lytton Road, Lahore, 1907. Dimensions are given in feet and inches. Source: Lahore Municipal Corporation.

The materials used on the exteriors of bungalows, too, were the same as those used on Indian houses. The usual treatment was to cover the exterior walls in a thin coat of lime plaster and paint or whitewash them a light color. Alternately, exterior walls could be finished with *surkhi,* a reddish plaster made from pulverized bricks. On buildings plastered with *surkhi,* mortar lines were sometimes inscribed into the finish coat to replicate the appearance of unplastered English bricks, thereby lending an air of decorative refinement to the building. Other decorative features were added to the bungalow's exterior that reflected European styles common in the nineteenth century, including neoclassical and Gothic-revival ornament. Notably, however, as we saw in chapter 4, the same practice was adopted by builders of Indian houses in the city by the end of the nineteenth century as well.

Applied stylistic features aside, the mundane features of bungalow construction thus served to distance them from the "small cozy" English houses Nawab Mehdi Hasan Khan described in London as "the kind of abode[s] in which our retired Lieutenant Governors live." These kinds of material differences are important, as historian Dell Upton argues, since conventions of construction help establish "a context or system of common understanding" within which visual clues to meaning become more or less obvious and where "allusions suffice."[34] In the colonial context, a distinctly different system of building conventions from those present in England lent bungalows an air of strangeness that was often commented upon: "The exterior of the bungalow will, I doubt not, be sufficient to impress you with a feeling of *absence from old England,*" wrote Colesworthy Grant, in his 1862 guide to Anglo-Indian domestic life; "that it is 'no your ain [own] house, you'll 'ken [know] by the rigging o't."[35]

As was true with locally crafted furniture, British writers regularly complained that buildings constructed by Indians were inadequately built and sloppily finished, which made the bungalow seem even further from the English ideals of decorum and refinement a home was supposed to both reflect and help produce in its occupants. Rudyard Kipling, whose father Lockwood worked at improving Indian craftsmanship in his role as principal at the Mayo School of Art and was critical of all poorly executed work, was perhaps unusually sensitive to this kind of issue by virtue of his father's vocation. While still resident in Lahore, Kipling put the following words in the voice of a short-story character:

> All the work that I have seen turned out by Native hands is bad. Doors don't come up properly to the jambs; windows are never straight; there is no finish in the roofs. Floors and plinths are badly put down, and timber is wastefully misused without any increase in strength. Native hinges and locks, and ironwork more generally, are all abominations to English eyes. There is no correct rabbeting, mortising, mitering, dovetailing or joinery of any sort in the land—as far as I have seen; and this disgusts me a good deal.... This slackness and want of straight lines goes all over India. The very keys on the railway lines seem as if they had been hammered in by a man who did not know which end of the hammer he ought to use. Every thing here is raw, unfinished, misjointed, slack, and wrongly built. The Anglo-Indians have a beautifully expressive word for all this—"*kutcha.*" Everything is "*kutcha*"—which means everything is just as an English workman would not turn it out.[36]

The relative simplicity of bungalow design, when compared to more elaborately conceived traditional Indian houses, was seen to be part of the problem: "Simplicity is no doubt to be desired," wrote Lockwood Kipling in a study on Indian carpentry, "but plain doors with frames of different sizes, windows and doors that would not shut, or if once shut refuse to open—characteristics of the average tarkhan's [carpenter's] work, do not go well with a severe simplicity, which, to be tolerable, must be perfect as regards joinery and finish."[37] Whereas the bungalow was meant to provide a setting for cultivating and displaying refined manners and tastes, its physical appearance played a role in creating a pervasive and often-announced sense of anxiety instead. The bungalow's walls, rooms, doors, and furnishings became a focus of annoyance; they also became vexing reminders, as we will see shortly, of the copresence of different sensory qualities, meanings, and values tied to more-local histories of production and use.[38]

THE SOCIAL ORGANIZATION OF DOMESTIC SPACE

Bungalows seemed inadequate for reasons other than perceived deficiencies in their material qualities, however. The standard arrangement of spaces in a bungalow made the orchestration of expatriate British home life difficult to manage. Most bungalows were built near the center of an enclosed plot of sufficient area to ensure a free flow of breeze (Figure 5.6). Servants' quarters and animal, vehicle, and other kinds of storage sheds were arrayed along one edge of the plot out of view from the main rooms of the house, and a separate structure placed closer to the main dwelling was used as a kitchen. As was true of Clark's little sketch that opened the discussion in this chapter, the rooms of a bungalow dwelling were almost always arranged with biaxial symmetry. Each corner of the roughly square building contained a rectangular room with smaller auxiliary spaces attached to it (used for bathing and dressing when the room was a bedroom). The corner rooms along one side of the bungalow either shared a common wall or shared walls with an intervening room and were separated from the attached rooms on the other side by a central hall that might be divided into two or more separate spaces. The rooms of the central hall were used for dining and entertaining guests.

Despite the bungalow's strict symmetry, the central hall intersected with the outer walls at two opposite ends, forming the front of the structure on one side and the back at the other. Ceilings in the central hall were usually taller than those over the suite of rooms on either side to facilitate ventilation through clerestory apertures opening on to the center of the house. In a humbler structure the central hall might be omitted altogether, leaving a four-square plan that nevertheless retained the front/back distinction. A projecting porch sometimes marked the front facade and served as a covered entryway. In most cases, a broad verandah surrounded the bungalow on three or four sides, and the whole building was raised several feet above the ground on a masonry plinth.

The front and back of the bungalow established an imaginary axis that divided more public functions in the house from those that were considered to be more private. Thus,

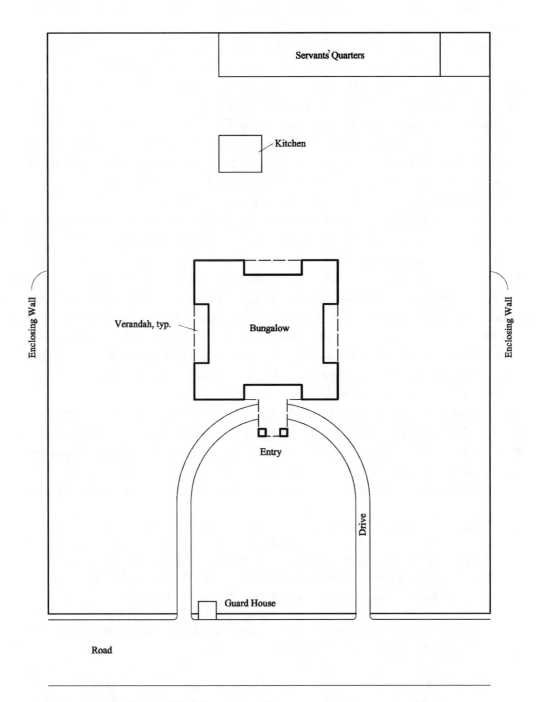

Figure 5.6. Drawing of a typical bungalow compound.

the vertical segregation of activity described above by Nawab Mehdi Hasan Khan for a typical London row house was accomplished horizontally in the bungalow. Rooms at the front of the house were used for entertaining visitors or overnight guests, and in the case of a government officer's residence, at least one room had to be set aside as a place for meeting the area's residents on matters concerning local governance (called the *"kutchery"* in Clark's plan; see Figure 5.1).[39] Not only was this often a necessity in out-of-the-way stations where a separate office could not be provided, but making the home a locus of authority aligned well with British ideas about the efficacy of "personal" government in the colony: "All Oriental peoples have a strong predilection for personal government," wrote the author of a government guide to officer etiquette, "and are much more amenable to order and control when they recognize the personal source of such control than when it appears to them in the light of a mere mechanical emanation, not from a man but from an office." The presence of an office in the bungalow meant that residence and office functions coexisted in the same structure, adding a further layer of complexity to the building's program of use: "The first difficulty which a junior officer encounters will be that of distinguishing between the various classes of Indians who visit him—to whom to offer a chair, with whom to shake hands, etc.," wrote the same author. Among the many things a new officer had to learn was which visitors were allowed to wear shoes in the office, how to address assembled petitioners on the verandah when no time was left in the day to meet them, and how to end an interview: "It must be remembered that ordinarily speaking an Indian visitor of the old school will not go until he is given leave to do so, therefore the host must himself indicate when he considers it is time to terminate the interview."[40]

Complicating matters further was the fact that nineteenth-century Anglo-European middle-class ideals of proper domestic arrangements preferred to make clear separations between less- and more-private spaces in the house, between servants and family members, and between people of different sexes and ages. It was desirable that the various spaces in the home segregated different activities from one another and provided a separate space for each:

> It is a first principle with the better classes of English people that the Family Rooms shall be essentially private, and as much as possible the Family Thoroughfares [hallways]. It becomes the foremost of all maxims, therefore, however small the establishment, that the Servants' Department shall be separated from the Main House, so that what passes on either side of the boundary shall be both invisible and inaudible on the other. . . . In short, whether in a small house or a large one, let the family have free passage without encountering the servants unexpectedly, and let the servants have access to all their duties without coming unexpectedly upon the family or visitors.[41]

Bungalows were unable to satisfy this need, since the relations of domestic labor they were supported by and the physical distribution of spaces they housed constantly worked against the ideal. One of the key points of conflict, of course, was the disposition of household servants.[42] Even a relatively modest British household in India maintained several specialized servants to conduct the daily labor of the house, from cooking, gardening, and cleaning out the house's rooms to serving as wet nurses and *ayah*s (nannies) for European infants and children. The copresence of Indian servants in the innermost recesses of the home, however, was thought to expose its occupants to a range of social (and physical) dangers brought about through racial mixing. As Ann Laura Stoler argues, "middle-class colonials . . . embodied a set of fundamental tensions between a culture of whiteness that cordoned itself off from the native world and a set of domestic arrangements and class distinctions among Europeans that produced cultural hybridities and sympathies that repeatedly transgressed these distinctions."[43] These tensions included concern over the possibility that European children would develop overly affectionate ties to their Indian nannies and acquire bad habits of personality (or even take on pernicious Indian racial traits through the medium of their wet nurses' milk) and the fear of servants' sexual profligacy or of their becoming a source of sexual arousal for their colonial employers.[44] And it was feared that letting down one's vigilance over personal demeanor in an unguarded moment might also incite insurrection or ridicule, either of which could quickly dismantle the social distance that separated ruler from ruled.

The layout of bungalows mediated these threats imperfectly, since one of their distinctive spatial features was a direct and porous connection between the interior of the house and the verandah outside. The need for ventilation militated against the use of interior hallways that could separate and channel the flow of activity from one space to the next. Less-private rooms of the house often opened directly onto more-private ones, therefore, without the intervening buffer provided by a hallway (Figure 5.7). The ability to open the interior rooms of the house to cooling breezes during the summer was indeed one of the critical design features of bungalows. Clark's sketch design, along with his documentation of temperature differentials between outside and inside, draws particular attention to this feature. The encircling verandah was an important device for this purpose, since it cooled air in immediate proximity to the house and provided an open but covered space for use in the evenings and cooler months of the year. Verandahs served some of the same functions an interior hallway did, since most rooms of the house opened onto them either directly through doorways or at least visually through windows. But verandahs were also spaces for conducting a range of household labor, and servants often slept there at night or rested in their shade during the day. This weakened their usefulness as a separating device, providing obvious opportunities for spatial transgression.

The uncanny associations provoked by the almost continual presence of servants in and around the bungalow, and the difficulty of policing their movements, formed a regular theme in Rudyard Kipling's literature. In his short story "The House of Shadows" (1887), Kipling portrayed the sense of anxiety these difficulties could lead to. Here, as elsewhere, Kipling used a popular late nineteenth-century literary device, the "haunted house" story,[45] to evoke a distinctly colonial "grievance":

> A woman has died and a child has been born in it, but these are accidents which may overtake the most respectable establishments. No sensible man would think of regarding

them. Indeed so sound is my common sense, that I sleep in the room of the death and do my work in the room of the birth; and I have no fault to find with either apartment. My complaint is against the whole house; and my grievance, so far as I can explain it in writing, is that there are far too many tenants in the eight, lime-washed rooms for which I pay seventy five rupees a month. . . . At breakfast, in the full fresh daylight, I am conscious that some one who is not the *khitmutgar* [butler] is watching the back of my head from the door that leads into my bedroom; when I turn sharply, the *purdah* [curtain] is dropped and I only see it waving gently as though shaken by the wind. . . . His feet make no noise, but I can hear in the hot, still night the jar of the *chik* [reed blind] as he comes into the verandah, and the lifting of the *purdah* over the drawing room door. I would endure the people who hide in the corners of the lamproom and rush out when my back is turned, the persons who get between the almirah and the wall when I come into my dressing-room hastily at dusk, or even the person in the garden who slides in and out of the *ferash* trees when I walk there, if I could only get rid of the *Man in the Next room.* There is no sense in him, and he interferes sadly with one's work. I believe now that if he dared he would come out from the other side of the *purdah* and peep over my shoulder

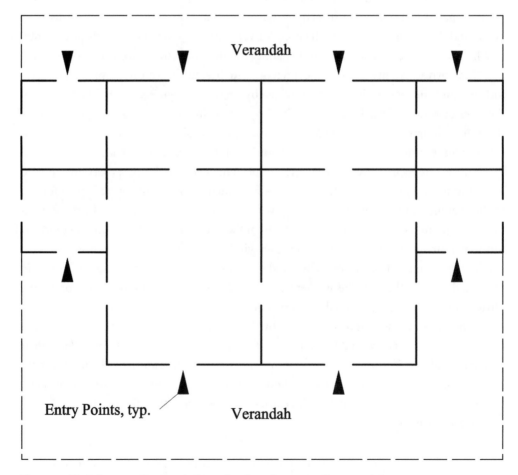

Figure 5.7. Typical entry points into the bungalow from the surrounding verandah.

to see what I am writing. But he is afraid and is now twitching the cord that works the ventilating window.... You will concede, will you not, that this is annoying, particularly when I know that I am officially the sole tenant. No man, visible or invisible, has a right to spy upon my outgoings or incomings.[46]

As in the earlier quotation from Kipling's story about Martyn, physical features of the bungalow are prominent in this passage. The Anglo-Indian nomenclature used for these features and the emotional content Kipling evokes in the story work in unison to characterize a form of unhomely anxiety. In the end, Kipling's narrator abandons his bungalow for a revivifying spell at a "hill-station."[47] While this was a remedy many Europeans could and did resort to in India, more immediate approaches to the same problems were required. Foremost among these was a search for methods of governing servant (and tenant) conduct in the colonial household, a task both announced by and facilitated through the ubiquitous publication of guides to household management from the mid-nineteenth century onward in India.

SETTING THE HOUSEHOLD RIGHT

The Anglo-Indian household guide was a hybrid text. Part nineteenth-century "book of manners," part domestic science text, and part colonial folk ethnography, the household guide was primarily focused on techniques for managing Indian servants and converting unfamiliar settings and foods into a reasonable facsimile of their English equivalents. The social environment of an English residence, adapted to conditions of life in a colonial setting, was likened to a microcosm of empire in these works, and household guides often worked to establish parallel qualities between the two. "Here, as there [in England], the end and object is not merely personal comfort, but the formation of a home," wrote Flora Annie Steel, "that unit of civilization where father and children, master and servant, employer and employed, can learn their several duties."[48]

Mirroring in miniature the ordering of imperial relations more generally, order in the colonial home depended in part upon classificatory schemes that divided servants according to race, religion, and gender. In *Anglo-Indian Domestic Life* (1862), Colesworthy Grant devoted several pages to a hierarchically ranked list of all the domestic servants found in a colonial home. Each type of servant was described according to his or her "race" and social standing in Indian society, along with the problems and benefits of service according to each. In her guide, Steel wrote that "an attempt has been made to assimilate the duties of each servant to those of his or her English compeer, and thus to show the new-comer where fault lies."[49]

Discipline over the self, no less than over servants, forms another central leitmotif in the household guide genre. "The pen wearies," wrote Francis Hogg, a British physician who served in Meerut, "in repeating the warnings against gross feeding, bottled beer, meat tiffins, wet clothes, lawn tennis or badminton on damp grass, thin boots or stockings, [and] scanty under-clothing during the rains." Bodily health and architectural order worked in combination to form Hogg's tableau of the ideal colonial family: "A smart, clean, wholesome, well-proportioned infant, with ruddy hands and feet . . . [with a] cool, well-shaped head, firm limbs, expansive chest, unblemished skin and happy expression; the sensible enjoyment of judicious food, fresh air, the cleansing bracing bath, the tranquil sleep and freedom from fretful pain . . . [parents that are] healthy, the father steady, the mother strong, the house clean, in good repair, the drainage satisfactory, [and] no over-crowding." Any momentary breach in the exercise of due diligence over this pleasant tableau, however, and the "cruel shadow" of death could intrude, dragging a host of distasteful practices in its wake: "When trouble comes then follows scraping, cleansing, white washing, lime washing, fumigation with chlorine, nitrous acid, or sulphurous acid gas, the boiling of bedding and the pulling the place to pieces which might all have been avoided."[50] By exhorting their readers to exercise personal vigilance over health, cleanliness, and diet, household guides frankly acknowledged that living in India demanded a high level of personal discipline in order to comport one's body safely.

The idea that colonial household manuals are best read as exemplars of Foucauldian disciplinarity—both by normalizing the colonial family and by establishing the everyday practices through which colonial power could be dispersed—is common in the secondary literature, not surprisingly.[51] Even if the Foucauldian reading has merit, however, we have to acknowledge at the same time that household guides presented a matrix of *overlapping* disciplines in the bungalow, rather than depicting a single type. The spatial practices the servants engaged in around the bungalow are rendered quite thinly in these manuals as the products of "custom" or "habit"—in short, as timeworn cultural predilections. But they emerge clearly, nevertheless, as a primary object of concern, and a range of techniques is suggested in order to root them out. "Pay periodic visits of inspection to [the servants'] quarters," wrote the author of a 1906 manual, "to see that a few obvious sanitary rules are not neglected."[52] The same author argued that such inspections were best conducted on the Sabbath, for reasons that did not need elaboration. In her book, Steel warned that "it is as well . . . to eat your breakfast in peace before venturing into the pantry and cook-room." But do so nevertheless, she suggested, lest the mistress of the house discover "the khitmatgar using his toes as an efficient toast-rack."[53]

Indeed, one underlying theme of these works is that of the Indian servant occupying the colonial domicile with a far greater degree of comfort than its British tenants. Vigilance has to be maintained, Steel wrote, to keep servants from "turning your domain into a caravanserai for their relations to the third and fourth generation." In another passage, she warned that "few mistresses have been long in India without having had the trouble of scandals between the ayah and the other servants."[54] Hogg warned his readers against selecting the wrong Indian wet nurse and urged his readers to "keep away [her] friends and relations," if at all possible, since one could hardly afford "a drunken, jealous, or extortionate husband eternally hanging about the premises."[55] Put somewhat differently, while the household guidebook provided a systematized base of knowledge for establishing imperial forms of order in miniature, it also revealed that more than one mode of sociality, and more than one domestic sensorium, were present in the bungalow compound.

BEING AT HOME

For many British residents, to live in a colonial bungalow was to hold a strange but powerful world tenuously at bay. The architecture of the dwelling made that task all the more difficult, with its perceived lack of refinement, its easily transgressed zones of privacy, and its absolute dependence on native labor for its operation and maintenance. Social relations between servants and masters presented further layers of vulnerability, from the potential for undue exposure of a tenant's intimate life to the seeming inaccessibility of servants' languages and habits. I have emphasized in this chapter how these things could lead to a sense of anxiety, to a disquieting feeling of unsettledness. I want to conclude by pointing to one further sensibility that emerges in the nineteenth century and that would continue through the end of British rule: the idea that the bungalow—as was indeed true of most of the new spaces in the colonial city—was more naturally suited to Indian communities than it was to the British community. Once again, it is Kipling who provides an eloquent, if perhaps unintended, expression of this idea.

In Kipling's 1891 short story "Naboth," a British tenant gradually loses control over his bungalow compound to an artful encroacher. The natural, almost inexorable expansion of the "native" world into the British tenant's private domain captures for me the sense of how Indian subjects were perceived to feel at home in newly fashioned colonial territory with an ease and inevitability that eluded the British community. At the opening of the story, the British narrator encounters a thin and impoverished beggar ("Naboth") standing in the corner of his bungalow garden. In response to Naboth's humble solicitation, the narrator gives him a rupee.[56] The next morning Naboth is "a little fatter," and our narrator finds him curled "into knots in the front verandah" (139). Naboth next begs to establish a "sweetmeat-pitch" near the house, which the narrator also allows. From this point onward, inexorably, Naboth's operations begin to expand:

> There is a short carriage-road from [my] house to the Mall, which passes close to the shrubbery. Next afternoon I saw that Naboth had seated himself at the bottom of the slope, down in the dust of the public road, and in the full glare of the sun, with a starved basket of greasy sweets in front of him. . . . Next day he had moved himself up the slope, nearer to my shrubbery, and waved a palm-leaf fan to keep the flies off the sweets. So I judged that he must have done a fair trade. Four days later I noticed that he had backed himself and his basket under the shadow of the shrubbery, and had tied an Isabella-coloured [brownish yellow] rag between two branches to make more shade. There were plenty of sweets in his basket. I thought that trade must certainly be looking up. (140–41)

An opportunity for further expansion comes along shortly, when a nearby plot of land is taken up for the construction of a new "Chief Court."[57] With the prospect of hundreds of "coolies" laboring on the project, Naboth invests in all the proper accoutrements of a merchant, including "a huge, fat, red-backed account-book and a glass inkstand" (141). Like the debtor entries in his account books, Naboth's presence in the bungalow compound grows: "[Naboth] had hacked away more of my shrubbery, and owned another and a fatter account-book," Kipling wrote; "eleven weeks later Naboth had eaten his way nearly through the shrubbery, and there was a reed hut with a bedstead outside it, standing in the little glade that he had eroded" (142). With talent and alacrity, Naboth encroaches further, exposing the narrator to "Municipal" scrutiny while, at the same time, securing more privacy for himself:

> Six weeks and two days later a mud wall had grown up at the back of the hut. There were
> fowls in front and it smelt a little. The Municipal Secretary said that a cess-pool was form-
> ing in the public road from the drainage of my compound, and that I must take steps to
> clear it away. . . . Four months later the hut was *all* mud walls, very solidly built, and
> Naboth had used most of my shrubbery for his five goats. . . . A week later he hired a man
> to make several dozen square yards of trellis-work to put round the back of his hut, that
> his women-folk might be screened from the public gaze. The man went away in the eve-
> ning, and left his day's work to pave the short cut from the public road to my house. (143)

The story ends with the narrator arriving home late at night, unaware of the new construction, only to send his horses and carriage "stamping and plunging" into the new "bamboo net-work" (144). This puts an end to Naboth's undue encroachments, and to his presence in the narrator's life. "Naboth is now gone," the story ends, "and his hut is ploughed into its native mud. . . . I have built a summer-house to overlook the end of the garden, and it is as a fort on my frontier whence I guard my Empire. I know how Ahab felt. He has been shamefully misrepresented in the Scriptures" (144).

Kipling began this story by labeling it an "allegory of Empire," and he had made it clear by the end that the bungalow compound was that empire in miniature.[58] Naboth's progress in the story—like that, allegorically, of Indian subjects in general—was due to the narrator's liberal generosity: "Remember," Kipling wrote, "there was only Naboth, his basket, the sunshine, and the gray dust when the sap of my Empire first began" (140). Kipling suggests here that like Indian subjects in the empire at large, Naboth took advantage of the narrator's generosity via a steady unfolding of natural, but corrupt, human instincts. The violent action that brings an end to Naboth's encroachment is then no more than the restoration of rights to private property under a liberal system of rule. With such direct analogies framing both ends of the story, the conclusion Kipling drew could hardly have been different: In the imperial space of a bungalow compound, if not in the empire at large, even-tempered British authority wins out withal over native opportunism, acquisitiveness, and greed.

I would like to read the "allegory" somewhat differently, however, as Kipling must in part have intended. In the first place, the Old Testament story of Naboth (in 1 Kings, chapter 21), which was the source of Kipling's "allegory," is a biblical tale of retributive justice. In the Old Testament story, Naboth owns a vineyard (note the "trellis-work" in Kipling's story) annexed to King Ahab's palace, but he refuses to part with it when Ahab offers to purchase or make an exchange for it. The grounds for Naboth's refusal are that the vineyard is an "inheritance" from his ancestors. Ahab's wife Jezebel, however, conspires to acquire Naboth's property by publicly defaming him, which leads to his death by stoning. Jezebel's deceit and illicit attempt to acquire Naboth's property bring divine retribution on her children and family, and it is Naboth—not the king—who emerges as the one who was egregiously wronged.

Kipling's "Naboth" is on one level a reversal of the older story. Yet the central figure of Naboth, as the rightful occupant of land passed down to him by his "fathers," also retains the essential moral valence of the original. Literary critic Sara Suleri, in her reading of Kipling's story, sees "Naboth" as bearing "testimony to the dynamic of *powerlessness* underlying the telling of colonial stories" and to the essential precariousness of a colonial power that shares with its subject population a congruent "economy of desire."[59] That shared "economy of desire," in the context explored in this chapter, is a relatively complex longing to be at home, and it is only through a kind of guilt-ridden violence that it can be portrayed—in Kipling's story and elsewhere, perhaps—as the restoration of household order. While bungalow home life was shot through with anxiety and ambivalence over who, master or servant, was in the end more at home, in the newly forming urban spaces of the city beyond the bungalow compound that question received a much firmer answer. Chapter 6 explores this claim by moving out from the confines of British and Indian residential districts in Lahore to consider the city as a whole.

THINKING WITH THE CITY

Urban Writing in Colonial Lahore

6 Urban restructuring does not simply change the look of a city's buildings and roads; it also changes the way people imagine and understand their city. Governments have long realized this, which is partly why urban restructuring became an important tool of governance in colonial India: The colonial officials who planned and built urban space in British India hoped to produce a transformative physical milieu, one that would change how Indian residents thought about and lived in urban space. Throughout the colonial period in Lahore, as we have seen, both the look of the city and the sense its residents made of it changed, in large and small ways.

In this final chapter, I want to explore more fully the changes in the way Lahore's residents made sense of their city by examining a small number of fiction and nonfiction texts written in colonial Lahore that treated the city and its monuments as something more than mere brickwork and mortar. Each of the authors considered below saw the city itself as an important horizon of interpretation. Not every author interpreted the city in the same way, of course, and part of my emphasis in what follows will be to call attention to their differences. When read together, however, the works examined in this chapter reflect the gradual coalescence of a conviction, by the end of the nineteenth century, that studying the city would reveal the intangible qualities of the present—its centers of excellence and disrepute, its promises and pitfalls, and the shape of society's relationship to both its future and past. This was a new mode of imagining the city in Indian literature, one that grew out of the practices of urban restructuring that accompanied British rule. It emerged in parallel, however, with older modes of imagining and writing, and while the latter diminished over time, they never fully disappeared. Nevertheless, by the end of the nineteenth century a marked change had emerged in how writers used the city to reflect on issues of collective concern.

In the earliest work we consider, a local history of Lahore, author Noor Ahmad Chishti linked the city's monuments to a larger moral framework through claims and metaphors of genealogy. Important monuments or sites in Lahore acquired their status by physically embodying the lived and remembered relationships city residents maintained with their ancestors. Importantly, both the normative claims of Chishti's scholarship and the substantive authority for making them grew out of his own status as a participant in the collectivity. In the second work, an urban history of the city written one generation later, author Syad Muhammad Latif stood outside Chishti's moral framework to peer down on the city from above, a disembodied seer preoccupied most with the effects of things in the present. Whereas in Chishti's history historical monuments indexed living relationships (sometimes with figures no longer alive), in Latif's the most significant facts about Lahore's older monuments were archaeological, primarily their provenance and attribution. For Latif, it was Lahore's modern buildings and colonial institutions that held the most significance. A final work discussed in this chapter, a novel by Dina Nath written at the turn of the twentieth century, helps confirm this transformation; it also points, more importantly, to a new kind of lived relationship with the physical city that colonial restructuring made available.[1]

NARRATING THE USEFUL PAST

The idea that the city could be useful to "think with," in the particular sense I have just proposed, has a genealogy in the genre of "local" urban history, a new form of urban writing in nineteenth-century India.[2] This new genre drew Indo-Islamic and Anglo-European historiographic traditions together to focus on a subject that was novel to both: a meditation on the history of urban monuments and institutions in cities undergoing rapid colonial changes. These new urban histories forced the Indian scholars who wrote them to face new goals for the production of knowledge, new resources for compiling and disseminating historical texts, and new epistemological frameworks for explaining the past. They also provide evidence of a gradual change in the way India's cities became available for intellectual reflection.

During the early period of British rule, Europeans most often wrote India's history as a succession of dynasties and, occasionally, the monuments they each erected. These dynastic histories helped justify Britain's colonial undertaking ideologically by denigrating India's previous regimes and portraying Britain's role as that of replacing despotism with an enlightened form of government.[3] When British scholars began writing India's first urban histories in the 1840s, India's historic monuments were drawn into the narrative as evidence of the relative state of "civilizational" achievement or decline under various rulers and dynasties.

Indian historians working in the Sikh, Mughal, and earlier courts wrote histories as well, of course. Those histories, most in manuscript form, were written from different historiographic traditions than those practiced by the British and seldom isolated a particular city as their object of analysis.[4] Several of Punjab's historians indeed lived in Lahore, since the city had long been an important center of imperial patronage for scholarly works.[5] British officials were aware of this and exploited their skills from almost the first moment of contact with the Punjab. Local scholars provided knowledge to the colonial state for a variety of administrative and scientific purposes, and by the 1860s British officials had begun commissioning Indian historians in the city to document Lahore's architectural monuments and antiquities.

Punjab's nineteenth-century historians emerged from a particular scholarly milieu, one dominated by older aristocratic or spiritually endowed Muslim families and by Kayasth or Khatri Hindu families who adopted the Persian script.[6] Their histories were largely focused on the affairs of the Sikh court or dealt with descriptions of Punjab's economy, geography, and social customs.[7] While occasionally addressing urban phenomena, none of these works dealt with Punjab's larger cities in much detail. The first historical works concerned entirely with a single city emerged only at midcentury in Punjab, during a period when the European populations of cities like Delhi and Lahore began to grow and settle more permanently.

In part, these new urban histories were prompted by the antiquarian interests of the British patrons who encouraged and commissioned them. The historical tombs and monuments surrounding the outskirts of Delhi and Lahore regularly provided settings for novels, memoirs, and landscape paintings conceived in the picturesque and romantic traditions.[8] Equally important, however, was the perception that those same buildings were fast being eradicated to make room for a colonial city. Recording the city's older monuments was thus also an effort in "salvage" archaeology prompted by British concerns to record the city's architectural remains before they vanished for good. Finally, and most importantly for my argument, architectural monuments in Punjab's cities were increasingly seen as effective sites for the presentation of didactic messages, since abstract propositions about progress and cultural superiority could be revealed through monuments in tangible, material form. An urban history of a city's monuments could thus reveal the stark disjuncture between what British authors saw as an older regime of despotism and a modern regime of enlightened governance by comparing their material works.

In addition to providing a rationale for this new genre of urban historical writing, British patrons also helped establish its form. British civilians and officials often supplied encouragement and financial compensation to Indian authors. They also provided models to emulate, indirectly, through the promotion of European historical texts in colonial school curricula. For a variety of reasons, however, the first histories written were not well received by their British patrons. One of the earliest was Sayyid Ahmed Khan's *Asar-us-Sanadid* (Manifestations of the Noblemen), an account of the city of Delhi composed in the Urdu language.[9] Sayyid Khan first published his history in 1846, illustrating the book's six hundred pages of text with more than a hundred lithograph prints. The book described Delhi's historical palaces, shrines, and religious buildings and included a 250-page account of "cultural life" in the city that described the city's fairs and festivals, bazaars, and places for community gathering. Shortly after the book's initial publication, Sayyid Khan presented a copy to A. A. Roberts, Delhi's district magistrate and collector. Roberts, in turn, presented the book to the Royal Asiatic Society in London. On the suggestion of a member of the society, Roberts undertook an English translation of the book that for unknown reasons was never completed. In the preface to a later edition, however, Sayyid Khan claimed that the process of translating the work into English brought out "defects" in the original.[10] The nature of those defects is perhaps summarized best by Indian architectural historian Ram Nath, who edited and translated the book into English in 1979: "There was much confusion in the arrangement of the data," according to Nath, "and in the absence of a scientific classification *the wood was lost into the trees.*"[11]

Nath's 1979 assessment, that in Sayyid Khan's original book, "the wood was lost into the trees," reflects more than a difference of opinion about the way a book should be organized. Using the same metaphor, we might view Sayyid Khan's concentration on trees in terms of the forest his work quietly presupposed. Put another way, the broader significance of the details recorded by Sayyid Khan—a significance that his British readership found missing—needed little elaboration for an Indian readership, since the mode of description he used established the context automatically. That context drew on an earlier tradition of Indo-Islamic historical writing, in particular a mode Christopher Bayly has described as "genealogical."[12] This historiographic tradition assumed that certain known families and individuals embodied innate moral and spiritual qualities and that these qualities could be invoked for a reader simply by reciting lines of descent. More importantly, perhaps, the qualities did not need to be specified: Listing the names was enough to invoke them.

The invocation of a chain *(silsila)* of spiritual ancestors at the outset of biographical and other historical accounts is a stable feature of Islamic historiographic writing.[13] On the Indian subcontinent, as elsewhere, this formula remained common well into the twentieth century.[14] The codification of attitudes of esteem, deference, and reverence toward some social classes or types of behavior and of contempt, censure, or dismissal toward others was a feature of South Asian literatures more generally. These were the codes that mattered in a social milieu where distinction devolved largely upon one's personal or familial comportment and location in a nexus of hierarchical relationships.[15]

What is most interesting for our purposes is the way this new genre of nineteenth-century urban history enunciated similar codes but transposed them onto material artifacts. The "useful past" in these accounts was a history of buildings written largely as a history of men of standing, most of whom, importantly, were no longer alive.[16] Something of this tradition of enquiry underlay Sayyid Khan's description of Delhi's buildings, monuments he referred to as "Manifestations of the Noblemen." What appeared to an outside reader of his text as a directionless mingling of details, in other words, meant something quite different to readers familiar with Indo-Islamic historiographic formulas. Both the mode of writing and the object of analysis differed in these texts from contemporary British histories, a difference that was reduced over time but never entirely eliminated.

CHISHTI'S ENCYCLOPEDIA

Sayyid Khan's book was an important precedent for Lahore resident Noor Ahmad Chishti's *Tahqiqaat Chishti: Tarikh-e-Lahor ka Encyclopedia* (Chishti's Inquiries: An Encyclopedia of

Lahore's History), the first comprehensive urban history undertaken on Lahore, published for the first time in 1867. The book was written on the suggestion of William Coldstream, a British assistant commissioner whose "urging and creative support," Chishti claimed, "did not leave any space to refuse."[17] Chishti wrote his almost-nine-hundred-page book in a literary Persianate Urdu. The first half of the book presented a chronological account of the dynasties that ruled in Lahore from the first millennium CE through the time when the East India Company replaced the Sikh kingdom as sovereigns—a staple account that would have been available to Chishti in manuscript histories kept in the city. The second half of the book, however, described the monuments situated in the city and its environs, an account Chishti pieced together through personal observation, stories told to him by the city's inhabitants, and an analysis of inscriptions found on the monuments themselves.

There is much in Chishti's book that suggests he wrote it with an awareness of the kind of criticism Sayyid Khan's earlier work had received. There is also much in *Tahqiqaat Chishti* that retains some of the earlier work's "haphazard" features, that sense of a wood "lost into the trees." While Chishti's organizational schema was broadly chronological, the buildings he described in the book's later sections were presented in no strict chronological sequence. Similarly, Chishti seems to have relied extensively on "legends" and "hearsay" to flesh out his account, something a contemporary British reviewer commented upon disparagingly:

> The object of [Chishti's encyclopedia] is excellent; and if a second edition be called for, it might be made a really useful work. As it is, the book is needlessly long, containing, in 872 closely printed pages, descriptions of very unimportant places, such as tombs of persons long forgotten by most people and insignificant little *takia*s [stands or platforms occupied by a holy person]. It appears, too, to be very hastily written. Not only are there numerous grammatical and other mistakes, but the inaccuracy of some of the descriptions would lead one to suppose they were written from information derived secondhand. Nowhere is there any mention of authority for any statement.[18]

Secondhand information, hearsay, and legends were respectable forms of evidence in Indo-Islamic historiographic tradition, however, which may help explain why both Chishti and Sayyid Khan relied on them for information. Recitation, memorization, and oral testimony were all practices with a long history of technical refinement in the subcontinent, and oral evidence was considered authoritative when it derived from a reliable source. "As with legal witnessing," writes Brinkley Messick in his study of nineteenth-century historical texts from Yemen, "the authoritative contributions of historical accounts centered on what the author had personally seen or had heard from reliable individuals. Historians used to open their accounts as if they were giving oral testimony."[19] The epistemological status of "hearsay" in the constitution of a text like Chishti's thus depended on which perspective one viewed the text from, and his text engaged more than one perspective.

Chishti organized his descriptive account of Lahore's monuments typologically rather than chronologically, with chapter titles such as "Destroyed Graves," "Gardens," "Temples and Buildings of Non-Muslim Fakirs [mendicants]," and "Graves of Sufis and Ancients." Within an individual entry, Chishti was concerned most with stories of the building's founders, their reasons for dedicating or building the structure, and the families who subsequently and currently occupied, embellished, worshipped, or lay buried within it. Chishti often prefaced a description with the clause "it is said that" or "I have heard it told," substantiating his British reviewer's suspicion that he compiled many entries by interviewing local residents or the caretakers of shrines. Chishti's source of knowledge was thus both affective and embodied, deriving its authority and relevance through social relationships rather than scientific methodology.[20] As noted by his British critic, the range of buildings Chishti described was broad, from the humble dwellings of religious devotees located within a larger complex to the details (including inscriptions) of Lahore's more famous monuments. The "house *[makaan]* of Shaboot Shah," an example of the former type, was described in the following terms:

> The appearance of this building is thus: a dignified *[balan]* brick enclosure some twenty-two *gaz* [a measure roughly equal to the English yard] in length, and seven *gaz* tall, which is entered and exited through a door placed in the northern wall. The door has a white wooden threshold. Inside, on the western side of the enclosure, there is a courtyard open along two sides. In this courtyard, *it is said,* lies a tank built by Sai Shaboot Shah. At the northern end of the courtyard is a small chamber whose ceiling is covered entirely with *surkhi.* Inside, on the west, lies another chamber. Nowadays the latter structure belongs to a female mystic named Dhin Shah, a devotee of Hussain Ali Shah, *saj-jaada nashin* [spiritual heir to the saint] whose memorial is kept by the mystic and her companions. On the northern border of the enclosure lies another courtyard with three bricked-in windows running along the outer wall. Inside this court are two small basins, and to the east a stairway ascends giving exit.[21]

Qualitative terms like *balan* could be used to describe people as well, and the parallelism between people and monuments in Chishti's account was not incidental. To call something or someone "dignified" was to invoke a familiar set of values, ones that were broadly shared within Chishti's social milieu. The value of his account for this community, the "useful past" his book annotated, acquired its usefulness through the adept way known people or groups were linked to the buildings they or their ancestors had erected. To name and locate a monument in this tradition was simultaneously to invoke human qualities remembered and made manifest in the names themselves and to situate a physical place in relation to the people for whom it held meaning. Buildings were known by the people who used them, by where a particular saint's followers gathered and communed with one another, or by their proximity to an important, honorable, or pious woman or man. In this way, spatial relations of proximity overlapped with genealogical lines of descent in a matrix with clear centers of temporal and spatial importance. Chishti's textual strategy thus played a constitutive role in the way the text was received by its readers and a rhetorical role in establishing the qualifications of its author.

For Chishti the most important things to know about Lahore were related to the spatial disposition of the city's ancestors. Particular locations in the city acquired significance through their association with historical figures, the most important of whom were regularly made present through practices of remembrance, including the celebration of saints' days near the precincts of tombs, festivals, and camping and worshipping at temples and shrines. The copresence in time and space of the city's ancestors that animated so much of Chishti's text was not, properly speaking, history according to Anglo-European historical epistemology.

The universe of signification that structured Chishti's encyclopedia was, therefore, both a source of value to one group of readers and a limitation to another. His language was intelligible only to a tiny literate elite in the city, after all, and his book would have enjoyed very limited circulation among the city's Indian residents. In addition, the book's patron—a British government official—wished to record Lahore's rapidly disappearing monuments, not the people for whom their use still held meaning. Pious saints and mystics peopled Chishti's account of Lahore, yet by calling the book an "encyclopedia" he also gave notice that his work had other purposes. Chishti was thus engaged in a bit of writerly innovation; in many ways, however, the audience for his text did not exist. Later historical accounts largely dismissed the past that mattered to Chishti. Indeed, Chishti's encyclopedia received only lukewarm praise from Coldstream, who had originally commissioned the book: "When a thorough analysis of all Lahore's ancient monuments is one day written," Coldstream wrote, "Chishti's book will provide invaluable assistance."[22]

LATIF'S CAMERA OBSCURA

The kind of work Coldstream had in mind was written twenty-six years after *Tahqiqaat Chishti*. This was Syad Muhammad Latif's *Lahore: Its History, Architectural Remains, and Antiquities, with an Account of Its Modern Institutions, Inhabitants, Their Trade, Custom, &c.* (1892), an account of Lahore's buildings, both historic and modern, written in English.[23] Like Chishti, Latif was a government official, employed as judicial assistant commissioner of Gurdaspur District in Punjab. Latif's inclusion of Lahore's modern buildings and institutions, however, signaled an important difference between Chishti's outlook and his own. While some of Lahore's colonial buildings (such as the railway station, Lawrence and Montgomery Halls, and Government College, among others) were complete at the time Chishti wrote, Latif's book documents the city at a point in time when nearly all of Lahore's major colonial institutions were complete or under construction. By the time Latif wrote, in other words, Lahore had acquired a new geography, and the open plain outside the Old City had taken on new forms and meanings. There was a concerted attempt in Latif's account to draw the new and the old together within the framework of the text. It is equally apparent, however, that for Latif, as for many British commentators we have encountered in this book, the two had little in common.

A quotation on the frontispiece of Latif's book foretold an important shift in the way Lahore's history would be told: "What exhibition could be found more interesting than a Camera-Obscura, which should reflect past incidents of historical or private interest, and recall, with the vividness and minuteness of life, at least, the extent and characteristics of long past ages!"[24] Here, then, was the promise of forest rather than just trees. As much of the remaining text makes evident, Latif's work emphasized didactic purposes that Chishti's account left unspecified. The emphasis on exhibition and sight in the book's frontispiece was redoubled by the importance placed on vision in his introduction:

> I have laid a panorama of the city before the reader with an object far more important than the mere gratification which the study of a new work . . . may afford. It is to give a useful lesson to my countrymen, that they may, by its study, be enabled to *look impartially around them* and see of Lahore that which is really worth seeing in it, seeing and carefully weighing.[25]

Latif's narrative perspective viewed the city from above, from a putatively objective vantage point focused on the present rather than the past. For Latif the city was made up of objects to be seen and weighed, and each section of his book is prefaced with the same basic message: British rule had bestowed civility and peacefulness on the Punjab, and these qualities could be perceived most clearly by observing the colonial government's material works. Latif addressed his book to his fellow "countrymen," to an Indian readership he saw as inherently slow to adopt progressive changes and as still encumbered by superstitions and "ideas [from] primitive life."[26] The fault lines he perceived in his own society were drawn between the "educated classes" and everyone else, and for Latif the colonial landscape of Lahore cogently revealed the superiority of British science and rules of law over the works of Punjab's earlier rulers.

The city was useful for Latif not merely as a spatial record of pious deeds and people, therefore. For Latif, the city became a heuristic device for illustrating less tangible qualities. In his text, the city's "exhibitions" and exemplary modern industries powerfully evoked the qualities of "progress," "enlightenment," and "harmony":

> What a marvelous change has the comparatively short period of British rule brought about! It is interesting to compare the present with the past condition of things, for, if this is done impartially, it is impossible not to be struck with admiration. An age of violence and rapine has given place to one of peace and harmony; an age of ignorance has been followed by one of enlightenment. It is an age of exhibitions, of progress and of prosperity. . . . [For example] I have, in these pages, given you a full description of [Lahore's] railway workshops. Consider the great works executed there by means of science, and compare them with the rude and unpolished works of your own smiths. But for our knowledge that the ponderous works turned out there are the results of science, we should have thought they were the works of giants.[27] [Figure 6.1]

For all of the differences of emphasis reflected in Latif's and Chishti's accounts, however, both writers compiled their works in a remarkably similar manner. After mentioning his debt to Chishti's earlier book—a work that "notwithstanding its shortcomings," Latif wrote, "is not altogether devoid of merit"—Latif described his method of inquiry into the city's history, one that would have been quite familiar to someone like Chishti: "I conceived that I could not do better," Latif wrote, "than make personal inquiries from old residents of the city, men of letters and knowledge, and intelligent and aged men residing in the neighborhood."[28] He compared this information with accounts in older manuscript works (which he scrupulously listed), especially the biographies of saints and other eminent men of the province. Therefore Latif, like Chishti, was able to call on a range of texts, personal narratives, and "affective" knowledge while compiling his history despite the new epistemological bases of his text. If Latif's presentation of Lahore reflected features of the colonial spatial imagination, then it did so without erasing an older way of knowing and being part of a city, one still tied to older institutions and notions of urban community.

LIVING THE LAHORE LIFE

When Chishti was encouraged to write about the historical buildings of Lahore, the abodes of the city's ancestors that lay on the plains outside the city received his most sustained and careful attention. By the time Latif wrote, it was precisely these plains whose meanings were being altered, since the buildings and streets of the colonial city were gradually being erected across them. No longer merely the spatial repository of the city's extended temporal community, the plains outside the city during the late nineteenth and early twentieth centuries were being ineluctably drawn into a new, overlain landscape of colonial institutions and

Figure 6.1. Locomotive shed of the North-Western Railway workshops, Lahore, circa 1919. Copyright The British Library Board. OIOC Photo 335/15(12); all rights reserved.

residences, into new configurations of power articulated through a forceful reorganization of space.

We are left to ask what it might have meant to live in that reconfigured space at the turn of the twentieth century for someone like Latif or for members of the literate middle-class milieu that he was part of. While sources that might provide answers to this question are rare in Lahore's fragmentary archive, the question does emerge in Lahori author Dina Nath's 1899 novel *The Two Friends: A Descriptive Story of the Lahore Life*.[29] The two friends of the book's title are Rama and Nath, two recent college graduates from Lahore deep in the throes of youthful angst. The two are close friends, but they have different human qualities. Rama is impetuous, prone to bad behavior, and "the foremost dandy in Lahore"; Nath is genuine and earnest, a child of nature fond of long rambles through Lahore's Lawrence Gardens. This juxtaposition of the bad and the good, often projected onto the worldly and the spiritual, is the novel's generative grammar for a series of moral lessons.

One could read *The Two Friends* as a didactic novel shedding light on Punjab's late nineteenth-century quasi-religious institutions of civil society. Nath is a member of the Arya Samaj, whose DAV College was discussed in chapter 3. The novel's lessons make up a catalog of social issues championed by the Arya Samaj at the time, including the acceptance of (virgin) widow remarriage, the importance of vegetarianism, and the deleterious effect of all things "un-Indian" on the moral character of youth. This kind of reading might proceed by looking at the content of the "good" and the "bad" in the story, the first embodying Arya Samajist principles and the latter embodying their matter-of-fact opposites. Instead, my reading will question the nature of the hinge that simultaneously separated and connected the good and the bad, that particular condition of social and material flux that prompted Nath to pose opposites in the first place.

In the context of the novel, the source of this flux is the newly cosmopolitan nature of the city. Nath's novel intersects with Lahore's colonial transformations most legibly in the figure of the Lahori "student," a figure that drives the novel's action and provides a device for linking the experience of Lahore's "newness" to a meditation on the effects of education. At the start of the novel, Rama and Nath meet one another for a walk through Lawrence Gardens. Here they engage in a lively repartee, "giving to every passerby a suitable certificate according to his or her credentials, gossiping over all those topics which enjoyed public attention, now thoughtful, the next moment hilarious, in short making merry in a tremendous method" (25). Later they stroll beyond the park along Mall Road to Gol Bagh, "that rendezvous of students" just beyond the Mayo School of Art, where small groups of youths "hover like fairies in celestial regions" (111). At the nearby Hindu Hotel, a place distinguished by "five or six imperfect chairs, two antiquated tables, one reading lamp, and a few solitary books," a "medley of riotous youth" are gathered together for a weekly session of "cracking immoral jokes, using the first rate slang, discussing all impious topics, ridiculing their betters, fighting hand to hand, and in fact whatnot" (33). Despite this irreverent attitude, however, the student persona has a "curious magic" about it, Nath writes, something that commands the attention of others:

Go where you will in this religious assembly or that, in all social conferences, in patri-otic meetings, in political institutions, in private clubs or in public entertainments, the same singular youth of a talkative nature is visible. He seems all-pervading. No subject of critical importance but he puts his opinion about it, no question of even the least moment where he fails to argue . . . nor again is his enthusiasm lost, for people seem to hear him with relish. There is a curious magic about him. (58)

This rendering of the student resonates with descriptions found in other written accounts from the time. In an article in the *Punjab Magazine* from 1890, author Iqbal Kishan described a trip through the civil station's Anarkali Bazaar. There, Kishan noticed several clusters of students "at a little distance from each other," discussing "topics of vital impor-tance, such as the transmigration of the soul, the existence of God, Christianity, the so-called Aryanism, and a number of other similar questions."[30] These representations commonly describe the privileged habitat of the student as lying squarely within the spaces carved out by Lahore's incipient civil society: the city's parks, clubs, and voluntary social gatherings. The student's mode of presence in these accounts, and his defining subjectivity, is that of a searching—even sassy, perhaps—critic. These descriptions remind us that Nath's "singular youth of a talkative nature" inhabits the same settings, and embodies the same attitudes, that have long been associated with a discourse on European modernity. Michel Foucault has written, for instance, that among other things, the "attitude of modernity" entails a type of continuous philosophical critique that "simultaneously problematizes man's relation to the present, man's historical mode of being, and the constitution of the self as an autonomous subject."[31] The characters in Nath's novel nevertheless embody a range of differences from that discourse that derive from the particular nature of social life in a colonial metropolis.

A CITY OF REALMS

These differences emerge in the way Nath treats Lahore as a tangible assemblage of spaces and buildings that nevertheless conceal a range of intangible qualities. Like the characters Rama and Nath, Lahore too is described as a city with two opposing qualities. On the one hand, it is a city whose "whole climate seems choked with sin and grime"; on the other hand, it is a city filled with "brilliant sights, brilliant people; everything brilliant to boot" (62, 113). Moreover, Nath systematically attaches these two different qualities to distinct areas within the city, respectively, to Lahore's Old City and the civil station beyond. The division between these two different districts was as spatially abrupt in real life—the Old City was only acces-sible behind its high masonry walls through thirteen well-spaced gates—as it was concep-tually abrupt in the novel. Passing from the Old City to the civil station outside, the narrator tells us, one's "heart dances with a perfect sense of freedom, for freedom it certainly is to escape from the deafening turmoil of the town" (113).

Echoing colonial attitudes toward urban sanitation, the novel describes the Old City as being "[as] poisonous as the deadliest herb yet untested by medical criticism" and "[as] polluted as the most dangerous effervescence from a marshy ground" (58). By the turn of the twentieth century, this roughly four-square-mile area was home to more than 150,000 people.

> Why! With its dirty and dingy streets where sunlight is conspicuous by entire absence, with its baffling and crooked lanes defiant to remembrances of memory, with its "bazaars" where none but men of stout physique and stouter heart can manage way and lastly though not leastly with the shrewd typical "Lahori," sly of look, cunning by temper and sloth of movement—with all these sights [the Old City] is wonderful. . . . It has roads whereupon sanitation is totally prohibited, it has gates with entrances guarded by huge masses of filth enough to frighten away every body (provided though he be with the most indifferent nasal organ), it has wretched streets, ruined houses, tottered walls and in fact whatnot. (112)

Contrast this description with that of the civil station, where the "capital [city] has its redeeming points" (112). Here is how the narrator in Nath's novel describes it:

> I dare not depict the multifarious charms of this exquisite road—the "Upper Mall." Its beauty is indescribable. . . . It is verily a road for the European community. All sort of White people can be had here. (115) [Figure 6.2]

While Nath mentions Lahore's government institutions obliquely in his text, the spaces of public resort in the civil station receive his most sustained attention. This is where the city's communities come together in all their diversity, with people of different races and places of origin all mingled together:

> Take for instance Anarkali, it is a good "bazaar" out and out. The shops are clean and respectable. In the evening time when the student folks give up their studies for a little recreation, it presents an extremely busy aspect. Even the dry-as-dust Lahori yields to the temptation of an evening ramble. Side by side with the spirited Native student, giving vent to his English in a very destructive fashion, may be seen the Herculean rustic

Figure 6.2. Mall Road outside the Punjab Chief Court building, circa 1930. A statue of John Lawrence, wielding a sword in one hand and a pen in the other, appears at left. Copyright The British Library Board. OIOC Photo 627/66; all rights reserved.

who has come to see the metropolis from the adjacent village. There again we see the N.W.P. [North-West Provinces] man whose tongue runs with a locomotive velocity, so fluently, so hurriedly as to leave the audience in a dilemma whether the speaker was using Latin or his own vernacular. Here and there the redcoated, bare-legged Highlander soldier from [Mian Mir] Cantonment can be seen walking always and invariably in a tipsy but wherewithal a strutting mode. Amongst this variety of people may also be found the famous Lahori "goonda" (lit. Scoundrel) with his pick-pocket looks and sullen scowling cut-throat face—a hated bully. (113)

Lahore's civil station is also where the white community is most abundantly in evidence. The narrator notices "old [white] folks bent double on the account of the ravages of age," and "stout gentlemen superfluously red but often very handsome. . . . grown up misses barely on the verge of womanhood but already looking wise and serious" (114). Montgomery Hall, just behind the entrance to the Lahore Botanical Garden, is "verily a talismanic lodge" for Europeans, we are told, a place where "all around us we see civilization and excellence" (115). Another staple of Victorian urban desire, the "lady cyclist," finds a place in Nath's text in the person of the "brave and killing—Sarah Fairborn," whom "God alone knows how much we admire" (114). Although the European community in Lahore never exceeded a few hundred people at any time during the nineteenth century, *The Two Friends* underscores their conspicuous presence in the civil station and Nath's ambivalent attitude toward them.

The different urban qualities of Lahore framed in Nath's text are thus held together more or less according to an inside/outside, older city/newer city binary. This image of the city separated into two different physical realms helps the author foreground two different social dimensions of the city as well. The civil station reveals the city's community in its horizontal dimensions—its different races, classes, and genders. Here, side by side with the "Herculean rustic," the bare-legged British soldier swaggers along in his tipsy, but "strutting" manner. Conversely, the vertical dimensions—those aspects of community that extend forward and backward in time—appear most clearly in the quarters of the Old City. This, for example, is the site of the tomb of Ranjit Singh, a figure whose spirit "lives [on] in a potent and *omni-present* condition" (111; emphasis added). Though the physical quality of the Old City leaves much to be desired, its very degradation reveals a place "fallen from thy glorious traditions, from thy ancient lineage, [and] from thy past splendor" (60).

Clearly, Nath's conceptualization of the city as divided into two disparate zones was compatible with British colonial attitudes at the time about the difference between the "native" city and the civil station, or between "Black Town" and "White Town" as these areas were sometimes labeled on city maps.[32] His conceptualization also shares something with more recent academic paradigms that describe the "dual" nature of colonial cities as one of their defining features. This idea became common in both planning and urban geographic literature from the 1970s onward, as researchers attempting to define the "colonial city" as a generic urban type focused on the unequal binary division, based primarily on racial segregation, of urban space, infrastructure, and amenities in these cities.[33] What these two ways of imagining the city have in common, however, is not so much an empirical object—

the colonial city—with relevant identifiable features. What they share more centrally is a particular perspective from which to view the city, one that seeks the confirmation of abstract principles in the shape of its visible features. Thus the dual-city theorist apprehends social inequality in the disparate morphologies of "native" and "European" urban districts, in much the same way that Dina Nath apprehends an abstract sense of "freedom" by passing from one district to the other ("for freedom it certainly is to escape from the deafening turmoil of the town"). While separated in time, genre, and locus of enunciation, these examples share a distinctive perspective.

As I hope to have shown in this chapter, and throughout this book more generally, that perspective was not something that came about naturally; nor was it a simple reflection of "reality" in any uncomplicated way. It was a perspective that had to be taught and learned, shaped to accommodate specific Indian contexts, and made able to demonstrate its relevance among, and in relation to, other traditions of thinking about the city. This was a key element in the process that made Lahore "modern," as both a constructed and an imagined city, and we can see it emerging clearly by the turn of the twentieth century.

THINKING WITH THE COLONIAL CITY

For many literate middle-class residents of Lahore, therefore, physical monuments and the organization of urban space became increasingly emblematic of deeper, less visible principles. Notably, it was the newer, colonial part of Lahore that was best suited to portraying the maelstrom of new and old attitudes and ideas that made living the "Lahore Life," for Dina Nath at least, something of consequence. We might say that for Nath, the elusive nature of Lahore's modernity was located—both rhetorically and materially—in the landscape of the newly growing metropolis, in its crowds and new surfaces, both of them full of promise and risk.[34] Lahore's colonial urban fabric was the constitutive ground for the urban histories and novel analyzed above, a newly ordered city that lent itself to a didactic narrative as a material manifestation of what were otherwise conceptual developments—for Latif, a newly turned-out locomotive was both a material marvel *and* an emblem of progress and prosperity. The spatial imagination that accompanied that evolution—one shared, at least, by the literate middle classes who were its subjects—worked by drawing analogies between particular materialities and arrangements of space, on the one hand, and the moral qualities that were seen to accompany them, on the other. Importantly, however, as with all synthetic conceptual schemata, this spatial imagination was never a simple replacement for older or less systematic conceptions. Both the city itself and the various manners and styles of appropriating it for thought retained links to other histories and ways of organizing social life, some substantially older and others just beginning to emerge.

Few today would hesitate in agreeing that the physical city is partially constituted through imagination. However, the relationship between morphology and imagination is never everywhere the same. The histories and novel we examined converged on a didactic paradigm, one that envisioned subject-altering effects emanating from the city's material works. It is notable that Latif's and Nath's texts stretched to reach closure on what the new parts of Lahore embodied long before the effects of those changes had become clear. Latif's conviction in 1892 that "an age of violence and rapine has given place to one of peace and harmony," or Nath's claim in 1899 that to escape the town was to attain freedom, seem as politically naive from our vantage point today as they must have seemed sketchily hopeful at the time of their initial writing. Rapid change perhaps does this to certain kinds of writers: It produces an urge to see a future manifest now, rather than an unfinished process unfolding.[35] Nevertheless, by the turn of the twentieth century Lahore had reached a kind of formal and spatial fixedness that had been elusive even ten years earlier.

The forces that produced that new urban form were not always as forceful or destructive as scholars sometimes assume. Without minimizing the severity of the violence and dehumanization required to maintain colonial rule in India (as with colonial rule elsewhere in the world), these are not the only dimensions of colonial power useful for understanding the complex processes that constituted colonial urbanism. Colonial officials who proposed the kinds of projects described in this book assumed that the shaping of proper sentiments, rather than the imposition by force of radically new forms of social organization, was the most effective means to create a proper milieu for the conduct of society. Their goal was nothing less than to create a new kind of person, and the material environment was thought crucial to the task.

The idea that a properly ordered material environment could foster societal change has been a cornerstone of state policy wherever modern Anglo-European governments ruled, whether at home or abroad. This idea was as central to early republican efforts to shape a national landscape in the United States or to nineteenth-century urban reforms in England as it was to the reshaping of colonial Rabat by French urban planners or to the reshaping of nineteenth-century Cairo by British and Egyptian engineers.[36] In this sense, there is nothing particularly "colonial" about the idea itself. The application of materialist reform in colonial settings was distinctive, however, in at least one important way: Europe's encounter with the "strange and unfamiliar" worlds of its overseas colonies gradually unsettled the assumption that materialist reform entailed principles—and produced effects—that were *universal* in nature. In a setting where the very foundation of knowledge and moral judgment—that is, experience derived from the sensate apperception of a material world—was no longer patterned along familiar lines, the endpoint of materialist reforms could never be ascertained with certainty. Put another way, the appeal of "object lessons," model schemes, and exemplary material works lasted far longer in colonial contexts than did any certainty regarding their effects.

This was not simply a matter of local specificity running up against the universalisms inherent to liberal theory, however. Once the techniques and assumptions of materialist reform spread to larger segments of colonial populations, reaching deeper into local societies, they increasingly had to contend with other imagined relationships between society and the material world and with other ways of positing moral growth. The result was not that "local" or "indigenous" practices formed an obdurate Other standing resolutely outside of modernity. Nor, as we have seen, did "local" practices simply dissolve under the continuous application of a particular form of Anglo-European reason. When colonial subjects gradually embraced the tenets of materialist reform, moreover, the results of that embrace were not prefigured in the West. Rather, the "local" and contingent became constitutive of— rather than remaining external to—the diverse expressions of modernity that emerged.

I have intentionally left the term "modernity" singular in the last passage rather than making it plural, even though throughout this book I have tried to emphasize the diversity of practices, intellectual traditions, and forms of agency that underlay Lahore's transformation into what I have called a "modern" city. This runs counter, perhaps, to a considerable body of recent scholarship that asserts the relevance of "alternative," "indigenous," or simply "Other" forms of modernity against any singular definition. These "plural" forms of modernity redress an older, largely discredited, but still hegemonic idea that modernity was invented in Europe and became, indeed, "the principle of Western society *as such.*"[37] Critics of the latter idea rightly point to the development of modern social formations in colonial settings that, while coeval with similar developments in the West, were differently configured, and often forged in opposition to, those same developments.[38] The call for acknowledging "multiple modernities" entails an ethical assertion that there is more than one way to be modern in the world and more than one historical path to its realization. It is an argument against the idea of modernity as a monolithic or self-contained phenomenon, one that sees it "fissured with paradox and incompleteness," incapable of being fully secured, and conveyed in "restless, discontinuous cultural interactions that create impure, syncretic subjects."[39] As David Scott has written, this argument "answers the demand for an understanding of the making of the modern world that refuses the progressivist teleologies of developmentalism and the moral prejudices of Eurocentrism, and focuses our attention on the agency of the non-Western subalterns themselves and what they make with what they have."[40] While in some hands the multiple-modernities argument occasionally drifts toward a less compelling version of cultural relativism, I admire both the political commitment that underlies advocacy for this position and the important scholarship many of its advocates have produced.

Nevertheless, I want to hold on to a notion of modernity in the context of the colonial city that, while acknowledging cultural difference, incomplete processes, and multiple kinds of experience, does not lose sight of the powerful way European colonialism set forces into motion that converged in a *particular* direction, forces that appear elsewhere in cities across the world at around the same time and that manifest in similar ways.[41] While the number of ways the small but powerful group of people discussed in this book worked on, recorded, governed, inhabited, and imagined colonial Lahore was diverse, and sometimes radically so, the result of their actions was to gradually produce a recognizable "kind" of city. Whether we wish to call this a "modern" city, as I have done for the purposes of this book, or use some other term, the urban sensibilities expressed about it in the archival record we have left to us are similar to those expressed about modern cities elsewhere at the time. Put somewhat differently, making Lahore modern meant making the city more, rather than less, like an increasingly prevalent type. This is not the same as saying that urban life in India, once colonized by the British, gradually but inevitably assimilated to a homogeneous Western pattern. Rather, it is to acknowledge that the colonial practices that brought a modern form of urbanism to Indian cities increasingly constituted the very grounds through which difference, resistance, incompletion, paradox, or creativity could be recognized *as such* in an urban setting.

NOTES

INTRODUCTION

1. Quoted in Latif, *Lahore*, 98.

2. Quoted in ibid.

3. Quoted in ibid., 99.

4. Ibid., 252, 100.

5. Government of India, *Imperial Gazetteer of India, Provincial Series, Punjab*, 2:23–27.

6. While urbanization in general increased during the British period, urban growth was unevenly distributed. With the increasing centralization of administration following the transfer from British East India Company to Crown rule in 1858, larger administrative and service cities tended to grow at the expense of smaller towns. The construction of the Indian railways, beginning in the 1850s, also helped redistribute population and wealth toward towns located at railheads; in those towns and cities that the railway bypassed, populations commonly declined. See Bayly, *Rulers, Townsmen, and Bazaars*, esp. chapter 12; Yang, *Bazaar India*. On the dynamics of urbanization in the Punjab, see Banga, "Polity, Economy, and Urbanization in the Upper Bari Doab, 1700–1947," 192–205; Reeta Grewal, "Urban Revolution under Colonial Rule," 438–54.

7. Until 1833, when the East India Company's charter was revised, British holdings in India were divided into three relatively independent administrative provinces, or "presidencies": Calcutta, Madras, and Bombay. The seat of government for each of these provinces was established in a new port city that shared its name with the province, hence the term "presidency capitals" for each of these three cities.

8. While I am fully aware that any attempt to define *the* modern city will meet with a rousing clatter of objections—from charges of sloppy oversimplification to those of willful totalization—it is surprising how frequently past efforts to declare such a definition have converged around a few main themes. I think the ones I have listed here represent an incomplete, but venerable, short list. See, for example, Blumenfeld, "The Modern Metropolis," 40–57. For a more recent defense of the decision to use the arguably exhausted terminology of "modern" and "modernity" to analyze urban culture—one whose

elegance I admire, yet whose sense of urgency I do not fully share—see Donald, *Imagining the Modern City*, 19–24.

9. See Donald, *Imagining the Modern City*, 19–24. Also see Coleman's short but informative introductory essay in his *Idea of the City in Nineteenth-Century Britain*, and Williams, *The Country and the City*.

10. See Marshall Berman's perceptive treatment of this theme in his *All That Is Solid Melts into Air*. Art historian Timothy J. Clark, in his *Painting of Modern Life*, provides a memorable analysis of how the twinned poles of promise and danger received figuration in avant-garde painting in Paris.

11. Çelik, *Urban Forms and Colonial Confrontations*, 3–4.

12. Cited in ibid., 4.

13. The Westernization hypothesis grew in tandem with modernization theory during the 1960s and '70s. Some analyses see the process of progressive modernization—like Westernization—as being most advanced in the middle and upper classes and see the urban poor (like their rural counterparts) as lagging behind and thus in some ways more culturally "authentic." For a representative study of this type of analysis that considers the nexus between "modernization," "Westernization," and urbanism in South Asia, see Qadeer, "Do Cities 'Modernize' the Developing Countries?" More recent architectural histories have deployed a fairly standard version of the "Westernization" hypothesis as well; see, for example, Tillotson, *The Tradition of Indian Architecture*, and Morris, *Stones of Empire*.

14. Upton, "The Tradition of Change."

15. I am leaving aside the difficulties of defining what "West" and "non-West" might refer to—in particular—when either of these terms is used, something that is usually left unspecified. See King, *Spaces of Global Cultures*, 68–69.

16. See Asad, "Modern Power and the Reconfiguration of Religious Traditions," 4–5.

17. Stuart Hall, "Cultural Identity and Diaspora," 394.

18. Ibid., 395.

19. See Mahmood, *Politics of Piety*, 199.

20. Chakrabarty, *Provincializing Europe*, 72. Page numbers in parentheses in the following passage refer to this work.

21. Chishti, *Tahqiqaat Chishti* [Chishti's Inquiries].

22. Rabinow, *French Modern*, 278.

23. This is a central thematic of Joe Nasr and Mercedes Volait's 2003 edited volume, *Urbanism Imported or Exported*. Monographs that centrally address this theme in contexts other than India include Yeoh, *Contesting Space* (1996); Bozdogan, *Modernism and Nation Building* (1996); Çelik, *Urban Forms and Colonial Confrontations* (1994); Crinson, *Modern Architecture and the End of Empire* (1996). Recent monographs that take up questions of cultural difference and authenticity in a postcolonial urban and architectural context include Kusno, *Behind the Postcolonial* (2000), and Vikramaditya Prakash, *Chandigarh's Le Corbusier* (2002).

24. Hosagrahar writes, "The remarkable features of Delhi's modernity were the circumstances of its arrival, its imposition by colonial forces, and its adaptation to local conditions." Hosagrahar, *Indigenous Modernities*, 190.

25. Ibid., 7.

26. Ibid., 45.

27. Ibid., 190.

28. Swati Chattopadhyay, *Representing Calcutta*, 178.

29. Ibid., 275.

30. Ibid., 275.

31. Ibid., 3.

32. Loudon, *An Encyclopedia of Cottage, Farm, and Villa Architecture and Furniture*, 3.

33. Kingsley, *Sanitary and Social Lectures and Essays*, 187.

34. Foucault, *Discipline and Punish*, 136–37.

35. Mitchell, *Colonizing Egypt*; Arnold, *Colonizing the Body*; Yang, "Disciplining 'Natives'"; Satadru Sen, *Disciplining Punishment*.

36. Foucault, *Discipline and Punish*, 135.

37. David Scott, "Colonial Governmentality," 193.

38. Stokes, *The English Utilitarians and India*.

39. Ibid., 32.

40. Ibid., 46.

41. Mandelbaum, *History, Man, and Reason*, 141, 146.

42. The idea that natural objects existed in a "purer" state than products formed by human industry was one Pestalozzi shared with a number of Enlightenment thinkers. Most of Pestalozzi's biographers highlight the obvious influence of Jean Jacques Rousseau's writings (particularly the novel *Émile*) on Pestalozzi's thought. The most thorough compilation of nineteenth-century writings on Pestalozzi and Pestalozzianism is in Barnard, *Pestalozzi and His Educational System*.

43. Calkins, *Primary Object Lessons for a Graduated Course of Development*, preface.

44. On the Lancasterian system of schooling, also called the "monitorial system" or the system of "mutual education" for its reliance on student monitors instead of trained teachers, see Markus, "The School as a Machine," and Upton, "Lancasterian Schools, Republican Citizenship, and the Spatial Imagination in Early Nineteenth-Century America."

45. Sengupta, "An Object Lesson in Colonial Pedagogy," 99.

46. Macaulay, *Macaulay: Prose and Poetry*, 729.

47. Government of Punjab, "Report on the Publications Registered in the Punjab under Act XXV of 1867 during the Year 1886," Home Department Proceedings (General), nos. 16–17 (July 1887): n.p.

48. Uday Singh Mehta, among others, has elegantly documented the "deployment of the metaphor of childhood" by nineteenth-century British liberal theorists to describe the character of Indian mental development. Mehta writes that the theme of India's childhood "is the fixed point underlying the various imperial imperatives of education, forms of governance and the alignment with progress." Mehta, *Liberalism and Empire*, 31.

49. Crary, *Suspensions of Perception*, 27.

50. Mead, *Movements of Thought in the Nineteenth Century*, 386–91.

51. Dhingra, "Indian Sanitation: A Personal View," 320.

1. AN URBAN PALIMPSEST

1. Suleri, *Meatless Days*, 54.

2. Government of Punjab, *Report of the Lahore and Amritsar Improvement Trust Committee*, 2.

3. Masudul Hasan, *Guide to Lahore*, 33.

4. Suleri, *Meatless Days*, 54.

5. Keep, McLaughlin, and Parmar, "Palimpsest."

6. Rudyard Kipling, *In Black and White*, 35.

7. Thornton, "Lahore," 112.

8. Anand Yang discusses the role precolonial features of Patna played during that city's colonial period in his *Bazaar India,* esp. 105–6.

9. Chetan Singh, *Region and Empire,* 173; also see K. N. Chaudhuri, "Some Reflections on the Town and Country in Mughal India."

10. Bayly, *Rulers, Townsmen, and Bazaars,* 190–93.

11. J. S. Grewal, "Historical Writing on Urbanisation in Medieval India," 78.

12. Chetan Singh, *Region and Empire,* 175.

13. Thornton, "Lahore," 114.

14. Akbar relocated his court from Fatehpur Sikri to Lahore in order to further Mughal power in the northwest following the death of his half brother in Kabul in 1585. See Richards, *The Mughal Empire,* 49–52.

15. On the original extent of the pre-Mughal city, see Pakistan Planning and Architectural Consultants, Ltd. (PEPAC), *The Walled City of Lahore.* Malik Ayyaz, who served under Mahmud of Ghazni, is said by legend to have built the original walls and fort of Lahore following Mahmud's conquest of the Punjab in 1023 CE. Ali Hajveri, better known as Data Ganj Bakhsh (Conferrer of Treasure), was a renowned scholar from Ghazni who also settled in Lahore following Mahmud's conquest. Hajveri's most important work was the *Kashf-ul Mahjub* (Revelation of the Hidden), which remains a central text in Sufism. Qutb ud-din Aibak (1150–1210), a Turkish slave under the Central Asian ruler Muhammad Ghuri (1160–1206), rose to the rank of sultan and is considered to be the first Muslim ruler of India. He died in Lahore, following a horseback riding accident, after only four years of rule. Syed Muhammad Ishaq, better known as Miran Badshah, was a Persian saint who died in Lahore in 1384.

16. Syad Latif, *Lahore,* 27.

17. The most important accounts of Lahore by Europeans from this period include Bernier, *Travels in the Mughal Empire;* Thévenot, *The Travels of Monsieur de Thévenot into the Levant;* Manrique, *Travels of Sebastian Manrique;* Steel and Crowther, "A Journal of the Journey of Richard Steel and John Crowther"; and Tavernier, *Travels in India.*

18. Fazl, *Ain-i Akbari,* 317.

19. Manucci, *The General History of the Mughal Empire,* 2:186.

20. Naqvi, *Urbanization and Urban Centers under the Great Mughals,* 18.

21. Blake, *Shahjahanabad,* 44–51.

22. PEPAC, "The Walled City of Lahore," 5.

23. A notable exception, of course, is Akbar's short-lived capital at Fatehpur Sikri, which was built on a site chosen for its proximity to Salim Chishti's tomb.

24. See Hussain, Rehman, and Wescoat, *The Mughal Garden;* Koch, "The Mughal Waterfront Garden"; Koch, "Mughal Palace Gardens from Babur to Shah Jahan"; Wescoat, "Gardens versus Citadels."

25. Naqvi, *Urbanization and Urban Centers under the Great Mughals,* 101.

26. Wescoat, "Gardens, Urbanization, and Urbanism in Mughal Lahore," 144.

27. Latif, *Lahore,* 95.

28. Nineteenth-century historians estimated the probable circumference of Mughal-era Lahore, including its suburbs, to be about sixteen miles. The circumference of the city wall has been about three miles since Akbar's time. See Thornton, "Lahore," 112.

29. See Blake, *Shahjahanabad;* Asher, *Architecture of Mughal India,* 51–67.

30. There is some scholarly disagreement on this point. Urban planner Samuel Noe, for one, has described the "Mughal city" as a version of the classic "Islamic city," using Lahore and Delhi as

paradigmatic examples of the former. See Noe, "Old Lahore and Old Delhi," and Noe, "Shahjahan-abad." Stephen Blake speculates that the layout of Shahjahanabad was based on a combination of Islamic cosmological ideas and more local Hindu sources. In addition, Blake finds in Shahjahanabad a microcosm of the "patrimonial-bureaucratic" state. See Blake, *Shahjahanabad*, 32–34. The point of departure for Blake is Max Weber's thesis on the nature of the patrimonial-bureaucratic state and his contention, on the evidence of Bernier's *Travels in the Mughal Empire*, that Mughal India lacked urban community, in the European sense of the term, since Mughal society and polity lacked autonomous mercantile and municipal corporations.

31. Several scholars have examined ancient Hindu and Buddhist manuscripts that purport to explain the layout of ancient and medieval towns in India, including Gawda, *Urban and Regional Planning*; Ghosh, *The City in Early Historical India*; and R. S. Sharma, "Urbanism in Early Historic India." Historian Brajadulal Chattopadhyay notes, however, that these prescriptive texts have never been successfully correlated with other types of evidence for any but the most ancient of Indian cities. See Brajadulal Chattopadhyay, *The Making of Early Medieval India*, esp. 155–56. Also see Bafna, "On the Idea of the Mandala as a Governing Device in Indian Architectural Tradition."

32. Bernier, *Travels in the Mughal Empire*, 245.

33. Ibid., 246; emphasis added.

34. Ibid., 366.

35. Ibid., 367, 367–68, 367.

36. See Koch, "Mughal Palace Gardens from Babur to Shah Jahan"; Asher, *Architecture of Mughal India*. John Richards described Akbar's planned city of Fatehpur Sikri as "an urban form in transition between camp and imperial metropolis." See Richards, *The Mughal Empire*, 29.

37. Bernier, *Travels in the Mughal Empire*, 246, 284–85, 285.

38. On the Mughal development of gardens and suburbs in Lahore, see Wescoat, "Gardens, Urbanization, and Urbanism in Mughal Lahore," and Wescoat, "Toward a Map of Mughal Lahore."

39. Sheikh Rahim Ali, cited in Naqvi, *Urbanization and Urban Centers under the Great Mughals*, 20. It is likely that the traveler meant that people were confined within the walls of the Old City rather than within the citadel itself.

40. There is little urban-historical scholarship on Amritsar, despite the historical importance of this city to the Sikh faith and to the Punjab more generally. See, however, Fauja Singh, *The City of Amritsar*; Gauba, *Amritsar*; J. S. Grewal, *The City of the Golden Temple*; Datta, *Amritsar Past and Present*.

41. Ranjit Singh has inspired more than a few biographies. Two that stand out from among others, for different reasons, are J. S. Grewal's scholarly *Maharaja Ranjit Singh* and Khushwant Singh's more adventurous *Ranjit Singh*.

42. Bayly, *Empire and Information*, 136. On the partial continuance of Mughal administrative personnel under subsequent rulers, see Baden Powell, *The Land Systems of British India*. For a nuanced account of Sikh adaptations, see Banga, "Formation of the Sikh State." Urban administration under the Mughal Empire is discussed in Blake, *Shahjahanabad*; Naqvi, *Mughal Hindustan*; Naqvi, *Urbanisation and Urban Centers under the Great Mughals*; and Hambly, *Cities of Mughal India*.

43. Chishti, *Tahqiqaat Chishti*; Griffen, *The Rajas of Punjab*; Massey, *Chiefs and Families of Note in the Punjab*; Latif, *Lahore*.

44. J. S. Grewal, *In the By-Lanes of History*, 25; Naqvi, *Urbanisation and Urban Centers under the Great Mughals*, 99.

45. Richards, *The Mughal Empire*, 92.

46. Habib, *Essays in Indian History*, 99–101.

47. Kozolowski, *Muslim Endowments and Society in British India*, 21–32.

48. Sikh and Mughal relations were mostly antagonistic during the seventeenth and eighteenth centuries. Syad Muhammad Latif's 1892 history provides numerous anecdotal accounts of Sikh desecration of Mughal buildings in the city, including the alleged looting of stone from Jahangir's tomb complex in Shahdara for reuse on the Golden Temple in Amritsar. Latif's narrative of this occurrence is typical: "The building suffered much at the cruel hands of Lahna Singh, one of the three sirdars who governed Lahore before the establishment of the Sikh monarchy, and by the ruthless vandalism of Maharaja Ranjit Singh, who stripped it of most of its choicest ornaments to decorate the Sikh temple at Amritsar." Latif, *Lahore*, 107.

49. Habib, *Essays in Indian History*, 94–100.

50. Jyoti Hosagrahar has documented the fate of several large Mughal-era *haveli*s in Delhi after the arrival of the British. In addition to the breakup and dispersal of the older buildings, Hosagrahar documents the emergence of a new, smaller, and more modest form of *haveli* during the nineteenth century in the city. See Hosagrahar, *Indigenous Modernities*, chap. 2.

51. Latif, *Lahore*, 230.

52. Jacquemont, *The Punjab a Hundred Years Ago*, 57.

53. Quoted in Latif, *Lahore*, 98.

54. Barr, *Travels from Delhi to Punjab and Cabul with the Mission of Lieutenant Colonel Sir C. M. Wade*, 37–38.

55. For an elegant exposition of this principle in action in a different cultural setting, see Harding, "Space, Property, and Propriety in Urban England."

56. Naqvi, *Urbanisation and Urban Centers under the Great Mughals*, 14.

57. An eighteenth-century Persian text by Ali Muhammad Khan, the last Mughal *diwan* (treasurer) of Gujrat, provides a description of the *kotwal*'s duties as these were related in a *farman* (imperial letter, order, communication) from Akbar: "The *kotwal* with the help of clerks should make a list of the house and buildings of the place, and enter under each house its inhabitants, stating what sort of men they are, how many of them are *bazaaris* [sellers in the bazaar], how many are artisans, how many are soldiers, how many dervishes. Taking security from every house, he should ensure their mutual co-operation, and defining the mohallas, he should appoint a headman for each mohalla, by whose advice all things should be done there. . . . when a guest arrives, be he a kinsman or a stranger, it should be reported to the headman of the ward." Cited in Sarkar, *Mughal Administration*, 59–60. The full title of this manuscript is *Mirat-i-Ahmad* (1761), by Ali Muhammad Khan. See Sarkar, *Mughal Administration*, 58–59; 249–50.

58. See Kozolowski, *Muslim Endowments in India*, 109.

59. Whitworth, *An Anglo-Indian Dictionary*, 171.

60. On the British use of *mohalladar*s in colonial Patna, see Yang, *Bazaar India*, 97–98. On the partial continuance of Mughal administrative personnel under subsequent rulers more generally, see Baden Powell, *The Land Systems of British India*. For a nuanced account of Sikh adaptations to the Mughal administrative system see Banga, "Formation of the Sikh State."

61. Wilson, *A Glossary of Judicial and Revenue Terms, and of Useful Words Occurring in Official Documents Relating to the Administration of the Government of British India*, 272.

62. The Bandhari documents portray salient features of trade in urban land that can be reasonably extended to the study of Lahore. Grewal writes that "there is no reason to assume that some extraordinary and unusual situation existed in [Batala]. What is true of Batala could be true of many

other towns in the Punjab and even outside the Punjab. The question of proprietary rights in Batala, therefore, has much more than a local significance." J. S. Grewal, *In the By-Lanes of History*, 40.

63. J. S. Grewal, *In the By-Lanes of History*, 43.

64. See Document 3 in ibid., 125–29.

65. J. S. Grewal, *In the By-Lanes of History*, 30; see Document 14, 195–200.

66. An Indian traveler to Shahjahanabad (Delhi) during the early eighteenth century documented a single street in the city with the following contiguous properties: "On one side, the shop of a *halwai* (sweetmeat seller), Kucha Bazaar Imli, Mohalla and Kucha of Pati Ram, Bangla of Hafiz Fida, Kucha Murghian (birds and fowl), residents of ryots *(makan-i-riaya)* [tenant farmers], houses of Kashmiri Pandits, *haveli* of Dudhadhari, house of Lala Gulab Rai Pandit, the Tahsildar of Palam proper, Kucha of Mai Das, Than of Panj Piran, Kucha of Shidi Qasim, which leads to the Kucha of Pati Ram [etc.]." From the travel account of Dargah Quli Khan (1738), quoted in S. Hasan, "The Morphology of a Medieval Indian City," 89.

67. Francisco Pelsaert, a Dutch traveler who visited India in the early seventeenth century as an employee of the Dutch East India Company, noted that during the expansion of Agra under Akbar's reign people from all walks of life vigorously bought urban property in the city: "Everyone acquired and purchased the plot of land which suited or pleased him best. . . . Hindus mingled with Moslems, the rich with the poor." Pelsaert, *Jahangir's India*, 1–2.

68. J. S. Grewal, *In the By-Lanes of History*, 74.

69. Ibid., 250.

70. Latif, *Lahore*, 83.

71. See Cynthia Talbot, "Inscribing the Other, Inscribing the Self."

72. Latif, *Lahore*, 114. The British restored use of Badshahi Mosque in 1856 following vigorous petitioning by the city's Muslim community.

73. Duguid, *Letters from India and Kashmir*, 147–48, 156.

74. Goulding, *Old Lahore*, 12–13.

75. Aijazuddin, *Lahore*, 151.

76. Shorto, "A Tomb of One's Own." Also see Shorto, "Public Lives, Private Places."

77. Latif, *Lahore*, 283.

78. In 1857–58 Indian troops and their sympathizers rebelled against British occupation of the subcontinent. During the rebellion, European quarters and institutions in towns and cities across India were forcibly occupied by Indian rebels, and a number of Europeans were killed before the British army ruthlessly restored control. The rebellion (or "mutiny," as British historians have often called it) led to the replacement of the British East India Company's de facto rule over much of India by formal and direct British rule. Punjab remained largely loyal to the British during the rebellion, providing Indian troops and materiel for the British side. On the rebellion in Punjab, see Major, *Return to Empire*, esp. chapter 6. On the rebellion more generally, see Thomas Metcalf, *The Aftermath of Revolt*.

79. The Lahore Railway Station was designed by William Brunton, chief engineer for the Punjab section of the Sind, Punjab, and Delhi Railway (SP&DR). The station both looked and functioned like a fortress. In addition to the functional medieval battlements, designed to allow the station to be defended by a small armed force, the interior of the building could be sealed off in an emergency with heavy iron sliding doors. Plans, elevations, and construction details for the station are published in Bahadur, "New Railway Station at Lahore," 207–8 and accompanying plates 24 and 25.

80. Nagi, *Ancient Lahore*, 111.

2. A COLONIAL SPATIAL IMAGINATION

1. See, among others, Williams, *The Country and the City;* Coleman, *The Idea of the City in Nineteenth-Century Britain;* Dyos and Wolff, *The Victorian City.*

2. Williams, *The Country and the City,* 289.

3. In this regard, see Swati Chattopadhyay's discussion of the differences between picturesque aesthetics in Great Britain and India during the late eighteenth and early nineteenth centuries, with particular reference to landscape painting, in her *Representing Calcutta,* esp. chap. 1.

4. Swati Chattopadhyay, "'Goods, Chattels, and Sundry Items'"; Glover, "'An Absence of Old England'"; Kennedy, *The Magic Mountains;* Sinha, "Britishness, Clubbability, and the Colonial Public Sphere."

5. A very important exception, however, was British intervention in the walled city of Delhi, which will be discussed in more detail below.

6. Upton, "Lancasterian Schools, Republican Citizenship, and the Spatial Imagination in Early Nineteenth-Century America," 239.

7. Taylor, *Modern Social Imaginaries,* 23.

8. Poovey, "The Liberal Civil Subject and the Social in Eighteenth-Century British Moral Philosophy," 132.

9. On the influence of utilitarianism in British India, see Mehta, *Liberalism and Empire;* Thomas Metcalf, *Ideologies of the Raj;* Stokes, *The English Utilitarians and India;* Zastoupil, *John Stuart Mill and India.*

10. The enumeration and classification of social phenomena was not an invention of British colonialism in India. As historians have shown, previous Indian states (including the Mughal) conducted censuses, classified populations according to social categories, and made careful inventories of land and other productive resources. See Bayly, *Empire and Information;* Peabody, "Cents, Sense, Census: Human Inventories in Late Precolonial and Early Colonial India." The enumerative and classificatory practices of British colonial rule were often generative, however, in the sense that they discursively produced many of the forms and objects they purported to simply describe. See Cohn, *Colonialism and Its Forms of Knowledge.* On the continued political effects of colonial enumerative practices in India, see Appadurai, *Modernity at Large: Cultural Dimensions of Globalization,* 114–35.

11. Bain, *The Emotions and the Will,* 266, 272, 266, 308. Bain was a prominent Scottish utilitarian philosopher and psychologist whose relationship to colonial India was significant but indirect (he was a close friend of John Stuart Mill and wrote biographies of both John Stuart and James Mill). Bain's textbook *Mental and Moral Science* (1868) was translated into Hindi for use by students at Punjab University shortly after its publication. See John Lockwood Kipling, *Lahore as It Was,* 53.

12. Quoted in Schmiechen, "The Victorians, the Historians, and the Idea of Modernism," 305.

13. Login, *Sir John Login and Duleep Singh,* 169.

14. On the intertwining of agriculture and civilizational development in imperial historiography, see Musselman, "Swords into Ploughshares"; Comaroff and Comaroff, *Ethnography and the Historical Imagination,* 246–50. The biblical passage is from the Old Testament: "And He shall judge among the nations, and shall rebuke many people: and they shall beat their swords into plowshares, and their spears into pruninghooks: nation shall not lift up sword against nation, neither shall they learn war any more." Isa. 2:4, King James Version.

15. Reginald Smith, *Life of Lord Lawrence,* 281.

16. Malleson, *The Indian Mutiny of 1857,* 44.

17. Saunders, quoted in Government of Punjab, *Gazetteer of the Lahore District, 1883–84,* 130.

Because of the imagined presence of "martial races" in the Punjab, for some of whom the sword held special symbolic significance, allusions to the conversion of "swords" lent this biblical motif added resonance in the Punjab's colonial context. On the British idea that Sikhs and other groups in the Punjab were innately "martial races," see Fox, *Lions of the Punjab*; MacMunn, *The Martial Races of India*; Streets, *Martial Races*. Tony Ballantyne has discussed how swords acquired a symbolic importance for Punjab's Sikhs that went beyond purely military meanings. Ballantyne writes that "members of the early Khalsa [orthodox Sikh order] frequently carried and paid respect to five weapons: the sword, bow, musket, quoit and dagger. Guru Hargobind is believed to have worn two swords, one called *piri*, which symbolized his spiritual mission, and the other, *miri*, which designated his struggle against Mughal tyranny. *Miri-piri* is now taken as the injunction for Sikhs to fight against oppression and injustice." Ballantyne, "Entangled Pasts."

18. Goswami's 2004 book, *Producing India*, emphatically underscores this point. Especially in the post-1857 period, when mercantilist practices gave way to what Goswami calls "territorial colonialism" following the transfer of Indian governance to direct rule by Britain (from the East India Company), such things as the nationalization of forests, confiscation of commons through eminent domain, and massive investment in roads, railways, and canal irrigation "profoundly shaped the administrative hierarchy and internal organization of the state" (56). The subsequent expansion of land surveying and registration "made the 'record of everything which concerns the agricultural and social habits of the people' into 'an immense business.'" Goswami, citing B. H. Powell, 56. The post-1857 period also saw a proliferation of revenue handbooks, glossaries of agricultural terms, and ethnographic accounts of agricultural practices that have no urban parallel.

19. The classic contemporary statement is found in Tupper, *Punjab Customary Law*. Tupper first codified a system of tribal customary law that would be used to adjudicate all noncivil cases in the province. The justification for designating "tribes" as the fundamental unit of society is given its fullest articulation in this work. In 1883, drawing partially on Tupper's work, Denzil Ibbetson published *Punjab Castes*, a separate monograph based on the chapter "The Races, Castes, and Tribes of the People" in his report on the 1881 census. Ibbetson wrote that "the tribe appears to me to be far more permanent and indestructible than the caste. . . . in [large areas of the Punjab] the broader distinctions of caste have become little more than a tradition or a convenient symbol for social standing, while the tribal groups are the practical units of which the community is composed." Ibbetson, *Punjab Castes*, 16. Also see Fox, *Kin, Clan, Raja, and Rule*; Gilmartin, *Empire and Islam*.

20. See Muhammad Chaudhury, *Justice and Practice*; Gilmartin, "Customary Law and Shari'at in British Punjab."

21. Gilmartin, *Empire and Islam*, esp. chaps. 1 and 2.

22. On the role an idealized rural past played in nineteenth-century constructions of Englishness, see Helsinger, *Rural Scenes and National Representation*; Marsh, *Back to the Land*.

23. Comaroff and Comaroff, *Ethnography and the Historical Imagination*, 190–91.

24. "Diversity of ranks" is a biblical concept naturalizing differences in human endowment (such as gender, social station, or spiritual attainment) as a dimension of divine unity. The concept was important in Anglican discourse on society and in Enlightenment philosophy more generally.

25. See Ali, *Punjab under Imperialism*; Gilmartin, *Empire and Islam*; Barrier, *The Punjab Alienation of Land Bill of 1900*; Jones, *Arya Dharm*; Major, *Return to Empire*.

26. Tupper, *Punjab Customary Law*, 19–20.

27. See Royal Commission on the Sanitary State of the Army in India, *Report of the Commissioners Appointed to Inquire into the Sanitary State of the Army in India*. Also see Florence Nightingale's

famous summary of the report in her *Observations on the Evidence Contained in the Stational Reports Submitted to Her by the Royal Commission on the Sanitary State of the Army in India*. On the Punjab survey, see Hume, "Colonialism and Sanitary Medicine."

28. Arnold, *Colonizing the Body*, 36–43; 72–80. On the impact of sanitary science on the planning and construction of military cantonments in India, see King, *Colonial Urban Development*, chap. 5.

29. Poisonous air (miasma) emanating from putrefaction and carried in the air was the central cause of illness according to the "miasmic" theory of disease prevalent at the time. This theory, popularized by German chemist Justus Liebig in the 1850s, maintained that once the poison entered a human body, it could catalyze a process of fermentation, or "zymosis," that led to the most fatal kinds of disease, including malaria, cholera, and enteric fevers. By the 1870s Liebig's theory of disease etiology had come to be generally accepted in British India, and public health measures were aimed primarily at preventing "zymotic" diseases. The water-borne theory of disease, developed by Englishman John Snow in 1853, competed somewhat with the miasmic theory by insisting that water (as opposed to air) was the sole medium in which some diseases—notably cholera—could be propagated. While controversial at first, Snow's research findings were also generally accepted by the 1870s. See Harrison, *Public Health in British India*, 51–52.

30. Harrison, *Public Health in British India*, 77.

31. Government of Punjab, *Gazetteer of the Lahore District, 1883–84*, 170; Arnold, *Colonizing the Body*, 70.

32. Government of Punjab, "Report of the Committee for the Inspection of Villages within a Radius of Five Miles of Meean Meer Cantonments," Home Department Proceedings (Medical and Sanitary), no. 5, (May 1878), 422–34. Page numbers for further quotations on the villages surrounding the cantonment outside Lahore are given in parentheses.

33. Only the term "village" is English. *"Mohalla"* comes from Arabic and denotes an urban quarter or district; *"mandi"* is a Hindi term for a specialized market; *"kila,"* from Arabic, and *"kot"* from Sanskrit, both denote a fort or stronghold; *"pind"* is a Punjabi word for an agricultural village; and *"bazaar"* is Persian for urban marketplace. All these terms are still in common use in the Punjab.

34. Government of Punjab, "Report of the Committee for the Inspection of Villages within a Radius of Five Miles of Rawalpindi Cantonments," Home Department Proceedings (Medical and Sanitary), no. 13 (April 1879): 287.

35. Ibid.

36. On Victorian ideas about the relationship between body tone, expression, and inner states (including states of health), see Hartley, *Physiognomy and the Meaning of Expression in Nineteenth Century Culture.*

37. Quoted in Government of Punjab, *Gazetteer of the Lahore District, 1883–84*, 45.

38. Steven Marcus, "Reading the Illegible," 1:266.

39. Quoted in Government of Punjab, *Gazetteer of the Lahore District, 1883–84*, 45.

40. Godwin, *Town Swamps and Social Bridges*, 61.

41. George Millen, quoted in Bellamy and Williamson, *Life in the Victorian Village*, 1:20, 22, 24.

42. Government of Punjab, "Proposed Village Sanitation Act for the Punjab," Home Department Proceedings (Medical and Sanitary), no. 12 (January 1894): 10.

43. Government of Punjab, "Village Sanitation and Formation of a Provincial Sanitary Board," Home Department Proceedings (Medical and Sanitary), no. 16 (January 1888): 205.

44. Ibid., 264.

45. Ibid., 210.

46. See Singha, *A Despotism of Law;* Yang, "Dangerous Castes and Tribes"; Major, "State and Criminal Tribes in Colonial Punjab"; Arnold, "Crime and Crime Control in Madras, 1858–1947." On the negative attitudes Europeans held toward mobile groups in nineteenth-century Asia, see Ludden, "Maps in the Mind and the Mobility of Asia."

47. Government of Punjab, "Memorandum of Suggestions Regarding the Report of the Criminal Tribes of the Punjab," Home Department Proceedings (Police), no. 9 (October 1914): 104.

48. Ibid., 103; emphasis added.

49. Government of Punjab, "Mina Tribe of the Gurgaon District," Home Department Proceedings (General), no. 5 (October 1873): 773.

50. Poovey, *Making a Social Body,* 35.

51. These included a desire to permanently settle Punjab's pastoral tribes, whose wandering lifestyle and perceived propensity for cattle theft threatened British notions of a stable yeoman peasantry in the countryside; a desire to reward decommissioned soldiers and officers from the colonial army; and a desire to provide opportunities to enterprising capitalists who could organize the economies of colony towns on a profitable basis. A fuller account of colonization in the Punjab appears in Ali, *Punjab under Imperialism;* also see Gilmartin, *Empire and Islam.*

52. Gilmartin, *Empire and Islam,* 132–33.

53. Punjab's canal-colony towns were roughly coeval, therefore, with the earliest planned suburban developments outside India's major cities. On planned suburban developments outside Delhi, which began in the late 1880s, see Hosagrahar, *Indigenous Modernities,* 122–32.

54. Government of Punjab, *Gazetteer of the Chenab Colony, 1905,* 149–51.

55. Oriental and India Office Collection (hereafter OIOC), V/26/315/1, 37, British Library, London; emphasis added.

56. Government of Punjab, Home Department Proceedings (Medical and Sanitary), no. 15 (1905): n.p.

57. Government of Punjab, "Proposed Codification of the Customary Law of the Punjab," Home Department Proceedings (Judicial), no. 6 (April 1907): 15; emphasis added.

58. Royal Commission on the Sanitary State of the Army in India, *Report of the Commissioners Appointed to Inquire into the Sanitary State of the Army in India,* 19:81.

59. Rudyard Kipling, "Typhoid at Home," 73.

60. This theme is developed in Markus, "The School as a Machine"; Davidoff and Hall, *Family Fortunes;* Poovey, *Making a Social Body;* and Thompson, *The Rise of Respectable Society.*

61. Chadwick, *Report on the Sanitary Condition of the Labouring Population of Great Britain,* 194.

62. Loudon, *An Encyclopedia of Cottage, Farm, and Villa Architecture and Furniture,* 3.

63. Godwin, *Town Swamps and Social Bridges,* 6.

64. Swati Chattopadhyay's discussion of British efforts to represent the spatiality of cholera in Calcutta underscores a similar theme. See her *Representing Calcutta,* 68–75.

65. Jacquemont, *The Punjab a Hundred Years Ago,* 57; emphasis added.

66. Government of Punjab, "Report by the Sanitary Commissioner, Punjab, on the Sanitary Conditions of Lahore," Home Department Proceedings (Medical and Sanitary), nos. 5–10 (February 1897): n.p.

67. In nineteenth-century Egypt, "teams of Bedouin were organized to heave and push the writer or tourist to the top [of the pyramids at Giza], where two more Bedouin would carry the European on their shoulders to all four corners, to observe the view. . . . the minaret presented itself similarly to even the most respectable European as a viewing tower, from which to sneak a panoptic

gaze over a Muslim town." Mitchell, *Colonizing Egypt,* 24. Mitchell points out that the "panoptic" view not only showed the scene in its entirety to a viewer but also, importantly, protected the foreign viewer's anonymity; the pleasure of the view hinged, in part, on the fact that "one could see and yet not be seen" (ibid.).

68. The following passages all come from Rudyard Kipling's story "The City of Dreadful Night."

69. See Blunt, "Imperial Geographies of Home"; Cohn, *Colonialism and Its Forms of Knowledge;* Inderpal Grewal, *Home and Harem;* Pratt, *Imperial Eyes;* and Suleri, *The Rhetoric of English India.*

70. For a fuller discussion on the operation of the census in Punjab, see Barrier, *The Census in British India.*

71. Government of India, *Census of India, 1891,* 19:6; emphasis added.

72. Ruchi Ram Sahni, who attended the university and later taught in Lahore, wrote about his experience as a census enumerator in the 1881 census in Lahore. See Sahni, "Self-Revelations of an Octogenarian," 123–24.

73. Government of India, *Census of India, 1891,* 19:8.

74. Ibid, 19:6; emphasis added.

75. Government of India, *Census of India, 1901,* 19:26.

76. Government of Punjab, *Report on the Punjab Sanitary Conference, 1913,* 2:164.

77. Ibid., 2:7.

78. Government of Punjab, "Drainage of Village Mozang, Lahore District," Public Works Department (General), Memo 860 (November 1887): n.p.

79. Government of Punjab, "Drainage and Etc. of the Village of Mozang in Lahore," Home Department Proceedings (Medical and Sanitary), no. 10 (March 1890): n.p.

80. Ibid.; emphases added.

81. Government of Punjab, "Report by the Sanitary Commissioner, Punjab, on the Sanitary Condition of Lahore," Home Department Proceedings (Medical and Sanitary), no. 10 (February 1897): 49.

82. Mehta, *Liberalism and Empire,* 69.

83. This stands in contrast to the British occupation and alteration of urban space in the older walled district of Delhi. Both military officials and civilians lived in Delhi throughout the nineteenth century, and the colonial government built, among other things, a clock tower, a town hall, a hospital, a railway station, and several new streets in the city. However, most of this construction took place after the quelling of the 1857 rebellion of Indian troops against their British officers, an India-wide event in which Delhi was a major battlefield. In the wake of the rebellion, Delhi was forcibly depopulated, and large swaths of the city were demolished for both punitive and defensive reasons. Depopulation, demolition, and strict controls over resettlement made post-1857 Delhi adequately "legible" in the sense described above. See Naryani Gupta, *Delhi between Two Empires, 1830–1931,* and Naryani Gupta, "Military Security and Urban Development." On British redevelopment of urban space in Delhi's Old City, see Hosagrahar, *Indigenous Modernities,* 47–81.

84. This was true, for example, during campaigns to inspect and disinfect homes in known plague or cholera locations. See Arnold, *Colonizing the Body,* 211–29.

85. Georges-Eugène Haussmann's reconstruction of Second Empire Paris (beginning in 1864) led a number of similar urban reconstruction projects across Europe. See Pinkney, *Napoleon III and the Rebuilding of Paris;* Olson, *The City as a Work of Art;* Harvey, *Paris.* London, traditionally resistant to large-scale schemes of reorganization, presented a somewhat different case. See Port, "Government and the Metropolitan Image."

86. For the case of Lucknow, see Oldenburg, *The Making of Colonial Lucknow, 1856–77.* Some

scholars have argued that lessons learned during the uprising of 1857 led the British to pursue a hands-off policy toward the private affairs of Indian subjects—including toward intervening in Indian neighborhoods. This position has been argued most fully by Thomas Metcalf in *The Aftermath of Revolt*. Others have argued, conversely, that the priorities of modern governance, and especially the emphasis on public health in the late nineteenth century, prompted an increase—rather than a decrease—in government interventions into the lives of Indian subjects after the rebellion. This is a central argument of Veena Oldenburg's *The Making of Colonial Lucknow, 1856–77*. Much the same argument is made by David Arnold in *Colonizing the Body*.

3. COLLABORATIONS

1. Cust, "History of the Conquest of the Panjab." Cust's comments were written in February 1846.

2. This assumption has been made often. Sunil Khilnani's description of the colonial city, to cite but one well-written and well-received example, expresses a common view: "The rectilinear securities of the European station became a notional norm for the entire [colonial] city," Khilnani writes; "the city embodied in the precise assignments of space within British civil and military lines did not mesh with any Indian conceptions, and Indians played little part in defining its meanings. . . . The colonial conception was imposed." See Khilnani, *The Idea of India*, 118.

3. On the inherently collaborative nature of colonial urban development in Bombay, see Chopra, "The City and Its Fragments."

4. See Christopher, "Urban Segregation Levels in the British Overseas Empire and Its Successors, in the Twentieth Century." Christopher notes that despite their overwhelming political dominance, Europeans in India never "converted this [advantage] into legally-based structural segregation" (101).

5. *Nazul* properties were similar to what might be called "commons" in English terminology, land whose control and rights to income were vested in the collective (in this case the ruling power) rather than individual owners. *Nazul* land in Lahore included several abandoned (and subsequently reused) buildings and several small plots of (mostly agricultural) land in and around the Old City. Income from *nazul* properties originally went to the Lahore municipality, but rule changes in 1871 reassigned this income to the provincial government. Each of the offices occupying *nazul* property were provincial, rather than municipal, establishments. See Government of Punjab, *Gazetteer of the Lahore District 1882–83*, 116.

6. Proposals to construct a new church near Anarkali's Tomb were first floated in the early 1860s. In 1867, when Lahore was separated from the head church at Calcutta and made a separate diocese, work on the foundations for a new church had already begun. At that point the need for a larger building, which would become the diocesan cathedral, prompted a search for a new site elsewhere in the civil station. In 1874, under the direction of Lieutenant Governor Robert Montgomery, a site was secured on an irregularly shaped plot of land near Mall Road. After inspecting the new site, Lahore's bishop, Thomas Valpy French, successfully argued for a much grander building. While French was on leave in London, sometime in the late 1870s, he consulted a prominent English church architect—John Oldrid Scott, Sir Gilbert Scott's son—about plans for a new cathedral. A short time later, Scott was given the commission. See Latif, *Lahore*, 13.

7. Government of Punjab, "Report Showing the Action Taken in Connection with the Celebration of the Jubilee of Her Majesty the Queen Empress in the Various Centers in the Jurisdiction of the Punjab," Home Department Proceedings (General), no. 8 (May 1887): 146.

8. Ibid., 146.

9. Dell Upton has underscored how the seeming comprehensiveness of built artifacts often obviates verbal or other efforts to convey meaning: "Compared with the ephemeral nature of human consciousness and social action," Upton writes, "the continuity of the material world and its apparent unchangeability seem to promise constant or certain meaning." See Upton, "Seen, Scene, and Unseen," 176.

10. Latif, *Lahore*, 310.

11. Goulding, *Old Lahore*, 41.

12. Latif, *Lahore*, 309.

13. I use the concept of "heterotopia" in the sense discussed by Michel Foucault in his "Of Other Spaces," 24.

14. Horticultural societies were common in large cities in the British Empire. In India the earliest gardens were built in Calcutta and Bombay. For an excellent case study of a British Agri-Horticultural Society garden in Singapore, see Reisz, "City as Garden."

15. Ian Kerr, "The Agri-Horticultural Society of the Punjab, 1851–71."

16. Latif, *Lahore*, 314–15.

17. Ian Kerr, "The Agro-Horticultural Society of the Punjab," 256.

18. Latif, *Lahore*, 314.

19. Ramachandra Guha, *A Corner of a Foreign Field*; Majumdar, *Lost Histories of Indian Cricket*.

20. Elinor Tollinton, OIOC MSS Eur D 1197. Tollinton's memoir was written in 1988; her descriptions of the garden are from about 1915.

21. Government of Punjab, "Appeal for Further Subscriptions towards the Aitchison College," Home Department Proceedings (General), nos. 10–12 (May 1889): 2.

22. Ibid.

23. All the students at Ambala were wards of the court from Ambala and surrounding districts, children whose estates were managed by the colonial government while they were in their minority (until eighteen years old). These included both sons of prominent families within British Punjab and members of the ruling families of Punjab's autonomous princely states. During the decade 1875–85, at least seven rulers of Punjab's princely states were, or had been, minor wards of the court.

24. Government of Punjab, "Appeal for Further Subscriptions towards the Aitchison College," Home Department Proceedings (General), nos. 10–12 (May 1889): 1.

25. Ibid.

26. Goffman, *Asylums*.

27. Thomas Metcalf, *An Imperial Vision*, 68; 129–30. Metcalf notes that all but one of the student residences at Ajmer were designed by British engineers and overseen by British agents to the princely states. The princes themselves, Metcalf writes, "did no more than comment on details of the design, or occasionally, protest the cost of the structures the British were putting up for them" (130).

28. Akhtar, "The Journey from Government Wards Institution Amballa City, 1864, to Punjab Chiefs College."

29. Government of Punjab, "Appeal for Further Subscriptions towards the Aitchison College," Home Department Proceedings (General), nos. 10–12 (May 1889): 4.

30. Rudyard Kipling, describing the raja's palace at Amber, wrote, "The crampt and darkened rooms, the narrow smooth-walled passages with recesses where a man might wait for his enemy unseen, the maze of ascending and descending stairs leading nowhere, the ever-present screens of marble tracery that may hide or reveal so much—all these things breathe of plot and counter-plot,

league and intrigue. In a living palace where the sightseer knows and feels that there are human beings everywhere, and that he is followed by scores of unseen eyes, the impression is almost unendurable." *From Sea to Sea*, 1:20.

31. Government of Punjab, "Design for the Punjab Chiefs' College Building," Home Department Proceedings (General), no. 36 (May 1886): 1.

32. Each designer received one thousand rupees for his original submittal, and Jacob received an additional five hundred rupees for his revised plans, working drawings, specifications, and cost estimates. Singh and Kipling split their half of the honorarium between them and agreed to wait for the money pending Jacob's successful completion of the project. The latter condition gave Kipling some pause since, as he put it, "it is not clear how the honorarium it is proposed to give us would be affected by the 'receipt and acceptance of Colonel Jacob's completed plans and specifications.' We go completely out of the coach at the beginning, and have no control over or concern in Colonel Jacob's designs." Government of Punjab, "Design for the Punjab Chiefs' College Building," PPAP Home Department Proceedings (General), no. 38 (May 1886): 2. The committee acknowledged Kipling's point but urged him to accept their condition since they could not afford to spend any money without being sure of receiving an acceptable design. Kipling's and Singh's assent to this condition reflected, thus, their trust in the committee's optimism that Jacob would ultimately succeed.

33. Thomas Metcalf, *An Imperial Vision*, chaps. 3, 4. Also see Tillotson, *The Tradition of Indian Architecture*, 46–59.

34. Gwendolyn Wright traces a similar shift in French urban policy in Vietnam under the direction of Ernest Hebrard at the beginning of the twentieth century, when "the decision to rely on large-scale, coordinated complexes of buildings and the specification that individual structures respond more visibly to their local context signaled a major shift from nineteenth-century colonial practice." Wright, "Tradition in the Service of Modernity," 332. In French Indochina, however, Wright traces this shift to a willing, if superficial, concession by the French to nationalist demands for more autonomy and respect. In both the Vietnamese and Indian cases, however, architectural style was seen as a political resource.

35. See Cohn, "Representing Authority in Victorian India."

36. Government of Punjab, "Appeal for Further Subscriptions towards the Completion of the Aitchison College," Home Department Proceedings (General), no. 10 (May 1889): 1.

37. For comparison, see David Lelyveld's excellent history of the Muhammadan Anglo-Oriental College in Aligarh, established in 1875, in his *Aligarh's First Generation*, esp. 147–203.

38. Bernard Cohn suggests that the relative ranking of different groups in India became increasingly systematic following the rebellion of 1857 and the royal proclamation in 1858 that vested sovereignty of India in Queen Victoria. Cohn writes, "[This proclamation] ended the ambiguity in the position of the British in India as now the British monarchy encompassed both Britain and India. A social order was established with the British crown seen as the centre of authority, and capable of ordering into a single hierarchy all of its subjects, Indian and British." Cohn, "Representing Authority in Victorian India," 180.

39. Lahore Municipal Committee, Old Record Room, "Plans Scrutiny of All Buildings and Appointment of a Building Inspector," case no. III-1/176 (July 1907): 19.

40. Steel, *The Garden of Fidelity*, 81–82.

41. Anthony King discusses the more formalized criteria on which (mostly) colonial officers were assigned rank, along with the spatial accommodations this system entailed, primarily with reference to New Delhi. See his *Colonial Urban Development*, 240–53.

42. Thomas Metcalf, *An Imperial Vision*, 58–65.

43. Aijazuddin, *Lahore*, 129. On the interaction between English common-law jurisprudence and precolonial Indian legal traditions, see Appadurai, *Worship and Conflict under Colonial Rule;* Cohn, "Law and the Colonial State in India."

44. Dina Nath, *The Two Friends*, 25.

45. On the development of the middle class as a social formation under colonial rule in India, see Sanjay Joshi, *Fractured Modernity.*

46. Jones, *Arya Dharm*, 58; emphasis added.

47. See Jones, "The Bengali Elite in Post-Annexation Punjab."

48. Several historians of colonial Punjab have written useful social histories of this new group. See, for example, Gilmartin, *Empire and Islam;* Jones, *Arya Dharm;* Sanjay Joshi, *Fractured Modernity;* Ravinder Kumar, "Urban Society and Urban Politics"; Oberoi, *The Construction of Religious Boundaries;* Harish Sharma, *Artisans of the Punjab;* Sohal, "The Swadeshi Movement in the Punjab."

49. Government College offered degrees in English language and literature; Arabic, Sanskrit, and Persian; history and political economy; mathematics; mental and moral science; and physical science. Latif, *Lahore*, 308.

50. Ibid., 312.

51. Ibid., 313. On British arguments over the relative importance of European and "Oriental" knowledge and languages as a foundation for colonial educational institutions, see Viswanathan, *Masks of Conquest;* Zastoupil, *John Stuart Mill and India;* Stokes, *The English Utilitarians and India.*

52. Sahni, *Self-Revelations of an Octogenarian*, 139.

53. Ibid., 92, 93.

54. M. E. Fyson, "Good Memory," OIOC MSS Eur D 885/2, 88. On British attitudes toward the mixed-race Anglo-European (sometimes called Eurasian) community in India, see Bear, "Miscegenations of Modernity"; Mannsaker, "East and West"; Stoler, "Rethinking Colonial Categories."

55. *Official Chronicle of Mayo School of Art*, 56.

56. Latif, *Lahore*, 325.

57. Engineering instruction was given both in England and in India. The Royal Indian Engineering College at Cooper's Hill, England (founded in 1871) was designed to train engineers, telegraphists, and forestry officers for positions in the public services in India, Burma, and elsewhere in the British Empire. Positions in the Indian Public Works Department were held open for the college's European graduates, with the exception of two positions annually that went to "subjects" of the British Empire. The training provided at Cooper's Hill, however, was considered inferior to that provided at Roorkee College of Engineering in India (founded in 1847), the oldest engineering college in the British Empire. Partially because of this, Cooper's Hill was closed in 1907. See OIOC L/PWD/8/243.

58. On architectural design and design culture in the Indian PWD, see Scriver, *Rationalization, Standardization, and Control in Design.*

59. Memorandum by H. H. Locke, July 26, 1873, in *Official Chronicle of Mayo School of Art*, 154; emphasis added.

60. Memorandum by H. H. Locke, *Official Chronicle of the Mayo School of Art*, 155. All the questions Locke poses were taken from the Calcutta University calendar of exams.

61. Government of India, Public Works Department, "Letter from the Secretary of Government, Bengal Public Works Department, to the Secretary, Government of India," January 23, 1886, OIOC L/PWD/8/91.

62. Obituary of Rai Bahadur Kanhayalal M.I.C.E., *Indian Magazine*, no. 208 (April 1888): 218.

63. Wheeler, *The History of the Imperial Assemblage at Delhi*, 71–72.

64. Government of India, Public Works Department, "Letter to the Secretary of State for India, Simla," July 29, 1882, OIOC L/PWD/6/99.

65. Bedi, *Harvest from the Desert*, 38, 39.

66. John Lockwood Kipling, "The Principal's Report on the Mayo School of Industrial Art, Lahore, for 1883–84," 54.

67. Ibid., 55.

68. On English art schools in colonial India, see Mitter, *Art and Nationalism in Colonial India, 1850–1922*; Guha-Thakurta, *Monuments, Objects, Histories*; Bagal, *Papers Relating to the Maintenance of Schools of Art in India as State Institutions*.

69. See Davey, *Architecture of the Arts and Crafts Movement*; Kornwolf, *M. H. Baillie Scott and the Arts and Crafts Movement*; Thomas Metcalf, *An Imperial Vision*; Tillotson, *The Tradition of Indian Architecture*.

70. Breckenridge, "The Aesthetics and Politics of Colonial Collecting"; Dutta, "The Politics of Display."

71. "Memorandum by the Honourable Sir Richard Temple, KCSI, on the Subject of Exhibition and Schools of Art and Design in India," October 24, 1873, in *Official Chronicle of the Mayo School of Art*, 143; emphasis added.

72. Ibid., 142.

73. Note from Richard Temple, Government of Punjab, "Industrial School of Art and Design at Lahore," Home Department Proceedings (General), no. 2 (January 1875): 5.

74. "Memorandum by the Honourable Sir Richard Temple," 142.

75. "Memorandum by H. H. Locke," July 26, 1873, in *Official Chronicle of the Mayo School of Art*, 151.

76. Havell, *The Basis for Artistic and Industrial Revival in India*, 25.

77. Orientalist scholars in the nineteenth century were aware of Indian architectural treatises, and many were translated into English during the nineteenth and twentieth centuries. None of these texts were considered suitable as resources for training in modern design, however. See Acharya, *An Encyclopedia of Hindu Architecture*, and Shukla, *Vastu-Sastra*. Both these works are multivolume sets. For more recent work on these textual traditions, see Bafna, "On the Idea of the Mandala as a Governing Device in Indian Architectural Tradition"; Kramrisch, "Traditions of the Indian Craftsman." Vibhuti Sachdev and Giles Tillotson have analyzed the city of Jaipur as exemplifying many of the principles of *vastu vidya*, a body of Indian architectural theory that some trace back to the Vedic period, in their *Building Jaipur*. Vibhuti Chakrabarti, in her *Indian Architectural Theory*, surveys the treatises with an eye toward demonstrating their continued relevance in contemporary architectural design practice.

78. John Lockwood Kipling, "The Principal's Report on the Mayo School of Art, Lahore, 1891–92," 87. This distinguished the Mayo School from the art schools in Bombay, Calcutta, and Madras, since students in the latter schools were drawn primarily from the middle classes. See Ata-Ullah, "Stylistic Hybridity and Colonial Art and Design Education."

79. John Lockwood Kipling, "The Principal's Report on the Mayo School of Industrial Art, Lahore, 1879–80," 41.

80. John Lockwood Kipling, "The Principal's Report on the Mayo School of Industrial Art, Lahore, 1891–92," 87.

81. Tarar, "Historical Introduction," 27.

82. Letter from F. J. E. Spring, cited in John Lockwood Kipling, "The Principal's Report on the Mayo School of Industrial Art, Lahore, 1887–88," 76.

83. Information on Bhai Ram Singh in this section derives from "New Indian Room at Osborne House," *Indian Magazine and Review* 264 (1892): 609–11.

84. Cited in Ata-Ullah, "Stylistic Hybridity and Colonial Art and Design Education," 79.

85. Maharishi Swami Dayanand Saraswati founded the organization in Bombay in 1875. The Lahore branch of the Arya Samaj was founded in 1877 following Dayanand's visit to Lahore, where he gave a series of lectures that were widely attended. On the history of the Arya Samaj in Punjab, see Jones, *Arya Dharm;* Shiv Gupta, *Arya Samaj and the Raj, 1875–1920.*

86. See Sethi, "The Creation of Religious Identities in the Punjab, c. 1850–1920."

87. The first members of Lahore's Arya Samaj included Lala Mulraj, M.A.; Lala Sri Ram, M.A.; Lala Bishan Lal, M.A.; Bhagat Ishar Das, M.A.; Lala Hansraj Sawhney, a lawyer; Lala Ishar Das, B.A.; Lala Dwarka Das, M.A.; Dr. Khazan Chand; and Dr. Bhagat Ram Sawhney. See Sri Ram Sharma, "Punjab in Ferment in the Beginning of the Twentieth Century."

88. Jones, *Arya Dharm.*

89. Lala Lal Chand, quoted in Sri Ram Sharma, *Mahatma Hansraj,* 36, 37–38.

90. Ibid., 52.

91. Oman, *Indian Life,* 88–91.

92. Quoted in Sri Ram Sharma, *Mahatma Hansraj,* 89.

93. Ibid., 90.

94. The Lahore Arya Samaj published two weekly newspapers, one in Urdu and one in English, from a press run by Lala Salig Ram. The English weekly was called the *Regenerator of Arya Varta* and became an unofficial organ of the organization.

4. CHANGING HOUSES

1. Comment by General Maclagan, published as an addendum to C. Purdon Clarke, "Some Notes upon the Domestic Architecture of India," 740. Page numbers in parentheses in the following discussion refer to this document.

2. Sir George Birdwood was the curator in charge of the India section of the South Kensington Museum (which was connected, as we have seen, to the Mayo School in Lahore) and a major figure in that branch of the English arts and crafts movement concerned with the indigenous arts of India. He also wrote the official handbook of the India section at the Victoria and Albert Museum, *The Industrial Arts of India.* In both his official and unofficial activities, Birdwood tirelessly supported the collection and preservation of Indian traditional crafts, arguing at the same time, however, that Asia had no "fine art" tradition—he once equated an Indonesian statue of the Buddha with a "boiled suet pudding." For further information on Birdwood's career and role in the arts and crafts movement, see Thomas Metcalf, *An Imperial Vision;* Guha-Thakurta, *The Making of a New "Indian" Art;* Tillotson, *The Tradition of Indian Architecture;* Skelton, "The Indian Collections."

3. Lala Kashi Ram, *Notes and Suggestions on Sanitation in the Punjab,* 12.

4. The practice of covering *parnala*s with dismantled tin boxes continues in areas of the city today. The author of a government report published in 1892 drew attention to the "recent" appearance of tin in the bazaars of the province: "One of the curiosities of recent trade is the new industry in tin.... Kerosene oil in large quantities comes in tin cases from Russia and America, and packing cases containing goods from Europe are often lined in tin. The kerosene oil tin is a cubical case about 9″ square and 14″ high, and is, or rather was, sold at a cheap rate." In addition to using tin as a building material, tinsmiths in the city converted kerosene tins into "lanterns, dispatch boxes, bird cages . . .

watering cans, lamps, cans for the growing manufacture of jams and preserves in the hills, kettles, jewel boxes for native ladies, and a greater variety of cases than at first blush would be thought possible." See Government of Punjab, *Report on the Material Progress of the Punjab during the Decade 1881–1891,* 39.

5. Government of Punjab, "Report by the Sanitary Commission, Punjab, on the Sanitary Condition of Lahore," Home Department Proceedings (Medical and Sanitary), nos. 1–5 (February 1897): 49.

6. Frederick S. Growse, who worked in the PWD near Delhi during the 1870s, described local bricks being sold for as little as one-tenth the price of the "government" brick. Growse, *Mathura,* 497.

7. The difference in cost was roughly 25 percent. Rai Bahadur Ganga Ram, in his *Pocket Book of Engineering for Sub-Divisional Officers, Mistrees, and Contractors,* 3, quotes prevailing building rates of twenty-five rupees per hundred cubic feet for brickwork in lime mortar, and eighteen rupees per hundred cubic feet for brickwork in mud mortar.

8. Jya Ram, "Food, Dress, and Dwelling Houses in the Delhi District," 14–15.

9. E. D. Maclagan, whose census report we encountered in chapter 2, gave the following advice to future census takers when labeling the doors of shops with census numbers: "The number should never be painted on the door, because it can then never be seen except when the door is shut. The numbers were often put on shop doors and when the shopkeeper opened his shop he swung back his door and piled up a huge assortment of goods in front of it, so that it took some minutes of fuss and bother to ascertain whether the number had been affixed." Government of India, *Census of India, 1891,* 19:5.

10. On municipal sanitation and "sitters," see Government of Punjab, "Proposed Amendments to the Bye-Laws of Simla Municipality," Home Department Proceedings (Municipal), no. 29 (October 1894): n.p. The idiom describing a woman "sitting on a stool" *(pirhi baithi)* in the bazaar as a prostitute was recorded in a Punjabi language textbook written by Pandit Sardha Ram in 1875. The book was intended to illustrate local customs and idioms in the region, using the conceit of an out-of-town visitor moving around the city asking a local guide about the things being done and said. In 1898 the book was translated into English "for the benefit of those English people who may wish to understand all the Panjabi customs." See Jawahir Singh, *Punjabi Bat-chit,* 132.

11. Scidmore, *Winter India,* 248, 250.

12. Compton, *Indian Life in Town and Country,* 49.

13. Jya Ram, "Food, Dress, and Dwelling Houses," 17.

14. Gopal Das Bhandari, cited in Government of Punjab, *Report on the Punjab Sanitary Conference, 1913,* 1:165.

15. Jya Ram, "Food, Dress, and Dwelling Houses," 17.

16. Government of India, *Census of India, 1901,* 19:28.

17. Gordon C. Walker, quoted in Roy, *A Brief History of Lahore and Directory,* 28.

18. Compton, *Indian Life in Town and Country,* 45, 45, 102.

19. Government of Punjab, *Report on the Working of Municipalities in the Punjab during the Year 1911–1912,* 2.

20. Jyoti Hosagrahar documents the impact of public health discourse on the architecture and urban layout of colonial-era Delhi, and of resistance to those impacts on behalf of the indigenous population, in her *Indigenous Modernities,* esp. chapter 4. Also see Yeoh, "Sanitary Ideology and the Control of the Urban Environment"; Prashad, "The Technology of Sanitation in Colonial Delhi"; Yeoh, *Contesting Space;* King, *Colonial Urban Development;* and Oldenburg, *The Making of Colonial Lucknow.*

21. In 1890, in order to serve on the Municipal Committee, one had to be a male taxpayer who owned immovable property in the city valued at ten thousand rupees or more, have a minimum monthly income of two hundred rupees (unless a university graduate, in which case a minimum income of one hundred rupees a month would suffice), and not belong to "any sect or caste such as Mehtar, Chamar, Butcher, Kanjar, Mirasi, &c., with whom Hindus and Muhammadans and also Christians object to mix." See Government of Punjab, "Proposed Qualifications for Municipal Committee Members in Multan," Boards and Committees Department (General), no. 48 (June 1890): n.p. The Punjab Municipal Act of 1867 provided for the appointment to the Municipal Committee of both official and nonofficial members from the British and Indian communities, with the district commissioner as the committee president. A revised act in 1870 provided for the election of some committee members and the appointment of others, but it was not until 1882, following Lord Ripon's Resolution on Self-Government, that municipal elections were undertaken regularly in the city. In 1884, the Municipal Act was amended to provide for the election of the president as well. In 1891, a further revision set fixed proportions for electing Muslim, Hindu, and Christian members to the committee. See Government of Punjab, *Report on the Working of Municipalities in the Punjab during the Year 1893–94*, 2.

22. The regulation of building construction in Lahore was at first limited to buildings within the civil station, with little or no oversight on construction in the Old City. Controls over building activity in the Old City were systematically enforced only after the passage of a revised Punjab Municipal Bill, in 1911. In 1906, the last year systematic records seem to have been kept, the municipal engineer's office in Lahore reviewed 554 plans for new buildings in the civil station, but none for buildings under construction in the Old City. See Lahore Municipal Committee, "Plans Scrutiny of All Buildings and Appointment of a Building Inspector," case no. III-1/176–07 (1907): 39.

23. Harrison, *Public Health in British India*, 181.

24. Chadwick, *Report on the Sanitary Condition of the Labouring Population of Great Britain*. Also see Gavin, *Sanitary Ramblings, Being Sketches and Illustrations of Bethnal Green*.

25. Government of Punjab, "Report by the Sanitary Commissioner, Punjab, on the Sanitary Condition of Lahore," Home Department Proceedings (Medical and Sanitary), nos. 1–5 (February 1897): 49.

26. Hume, "Colonialism and Sanitary Medicine," 710.

27. The history of indigenous medical practice in relation to colonial medicine and health policy in the Punjab is discussed in Hume, "Rival Traditions." Also see Barbara Metcalf's study of an influential modernizing *hakim* in Delhi during the late nineteenth and early twentieth centuries, "Hakim Ajmal Khan."

28. Works of this kind published and distributed in Lahore include *Mukhtasar Risala-e-Hafiz-e-Sehat* [Various Essays on Good Health]; Beli Ram, *Hadi-i Sehat* [A Guide to Health]; Ganga Ram, *Lecture-e-Sehat* [A Lecture on Health]; and *Zindagi, Raushni aur Safai* [Life, Light, and Cleanliness]. Urdu pamphlets on smallpox, cholera, and plague (by Indian and British authors) were also produced and distributed in the city from the 1890s onward. For examples, see *Chechak* [Smallpox]; Bellew, *Vaccination Kyunkar Kiya Jata Hai* [Why Is Vaccination Done?]; *'Ilaaj-e-Heza* [A Treatment for Cholera]; Adir, *Chuha aur Plague, Billi aur Chuha, aur Mohafiz-e-Jaan Tika* [Rat and Plague, Cat and Rat, and a Guard].

29. Serious plague epidemics occurred in Punjab in 1897, 1903, 1904, and 1907. In the 1904 epidemic, 364,740 people died of the disease in the province, with over 1,750 deaths being reported in Lahore alone. In 1907, plague killed over 675,000 in the province. See Bamber, *Report on the Sanitary*

Administration of the Punjab and Proceedings of the Sanitary Board for the Year 1904, 9; Catanach, "Plague and the Indian Village, 1896–1914." By 1907 the rat flea had been isolated as the carrier of bubonic plague. In 1908, "rat-proof" building methods were urged for use in all government structures. A "rat-proof" building had solid eight-inch concrete floors raised two feet off the ground on a packed-earth plinth, with projecting tile copings at the threshold of every ground-level door. See Government of Punjab, "Sir Bradford Leslie's Proposal for Building Rat-Proof Dwellings in Plague Stricken Villages and along the Southern Punjab Railway (1908)," Home Department Proceedings (Medical and Sanitary), nos. 16–23 (September 1910): n.p.

30. Adir, *Chuha aur Plague Billi aur Chuha aur Mohafiz-e-Jaan Tika.*

31. Lala Kashi Ram, *Notes and Suggestions on Sanitation in the Punjab,* 3. Ram was secretary and member of the sanitary committee of the *Anjuman-i Punjab,* a voluntary social organization founded in 1865 in Lahore.

32. Ibid., 10.

33. Dhingra, "Sanitation in India," 415. On the zymotic theory of disease adduced in Dhingra's quotation see Harrison, *Public Health in British India,* 51–52; Rosen, "Disease, Debility, and Death."

34. Lala Kashi Ram, *Notes and Suggestions on Sanitation in the Punjab,* 17, 28.

35. Government of India, *Census of India, 1911,* 26.

36. Lala Kashi Ram, *Notes and Suggestions on Sanitation in the Punjab,* 12, 13.

37. Charu Gupta, *Sexuality, Obscenity, Community,* 123. The scholarship on women's reform in the late nineteenth and early twentieth centuries is extensive, though much of it is focused on the role negotiations over women's status and cultural position played in early nationalist politics. The idea that the domestic sphere increasingly became associated with the inner, spiritual essence of Indian national culture has been most fully elaborated in Chatterjee, *The Nation and Its Fragments.* Gail Minault has written on the world of the north Indian *zenana* as both a material and social space in her "Other Voices, Other Rooms."

38. On Sikh and Hindu reform in the Punjab, see Malhotra, *Gender, Caste, and Religious Identities.* On Muslim reform, see Minault, *Secluded Scholars.* On the difference between Hindu and Muslim practices of *purdah,* see Vatuk, "Purdah Revisited."

39. Minault, "Other Voices, Other Rooms," 118. See also Talwar, "Feminist Consciousness in Women's Journals in Hindi, 1910–20." For a study of the many ways women resisted the everyday forms of patriarchal oppression in their lives, see Oldenberg, "Lifestyle as Resistance."

40. "Hygiene in the Zenanas of India," 484–85.

41. Lala Kashi Ram, *Notes and Suggestions on Sanitation in the Punjab,* 11.

42. See Minault, "Hali's *Majalis un-Nissa.*" Minault translated Hali's text in Minault, *Voices of Silence.*

43. Maulana Ashraf 'Ali Thanawi, *Bihishti Zewar,* quoted in Barbara Metcalf, *Perfecting Women,* 334.

44. The *Mirat ul-'Arus* was immensely popular and was widely distributed. It won a government prize the year it was published (1869), and the provincial government then "bought 2000 copies of the book and recommended its adoption as a textbook in vernacular schools for girls." Minault, *Secluded Scholars,* 35.

45. Ahmad, *The Bride's Mirror,* 105–6. In his 1911 census report, Harikishan Kaul made note of the way house interiors were changing in the Punjab, using language that bears comparison to the passage I cite in the text from *Mirat ul-'Arus:* "In the houses of the better classes, the old carpet and great pillow have been replaced by tables, chairs, cushioned armed chairs and sofas, and a corresponding

change has occurred in the toilet, dining room and other furniture. . . . Enameled plates and tumblers are found in abundance, particularly in Mohammedan houses, dishes and cooking utensils of metal are replacing earthen articles, and most houses are proud of possessing a wooden box, or a steel trunk of sorts, as the receptacle of the family belongings, instead of the old cane basket." See Government of India, *Census of India, 1911,* 28.

46. Chatterjee, "The Nationalist Resolution of the Women's Question," 239.

47. K. C. Joshi, *Joshi's Modern Designs,* i. The original work was in Urdu; the English translation was published the same year. Page numbers for further quotations from this work are given in parentheses in the text.

48. E. D. Maclagan, cited in Government of Punjab, *Report on the Material Progress of the Punjab during the Decade 1881–1891,* 20.

49. Based on figures in Government of Punjab, *Gazetteer of the Lahore District, 1883–84,* 192.

50. Government of Punjab, "Review of the Sanitary Administration Report for 1890," Home Department Proceedings (Medical and Sanitary), no. 3 (June 1891): 30.

51. Government of Punjab, *Gazetteer of the Lahore District, 1893–94,* 93–94.

52. Pook, *Lahore,* 46, 47.

53. Government of India, *Census of India, 1911,* 29.

54. A. E. Barton, deputy commissioner of Hoshiarpur, cited in Government of Punjab, *Report on the Punjab Sanitary Conference,* 2:147.

55. C. J. Halifax, "Notes on Original Works of Importance Which Seem to Be Urgently Necessary for the Lahore Municipality, and the Provision of Funds for These Works," Lahore Municipal Committee, Old Records, General File (4 April 1905): 6.

56. Michael O'Dwyer, cited in Government of Punjab, *Report on the Punjab Sanitary Conference,* 2:5.

57. Government of Punjab, *Report on the Punjab Sanitary Conference,* 2:147.

58. In Lahore in 1919 the lieutenant governor of the province appointed the Improvement Committee. It had the purely advisory task of recommending "steps necessary for improving the utility and beauty of the main roads and public spaces of Lahore." A reconstituted Improvement Trust Committee was formed in 1925, "owing to the recrudescence on the Mall of vulgar hoardings, projections looking suspiciously like encroachments, and the neglected state of the Statue of the Queen Empress [at Charing Cross, in the civil station]." In 1935 this body became the Lahore Improvement Trust. See Government of Punjab, *Report on the Affairs of the Municipal Committee of Lahore,* 75–76.

59. Government of Punjab, "Town Improvement Act, 1922." The act provided for the establishment of improvement trusts in Punjab's municipalities, giving them responsibility for overseeing new layout plans and proposing schemes to ameliorate unsanitary developments in the city. The trusts' schemes were advisory and, if approved, would be enforced by the municipal committee or provincial government. Improvement trusts were first established at the end of the nineteenth century and continued to be established into the early decades of the twentieth. The first trust was established in Bombay (1898), followed by Mysore (1903), Calcutta (1911), and Hyderabad (1912). See Kopardekar and Diwan, *Urban and Regional Planning,* 38.

60. Government of Punjab, *Report of the Lahore and Amritsar Improvement Trust Committee,* 2, 7.

61. See Qadeer, *Lahore.* Qadeer, one of the few scholars to have studied urban development in Lahore during the twentieth century, labeled these new settlements "New Indigenous Communities" (NICs). Qadeer and others have written that NICs were segregated by religion, which is reflected in the names of the communities themselves: "In these New Indigenous Communities, segregation by

religious groups continued to persist. Krishan Nagar, Gowal Mandi, Mohni Road, Ram Nagar, were modern Hindu neighbourhoods, and correspondingly Islamia Park, Farooq Gunj, Garhi Shahu were predominantly Muslim residential areas" (83).

62. The early history of Model Town has not yet been well documented. See, however, Vandal, "The Dream and the Reality," and Masood Khan, "Cultural Transfers." Khan estimates, on the basis of a sample survey of early share certificates, that roughly two-thirds of shareholders "belonged to the administrative and judicial part of the colonial administrative system. Except for a few, these were at most second-echelon positions: police officers, revenue officers, engineers who manned the colonial railways, roads, buildings, and irrigation departments, the lower judiciary" (92). Interestingly, in the early years, up to 80 percent of shareholders lived outside Lahore at the time they purchased their shares; presumably these were Lahoris who intended to return to the city at retirement.

63. Tandon, *Punjabi Century*, 236.

64. While Howard emphasized that his circular garden-city plan was a "diagram only" and meant for it to be modified in actual use, his illustration of one "ward" plan in *Garden Cities of Tomorrow* was rendered in more precise geometric detail. In this illustration, many features of the ward, including the radial streets, neighborhood parks, industries at the perimeter, and large circular garden at the city's center, are drawn in careful detail. Historian Robert Fishman argues that despite their diagrammatic nature, there was "nothing merely mechanical" about Howard's plans: "Howard does not seem to have been familiar with the designs for geometric cities that utopian socialists had put forward earlier in the nineteenth century. Nonetheless the perfectly circular, perfectly symmetrical plan he devised for the Garden City bears a distinct resemblance to some of these. . . . the explanation, however, lies not in direct influence but in shared values. For Howard had inherited that tradition in English utopian thought in which it was assumed that society could be improved just as a machine could—through the appropriate adjustments. A properly functioning society would thus take on the precise and well-calculated look of a good machine." Fishman, *Urban Utopias in the Twentieth Century*, 41.

65. Ziffren, "Biography of Patrick Geddes."

66. Patrick Geddes, cited in Stalley, *Patrick Geddes*, 424–28. Elsewhere, in a report for Raja Holkar of Indore State, Geddes described the new suburbs he planned for Indore in language borrowed directly from Howard: "[In new garden suburbs] town and country conditions are peculiarly united and combined, with much of the advantages and economy of both, and with fewer than hitherto of the disadvantages of either." Geddes, *Town Planning towards City Development*, 76. Few of the layout plans Geddes drew for Indore's new suburbs show much formal symmetry. Even more than did Howard, Geddes emphasized the importance of adapting new construction to the particularities of a given site: "Variety arises as each suburb or village plan is worked out in detail," Geddes wrote, "since all existing natural and architectural features worth preserving have to be respected and utilized, such as good trees, existing homes and wells, temples and tombs, etc. as also open views of country or river." Geddes, *Town Planning towards City Development*, 77. For more on Geddes's role in India, see Peter Hall, *Cities of Tomorrow*, 263–70; Ferreira and Jha, *The Outlook Tower*. For excerpts of reports on particular cities, see Stalley, *Patrick Geddes* (report on Lahore); Tyrwhitt, *Patrick Geddes in India* (reports on various cities in India); and Geddes, *Town Planning towards City Development* (report on Indore).

67. Geddes, cited in Stalley, *Patrick Geddes*, 189, 425–26.

68. Architect and educator Masood Khan has noted that several different standard plans were available for purchase from the society some years after Model Town was initiated, all designed by architect M. C. Khanna. See Masood Khan, "Cultural Transfers," 102.

69. Tandon, *Punjabi Century*, 237–38; emphasis added.

70. Tom Rosin has documented similar changes in houses built shortly after independence in Jaipur, arguing that changes to the bungalow typology, over time, lead more and more toward an older *haveli* typology. See Rosin, "From Garden Suburb to Old City Ward."

71. Fishman, *Urban Utopias in the Twentieth Century*, 4.

72. Esmee Mascall, "All Change," OIOC MSS Eur C 427.

73. Tandon, *Punjabi Century*, 238.

5. ANXIETIES AT HOME

1. William Owens Clark, OIOC MSS Eur A 148/1.

2. Nawab Khan, Item, in *Punjab Magazine* 233 (1890): 28, 31.

3. Thomas Metcalf, *An Imperial Vision*, 9.

4. Rudyard Kipling, "The Enlightenments of Pagett, M.P.," 340.

5. See Catherine Hall, *Civilizing Subjects;* McClintock, *Imperial Leather;* Sinha, *Colonial Masculinity;* Stoler, *Race and the Education of Desire;* Chatterjee, *The Nation and Its Fragments;* Comaroff and Comaroff, *Ethnography and the Historical Imagination;* White, *The Comforts of Home.*

6. Stoler, *Race and the Education of Desire;* Thomas Metcalf, *Ideologies of the Raj*, 160–85.

7. Comaroff and Comaroff, *Ethnography and the Historical Imagination*, 280.

8. Steel, *The Complete Indian Housekeeper and Cook*, 11.

9. Rudyard Kipling, "The Private Services Commission," 237. Page numbers in parenthesis in the following paragraph refer to this story. Kipling's fictional and journalistic accounts of British home life in India provide an exceedingly rich archive on the topic. They are of particular use for this project, since so many of his fictional stories, and most of his journalistic writings, are set in mid-1880s Lahore. Kipling's oeuvre is complex, and my use of his writing in this chapter is aimed more at capturing the experiential qualities of British home life portrayed so often in his work than in assessing either Kipling's stature as a writer or his complex ideological relationship to the British Empire.

10. See Ranajit Guha, "Not at Home in Empire."

11. Government of India, *Census of India, 1911*, 29.

12. Anthony D. King pioneered the study of the bungalow as a distinctive colonial type in his *Colonial Urban Development*, 122–55. His later work *The Bungalow* analyzes the global diffusion of the bungalow-type house and the different interpretations of the type that accompanied its spread to settings outside colonies in the British Empire.

13. Goulding, *Old Lahore*, 74.

14. "Letter from Lady Maynard (Alfreda Horner Eppes) to Mrs. Richard Eppes (mother)," March 2, 1897, from Charing Cross Hotel, Lahore, OIOC MSS Eur F 224/12.

15. In an article published early in his career, Bernard Cohn studied the tenure of judges and collectors who served in the North-West Provinces from 1795 to 1850. The average length of service in these positions ranged from two to five years, though every district recorded several men who served in these positions for less than two years. "Among the most important group socially and economically—the officials—few stayed long in Benares [the provincial headquarters]," Cohn wrote; "their careers were made up of a series of postings over much of North India." Cohn, "The British in Benares," 169. Also see Maconochie, *Life in the Indian Civil Service.*

16. PWD housing is discussed in Scriver, *Rationalization, Standardization, and Control in Design;* Davies, *Splendours of the Raj;* King, "Colonial Architecture Re-visited"; Morris, *Stones of Empire;*

Stamp, "British Architecture in India, 1857–1947"; Thomas Metcalf, *An Imperial Vision.* Peter Scriver has completed the most detailed study to date of PWD buildings in India, especially in their relation to colonial institutional frameworks and professional knowledge cultures. Scriver writes, "The first order of concern in determining a standard for a particular office or dwelling type was the budget. All matters of status, class, caste and race could in fact be neatly codified in a simple scale of cost. If one occupied an official dwelling unit, no matter what type, one rented it at a fixed percentage of their salary. The fixed scale of salaries fixed the corresponding rate at which each specific rank and category of government servant was scheduled to pay for his accommodation. Amortized over a set period of time, and depreciated accordingly, the maximum recoverable cost for any such employment grade determined dwelling type could be calculated precisely." Scriver, *Rationalization, Standardization, and Control in Design,* 175.

17. Government of Punjab, "Rules Relating to the Construction or Purchase of Residences for Government Officials and the Rents to Be Charged for Such Buildings," Home Department Proceedings (General), no. 32 (October 1896): n.p. In addition, the PWD regularly charged an "establishment fee" of 23 percent of the building cost for new construction (and maintenance), which drove the prices of government-owned housing higher still. See Government of Punjab, Home Department Proceedings (B Files) (Medical and Sanitary), no. 8 (August 1886): n.p.

18. Government of Punjab, "Construction of Residential Buildings for Government Officials," Home Department Proceedings (General), no. 35 (September 1904): n.p.

19. Girouard, *The Victorian Country House;* McCleod, *Style and Society;* Markus, *Order in Space and Society;* Davidoff and Hall, *Family Fortunes;* Poovey, *Making a Social Body;* Thompson, *The Rise of Respectable Society;* Sharon Marcus, *Apartment Stories.*

20. Schmiechen, "The Victorians, the Historians, and the Idea of Modernism," 287–316.

21. Quoted in Grier, *Culture and Comfort,* 7.

22. Growse, *Indian Architecture of Today as Exemplified in New Buildings in the Bulandshahr District,* v.

23. John Lockwood Kipling, quoted in Government of Punjab, *Monograph on Wood Manufactures in the Punjab: 1887–88,* 4.

24. Letter from Lady Maynard (Alfreda Horner Eppes) to Mrs. Richard Eppes, March 2, 1897, OIOC MSS Eur F 224/12.

25. On page 1 of the first issue of the *Bungalow: A Paper for Anglo Indian Homes* (January 4, 1896), published in Bombay, the editor wrote, "In bringing out *The Bungalow,* the Editor hopes to supply a much-felt want—a ladies paper that will devote itself to the interests of Anglo Indian Homes. There will be every month articles on 'The Home: how to beautify it,' with many hints on decoration, by a lady who has spent many years in Indian bungalows, Indian Cookery, with Recipes and Menus, 'Lessons on Home Dressmaking,' 'Gardening,' 'The Toilet,' fashions, etc. There will also be a column of ladies' private advertisement for articles for sale and exchange, and several prizes will be offered for competition each month." Also see Swati Chattopadhyay, "'Goods, Chattels, and Sundry Items.'"

26. Quoted in A. G. N. Verity, "The Kings in Imperial India, by A. G. N. Verity, A Grand Daughter," OIOC MSS Eur C 852/2, 85–86.

27. Esmee Mascall, "All Change," OIOC MSS Eur C 427: 27.

28. Ibid., 29.

29. Memoir by Mrs. Elinor Tollinton (b. 1909) née Astbury, OIOC MSS Eur D 1197.

30. Rudyard Kipling, "William the Conqueror," 205.

31. Government of Punjab, "Tour Programme of His Imperial Highness the Crown Prince of

Germany in the Punjab and Sanitary Arrangements in Connection Therewith," Home Department Proceedings (Medical and Sanitary), no. 242 (September 1910): 230–31.

32. In the 1901 census, 16,700 persons were listed as working in miscellaneous building trades in Punjab Province; by 1911, the number had risen to over 100,000, reflecting an increase of more than 500 percent. Trades that showed big increases during this period included cabinet makers and carriage painters (280 percent); thatchers, building contractors, house painters, tilers, plumbers, locksmiths (500 percent); traders in dyes, paints, and petroleum (200 percent); brick and tile makers (100 percent); and traders in furniture, carpets, curtains, and bedding (210 percent). Figures calculated from tables in Government of India, *Census of India, 1911*.

33. G. T. A., "The Traveler's Scrapbook," n.d. (ca. 1855), OIOC MSS Eur B 366.

34. Upton, *Holy Things and Profane*, 102.

35. Grant, *Anglo Indian Domestic Life*, 8.

36. Rudyard Kipling, *Kipling's India*, 188–89. The racialized notion that Indian craftsmanship is substandard may continue to resonate in some circles within Britain. The following appeared in "Princely Gaffe" in the *New York Times* of August 11, 1999: "Prince Philip, husband of Queen Elizabeth, said during a tour of a factory in Scotland that an unsophisticated fuse box looked 'as though it was put in by an Indian.' Racial equality groups expressed anger and Philip swiftly apologized."

37. John Lockwood Kipling, quoted in Government of Punjab, *Monograph on Wood Manufactures in the Punjab*, 5–6.

38. See Serematakis, *The Senses Still*, 136.

39. Also see King, *The Bungalow*, 36.

40. Government of Punjab, *Memorandum on the Subject of Social and Official Intercourse between European Officers in the Punjab and Indians*, 5, 6.

41. Kerr, *The Gentleman's House*, 74–75.

42. The Indian staff of a bungalow residence were frequent subjects of "memoir-like" accounts by Europeans, which usually portrayed them in an unflattering light. Perhaps the most famous work in this genre is Atkinson, *Curry and Rice on Forty Plates*. Atkinson's book includes forty watercolor plates of domestic scenes from a bungalow, most of which lampoon and exaggerate the physical and racial characteristics of typical bungalow staff, along with their perceived lassitude.

43. Stoler, *Race and the Education of Desire*, 112.

44. Ibid., chap. 5 passim. Stoler writes that "one seventeenth-century French doctor took as a given that breastmilk 'had the power to make children resemble their nurses in mind and body, just as the seed makes them resemble their mother and father'" (146).

45. For a succinctly sketched history of this genre as it relates to urban housing, see Sharon Marcus, *Apartment Stories*, esp. chap. 3. On the relationship between haunted house stories and Freud's elucidation of the "uncanny," which in many ways parallels the connection drawn here between Kipling's story and my emphasis on anxiety, see Vidler, *The Architectural Uncanny*.

46. Rudyard Kipling, "The House of Shadows," 246–48.

47. On the British hill station as a resort for Europeans, see Kennedy, *The Magic Mountains*; Kenny, "Climate, Race, and Imperial Authority."

48. Steel, *The Complete Indian Housekeeper and Cook*, 7.

49. Ibid., vi.

50. Hogg, *Practical Remarks Chiefly Concerning the Health and Ailments of European Families in India, with Special Reference to Maternal Management and Domestic Economy*, 10, 33, 55.

51. John and Jean Comaroff offer the following summary and qualification of this kind of

argument: "If the likes of Foucault are correct [a naturalized notion of domesticity] was an element in the making of a total moral order, a silent edifice in which family and home served as mechanisms of discipline and social control. Vested in dispersed regimes of surveillance and in the texture of everyday habit, goes the general argument, the doctrine of domesticity facilitated new forms of production, new structures of inequality. Still, we repeat, it did not prevail immediately or without resistance—nor everywhere in just the same way." Comaroff and Comaroff, *Ethnography and the Historical Imagination*, 267.

52. Calvert, *On the Preservation of Health for the Guidance of Young Officers on their Arrival in India*, 5.

53. Steel, *The Complete Indian Housekeeper and Cook*, 10, 2.

54. Ibid., 4, 67.

55. Hogg, *Practical Remarks*, 23.

56. Rudyard Kipling, "Naboth." Parenthetical references to page numbers in the following passage refer to this source.

57. The Kipling bungalow in Lahore was located close to Mall Road, and the Chief Court (discussed in chapter 3) had been completed a few years prior to the publication of this story.

58. The opening line of the story reads, "This was how it happened; and the truth is also an allegory of Empire" (139).

59. Suleri, *The Rhetoric of English India*, 2; emphasis added.

6. THINKING WITH THE CITY

1. The development of colonial-era "urban" fiction in north India—in which the city forms an important topos for events—has thus far received little scholarly attention, and my analysis in this chapter is, of course, tangential to that task. Historian Markus Daechsel has written provocatively on one urban genre, the detective novel, with special reference to Punjab. See Daechsel, "Zalim Daku and the Mystery of the Rubber Sea Monster." Also see Daechsel, *The Politics of Self-Expression*; Zelliot, "Literary Images of the Modern Indian City."

2. Earlier genres of urban writing that look to the physical city as a source of evidence for intangible qualities predate British rule on the subcontinent, of course. Perhaps the most immediately relevant (to our discussion) precolonial genre in north India was the *shahr ashob*, or "city disturber" literature. *Shahr ashob* literature came to India from Persia (and subsequently Ottoman Turkey) and is usually written in the form of a satire or lament on the declining qualities of a particular city and its prominent figures. The genre is most closely associated with the period of Mughal decline in the eighteenth and nineteenth centuries in India, and it is thus also coterminous with the early period of British rule. Many, perhaps most, *shahr ashob* compositions describe particular cities in generic terms rather than by referencing known monuments and places. They differ considerably, therefore, from the texts under examination below. See Petievich, "Poetry of the Declining Mughals"; Bernardini, "The *Masnavi-Shahrashubs* as Town Panegyrics"; Sunil Sharma, "The City of Beauties in the Indo-Persian Poetic Landscape."

3. This is the central tenet of James Mill's extremely influential *History of British India*. Subsequent European histories of India broadly accepted Mill's conclusions. On early British histories of India, see Thomas Metcalf, *Ideologies of the Raj*. The influence of Mill's *History* on subsequent historians (and on British colonial policy) is discussed by Mehta, *Liberalism and Empire*, esp. chap. 3.

4. A large variety of historiographic modes existed side by side in nineteenth-century India.

My intention in this section is to characterize one in particular, a mode I believe drew, in part, on Indo-Islamic formulas common to a number of more specialized historical genres, including the *tarikh* (history), *manaqib* (miracle stories), and *tasnif* (literary composition). See Sudipta Sen, "Imperial Orders of the Past."

5. In an early nineteenth-century Persian history of the region, Ganesh Das's *Char Bagh-i-Punjab* (The Heavenly Garden of Punjab), the author refers to the number of learned men in Lahore as "beyond description." See Grewal and Banga, *Early Nineteenth Century Panjab,* 32.

6. In the Punjab, Aroras and Khatris were the dominant merchant castes. They were also prominent in Mughal, Sikh, and British governments as clerks, scholars, and lower-level administrative personnel. Historical anthropologist Richard Fox writes that Aroras and Khatris "made up less than five percent of the Punjab's male population in 1891" but that "their literacy rate in 1891 was seven times higher than the average for all castes." See Fox, *Lions of the Punjab,* 126. For a discussion of the north-Indian Muslim scholarly milieu, see Lelyveld, *Aligarh's First Generation,* esp. chap. 2.

7. A representative sample of these earlier works on Punjab are discussed by Fauja Singh, "Two Contemporary Urdu Accounts of Mid-Nineteenth Century Punjab"; Bhagat Singh, "Ali-ud-Din Mufti"; and Gurbux Singh, "Society in the Punjab under Ranjit Singh, Mufti 'Ali Ud Din's Analysis." Also see Grewal and Banga, *Early Nineteenth Century Panjab.*

8. In the case of Lahore, one would have to include the work of Kipling, in particular, and Thomas Moore, whose *Lalla Rookh* (1829) is partly set in the city. Moore, unlike Kipling, never visited Lahore. On the relationship between romanticism and British writing on India more generally, see Suleri, *The Rhetoric of English India.* On the picturesque aesthetic in British paintings of India, with particular reference to Calcutta, see Swati Chattopadhyay, *Representing Calcutta,* esp. chap. 1, and Dirks, "Guiltless Spoliations."

9. I will be using Ram Nath's English translation of Khan's work. See Ram Nath, *Monuments of Delhi. Sanadid* is defined in Platts's Urdu/English dictionary as both "Princes, chiefs, lords, noblemen" and as "calamities, misfortunes, dangers, great or formidable events." *Asar* refers to vestiges, relics, manifestations, or traces. See Platts, *A Dictionary of Urdu, Classical Hindi, and English,* 746, 22. On Sayyid Ahmed Khan's broader role in late nineteenth-century Muslim society and his stewardship of the Muslim Anglo-Oriental College in Aligarh in particular, see Lelyveld, *Aligarh's First Generation.*

10. Ram Nath, *Monuments of Delhi,* xiv; the English title and translation are by Nath.

11. Ibid., v; emphasis added.

12. Bayly, *Empire and Information,* 20–25.

13. Two early genres of Muslim historical writing that continued well into the nineteenth century are biographical dictionaries and chronicles of the lives of saints, rulers, and other persons of note. Anthropologist Brinkley Messick writes that "the initial impetus for such works [as chronicles and biographical dictionaries] was to 'know the men,' enabling the critical assessment of the passage of authoritative knowledge through time." Messick, *The Calligraphic State,* 128. In a context where the authority of a text was judged largely on the basis of the chain of transmission through which it was constituted, enunciating the links in that chain served to identify and ground, in part, the authority on which a text was based.

14. Lewis, "First-Person Narrative in the Middle East"; Barbara Metcalf, "Narrating Lives."

15. This theme forms the main subject of a number of excellent essays, including both historical and contemporary case studies, in Ewing, *Shari'at and Ambiguity in South Asian Islam.*

16. I borrow the concept "useful past" from historian Michael Chamberlain, who uses the term to characterize biographical writing in elite circles in medieval Damascus. Biographies of men of

standing were a type of document carefully preserved from generation to generation in medieval Damascus, and few other documents were preserved and passed down with the same degree of care. The past encoded in biographies was "useful," Chamberlain suggests, because it bore claims to status—something that had to be constantly negotiated in a society with few "status producing" institutions. See Chamberlain, *Knowledge and Social Practice in Medieval Damascus, 1190–1350.*

17. Chishti, *Tahqiqaat Chishti* [Chishti's Inquiries], 14.

18. Government of Punjab, "Report on Vernacular Books Registered in the Punjab during the year 1867," Home Department Proceedings (General), no. 131 (September 1870): n.p.

19. Messick, *The Calligraphic State,* 125. While Messick studied Middle Eastern, not South Asian, traditions of historical writing, the two areas shared a substantial corpus of Islamic texts, practices, and institutional frameworks for the production and dissemination of knowledge that make their comparison in the present context a meaningful one.

20. I borrow the concept of "affective" knowledge from historian Christopher Bayly. This is a concept Bayly defines differently throughout his work, but most usefully (for my purposes) as knowledge that grows out of a kind of "sympathy which comes from ties of belief, of marriage and from a sense of inhabiting the same moral realm." Bayly, *Empire and Information,* 55.

21. Chishti, *Tahqiqaat Chishti* [Chishti's Inquiries], 888.

22. William Coldstream, preface to Chishti, *Tahqiqaat Chishti* [Chishti's Inquiries], 14. Coldstream's original comments were recorded in Urdu.

23. Latif wrote a similar book on Agra, published four years later. His book on Agra, unlike *Lahore*, concentrates overwhelmingly on the Mughal period of the city's history, relegating the history of "modern" Agra to a few short pages at the end. Latif, *Agra Historical and Descriptive, with an Account of Akbar and His Court and of the Modern City of Agra.*

24. The frontispiece quotation is attributed to Thomas H. Dyer, who wrote a book on Pompeii with a title that suggests certain similarities with Latif's book: *Pompeii: Its History, Buildings, and Techniques.*

25. Latif, *Lahore,* vii; emphasis added.

26. Ibid., 261.

27. Ibid., ix–x.

28. Ibid., v.

29. Parenthetical references hereafter refer to page numbers in *The Two Friends.*

30. Kishan, "Advice to Young Punjab," 35.

31. Foucault, "What Is the Enlightenment?" 312. The role played by civil society in the constitution of European modernity has been most fully discussed by Jürgen Habermas in his *Structural Transformation of the Public Sphere.*

32. See Swati Chattopadhyay, "Blurring Boundaries"; Neild, "Colonial Urbanism"; Marshall, "The White Town of Calcutta under the Rule of the East India Company"; Brown, "The Cemeteries and the Suburbs"; John Archer, "Paras, Palaces, Pathogens."

33. The dual-city model refers primarily to morphological differences between newer, expatriate districts of colonial cities and older areas of indigenous population. Early formulations of the dual-city model appear in Murphy, "Urbanization in Asia"; Horvath, "In Search of a Theory of Urbanization"; and McGee, *The Southeast Asian City.* Also see Ross and Telkamp, *Colonial Cities.* More recently, Karachi-based architect Yasmeen Lari and Mihail Lari assume the relevance of the concept in their book *The Dual City.* Anthony King, in addition to being an early contributor to the dual-city model, has traced its historiography in *Urbanism, Colonialism, and the World Economy.*

Also see Gwendolyn Wright's carefully historicized discussion of the deliberate creation of dual cities in French colonial Morocco under Hubert Lyautey in her *Politics of Design in French Colonial Urbanism*.

34. This stands in contrast to the countryside or village, settings that both literature and social-scientific analyses have long associated with timeless continuity. The countryside does appear in Nath's novel, if only as a present absence. When Rama, the bad seed, becomes aimless and aware of his detachment from Indian society during the course of the novel, he retreats to the countryside to think through his predicament. The sequence of events that follows from this nevertheless reveals that the countryside is a space that can only be sensed remotely: When Nath grows worried about Rama's sudden disappearance, he does not set out into the countryside to find him; instead, he takes out an ad in the *Civil and Military Gazette* beseeching his friend to return. The imagined relationship between the village and the city in the Indian context is discussed in Nandy, *An Ambiguous Journey to the City*.

35. This observation may be one line of connection between "colonial modernity" and a broader discourse on modernity fleshed out by scholars of nineteenth-century Europe. In his discussion of late nineteenth-century French novels that addressed Baron Haussmann's reconstruction of Paris (beginning in 1864), art historian Timothy Clark made the following observation: "It should give us pause straightaway that the best description of Haussmannization was written thirty years before the event. . . . We might say of these writers that they seem to *want* the city to have a shape—a logic and a uniformity—and therefore construct one from the signs they have, however sparse and unsystematic." Clark, *The Painting of Modern Life*, 33; emphasis in the original.

36. Mitchell, *Colonizing Egypt*; Poovey, *Making a Social Body*; Rabinow, *French Modern*; Upton, "Lancasterian Schools, Republican Citizenship, and the Spatial Imagination in Early Nineteenth-Century America."

37. Krishan Kumar, "Modernity"; emphasis added.

38. Programmatic statements in favor of pluralizing modernity appear in Taylor, "Two Theories of Modernity"; Eisenstadt, "Multiple Modernities"; and Gaonkar, *Alternative Modernities*. On the usefulness of this concept for studies in colonial urbanism, see King, *Spaces of Global Cultures*, chap. 4; also see Hosagrahar, *Indigenous Modernities*. Two provocative and important criticisms of the concept (and indeed of the overuse of the concept of "modernity" more generally) are found in Kelly, "Alternative Modernities or an Alternative to Modernity," and Cooper, *Colonialism in Question*, 113–49. My own thinking on this issue is indebted to David Scott's elegant assessment of what is at stake in pluralizing the term in his *Conscripts of Modernity*, esp. 112–19.

39. Rofel, *Other Modernities*, 15.

40. David Scott, *Conscripts of Modernity*, 114.

41. See David Scott, "The Trouble of Thinking," esp. 292–93.

BIBLIOGRAPHY

ARCHIVES

England

Oriental and India Office Collections (OIOCs), British Library, London
   Public Works Department Proceedings
   Mascall Papers (MSS Eur C 427)
   Fyson Papers (MSS Eur D 885/2)
   Tollinton Papers (MSS Eur D 1197)
   Clark Papers (MSS Eur A 148/1)
   Maynard (Eppes) Papers (MSS Eur F 224/12)
   Verity Papers (MSS Eur C 852/2)
   G.T.A., "The Traveler's Scrapbook" (MSS Eur B 366)

Pakistan

The Co-operative Model Town Society, Limited, Lahore
   Building Permit Files
Government of Punjab (Punjab Provincial Archives of Pakistan, Anarkali's
   Tomb, Civil Secretariat, Lahore)
   Boards and Committees Department (General)
   Home Department Proceedings (General)
   Home Department Proceedings (Jails)
   Home Department Proceedings (Judicial)
   Home Department Proceedings (Legislative)
   Home Department Proceedings (Medical and Sanitary)
   Home Department Proceedings (Municipal)
   Home Department Proceedings (Police)
   Public Works Department (General)
Lahore Municipal Corporation, Old Record Room Archives, Lahore
   Case Files

PUBLISHED WORKS

Acharya, Prasanna K. *An Encyclopedia of Hindu Architecture* (1927). Delhi: Low
   Price, 1998.

Adir, Gulam Nabi, comp. *Chuha aur Plague Billi aur Chuha aur Mohafiz-e-Jaan Tika* [Rat and Plague, Cat and Rat, and a Guard]. Lahore, 1890.

Ahmad, Nazir. *The Bride's Mirror.* Trans. G. E. Ward. London: Henry Frowde, 1903. Original title *Mirat ul-'Arus.*

Aijazuddin, F. S. *Lahore: Illustrated Views of the 19th Century.* Ahmedabad: Mapin, 1991.

Akhtar, Mazhar Pervez. "The Journey from Government Wards Institution Amballa City, 1864, to Punjab Chiefs College: Glimpses from the History" (2005). http://www.aitchison.edu.pk/uploads/9/history.doc (accessed February 12, 2006).

Ali, Imran. *Punjab under Imperialism, 1885–1947.* Princeton: Princeton University Press, 1988.

Appadurai, Arjun. *Modernity at Large: Cultural Dimensions of Globalization.* Minneapolis: University of Minnesota Press, 1996.

———. *Worship and Conflict under Colonial Rule: A South Indian Case.* Cambridge: Cambridge University Press, 1981.

Archer, John. "Paras, Palaces, Pathogens: Frameworks for the Growth of Calcutta, 1800–1850." *City and Society* 12, no. 1 (2000): 19–54.

Archer, Mildred. *Indian Architecture and the British: 1780–1830.* London: RIBA, 1968.

Arnold, David. *Colonizing the Body: State Medicine and Epidemic Disease in Nineteenth-Century India.* Berkeley and Los Angeles: University of California Press, 1993.

———. "Crime and Crime Control in Madras, 1858–1947." In *Crime and Criminality in British India,* ed. Anand Yang, 62–88. Tucson: University of Arizona Press, 1985.

Asad, Talal. "Conscripts of Western Civilization." In *Dialectical Anthropology: Essays in Honor of Stanley Diamond,* 2 vols., ed. Christine Gailey, 1:333–51. Gainsville: University of Florida Press, 1992.

———. "Modern Power and the Reconfiguration of Religious Traditions: Interview by Saba Mahmood." *Stanford Humanities Review* 5, no. 1 (1995): 1–18.

Asher, Catherine B. *Architecture of Mughal India.* 2nd ed. Cambridge: Cambridge University Press, 1992.

Asher, Catherine B., and Thomas Metcalf. *Perceptions of South Asia's Visual Past.* New Delhi: Oxford and IBH, 1994.

Ata-Ullah, Naazish. "Stylistic Hybridity and Colonial Art and Design Education: A Wooden Carved Screen by Ram Singh." In *Colonialism and the Object: Empire, Material Culture, and the Museum,* ed. Tom Barringer and Tom Flynn, 68–81. London: Routledge, 1998.

Atkinson, George Franklin. *Curry and Rice on Forty Plates; or, The Ingredients of Social Life at "Our Station" in India.* 5th ed. London: W. Thacker, 1911.

Bachelard, Gaston. *The Poetics of Space.* Trans. Maria Jolas. Boston: Beacon House, 1994.

Baden Powell, B. H. *The Land Systems of British India.* 3 vols. Oxford: Clarendon Press, 1892.

Bafna, Sonit. "On the Idea of the Mandala as a Governing Device in Indian Architectural Tradition." *Journal of the Society of Architectural Historians* 59, no. 1 (2000): 26–49.

Bagal, J. C. *Papers Relating to the Maintenance of Schools of Art in India as State Institutions.* Calcutta: Government Printing Press, 1898.

Bagchi, P. C. *Calcutta: Past and Present.* Calcutta: Calcutta University Press, 1939.

Bahadur, Rai Kunhya Lal. "New Railway Station at Lahore." *Professional Papers on Indian Engineering,* no. 1 (1863–64): 207–8.

Bain, Alexander. *The Emotions and the Will.* London: John W. Parker and Son, 1859.

Ballantyne, Tony. "Entangled Pasts: Colonialism, Mobility, and the Systematisation of Sikhism." http://www.cishsydney2005.org/images/ST6%20-%20Tony%20Ballantyne.doc (accessed January 19, 2006; no longer available at this site).

Ballhatchet, Kenneth. *Race, Class, and Sex under the Raj: Imperial Attitudes and Policies and Their Critics, 1793–1905*. New York: St. Martin's Press, 1980.

Bamber, C. J. *Report on the Sanitary Administration of the Punjab and Proceedings of the Sanitary Board for the Year 1904*. Lahore: Civil and Military Gazette Press, 1905.

Banga, Indu, ed. *The City in Indian History: Urban Demography, Society, and Politics*. Delhi: Manohar, 1994.

———, ed. *Five Punjabi Centuries: Polity, Economy, Society, and Culture: C. 1500–1990*. Delhi: Manohar, 1997.

———. "Formation of the Sikh State, 1765–1845." In *Five Punjabi Centuries: Polity, Economy, Society, and Culture: C. 1500–1990*, ed. Indu Banga, 84–111. Delhi: Manohar, 1997.

———, ed. "Polity, Economy, and Urbanization in the Upper Bari Doab, 1700–1947." In *Studies in Urban History*, ed. J. S. Grewal and Indu Banga, 192–205. Amritsar: Guru Nanak Dev University, 1978.

Barnard, Henry. *Pestalozzi and His Educational System*. Syracuse, N.Y.: C. W. Bardeen, 1906.

Barr, William. *Travels from Delhi to Punjab and Cabul with the Mission of Lieutenant Colonel Sir C. M. Wade* (1839). Delhi: Nirmal, 1987.

Barrier, N. Gerald. *The Census in British India*. Delhi: Manohar, 1981.

———. *The Punjab Alienation of Land Bill of 1900*. Durham, N.C.: Duke University Press, 1966.

Barringer, Tom, and Tom Flynn, eds. *Colonialism and the Object: Empire, Material Culture, and the Museum*. London: Routledge, 1998.

Bartholomew, J. G. *A Literary and Historical Atlas of Asia*. London: J. M. Dent and Sons, 1913.

Baucom, Ian. *Out of Place: Englishness, Empire, and the Locations of Identity*. Princeton: Princeton University Press, 1999.

Bayly, Christopher A. "Delhi and Other Cities of North India during the 'Twilight.'" In *Delhi through the Ages: Selected Essays in Urban History, Culture, and Society*, ed. Robert E. Frykenberg, 121–36. Delhi: Oxford University Press, 1993.

———. *Empire and Information: Intelligence Gathering and Social Communication in India, 1780–1870*. Cambridge: Cambridge University Press, 1996.

———. *Rulers, Townsmen, and Bazaars: North Indian Society in the Age of British Expansion, 1770–1870*. Cambridge: Cambridge University Press, 1983.

Bear, L. G. "Miscegenations of Modernity: Constructing European Respectability and Race in the Indian Railway Colony, 1857–1931." *Women's History Review* 3, no. 4 (1994): 531–48.

Bedi, Baba Pyari Lal. *Harvest from the Desert: The Life and Work of Sir Ganga Ram*. Lahore: Sir Ganga Ram Trust Society, 1940.

Bellamy, Liz, and Tom Williamson, eds. *Life in the Victorian Village: The Daily News Survey of 1891*. 2 vols. London: Caliban Books, 1999.

Bellew, H. W. *Vaccination Kyunkar Kiya Jata Hai* [Why Is Vaccination Done?]. Lahore, n.d.

Berman, Marshall. *All That Is Solid Melts into Air: The Experience of Modernity*. New York: Verso, 1982.

Bernardini, Michele. "The *Masnavi-Shahrashubs* as Town Panegyrics: An International Genre in Islamic Mashriq." In *Narrated Space in the Literature of the Islamic World*, ed. Roxane Haag-Higuchi and Christian Szyska, 81–94. Wiesbaden: Harrassowitz, 2001.

Bernier, François. *Travels in the Mughal Empire: AD 1656–68*. Trans. Irving Brock. Ed. Vincent A. Smith. 2nd ed. Delhi: Low Price, 1989.

Bhadra, Gautam. "Four Rebels of Eighteen-Fifty-Seven." In *Subaltern Studies: Writings on South Asian History and Society*, ed. Ranajit Guha, 4:229–75. New York: Oxford University Press, 1982.

Bhandari, Vivek. "Historicizing the 'Public': The Making of a Social Formation in Nineteenth Century Punjab." Ph.D. diss., University of Pennsylvania, 1998.

Birdwood, G. C. M. *The Industrial Arts of India.* London: Chapman and Hall, 1880.

Bishop, Ryan, John Phillips, and Wei Wei Yeo, eds. *Postcolonial Urbanism: Southeast Asian Cities and Global Processes.* New York: Routledge, 2003.

Blake, Stephen. *Shahjahanabad: The Sovereign City in Mughal India, 1639–1739.* Cambridge: Cambridge University Press, 1991.

Blumenfield, Hans. "The Modern Metropolis." In *Cities,* 40–57. New York: Alfred A. Knopf, 1965.

Blunt, Alison. "Imperial Geographies of Home: British Domesticity in India, 1886–1925." *Transactions of the Institute of British Geographers,* new series, 24, no. 4 (1999): 421–40.

Borthwick, Meredith. *The Changing Role of Women in Bengal, 1849–1905.* Princeton: Princeton University Press, 1984.

Bozdogan, Sibel. *Modernism and Nation Building: Turkish Architectural Culture in the Early Republic.* Seattle: University of Washington Press, 1996.

Breckenridge, Carol. "The Aesthetics and Politics of Colonial Collecting: India at World Fairs." *Society for Comparative Study of Society and History* 31, no. 2 (1989): 195–216.

Breese, Gerald, ed. *The City in Newly Developing Countries.* London: Prentice-Hall, 1972.

Brown, Rebecca. "The Cemeteries and the Suburbs: Patna's Challenge to the Colonial City in South Asia." *Journal of Urban History* 29 (January 2003): 151–72.

Calkins, N. A. *Primary Object Lessons for a Graduated Course of Development: A Manual for Teachers and Parents with Lessons for the Proper Training of the Facilities of Children.* New York: Harper and Brothers, 1861.

Calvert, J. T. *On the Preservation of Health for the Guidance of Young Officers on Their Arrival in India.* Calcutta: Bengal Secretariat Press, 1906.

Catanach, I. J. "Plague and the Indian Village, 1896–1914." In *Rural India: Land, Power, and Society under British Rule,* ed. Peter Rob, 216–43. London: Curzon Press, 1983.

Çelik, Zeynep. *Urban Forms and Colonial Confrontations: Algiers under French Rule.* Berkeley and Los Angeles: University of California Press, 1994.

Chadwick, Edwin. *Report on the Sanitary Condition of the Labouring Population of Great Britain* (1842). Edinburgh: Edinburgh University Press, 1965.

Chakrabarti, Vibhuti. *Indian Architectural Theory: Contemporary Uses of Vastu Vidya.* Richmond, U.K.: Curzon Press, 1998.

Chakrabarty, Dipesh. *Provincializing Europe: Post-Colonial Thought and Historical Difference.* Princeton: Princeton University Press, 2000.

Chamberlain, Michael M. *Knowledge and Social Practice in Medieval Damascus, 1190–1350.* New York: Cambridge University Press, 1994.

Chatterjee, Partha. "Colonialism, Nationalism, and Colonialized Women: The Contest in India." *American Ethnologist* 16, no. 4 (1989): 622–33.

———. *The Nation and Its Fragments.* Princeton: Princeton University Press, 1993.

———. "The Nationalist Resolution of the Women's Question." In *Recasting Women: Essays in Colonial Indian History,* ed. Kum Kum Sangari and Sudesh Vaid, 233–53. New Brunswick, N.J.: Rutgers University Press, 1990.

———. *Nationalist Thought and the Colonial World: A Derivative Discourse?* London: Oxford University Press, 1986.

Chattopadhyay, Brajadulal. *The Making of Early Medieval India.* Delhi: Oxford University Press, 1994.

Chattopadhyay, Swati. "Blurring Boundaries: The Limits of 'White Town' in Colonial Calcutta." *Journal of the Society of Architectural Historians* 59, no. 2 (2000): 154–79.

———. "'Goods, Chattels, and Sundry Items': Constructing 19th-Century Anglo-Indian Domestic Life." *Journal of Material Culture* 7, no. 3 (2002): 243–71.

———. *Representing Calcutta: Modernity, Nationalism, and the Colonial Uncanny.* London: Routledge, 2005.

Chaudhuri, K. N. "Some Reflections on the Town and Country in Mughal India." *Modern Asian Studies* 12, no. 1 (1978): 77–96.

Chaudhuri, Nupur. "Memsahibs and Motherhood in Nineteenth-Century Colonial India." *Victorian Studies* 13, no. 4 (1988): 517–536.

Chaudhury, Muhammad Azam. *Justice and Practice: Legal Ethnography of a Pakistani Punjabi Village.* Oxford: Oxford University Press, 1999.

Chechak [Smallpox]. Lahore: Chand Kapoor and Sons, n.d.

Chishti, Noor Ahmad. *Tahqiqaat Chishti: Tarikh-e-Lahor ka Encyclopedia* [Chishti's Inquiries: An Encyclopedia of Lahore's History] (1867). Lahore: Al-Fasl Nashraan-o-Tajran Kitab, 1996.

Chopra, Preeti. "The City and Its Fragments: Colonial Bombay, 1854 to 1918." Ph.D. diss., University of California at Berkeley, 2001.

Christopher, A. J. "Urban Segregation Levels in the British Overseas Empire and Its Successors, in the Twentieth Century." *Transactions of the Institute of British Geographers,* new series, 17, no. 1 (1992): 95–107.

Clark, Timothy J. *The Painting of Modern Life: Paris in the Art of Manet and His Followers.* New York: Alfred A. Knopf, 1985.

Clarke, C. Purdon. "Some Notes upon the Domestic Architecture of India." *Journal of the Society of Arts* 32, no. 1594 (June 8, 1883): 731–46.

Cohn, Bernard. "The British in Benares: A Nineteenth Century Colonial Society." *Comparative Studies in Society and History* 4, no. 2 (January 1962): 169–99.

———. *Colonialism and Its Forms of Knowledge.* Delhi: Oxford University Press, 1997.

———. "The Command of Language and the Language of Command." In *Subaltern Studies: Writings on South Asian History and Society,* ed. Ranajit Guha, 4:276–329. New York: Oxford University Press, 1982.

———. "Law and the Colonial State in India." In *History and Power in the Study of Law,* ed. J. Starr and J. Collier, 131–52. Ithaca, N.Y.: Cornell University Press, 1989.

———. "Representing Authority in Victorian India." In *The Invention of Tradition,* ed. Eric Hobsbawm and Terence Ranger, 165–210. Cambridge: Cambridge University Press, 1983.

Coleman, Bruce I. *The Idea of the City in Nineteenth-Century Britain.* London: Routledge and Kegan Paul, 1973.

Comaroff, John, and Jean Comaroff. *Ethnography and the Historical Imagination.* Boulder, Colo.: Westview Press, 1992.

Compton, Herbert. *Indian Life in Town and Country.* London: George Newnes, 1904.

Conran, W. L., and H. D. Craik. *Chiefs and Families of Note in the Punjab.* Rev. ed. Vol. 2. Lahore: Civil and Military Gazette Press, 1910.

———. *The Punjab Chiefs.* Rev. ed. (1909). Lahore: Sang-e-Meel, 1993.

Cooper, Frederick. *Colonialism in Question: Theory, Knowledge, History.* Berkeley and Los Angeles: University of California Press, 2005.

Cooper, Frederick, and Ann Laura Stoler, eds. *Tensions of Empire: Colonial Cultures in a Bourgeois World.* Berkeley and Los Angeles: University of California Press, 1997.

Crary, Jonathan. *Suspensions of Perception: Attention, Spectacle, and Modern Culture.* Cambridge: MIT Press, 1999.

Crinson, Mark. *Empire Building: Orientalism and Victorian Architecture.* New York: Routledge, 1996.

———. *Modern Architecture and the End of Empire.* Aldershot, U.K.: Ashgate Press, 2003.

Cust, Robert Needham. "History of the Conquest of the Panjab" (1898). *The Panjab Past and Present* 13, no. 1 (1979): 73–131.

Daechsel, Markus. *The Politics of Self-Expression: The Urdu Middle-Class Milieu in Mid-Twentieth Century India and Pakistan.* London: Routledge, 2006.

———. "Zalim Daku and the Mystery of the Rubber Sea Monster: Urdu Detective Fiction in 1930s Punjab and the Experience of Colonial Modernity." *Journal of the Royal Asiatic Society,* series 3, 13, no. 1 (2003): 21–43.

Datta, V. N. *Amritsar Past and Present.* Amritsar: Municipal Committee of Amritsar, 1967.

Davey, Peter. *Architecture of the Arts and Crafts Movement.* New York: Rizzoli, 1980.

Davidoff, Leonore, and Catherine Hall. *Family Fortunes: The Men and Women of the English Middle Class, 1780–1850.* Chicago: University of Chicago Press, 1987.

Davies, Philip. *Splendours of the Raj: British Architecture in India 1660 to 1947.* London: John Murray, 1985.

Deshpande, R. S. *Modern Ideal Homes for India.* Poona: R. S. Deshpande, 1939.

Dhingra, M. L. "Indian Sanitation: A Personal View." *Indian Magazine and Review* 372 (December 1901): 311–30.

———. "Sanitation in India." *Indian Magazine and Review* 372 (December 1901): 415.

Dirks, Nicholas B. "Guiltless Spoliations: Picturesque Beauty, Colonial Knowledge, and Colin Mackenzie's Survey of India." In *Perceptions of South Asia's Visual Past,* ed. Catherine Asher and Thomas R. Metcalf, 211–32. New Delhi: Oxford and IBH, 1994.

Donald, James. *Imagining the Modern City.* London: Athlone Press, 1999.

Dossal, Mariam. *Imperial Designs and Indian Realities: The Planning of Bombay City, 1845–1875.* Delhi: Oxford University Press, 1991.

Duguid, J. *Letters from India and Kashmir: Written in 1870; Illustrated and Annotated 1873.* London: George Bell and Sons, 1874.

Dulai, Surjit S. "The City in the History and Literature of the Punjab." *Journal of South Asian Literature* 25, no. 1 (1990): 139–59.

Dutta, Arindam. "Infinite Justice: An Architectural Coda." *Grey Room* 7 (2002): 40–55.

———. "The Politics of Display: India 1886 and 1986—Sites of Art History, Canons, and Expositions." *Journal of Arts and Ideas* 30–31 (December 1997): 115–45.

Dyos, H. J., and Michael Wolff, eds. *The Victorian City: Images and Realities.* London: Routledge and Kegan Paul, 1973.

Eisenstadt, Shmuel N. "Multiple Modernities." *Daedalus* 129, no. 1 (2000): 1–31.

Engels, Dagmar. "The Limits of Gender Ideology: Bengali Women, the Colonial State, and the Private Sphere, 1890–1930." *Women's Studies International Forum* 12, no. 4 (1989): 425–38.

Evenson, Norma. *The Indian Metropolis: A View toward the West.* New Haven: Yale University Press, 1989.

Ewing, Katherine P., ed. *Shari'at and Ambiguity in South Asian Islam.* Berkeley and Los Angeles: University of California Press, 1988.

Fazl, Abul. *Ain-i Akbari*. Trans. H. Blochmann. 2 vols. Delhi: Aadish Book Depot, 1965.

Ferreira, J. V., and S. S. Jha, eds. *The Outlook Tower: Essays on Urbanization in Memory of Patrick Ged-des*. Bombay: Popular Prakashan, 1976.

Fishman, Robert. *Urban Utopias in the Twentieth Century: Ebenezer Howard, Frank Lloyd Wright, and Le Corbusier*. New York: Basic Books, 1999.

Foucault, Michel. *Discipline and Punish: The Birth of the Prison* (1977). Trans. Alan Sheridan. New York: Vintage Books, 1995.

———. "Of Other Spaces." *Diacritics* 16, no. 1 (1986): 22–27.

———. "What Is the Enlightenment?" In Michel Foucault, *Ethics: Subjectivity and Truth*, ed. Paul Rabinow, 303–19. New York: New Press, 1997.

Fox, Richard G. *Kin, Clan, Raja, and Rule*. Berkeley and Los Angeles: University of California Press, 1971.

———. *Lions of the Punjab: Culture in the Making*. Berkeley and Los Angeles: University of California Press, 1985.

———, ed. *Urban India: Society, Space, and Image*. Monograph and Occasional Papers 10. Durham, N.C.: Duke University Program in Comparative Studies in South Asia, 1970.

Frykenberg, R. E. *Delhi through the Ages: Selected Essays in Urban History, Culture, and Society*. Delhi: Oxford University Press, 1993.

Gajrani, S. D. "Agrarian Unrest in the Doab Region: 1907." *The Panjab Past and Present* 14, no. 1 (1980): 146–58.

Gaonkar, Dilip P., ed., *Alternative Modernities*. Durham, N.C.: Duke University Press, 2001.

Gauba, Anand. *Amritsar: A Study in Urban History, 1840–1947*. Jalandhar: ABS, 1988.

Gavin, Hector. *Sanitary Ramblings, Being Sketches and Illustrations of Bethnal Green: A Type of the Condition of the Metropolis and Other Large Towns* (1848). London: Frank Cass, 1971.

Gawda, K. S. Rame. *Urban and Regional Planning*. Mysore: University of Mysore Press, 1972.

Geddes, Patrick. *Town Planning towards City Development: A Report to the Durbar of Indore*. Parts 1 and 2. Indore: Holkar State Printing Press, 1918.

George, Rosemary M. "Homes in the Empire, Empires in the Home." *Cultural Critique* 15 (1994): 95–127.

Ghosh, Amalananda. *The City in Early Historical India*. Simla: Indian Institute of Advanced Study, 1990.

Gilmartin, David. "Customary Law and Shari'at in British Punjab." In *Shari'at and Ambiguity in South Asian Islam*, ed. Katherine P. Ewing, 43–62. Berkeley and Los Angeles: University of California Press, 1988.

———. *Empire and Islam: Punjab and the Making of Pakistan*. London: I. B. Tauris, 1988.

———. "A Magnificent Gift: Muslim Nationalism and the Election Process in Colonial Punjab." *Comparative Studies in Society and History* 40, no. 3 (1998): 415–36.

———. "Scientific Empire and Imperial Science: Colonialism and Irrigation Technology in the Indus Basin." *Journal of Asian Studies* 53 (1994): 1127–49.

Girouard, Mark. *The Victorian Country House*. New Haven: Yale University Press, 1971.

Glover, William J. "'An Absence of Old England': The Anxious English Bungalow." *HomeCultures* 1, no. 1 (2004): 61–81.

———. "Objects, Models, and Exemplary Works: Educating Sentiment in Colonial Punjab." *Journal of Asian Studies* 64, no. 3 (August, 2005): 539–66.

Godwin, George. *Town Swamps and Social Bridges*. Intro. Anthony D. King (1859). Leicester, U.K.: Leicester University Press, 1972.

Goffman, Irving J. *Asylums: Essays on the Social Situation of Mental Patients and Other Inmates.* New York: Doubleday Anchor, 1961.

Goswami, Manu. *Producing India: From Colonial Economy to National Space.* Chicago: University of Chicago Press, 2004.

Goulding, H. R. *Old Lahore: Reminiscences of a Resident* (1924). Lahore: Sang-e-Meel, n.d.

Government of India. *Census of India, 1881.* Vol. 19, *Punjab and Its Feudatories,* pt. 1. Calcutta: Office of the Superintendent of Government Printing, 1882.

———. *Census of India, 1891.* Vol. 19, *Punjab and Its Feudatories,* pt. 1. Simla: Office of the Superintendent of Government Printing, 1892.

———. *Census of India, 1901.* Vol. 19, *Punjab,* pt. 1. Lahore: Civil and Military Gazette Press, 1902.

———. *Census of India, 1911.* Vol. 14, *Punjab,* pt. 1. Lahore: Civil and Military Gazette Press, 1912.

———. *Imperial Gazetteer Atlas of India.* Vol. 26. Oxford: Clarendon Press, 1931.

———. *Imperial Gazetteer of India, Provincial Series, Punjab.* 2 vols. Calcutta: Superintendent of Government Printing, 1908.

Government of Punjab. *Gazetteer of the Chenab Colony, 1904* (1905). Lahore: Sang-e-Meel, 1996.

———. *Gazetteer of the Chenab Colony, 1905.* Lahore: Punjab Government Press, 1906.

———. *Gazetteer of the Lahore District, 1882–83* (1884). Lahore: Sang-e-Meel, 1989.

———. *Gazetteer of the Lahore District, 1883–84* (1885). Lahore: Sang-e-Meel, 1989.

———. *Gazetteer of the Lahore District, 1893–94.* Lahore: Government of Punjab Press, 1895.

———. *Memorandum on the Disturbances in the Punjab, April 1919* (1920). Lahore: Sang-e-Meel, 1997.

———. *Memorandum on the Subject of Social and Official Intercourse between European Officers in the Punjab and Indians.* Lahore: Punjab Government Press, 1922.

———. *Monographs on Various Industries: Punjab.* Lahore: Punjab Government Press, 1884–1909.

———. *Monograph on Wood Manufactures in the Punjab: 1887–88.* Lahore: Civil and Military Gazette Press, 1889.

———. *Report of the Lahore and Amritsar Improvement Trust Committee.* Lahore: Superintendent of Government Printing, 1927.

———. *Report on the Affairs of the Municipal Committee of Lahore.* Lahore: Superintendent of Government Printing, 1931.

———. *Report on the Material Progress of the Punjab during the Decade 1881–1891.* Lahore: Punjab Government Press, 1892.

———. *Report on the Punjab Sanitary Conference, 1913.* Vol. 1, *Proceedings.* Vol. 2, *Correspondence and Papers.* Lahore: Punjab Government Press, 1913.

———. *Report on the Working of Municipalities in the Punjab [during various years].* Lahore: Punjab Government Press, 1893–1912 [annual reports].

———. "Town Improvement Act, 1922." In *Punjab Act IV of 1922.* Lahore: Superintendent of Government Printing, 1922.

Grant, Colesworthy. *Anglo-Indian Domestic Life: A Letter from an Artist in India to His Mother* (1862). Calcutta: Subornorekha, 1984.

Grewal, Inderpal. *Home and Harem: Nation, Gender, Empire, and the Cultures of Travel.* Durham, N.C.: Duke University Press, 1996.

Grewal, J. S. *The City of the Golden Temple.* Chandigarh, 1986.

———. "Historical Writing on Urbanisation in Medieval India." In *The City in Indian History,* ed. Indu Banga, 69–79. Delhi: Manohar Press, 1991.

———. *In the By-Lanes of History: Some Persian Documents from a Punjab Town.* Simla: Indian Institute of Advanced Study, 1975.

———. *Maharaja Ranjit Singh.* Amritsar: Guru Nanak Dev University, 1982.

Grewal, J. S., and Indu Banga, eds. *Studies in Urban History.* Amritsar: Guru Nanak Dev University, n.d.

———, trans. and eds. *Early Nineteenth Century Panjab: From Ganesh Das's Char Bagh-i-Panjab.* Amritsar: Guru Nanak University, 1975.

Grewal, Reeta. "Urban Revolution under Colonial Rule." In *Five Punjabi Centuries: Polity, Economy, Society, and Culture: C. 1500–1990,* ed. Indu Banga, 438–54. Delhi: Manohar, 1997.

Grier, Katherine C. *Culture and Comfort: Parlour Making and Middle-Class Identity, 1850–1930.* Washington, D.C.: Smithsonian Institution Press, 1997.

Griffen, Lepel. *The Punjab Chiefs.* Lahore, 1890.

———. *The Rajas of Punjab.* Lahore: Government of Punjab Press, 1870.

Groth, Paul. *Living Downtown: The History of Residential Life in the United States.* Berkeley and Los Angeles: University of California Press, 1994.

Groth, Paul, and Tod Bressi, eds. *Understanding Ordinary Landscapes.* New Haven: Yale University Press, 1997.

Growse, Frederick S. *Indian Architecture of Today as Exemplified in New Buildings in the Bulandshahr District.* Benares: Medical Hall Press, 1886.

———. *Mathura: A District Memoir.* 2nd. ed. Allahabad: North-western Provinces and Oudh Government Press, 1880.

Guha, Ramachandra. *A Corner of a Foreign Field: The Indian History of a British Sport.* London: Picador, 2002.

Guha, Ranajit. "Not at Home in Empire." *Critical Inquiry* 23, no. 3 (Spring 1997): 482–93.

———, ed. *Subaltern Studies: Writings on South Asian History and Society.* Vol. 4. New York: Oxford University Press, 1982.

Guha-Thakurta, Tapati. *The Making of a New "Indian" Art: Artists, Aesthetics, and Nationalism in Bengal, c. 1850–1920.* Cambridge: Cambridge University Press, 1992.

———. *Monuments, Objects, Histories: Institutions of Art in Colonial and Post-Colonial India.* New York: Columbia University Press, 2004.

Gupta, Charu. *Sexuality, Obscenity, Community: Women, Muslims, and the Hindu Public in Colonial India.* Delhi: Permanent Black, 2001.

Gupta, Naryani. *Delhi between Two Empires, 1830–1931: Society, Government, and Urban Growth.* Delhi: Oxford University Press, 1981.

———. "Military Security and Urban Development: A Case Study of Delhi: 1857–1912." *Modern Asian Studies* 5, no. 1 (1971): 61–77.

Gupta, Shiv Kumar. *Arya Samaj and the Raj, 1875–1920.* New Delhi: Gitanjali, 1991.

Haag-Higuchi, Roxane, and Christian Szyska, eds. *Narrated Space in the Literature of the Islamic World.* Wiesbaden: Harrassowitz, 2001.

Habermas, Jürgen. *The Structural Transformation of the Public Sphere: An Inquiry into a Category of Bourgeois Society* (1962). Trans. Thomas Burger. Cambridge: MIT Press, 1998.

Habib, Irfan. *Essays in Indian History: Towards a Marxist Perception.* New Delhi: Tulika, 1995.

Hall, Catherine. *Civilizing Subjects: Metropole and Colony in the English Imagination, 1830–1867.* Oxford: Polity Press, 2002.

Hall, Peter. *Cities of Tomorrow: An Intellectual History of Urban Planning and Design in the Twentieth Century.* 3rd ed. Oxford: Blackwell, 2002.

Hall, Stuart. "Cultural Identity and Diaspora." In *Colonial Discourse and Post-Colonial Theory: A Reader,* ed. Patrick Williams and Laura Chrisman, 392–403. New York: Columbia University Press, 1994.

Hambly, Gavin. *Cities of Mughal India: Delhi, Agra, and Fatehpur Sikri.* London: Elek, 1968.

Hansen, Karen, ed. *African Encounters with Domesticity.* New Brunswick, N.J.: Rutgers University Press, 1992.

Harding, Vanessa. "Space, Property, and Propriety in Urban England." *Journal of Interdisciplinary History* 22, no. 4 (Spring 2002): 549–69.

Harrison, Mark. *Public Health in British India: Anglo-Indian Preventive Medicine, 1859–1914.* Cambridge: Cambridge University Press, 1994.

Hartley, Lucy. *Physiognomy and the Meaning of Expression in Nineteenth-Century Culture.* Cambridge: Cambridge University Press, 2001.

Harvey, David. *Paris: Capital of Modernity.* London: Routledge, 2003.

Hasan, Farhat. "Indigenous Cooperation and the Birth of a Colonial City: Calcutta, c. 1698–1750." *Modern Asian Studies* 26, no. 1 (1992): 65–82.

Hasan, Masudul. *Guide to Lahore.* Lahore: Ferozsons, 1977.

Hasan, S. Nurul. "The Morphology of a Medieval Indian City: A Case Study of Shahjahanabad." In *The City in Indian History: Urban Demography, Society, and Politics,* ed. Indu Banga, 87–98. Delhi: Manohar, 1994.

Havell, E. B. *The Basis for Artistic and Industrial Revival in India* (1912). New Delhi: Usha, 1986.

Haynes, Douglas, and Gyan Prakash, eds. *Contesting Power: Resistance and Everyday Social Relations in South Asia.* Berkeley and Los Angeles: University of California Press, 1992.

Helsinger, Elizabeth. *Rural Scenes and National Representation: Britain, 1815–1850.* Princeton: Princeton University Press, 1999.

Hira, Bachan Singh. "The Upper Bari Doab: A Geographical Region." *Panjab Past and Present* 24, no. 2 (1990): 344–53.

Hogg, Francis D., M.D. *Practical Remarks Chiefly Concerning the Health and Ailments of European Families in India, with Special Reference to Maternal Management and Domestic Economy.* Benares: Medical Hall Press, 1877.

Horvath, Ronald J. "In Search of a Theory of Urbanization: The Colonial City." *East Lakes Geographer* 5 (1969): 60–82.

Hosagrahar, Jyoti. *Indigenous Modernities: Negotiating Architecture and Urbanism.* London: Routledge, 2005.

Howard, Ebenezer. *Garden Cities of To-morrow.* London: Swan Sonnenschein, 1902.

Hume, John C. Jr. "Colonialism and Sanitary Medicine: The Development of Preventive Health Policy in the Punjab, 1860 to 1900." *Modern Asian Studies* 20 (1986): 703–24.

———. "Rival Traditions: Western Medicine and *Yunan-i Tibb* in the Punjab, 1849–1889." *Bulletin of the History of Medicine* 51 (1977): 214–31.

Hunt, J. D., ed. *Garden History: Issues, Approaches, Methods.* Washington, D.C.: Dumbarton Oaks, 1992.

Hussain, Mahmood, Abdul Rehman, and James L. Wescoat Jr., eds. *The Mughal Garden: Interpretation, Conservation, and Implications.* Lahore: Ferozsons, 1996.

"Hygiene in the Zenanas of India." *Indian Magazine and Review* 250 (October 1891): 483–90.

Ibbetson, Denzil. *Punjab Castes.* 1883. Lahore: Sang-e-Meel, 1994.

'Ilaaj-e-Heza [A Treatment for Cholera]. Lahore: Lala Gobind Ram, 1905.

Indian Magazine. Obituary of Rai Bahadur Kanhaya Lal, M.I.C.E. No. 208 (April 1888): 218–220.

Jacquemont, V. *The Punjab a Hundred Years Ago: As Described by V. Jacquemont (1831) and A. Soltykoff (1842).* Trans. and ed. H. L. O. Garrett. Lahore: Punjab Government Record Office, 1935.

Jones, Kenneth W. *Arya Dharm: Hindu Consciousness in 19th-Century Punjab.* Berkeley and Los Angeles: University of California Press, 1976.

———. "The Bengali Elite in Post-Annexation Punjab: An Example of Inter-regional Influence in Nineteenth Century India." In *Punjab Past and Present: Essays in Honour of Dr. Ganda Singh,* ed. Harbans Singh and Gerald Barrier, 234–51. Patiala: Punjabi University, 1976.

———, ed. *Religious Controversy in British India: Dialogues in South Asian Languages.* Albany: State University of New York Press, 1992.

Joshi, K. C. *Joshi's Modern Designs.* Amritsar: Ber Badhar Joshi, 1937.

Joshi, Sanjay. *Fractured Modernity: Making of a Middle Class in Colonial North India.* New Delhi: Oxford University Press, 2001.

Kanhayalal. *Tarikh-e-Lahor* [History of Lahore] [1871?]. Lahore: Sang-e-Meel, 1990.

Kaviraj, Sudipta. "Filth and the Public Sphere: Concepts and Practices about Space in Calcutta." *Public Culture* 10, no. 1 (1997): 83–114.

Keep, Christopher, Tim McLaughlin, and Robin Parmar. "Palimpsest." In *The Electronic Labyrinth.* http://www3.iath.virginia.edu/elab/hfl0243.html (accessed June 1, 2006).

Kelly, John D. "Alternative Modernities or an Alternative to Modernity." In *Critically Modern: Alternatives, Alterities, Anthropologies,* ed. Bruce Knauft, 258–86. Bloomington: Indiana University Press, 2002.

Kennedy, Dane. *Islands of White: Settler Society and Culture in Kenya and Southern Rhodesia, 1890–1939.* Durham, N.C.: Duke University Press, 1987.

———. *The Magic Mountains: Hill Stations and the British Raj.* Berkeley and Los Angeles: University of California Press, 1996.

Kenny, Judith T. "Climate, Race, and Imperial Authority: The Symbolic Landscape of the British Hill Station in India." *Annals of the Association of American Geographers* 84, no. 4 (1995): 694–714.

Kerr, Ian J. "The Agri-Horticultural Society of the Punjab, 1851–71." In *Punjab Past and Present: Essays in Honour of Dr. Ganda Singh,* ed. Harbans Singh and N. G. Barrier, 252–72. Patiala: Punjabi University, 1976.

Kerr, Robert. *The Gentleman's House; or, How to Plan English Residences.* London: John Murray, 1864.

Khan, Masood. "Cultural Transfers: The Repossession of Architectural Form." *Environmental Design: Journal of the Islamic Environmental Design Research Center* 1–2 (1994–95): 84–103.

Khan, Nawab Mehdi Hasan. Item. *Punjab Magazine* 233 (1890): 28, 31–32.

Khan, Sayyid Ahmed. *Asar-us-Sanadid* [Manifestations of the Noblemen] (1846). Ed. Khalid Nasir Hashmi. Delhi: Central Book Depot, 1965.

Khilnani, Sunil. *The Idea of India.* New Delhi: Penguin Books India, 1998.

King, Anthony D. *The Bungalow: The Production of a Global Culture.* New York: Oxford University Press, 1995.

———. "Colonial Architecture Re-visited: Some Issues for Further Debate." In *Changing South Asia: City and Culture,* ed. Kenneth Ballhatchet and David Taylor, 99–106. Hong Kong: Asian Research Service, 1984.

———. *Colonial Urban Development: Culture, Social Power, and Environment.* London: Routledge and Kegan Paul, 1976.

———. *Spaces of Global Cultures: Architecture, Urbanism, Identity.* London: Routledge, 2005.

———. *Urbanism, Colonialism, and the World Economy: Cultural and Spatial Foundations of the World Urban System.* London: Routledge, 1991.

Kingsley, Charles. *Sanitary and Social Lectures and Essays.* New York: Macmillan, 1880.

Kipling, John Lockwood. *Lahore as It Was* (1876). Lahore: National College of Arts, 2002.

———. "The Principal's Report on the Mayo School of Industrial Art, Lahore [various dates]." In *Official Chronicle of the Mayo School of Art: Formative Years under J. L. Kipling, 1874–94,* comp. Nadeem Omar Tarar, ed. Samina Choonara. Lahore: National College of Arts, n.d. [2003].

Kipling, Rudyard. *A Choice of Kipling's Prose.* Ed. W. Somerset Maugham. London: Macmillan, 1952.

———. "The City of Dreadful Night." In *In Black and White,* 34–45. New York: Charles Scribner's Sons, 1907.

———. "The Enlightenments of Pagett, M.P." In *In Black and White.* New York: Charles Scribner's Sons, 1907.

———. *From Sea to Sea.* 2 vols. Norwood, Mass.: Norwood Press, 1899.

———. "The House of Shadows" (1887). In *Kipling's India: Uncollected Sketches, 1884–88,* ed. Thomas Pinney, 246–48. London: Macmillan, 1986.

———. *In Black and White* (1891). New York: Charles Scribner's Sons, 1907.

———. *Kipling's India: Uncollected Sketches, 1884–88.* Ed. Thomas Pinney. London: Macmillan, 1986.

———. "Naboth." In *In Black and White,* 139–44. New York: Charles Scribner's Sons, 1907.

———. "The Private Services Commission" (1887). In *Kipling's India: Uncollected Sketches, 1884–88,* ed. Thomas Pinney, 235–42. London: Macmillan, 1986.

———. "Typhoid at Home," *Civil and Military Gazette (Lahore),* February 14, 1885. Reproduced in *Kipling's India: Uncollected Sketches, 1884–88,* ed. Thomas Pinney, 69–77. London: Macmillan, 1986. Page numbers are to *Kipling's India.*

———. "William the Conqueror" (circa 1890). In *A Choice of Kipling's Prose,* ed. W. Somerset Maugham, 193–220. London: Macmillan, 1952.

Kishan, Iqbal. "Advice to Young Punjab." *Punjab Magazine* 50 (1892): 35–50.

Koch, Ebba. "Mughal Palace Gardens from Babur to Shah Jahan (1526–1648)." *Muqarnas* 14 (1997): 143–65.

———. "The Mughal Waterfront Garden." In *Gardens in the Time of the Great Mughal Empires,* ed. Attilio Petruccioli, 140–60. Leiden: E. J. Brill, 1997.

Kopardekar, H. D., and G. R. Diwan. *Urban and Regional Planning: Principles, Practice, and the Law.* Talegaon-Dabhade: Sundhanwa H. Kopardekar, 1994.

Kornwolf, James D. *M. H. Baillie Scott and the Arts and Crafts Movement: Pioneers of Modern Design.* Baltimore: The Johns Hopkins University Press, 1972.

Kozolowski, Gregory C. *Muslim Endowments and Society in British India.* Cambridge: Cambridge University Press, 1985.

Kramrisch, Stella. "Traditions of the Indian Craftsman." *Journal of American Folklore* 71, no. 281(1958): 224–30.

Kumar, Krishan. "Modernity." In *The Blackwell Dictionary of Twentieth-Century Social Thought,* ed. William Outhwaite and Tom Bottomore, 391–92. London: Blackwell, 1994.

Kumar, Nita, ed. *Women as Subjects: South Asian Histories.* Charlottesville: University Press of Virginia, 1994.

Kumar, Ravinder. "Urban Society and Urban Politics: Lahore in 1919." In *Five Punjabi Centuries: Polity, Economy, Society, and Culture: C. 1500–1990,* ed. Indu Banga, 190–220. Delhi: Manohar, 1997.

Kusno, Abidin. *Behind the Postcolonial: Architecture, Urban Space, and Political Cultures in Indonesia.* London: Routledge, 2000.

Lari, Yasmeen, and Mihail Lari. *The Dual City: Karachi during the Raj.* Karachi: Oxford University Press, 1996.

Latif, Syad Muhammad. *Agra Historical and Descriptive, with an Account of Akbar and His Court and of the Modern City of Agra.* Calcutta: Calcutta Central Press Company, 1896.

———. *Lahore: Its History, Architectural Remains, and Antiquities, with an Account of Its Modern Institutions, Inhabitants, Their Trade, Custom, &c.* (1892). Lahore: Sang-e-Meel, 1994.

Lelyveld, David. *Aligarh's First Generation: Muslim Solidarity in British India.* Princeton: Princeton University Press, 1978.

Lewis, Bernard. "First-Person Narrative in the Middle East." In *Middle Eastern Lives: The Practice of Biography and Self-Narrative,* ed. Martin Kramer, 20–34. Syracuse, N.Y.: Syracuse University Press, 1991.

Llewellyn-Jones, Rosie. *A Fatal Friendship: The Nawabs, the British, and the City of Lucknow.* Delhi: Oxford University Press, 1992.

Login, Lady Lena. *Sir John Login and Duleep Singh* (1889). Patiala: Languages Department Punjab, 1970.

Loudon, John Claudius. *An Encyclopedia of Cottage, Farm, and Villa Architecture and Furniture: Containing Numerous Designs for Dwellings, from the Villa to the Cottage and the Farm* (1833). 2nd ed. London: Longman, Brown, Green, Longman, 1853.

Ludden, David. "Maps in the Mind and the Mobility of Asia." *Journal of Asian Studies* 62, no. 4 (November 2003): 1057–78.

Macaulay, Thomas Babington. *Macaulay: Prose and Poetry.* Comp. G. M. Young. Cambridge, Mass.: Harvard University Press, 1952.

Maclagan, E. D. "The Earliest English Visitors to the Punjab, 1585–1628." *Journal of the Panjab Historical Society* 1, no. 2 (1912): 9–34.

MacMunn, George. *The Martial Races of India.* London. Sampson Low, Marston, 1933.

Maconochie, Evan. *Life in the Indian Civil Service.* London: Chapman and Hall, 1926.

Mahmood, Saba. *Politics of Piety: The Islamic Revival and the Feminist Subject.* Princeton: Princeton University Press, 2005.

Major, Andrew J. *Return to Empire: Punjab under the Sikhs and British in the Mid-Nineteenth Century.* Karachi: Oxford University Press, 1996.

———. "State and Criminal Tribes in Colonial Punjab: Surveillance, Control, and Reclamation of the 'Dangerous Classes.'" *Modern Asian Studies* 33, no. 3 (1999): 657–88.

Majumdar, Boria. *Lost Histories of Indian Cricket: Battles Off the Field.* London: Routledge, 2006.

Malhotra, Anshu. *Gender, Caste, and Religious Identities: Restructuring Class in Colonial Punjab.* New Delhi: Oxford University Press, 2002.

Malleson, G. B. *The Indian Mutiny of 1857.* London: Seeley, 1891.

Mandelbaum, Maurice H. *History, Man, and Reason: A Study in Nineteenth-Century Thought.* Baltimore: The Johns Hopkins University Press, 1971.

Mannsaker, F. M. "East and West: Anglo-Indian Racial Attitudes as Reflected in Popular Fiction, 1890–1914." *Victorian Studies* 24 (1980): 33–51.

Manrique, Sebastien. *Travels of Sebastien Manrique, 1629–1643.* Trans. Charles Eckford Luard. Oxford: Halkyut Society, 1927.

Manucci, Niccolao. *The General History of the Mughal Empire* (1709). 8 vols. Trans. William Irvine. London: John Murray, 1906.

Marcus, Sharon. *Apartment Stories: City and Home in Nineteenth-Century Paris and London.* Berkeley and Los Angeles: University of California Press, 1999.

Marcus, Steven. "Reading the Illegible." In *The Victorian City: Images and Realities,* 2 vols., ed. Harold James Dyos and Michael Wolff, 1:257–72. London: Routledge and Kegan Paul, 1973.

Markus, Thomas, ed. *Order in Space and Society: Architectural Form and Its Context in the Scottish Enlightenment.* Edinburgh: Mainstream, 1982.

———. "The School as a Machine: Working Class Scottish Education and the Glasgow Normal Seminary." In *Order in Space and Society: Architectural Form and Its Context in the Scottish Enlightenment,* ed. Thomas Markus, 201–61. Edinburgh: Mainstream, 1982.

Marsh, Jan. *Back to the Land: The Pastoral Impulse in England, from 1880 to 1914.* London: Quartet, 1982.

Marshall, P. J. "The White Town of Calcutta under the Rule of the East India Company." *Modern Asian Studies* 34, no. 2 (2000): 307–31.

Massey, Charles. *Chiefs and Families of Note in the Punjab.* Lahore: Government of Punjab Press, 1890.

McCleod, Robert. *Style and Society: Architectural Ideology in Britain, 1835–1914.* London: RIBA, 1971.

McClintock, Anne. *Imperial Leather: Race, Gender, and Sexuality in the Colonial Contest.* London: Routledge, 1995.

McGee, Terry G. *The Southeast Asian City: A Social Geography of the Primate Cities of Southeast Asia.* London: George Bell and Sons, 1967.

Mead, George H. *Movements of Thought in the Nineteenth Century.* Chicago: University of Chicago Press, 1936.

Mehta, Uday Singh. *Liberalism and Empire: A Study in Nineteenth-Century British Liberal Thought.* Chicago: University of Chicago Press, 1999.

Messick, Brinkley. *The Calligraphic State: Textual Domination and History in a Muslim Society.* Berkeley and Los Angeles: University of California Press, 1993.

Metcalf, Barbara D. "Hakim Ajmal Khan: *Rais* of Delhi and Muslim Leader." In *Delhi through the Ages: Selected Essays in Urban History, Culture, and Society,* ed. Robert E. Frykenberg, 299–315. Delhi: Oxford University Press, 1993.

———, ed. *Moral Conduct and Authority: The Place of Adab in South Asian Islam.* Berkeley and Los Angeles: University of California Press, 1984.

———. "Narrating Lives: A Mughal Empress, a French Nabob, a Nationalist Muslim Intellectual." *Journal of Asian Studies* 54, no. 2 (1995): 474–80.

———, trans. and comp. *Perfecting Women: Maulana Ashraf 'Ali Thanawi's Bihishti Zewar; A Partial Translation with Commentary.* Berkeley and Los Angeles: University of California Press, 1990.

Metcalf, Thomas R. *The Aftermath of Revolt: India 1857–1870.* Princeton: Princeton University Press, 1964.

———. *Ideologies of the Raj.* Cambridge: Cambridge University Press, 1994.

———. *An Imperial Vision: Indian Architecture and Britain's Raj.* Berkeley and Los Angeles: University of California Press, 1989.

Mill, James. *A History of British India.* London: J. Madden, Piper, Stephenson, and Spence, 1858.

Minault, Gail. "Hali's *Majalis-un-Nissa:* Purdah and Women Power in Nineteenth-Century India." In *Islamic Society and Culture: Essays in Honor of Professor Aziz Ahmad,* ed. Milton Israel, 39–49. Delhi: Manohar, 1983.

———. "Other Voices, Other Rooms: The View from the Zenana." In *Women as Subjects: South Asian Histories,* ed. Nita Kumar, 108–124. Charlottesville: University Press of Virginia, 1994.

———. "Sayyid Mumtaz 'Ali and *Tahzib un-Niswan:* Women's Rights in Islam and Women's

Journalism in Urdu." In *Religious Controversy in British India: Dialogues in South Asian Languages,* ed. Kenneth W. Jones, 179–199. Albany: State University of New York Press, 1992.

———. *Secluded Scholars: Women's Education and Muslim Social Reform in Colonial India.* Delhi: Oxford University Press, 1998.

———, trans. *Voices of Silence: English Translation of Khwaja Altaf Hussain Hali's "Majalis un-nissa" and "Chup ki dad."* Delhi: Chanakya, 1986.

Mitchell, Timothy. *Colonizing Egypt.* Cambridge: Cambridge University Press, 1988.

Mitter, Partha. *Art and Nationalism in Colonial India, 1850–1922: Occidental Orientations.* Cambridge: Cambridge University Press, 1994.

Morris, Jan. *Stones of Empire: The Buildings of the Raj.* 2nd. ed. Oxford: Oxford University Press, 1986.

Mukhtasar Risala-e-Hafiz-e-Sehat [Various Essays on Good Health]. Lahore, 1897.

Murphy, Rhodes. "Urbanization in Asia." In *The City in Newly Developing Countries,* ed. Gerald Breese, 58–75. London: Prentice-Hall, 1972.

Musselman, Elizabeth Green. "Swords into Ploughshares: John Herschel's Progressive View of Astronomical and Imperial Governance." *British Journal for the History of Science* 31 (1998): 419–35.

Nagi, Anis, ed. *Ancient Lahore: A Brief Account of the History and Antiquities of Lahore Written under the Instructions of Sir Robert Montgomery* (1860). Lahore: Gautam, 1994.

Nair, Janaki. "Uncovering the Zenana: Visions of Indian Womanhood in Englishwomen's Writings, 1813–1940." *Journal of Women's History* 2, no. 1 (1990): 8–34.

Nandy, Ashis. *An Ambiguous Journey to the City: The Village and Other Odd Ruins of the Self in the Indian Imagination.* New Delhi: Oxford University Press, 2001.

Naqvi, Hameeda Khatoon. *Mughal Hindustan: Cities and Industries, 1556–1803* (1958). 2nd ed. Karachi: National Book Foundation, 1974.

———. *Urbanisation and Urban Centres under the Great Mughals, 1556–1707: An Essay in Interpretation.* Vol. 1. Simla: Indian Institute of Advanced Study, 1972.

Nasr, Joe, and Mercedes Volait. *Urbanism Imported or Exported: Native Aspirations and Foreign Plans.* Chichester, U.K.: Wiley-Academy, 2003.

Nath, Dina. *The Two Friends: A Descriptive Story of the Lahore Life.* Lahore: Virjanand Press, 1899.

Nath, Ram. *Monuments of Delhi.* New Delhi: Ambika, 1979.

Neild, Susan. "Colonial Urbanism: The Development of Madras City in the Eighteenth and Nineteenth Centuries." *Modern Asian Studies* 13, no. 2 (1979): 217–46.

Nevile, Pran. *Lahore: A Sentimental Journey.* Karachi: Indus, 1993.

"New Indian Room at Osborne House." *Indian Magazine and Review* 264 (1892): 609–11.

Nightingale, Florence. *Observations on the Evidence Contained in the Stational Reports Submitted to Her by the Royal Commission on the Sanitary State of the Army in India.* London: Edward Stanford, 1863.

Nilsson, Sten. *European Architecture in India, 1750–1850.* New York: Taplinger, 1969.

Noe, Samuel. "Old Lahore and Old Delhi: Variations on a Mughal Theme." *Urbanism Past and Present* 12, no. 6 (1981): 1–20.

———. "Shahjahanabad: Geometrical Bases for the Plan of Mughal Delhi." *Urbanism Past and Present* 18, no. 9 (1984): 15–25.

Oberoi, Harjot. *The Construction of Religious Boundaries: Culture, Identity, and Diversity in the Sikh Tradition.* Delhi: Oxford University Press, 1997.

Official Chronicle of Mayo School of Art: Formative Years under J. L. Kipling, 1874–94. Comp. Nadeem Omar Tarar. Ed. Samina Choonara. Lahore: National College of Arts, n.d. [2003].

Oldenberg, Veena Talwar. "Lifestyle as Resistance: The Case of the Courtesans of Lucknow." In *Contesting Power: Resistance and Everyday Social Relations in South Asia,* ed. Douglas Haynes and Gyan Prakash, 23–61. Berkeley and Los Angeles: University of California Press, 1992.

———. *The Making of Colonial Lucknow, 1856–77.* Princeton: Princeton University Press, 1984.

Olson, Donald. *The City as a Work of Art: London, Paris, Vienna.* New Haven: Yale University Press, 1986.

Oman, John Campbell. *Cults, Customs, and Superstitions of India.* London: T. Fisher Unwin, 1908.

———. *Indian Life: Religious and Social.* London: T. Fisher Unwin, 1889.

Outhwaite, William, and Tom Bottomore, eds. *The Blackwell Dictionary of Twentieth-Century Social Thought.* London: Blackwell, 1994.

Pakistan Planning and Architectural Consultants, Ltd. (PEPAC). *The Walled City of Lahore.* Lahore: Lahore Development Authority, 1988.

Peabody, Norbert. "Cents, Sense, Census: Human Inventories in Late Precolonial and Early Colonial India." *Comparative Studies in Society and History* 43, no. 4 (2001): 819–50.

Pelsaert, Francisco. *Jahangir's India: The Remonstrantie of Francisco Pelsaert* (1626). Trans. W. H. Moreland and P. Geyl. Cambridge: W. Heffer and Sons, 1925.

Petievich, Carla. "Poetry of the Declining Mughals: The *Shahr Ashob.*" *Journal of South Asian Literature* 25, no. 1 (1990): 96–107.

Pinkney, David H. *Napoleon III and the Rebuilding of Paris.* Princeton: Princeton University Press, 1958.

Platts, John T. *A Dictionary of Urdu, Classical Hindi, and English* (1911). Lahore: Sang-e-Meel, 1994.

Pook, A. H. *Lahore: A Brief History and Guide with Notes on the Durbar Sahib.* Lahore: Faletti's Hotel, 1914.

Poovey, Mary. "The Liberal Civil Subject and the Social in Eighteenth-Century British Moral Philosophy." *Public Culture* 14, no. 1 (2002): 125–45.

———. *Making a Social Body: British Cultural Formation, 1830–1864.* Chicago: University of Chicago Press, 1995.

Port, M. H. "Government and the Metropolitan Image: Ministers, Parliament, and the Concept of a Capital City, 1840–1915." *Art History* 22, no. 4 (1999): 567–92.

Prakash, Ved. *New Towns in India.* Monograph and Occasional Papers 8. Durham, N.C.: Duke University Program in Comparative Studies in South Asia, 1969.

Prakash, Vikramaditya. *Chandigarh's Le Corbusier: The Struggle for Modernity in Postcolonial India.* Seattle: University of Washington Press, 2002.

Prashad, Vijay. "The Technology of Sanitation in Colonial Delhi." *Modern Asian Studies* 35, no. 1 (2001): 113–55.

Pratt, Mary L. *Imperial Eyes: Travel Writing and Transculturation.* London: Routledge, 1992.

Professional Papers on Indian Engineering. Vols. 1–20. Roorkee: Thomason Civil Engineering College Press, 1863–86.

Purchas, Samuel. *Hakluytus Posthumus; or, Purchas His Pilgrimes: Contayning a History of the World in Sea Voyages and Lande Travells by Englishmen and Others* (1625). Glasgow: J. MecLehose and Sons, 1905–7.

Qadeer, Muhammad A. "Do Cities 'Modernize' the Developing Countries? An Examination of the South Asian Experience." *Comparative Studies in Society and History* 16, no. 3 (1974): 266–83.

———. *Lahore: Urban Development in the Third World.* Lahore: Vanguard Books, 1983.

Rabinow, Paul. *French Modern: Norms and Forms of the Social Environment.* Cambridge: MIT Press, 1989.

Ram, Beli. *Hadi-i-Sehat* [A Guide to Health]. Lahore: Munshi Fakhar al Din, 1900.

Ram, Ganga. *Lecture-e-Sehat* [A Lecture on Health]. Lahore, 1899.

Ram, Jya. "Food, Dress, and Dwelling Houses in the Delhi District." *Punjab Magazine* 34 (1890): 14–35.

Ram, Lala Kashi. *Notes and Suggestions on Sanitation in the Punjab.* Rev. ed. Calcutta, 1884.

Ram, Rai Bahadur Ganga. *The Pocket Book of Engineering for Sub-Divisional Officers, Mistrees, and Contractors.* 3rd ed., rev. and enlarged. Lahore: Mufid-i-Am Press, 1894.

Raychaudhuri, Tapan, and Irfan Habib, eds. *The Cambridge Economic History of India.* Cambridge: Cambridge University Press, 1982.

Rehman, Abdul. *Historic Towns of Punjab: Ancient and Medieval Period.* Lahore: Ferozsons, 1997.

Reisz, Emma. "City as Garden: Shared Space in the Urban Botanic Gardens of Singapore and Malaysia, 1786–2000." In *Postcolonial Urbanism: Southeast Asian Cities and Global Processes,* ed. Ryan Bishop, John Phillips, and Wei Wei Yeo, 123–48. New York: Routledge, 2003.

Richards, John F. *The Mughal Empire.* The New Cambridge History of India I, 5. Cambridge: Cambridge University Press, 1993.

Rob, Peter, ed. *Rural India: Land, Power, and Society under British Rule.* London: Curzon Press, 1983.

Rofel, Lisa. *Other Modernities: Gendered Yearnings in China after Socialism.* Berkeley and Los Angeles: University of California Press, 1999.

Rose, H. A. *A Glossary of the Tribes and Castes of the Punjab and Northwest Frontier Province.* 1883. Delhi: Punjab National Press, 1970.

Rosen, George. "Disease, Debility, and Death." In *The Victorian City: Images and Realities,* ed. H. J. Dyos and Michael Wolff, 635–46. London: Routledge and Kegan Paul, 1973.

Rosin, Tom. "From Garden Suburb to Old City Ward: A Longitudinal Study of Social Process and Incremental Architecture in Jaipur, India." *Journal of Material Culture* 62, no. 2 (2001): 165–92.

Ross, R., and G. Telkamp, eds. *Colonial Cities.* Boston: Martinus Nijhoff, 1985.

Roy, G. K. *A Brief History of Lahore and Directory.* Lahore: G. K. Roy, 1916.

Royal Commission on the Sanitary State of the Army in India. *Report of the Commissioners Appointed to Inquire into the Sanitary State of the Army in India.* British Parliamentary Papers, House of Commons. *Sessional Papers,* vol. 19. London: Her Majesty's Stationary Office, 1863.

Rushbrook, Williams, L. F. *India in 1920: A Report Prepared for Presentation to Parliament in Accordance with the Requirements of the 26th Section of the Government of India Act 5 and 6, George V, Chapter 61.* Calcutta: Superintendent Government Printing Press, 1921.

Sachdev, Vibhuti, and Giles Tillotson. *Building Jaipur: The Making of an Indian City.* London: Reaktion Press, 2002.

Sahni, Ruchi Ram. "Self-Revelations of an Octogenarian." Unpublished ms. [in author's possession].

Sangari, Kum Kum, and Sudesh Vaid, eds. *Recasting Women: Essays in Colonial Indian History.* New Brunswick, N.J.: Rutgers University Press, 1990.

Sarkar, Jadunath. *Mughal Administration.* 4th ed. Calcutta: M. C. Sarkar and Sons, 1952.

Schmiechen, James A. "The Victorians, the Historians, and the Idea of Modernism." *The American Historical Review* 93, no. 2 (1988): 287–316.

Scidmore, Eliza Ruhamah. *Winter India.* London: T. Fisher Unwin, 1903.

Scott, David. "Colonial Governmentality." *Social Text* 43, no. 2 (1995): 191–220.

———. *Conscripts of Modernity: The Tragedy of Colonial Enlightenment.* Durham, N.C.: Duke University Press, 2004.

———. "The Trouble of Thinking: An Interview with Talal Asad." *Powers of the Secular Modern:*

Talal Asad and His Interlocutors, ed. David Scott and Charles Hirschkind, 243–303. Stanford: Stanford University Press, 2006.

Scott, James C. *Seeing Like a State: How Certain Schemes to Improve the Human Condition Have Failed.* New Haven: Yale University Press, 1998.

Scriver, Peter. *Rationalization, Standardization, and Control in Design: A Cognitive Historical Study of Architectural Design and Planning in the Public Works Department of British India, 1855–1901.* Delft, Netherlands: Publicatiebureau Bouwkunde of the Delft University of Technology, 1994.

Sen, Satadru. *Disciplining Punishment: Colonialism and Convict Society in the Andaman Islands.* Delhi: Oxford University Press, 2000.

Sen, Sudipta. "Imperial Orders of the Past: The Semantics of History and Time in the Medieval Indo-Persianate Culture of North India." In *Invoking the Past: The Uses of History in South Asia,* ed. Daud Ali, 231–57. Delhi: Oxford University Press, 1999.

Sengupta, Parna. "An Object Lesson in Colonial Pedagogy." *Comparative Studies in Society and History* 45, no. 1 (2003): 99.

Serematakis, Nadia, ed. *The Senses Still: Perception and Memory as Material Culture in Modernity.* Boulder, Colo.: Westview Press, 1994.

Sethi, Anil. "The Creation of Religious Identities in the Punjab, c. 1850–1920." Ph.D. diss., St. Catharine's College, University of Cambridge, 1998.

Sharma, Harish C. *Artisans of the Punjab: A Study of Social Change in Historical Perspective 1849–1947.* Delhi: Manohar, 1996.

Sharma, R. S. "Urbanism in Early Historic India." In *The City in Indian History: Urban Demography, Society, and Politics,* ed. Indu Banga, 9–18. Delhi: Manohar, 1994.

Sharma, Sri Ram. *Mahatma Hansraj: Maker of the Modern Punjab.* Lahore: Arya Pradeshik Pratinidhi Sabha, 1941.

———. "Punjab in Ferment in the Beginning of the Twentieth Century." *The Panjab Past and Present* 14, no. 1 (1980): 121–45.

Sharma, Sunil. "The City of Beauties in the Indo-Persian Poetic Landscape." *Comparative Studies of South Asia, Africa, and the Middle East* 24, no. 1 (2004): 18–26.

Shorto, Sylvia M. "Public Lives, Private Places: British Houses in Delhi, 1803–1853." Ph.D. diss., New York University, 2003.

———. "A Tomb of One's Own: Governor's House, Lahore." Paper presented at the 52nd Annual Meeting of the Society of Architectural Historians, Miami, Florida, June 14–18, 2000.

Shukla, D. N. *Vastu-Sastra: Hindu Science of Architecture* (1957). Delhi: Munshiram Manoharlal, 1995.

Sidhwa, Rustam Sohrabji. *The Lahore High Court and Its Principal Bar.* Lahore: Pakistan Times Press, 1967.

Singh, Bhagat. "Ali-ud-Din Mufti." *The Panjab Past and Present* 26, no. 2 (1992): 36–53.

———. "Ghulam Muhayy-ud-Din alias Bute Shah." *Panjab Past and Present* 26, no. 1 (1992): 134–49.

Singh, Chetan. *Region and Empire: Panjab in the Seventeenth Century.* Delhi: Oxford University Press, 1991.

Singh, Fauja. "Two Contemporary Urdu Accounts of Mid-19th Century Punjab." In *Proceedings from the Punjab History Conference, Ninth Session,* 128–32. Patiala: Publication Bureau Punjabi University, 1975.

———, ed. *The City of Amritsar.* Patiala: Punjabi University, 1990.

Singh, Gurbux. "Society in the Punjab under Ranjit Singh, Mufti 'Ali Ud Din's Analysis." In *Proceedings from the Punjab History Conference, Tenth Session,* 130–38. Patiala: Publication Bureau Punjabi University, 1976.

Singh, Harbans, and N. G. Barrier, eds. *Punjab Past and Present: Essays in Honour of Dr. Ganda Singh.* Patiala: Punjabi University, 1976.

Singh, Hari. "The Myth of Loyalty of the Punjab during the War, 1914–1918." In *Proceedings of the Punjab History Conference, Tenth Session*, 198–205. Patiala: Publication Bureau Punjabi University, 1976.

Singh, Jawahir, trans. *Punjabi Bat-chit: Textbook for Punjabi High School.* Lahore: Sri Akal Press, 1898.

Singh, Khushwant. *Ranjit Singh: Maharaja of the Punjab, 1780–1839.* Bombay: George Allen and Unwin, 1962.

Singha, Radhika. *A Despotism of Law: Crime and Justice in Early Colonial India.* Delhi: Oxford University Press, 1998.

Sinha, Mrinalini. "Britishness, Clubbability, and the Colonial Public Sphere: The Genealogy of an Imperial Institution in Colonial India." *Journal of British Studies* 40, no. 4 (2001): 489–521.

———. *Colonial Masculinity: The "Manly Englishman" and the "Effeminate Bengali" in the Late Nineteenth Century.* New York: Manchester University Press, 1995.

Skelton, Robert. "The Indian Collections: 1798 to 1978." *Burlington Magazine* 120 (1978): 297–304.

Smith, Browning. *Report on the Punjab Sanitary Conference, 1913: Part I: Proceedings.* Lahore: Punjab Government Press, 1913.

Smith, Reginald Bosworth. *Life of Lord Lawrence.* New York: Scribner's and Sons, 1883.

Sohal, Sukhdev Singh. "The Swadeshi Movement in the Punjab." *Panjab Past and Present* 26, no. 1 (1992): 129–33.

Stalley, Marshall, ed. *Patrick Geddes: Spokesman for Man and the Environment.* New Brunswick, N.J.: Rutgers University Press, 1972.

Stamp, Gavin. "British Architecture in India, 1857–1947." *Journal of the Royal Society of Arts* 129 (1981): 357–79.

Steel, Flora Annie. *The Complete Indian Housekeeper and Cook.* London: Macmillan, 1888.

———. *The Garden of Fidelity: Being the Autobiography of Flora Annie Steel, 1847–1929.* London: Macmillan, 1930.

Steel, Richard, and John Crowther. "A Journal of the Journey of Richard Steel and John Crowther." In Samuel Purchas, *Hakluytus Posthumus; or, Purchas His Pilgrimes: Contayning a History of the World in Sea Voyages and Lande Travells by Englishmen and Others* (1625), 519–24. Glasgow: J. MecLehose and Sons, 1905–7.

Stokes, Eric. *The English Utilitarians and India.* Oxford: Oxford University Press, 1959.

Stoler, Ann Laura. *Race and the Education of Desire: Foucault's History of Sexuality and the Colonial Order of Things.* Durham, N.C.: Duke University Press, 1995.

———. "Rethinking Colonial Categories: European Communities and the Boundaries of Rule." *Comparative Studies in Society and History* 31, no. 1 (1989): 134–61.

Streets, Heather. *Martial Races: The Military, Race, and Masculinity in British Imperial Culture, 1857–1914.* Manchester, U.K.: Manchester University Press, 2004.

Suleri, Sara. *Meatless Days.* Chicago: University of Chicago Press, 1989.

———. *The Rhetoric of English India.* Chicago: University of Chicago Press, 1992.

Suri, V. S. "Political, Territorial, and Administrative Changes in the Punjab from Earliest Times up to 1947." *Panjab Past and Present* 1, no. 1 (1967): 177–202.

Talbot, Cynthia. "Inscribing the Other, Inscribing the Self," *Comparative Study of Society and History* 37, no. 4 (1995): 692–722.

Talbot, Ian. *Punjab and the Raj, 1849–1947.* Riverdale, Md.: Riverdale Company, 1988.

Talwar, Vir Bharat. "Feminist Consciousness in Women's Journals in Hindi, 1910–20." In *Recasting Women: Essays in Colonial Indian History,* ed. Kum Kum Sangari and Sudesh Vaid, 204–32. New Brunswick, N.J.: Rutgers University Press, 1990.

Tandon, Prakash. *Punjabi Century: 1857–1947* (1961). Berkeley and Los Angeles: University of California Press, 1968.

Tarar, Nadeem Omar. "Historical Introduction." In *Official Chronicle of the Mayo School of Art: Formative Years under J. L. Kipling, 1874–94,* comp. Nadeem Omar Tarar, ed. Samina Choonara, 21–29. Lahore: National College of Arts, n.d. [2003].

Tavernier, J. B. *Travels in India.* Trans. V. Ball. London, 1889.

Taylor, Charles. *Modern Social Imaginaries.* Durham, N.C.: Duke University Press, 2004.

———. "Two Theories of Modernity." *Public Culture* 11, no. 1 (1999): 153–74.

Thévenot, Jean de. *The Travels of Monsieur de Thévenot into the Levant, Part III.* Ed. Surendranath Sen. Delhi: National Archives of India, 1949.

Thompson, F. M. L. *The Rise of Respectable Society: A Social History of Victorian Britain, 1830–1900.* Cambridge: Cambridge University Press, 1988.

Thornton, T. H. "Lahore: A Historical and Descriptive Note, Written in 1860." In *Old Lahore: Reminiscences of a Resident* (1924), ed. H. R. Goulding, 81–127. Lahore: Sang-e-Meel, n.d.

Tillotson, G. H. R. *The Tradition of Indian Architecture: Continuity, Controversy, and Change since 1850.* New Haven: Yale University Press, 1989.

"A Tour to Lahore [in 1809] by an Officer of the Bengal Army." *The Asiatic Annual Register* 10 (1809), reprinted in *Panjab Past and Present* 1, no. 1 (1967): 110–41. Page numbers in notes are from the reprinted article.

Tupper, C. L. *Punjab Customary Law.* 3 vols. Calcutta: Superintendent of Government Printing, 1881.

Tyrwhitt, Jaqueline, ed. *Patrick Geddes in India.* London: Lund Humphries, 1947.

Ufuq, M. Dwarka Prasad. *Risala-e-Tikka Manzum* [A Political Treatise on Vaccination]. Lucknow: Nazm Akbar, n.d.

Upton, Dell. *Architecture in the United States.* Oxford: Oxford University Press, 1998.

———. *Holy Things and Profane: Anglican Parish Churches in Colonial Virginia.* New Haven: Yale University Press, 1986.

———. "Lancasterian Schools, Republican Citizenship, and the Spatial Imagination in Early Nineteenth-Century America." *Journal of the Society of Architectural Historians* 55 (1996): 238–53.

———. "Seen, Scene, and Unseen." In *Understanding Ordinary Landscapes,* ed. Paul Groth and Tod Bressi, 174–79. New Haven: Yale University Press, 1997.

———. "The Tradition of Change." *Traditional Dwellings and Settlements Review* 5, no. 1 (1993): 9–15.

Vandal, Pervaiz. "The Dream and the Reality." *News International* [Pakistan], Sunday, June 24, 2001.

Vatuk, Sylvia. "Purdah Revisited: A Comparison of Hindu and Muslim Interpretations of the Cultural Meaning of Purdah in South Asia." In *Separate Worlds: Studies of Purdah in South Asia,* ed. Hanna Papanek and Gail Minault, 54–78. Delhi: Chanakya, 1982.

Vidler, Anthony. *The Architectural Uncanny: Essays in the Modern Unhomely.* Cambridge: MIT Press, 1992.

Viswanathan, Gauri. *Masks of Conquest: Literary Study and British Rule in India.* New York: Columbia University Press, 1989.

Wescoat, James L. "Gardens, Urbanization, and Urbanism in Mughal Lahore: 1526–1657." In *Mughal Gardens: Sources, Places, Representations, and Prospects,* ed. James L. Wescoat and Joachim Wolschke-Bulmahn, 139–69. Washington, D.C.: Dumbarton Oaks Research Library and Collection, 1996.

———. "Gardens versus Citadels: The Territorial Context of Early Mughal Gardens." In *Garden History: Issues, Approaches, Methods,* ed. J. D. Hunt, 331–58. Washington, D.C.: Dumbarton Oaks Research Library and Collection, 1992.

———. "Toward a Map of Mughal Lahore: An Outline of Cartographic Sources from 1590 to 1990." *Environmental Design: Journal of the Islamic Environmental Design Research Center* 1–2 (1993): 86–93.

———. "Waterworks and Culture in Metropolitan Lahore." *Asian Art and Culture* 8, no. 2 (1995): 21–36.

Wheeler, James Talboys. *The History of the Imperial Assemblage at Delhi* (1877). Delhi: R. K., 1982.

White, Luise. *The Comforts of Home: Prostitution in Colonial Nairobi.* Chicago: University of Chicago Press, 1990.

Whitworth, George C. *An Anglo-Indian Dictionary: A Glossary of Indian Terms Used in English, and of Such English or Other Non-Indian Terms as Have Obtained Special Meanings in India* (1842). Lahore: Sang-e-Meel, 1981.

Williams, Raymond. *The Country and the City.* New York: Oxford University Press, 1973.

Wilson, H. H. *A Glossary of Judicial and Revenue Terms, and of Useful Words Occurring in Official Documents Relating to the Administration of the Government of British India* (1855). Delhi: Munshiram Manoharlal, 1994.

Wright, Gwendolyn. *The Politics of Design in French Colonial Urbanism.* Chicago: University of Chicago Press, 1991.

———. "Tradition in the Service of Modernity: Architecture and Urbanism in French Colonial Policy, 1900–1930." In *Tensions of Empire: Colonial Cultures in a Bourgeois World,* ed. Frederick Cooper and Ann Laura Stoler, 322–45. Berkeley and Los Angeles: University of California Press, 1997.

Yang, Anand. *Bazaar India: Markets, Society, and the Colonial State in Bihar.* Berkeley and Los Angeles: University of California Press, 1998.

———. "Dangerous Castes and Tribes: The Criminal Tribes Act and the Magahiya Doms of Northeast India." In *Crime and Criminality in British India,* ed. Anand Yang, 89–107. Tucson: University of Arizona Press, 1985.

———. "Disciplining 'Natives': Prisons and Prisoners in Early Nineteenth Century India." *South Asia* 10 (1995): 29–45.

Yeoh, Brenda. *Contesting Space: Power Relations and the Urban Built Environment in Colonial Singapore.* Oxford: Oxford University Press, 1996.

———. "Sanitary Ideology and the Control of the Urban Environment." In *Ideology and Landscape,* ed. Alan R. H. Baker, 148–72. Cambridge: Cambridge University Press, 1992.

Zastoupil, Lynn. *John Stuart Mill and India.* Stanford: Stanford University Press, 1994.

Zelliot, Eleanor. "Literary Images of the Modern Indian City." In *Urban India: Society, Space, and Image,* ed. Richard G. Fox, 215–23. Monograph and Occasional Papers 10. Durham, N.C.: Duke University Program in Comparative Studies in South Asia, 1970.

Ziffren, Abbie. "Biography of Patrick Geddes." In *Patrick Geddes: Spokesman for Man and the Environment,* ed. Marshall Stalley, 3–101. New Brunswick, N.J.: Rutgers University Press, 1972.

Zindagi Raushni aur Safai [Life, Light, and Cleanliness]. Lahore: Publishers United, 1941.

INDEX

WILLIAM J. GLOVER is associate professor of architecture at the University of Michigan in Ann Arbor, where he teaches architectural and urban history. His writing has been published in *Journal of Asian Studies, HomeCultures, The Encyclopedia of Women in Islamic Countries,* and other publications.